CROCKETT JOHNSON

and

RUTH KRAUSS

Crockett JOHNSON and Ruth KRAUSS

HOW AN UNLIKELY COUPLE FOUND LOVE, DODGED THE FBI, AND TRANSFORMED CHILDREN'S LITERATURE

Philip Nel

UNIVERSITY PRESS OF MISSISSIPPI • JACKSON

Furthermore:
a program of the J. M. Kaplan Fund

Publication of this book was made possible, in part, by a grant from
Furthermore: a program of the J. M. Kaplan Fund.

Children's Literature Association Series

www.upress.state.ms.us

Designed by Peter D. Halverson

The University Press of Mississippi is a member of the Association
of American University Presses.

frontis: Ruth Krauss and Crockett Johnson on their front porch, 1959.
Image courtesy of Smithsonian Institution. Reproduced courtesy of
the *New Haven Register*.

First printing 2012
∞
Library of Congress Cataloging-in-Publication Data

Nel, Philip, 1969–
Crockett Johnson and Ruth Krauss : how an unlikely couple found
love, dodged the FBI, and transformed children's literature / Philip Nel.
p. cm. — (Children's literature association series)
Includes bibliographical references and index.
ISBN 978-1-61703-624-8 (cloth : alk. paper) —
ISBN 978-1-61703-636-1 (pbk. : alk. paper) —
ISBN 978-1-61703-625-5 (ebook) 1. Johnson, Crockett, 1906–1975.
2. Krauss, Ruth. 3. Children's literature, American—History and criti-
cism. I. Title.
PS3519.O224Z77 2012
813'.52—dc23
[B]   2012001106

British Library Cataloging-in-Publication Data available

To Karin,
who, for a dozen years, shared her spouse with this book

CONTENTS

CROCKETT JOHNSON

and

RUTH KRAUSS

INTRODUCTION

"Few stories are completely perfect," said the lion.

"That's true," said Ellen, leaving the playroom. "And otherwise it's a wonderful story. Thank you for telling it to me."

—CROCKETT JOHNSON, *The Lion's Own Story* (1963)

When a stranger knocked on Crockett Johnson's front door one mild Friday in August 1950, he was not expecting was a visit from the FBI.

Stepping out onto his porch, Johnson spoke with one federal agent while another surreptitiously snapped his photograph. As he stood there politely answering their questions, he had no idea that the bureau had for months been opening his mail, monitoring his bank account, and noting the names of anyone who visited or phoned.[1]

For the previous five years, Johnson and his wife, Ruth Krauss, had been living quietly in Rowayton, a small coastal community in Norwalk, Connecticut. They had been married for seven years. He was famous for writing *Barnaby* (1942–52), the epitome of the thinking person's comic strip. In a few years' time, he would begin writing what would become his best-known book, *Harold and the Purple Crayon*. She was gathering material for her eleventh children's book, *A Hole Is to Dig* (1952), the classic that launched the career of Maurice Sendak.

Despite (or perhaps because of) their modest acclaim, the FBI had begun keeping tabs on Johnson and Krauss in April 1950. By the time the investigation concluded five years later, the FBI had amassed a file so detailed that it mentioned an interview with the manager of the Baltimore apartment building where Krauss's mother lived.

Situated at the intersection of art, politics, and commerce, the lives of Krauss and Johnson lead us into a lost chapter in the histories of children's books, comics, and the American Left. During the McCarthyist 1950s, left-wing artists and writers, shut out of many fields, found success in children's literature. Only two children's authors were called to testify before the House

Un-American Activities Committee (HUAC), and both received no questions about their radical work for children. As a result of her refusal to cooperate with the committee, Helen Kay had her decidedly apolitical *Apple Pie for Lewis* (1951) banned from U.S. overseas libraries. Questioned by HUAC about a handful of radical poems he wrote for adults in the 1930s, Langston Hughes suddenly faced a huge loss of income two decades later: His publisher, Henry Holt, canceled his contracts, and schools stopped inviting him to speak. He returned to writing for younger readers, creating six books for children. Anticommunist crusaders simply did not see "kiddie lit" as a field important enough to monitor. As left-leaning children's author Mary Elting Folsom put it, "Our trade was so looked down upon that nobody bothered with us." Even as the FBI was watching them, Crockett Johnson and Ruth Krauss could and did make a good living writing for children.[2]

It was a good time to be writing for younger readers: Thanks in part to the baby boom, the American children's book business was thriving. Between 1950 and 1960, total annual sales nearly tripled, reaching a record high of eighty-eight million dollars in 1960. The decade of *Harold and the Purple Crayon* and *A Hole Is to Dig* was also the decade of C. S. Lewis's *The Lion, the Witch, and the Wardrobe* (1950), Astrid Lindgren's *Pippi Longstocking* (English translation, 1950), E. B. White's *Charlotte's Web* (1952), Kay Thompson's *Eloise* (1955), Syd Hoff's *Danny and the Dinosaur* (1958), and several Dr. Seuss standards: *Horton Hears a Who!* (1954), *How the Grinch Stole Christmas!* (1957), and *The Cat in the Hat* (1957). In the 1950s, Leo Lionni, Richard Scarry, Maurice Sendak, and Crockett Johnson debuted as children's authors. The decade launched careers and classics.[3]

Two of the decade's best children's book creators were also best friends. Theirs was a love story of complementary opposites. Nearly six feet tall and with the build of an ex-football player, Crockett Johnson was a gentle giant, a soft-spoken man with a wry sense of humor. A slender five feet, four inches tall, Ruth Krauss was outspoken and exuberant, an original thinker who nonetheless harbored doubts about her creative gifts. Where Krauss could be anxious, Johnson was always calm. Their backgrounds differed, too. She was a secular Jew from a bourgeois Baltimore family; the son of two immigrants, he was a lapsed Methodist who grew up in working-class Queens. As Krauss wrote in *A Moon or a Button* (1959), she and Johnson were two "people on a long winding road and they meet in the middle."

Between them, they created more than seventy-five books, many of which became classics. Five of Johnson's seven books about Harold and his purple crayon have remained in print for more than fifty years, and the series has inspired many other books and authors. A May 2010 episode of *The Simpsons* has Harold draw the opening credits' couch scene, and Homer tells Harold, "Draw me some beer." Two-time Caldecott Award winner Chris Van Allsburg thanked "Harold, and his purple crayon" in accepting the Caldecott for *Jumanji* (1981). Rita Dove, U.S. poet laureate from 1993 to 1995, has written that she could "take the path of Harold's purple crayon / through the bedroom window and onto a lavender / spill of stars." In 1995, Michael Tolkin, screenwriter of *The Player* (1992) and *Deep Impact* (1998), wrote a screenplay for *Harold and the Purple Crayon*, a favorite of his and of Spike Jonze, who signed on to direct. Though the film was never made, Jonze went on to direct such inventive and offbeat films as *Being John Malkovich* (1999), *Adaptation* (2003), and *Where the Wild Things Are* (2009).[4]

Harold and the Purple Crayon has captivated so many people because Harold's crayon not only embodies the imagination but shows that the mind can change the world: What we dream can become real, nothing can become something. The book's succinct expression of creative possibility tells readers that although they may be subject to forces beyond their control, they can improvise, invent, draw a new path. Many earlier works explored the boundaries between real and imagined worlds—Chuck Jones's *Duck Amuck* (1953), Saul Steinberg's *New Yorker* cartoons of the early 1950s, René Magritte's *The Human Condition 1* (1933), and Winsor McCay's *Little Nemo in Slumberland* (2 May 1909), among others. But Johnson distilled this idea into its simplest and most profound form. His Harold lives in the existential uncertainty of the blank canvas: There is no world except that which he makes. A small god in a white romper, Harold uses art to create the heavens and the earth, dragons and apple trees, tall buildings and nine kinds of pie. Explaining why *Harold and the Purple Crayon* is the children's art book she recommends above all others, Jackson Pollock biographer Deborah Solomon writes that it suggests that "one well-worn, stubby crayon could allow you to dream up a whole universe. Which of course it can. There's no better art history lesson than that."[5]

Where Johnson's feeling for a child's creativity emerged in his artist hero, Ruth Krauss conveyed her respect by bringing real children's voices into her work and in so doing changed the way authors write for young people. In her *Here and Now Storybook* (1921), Lucy Sprague Mitchell reproduced child-authored tales in the child's own words. In *A Hole Is to Dig*, Krauss went a step further, transforming children's startling, spontaneous utterances into poetry. Because she treated them as her equals, children accepted Krauss as one of them, confiding in her, telling her stories, or just playing while she watched. She listened, wrote down what they said, and used her poet's ear to select phrases that displayed a natural, unrehearsed lyricism ("A dream is to look at the night and see things" and "A sea shell is to hear the sea") or a sense of humor ("Rugs are so dogs have napkins," "A tablespoon is to eat a table with," and "Mud is to jump in and slide in and yell doodleedoodleedoo"). Her carefully chosen quotations, juxtaposed with Sendak's illustrations of scruffy, uninhibited children, helped pave the way for books that respect children's tough, pragmatic thinking and unorthodox use of language.

Krauss's influence has been so pervasive as to have become invisible: Contemporary readers take for granted that there have always been vital, spontaneous, loose-tongued children in children's books. There haven't. Krauss did not invent these children, but she did give them a place in children's literature. After her success, everyone else started writing books featuring such children. Some of those authors misread Krauss, finding in her work an occasion for selling sentimental, easily assimilated homilies, such as Joan Walsh Anglund's *Love Is a Special Way of Feeling* (1960) and *Spring Is a New Beginning* (1963). Other authors, however—Kevin Henkes, Lane Smith, and Laurie Keller, to name a few—understood what Krauss was up to. Without sentimentality, she respected what Sendak calls "the natural ferocity of children" and, as Barbara Bader aptly notes, "grasped intuitively what the great Russian children's poet Kornei Chukovsky spent his life studying, 'the whimsical and elusive laws of childhood thinking.'" That is why children liked her work and why adult writers of children's books continue to be influenced by it.[6]

A favorite of graphic novelists today and of the culturally influential in its day, Johnson's *Barnaby* betrays its author's wide-ranging interests—political satire, popular culture, classic literature, modern art, and mathematics. Its subtle ironies and playful allusions never won a broad following, but the adventures of five-year-old Barnaby Baxter and his bumbling con artist of a fairy godfather were and remain critical favorites. Confessing her love of *Barnaby* in 1943, Dorothy Parker thought it better than its genre, closer to Mark Twain than to comics: "I suppose you must file *Barnaby* under comic strips, because his biography runs along in strip form in a newspaper. I bow to convention in the matter. But, privately, if the adventures of Barnaby constitute a comic strip, then so do those of Huckleberry Finn." While Parker's low estimation of comics reflects the prejudices of the day, her evocation of a classic American novel still resonates: *Barnaby* is full of Johnson's delight in language. Using typeset dialogue, a technique unprecedented in comics, enabled him to include what he estimated to be 60 percent more words, giving Mr. O'Malley more room to indulge in rhetoric that, as one critic put it, combines the "style of a medicine-show huckster with that of Dickens's Mr. Micawber."[7]

Barnaby's deft balance of fantasy, political commentary, sophisticated wit, and elegantly spare images expanded our sense of what comic strips can do. The missing links between George Herriman's *Krazy Kat* (1913–44) and Walt Kelly's *Pogo* (1948–75), Johnson's *Barnaby* and Al Capp's *Li'l Abner* (1934–77) form the bridge to those idea-driven comics that followed. As a daily topical strip, *Li'l Abner* precedes *Barnaby* and exerts its own influence on subsequent satirical strips—especially *Pogo* and *Bloom County* (1980–89). But Crockett Johnson's understated style, keen intellect, and feeling for the imaginary landscape of children all work to place *Barnaby* in a class by itself. With subtlety and economy, *Barnaby* proved that comics need not condescend to their readers. Its small but influential readership took that message to heart. As Coulton Waugh noted in his landmark *The Comics* (1947), *Barnaby*'s audience may not "compare, numerically, with that of the top, mass-appeal strips. But it is a very discriminating audience, which includes a number of strip artists themselves, and so this strip stands a good chance of remaining to influence the course of American humor for many years to come." His words were prophetic. *Barnaby*'s fans have included *Peanuts* creator Charles Schulz, *Family Circus* creator Bil Keane, and graphic novelists Daniel Clowes, Art Spiegelman, and Chris Ware.[8]

Although Johnson and Krauss were never quite household names, their works were well known from the 1940s through the 1960s. If we measure lives through their influence and intersection with important figures and movements, then these two names deserve to be better remembered today. Their circle of friends and acquaintances included some of the most important cultural figures of the twentieth century. Abstract painter Ad Reinhardt and *New Yorker* cartoonist Mischa Richter were close friends of Johnson's. Krauss studied anthropology under Margaret Mead and poetry under Frank O'Hara and Kenneth Koch. Harper's innovative, influential Ursula Nordstrom edited their works and nurtured their unique talents. Johnson, Krauss, and Nordstrom all served as mentors to Sendak.

When referring to Crockett Johnson or Ruth Krauss, I use the name that best suits the situation. Krauss is "Ruth" in a personal context and "Ruth Krauss" or "Krauss" in a public one. Similarly, in public, Johnson is "Crockett Johnson" or "Johnson." In the realm of the personal, Johnson is "Dave" because all of his friends and associates called him by his given name. During the decade it took to write this book, I interviewed more than eighty people, conducted research at more than three dozen archives and special collections, read everything I could find written by or about Johnson and Krauss, and consulted hundreds of additional books and articles to situate their lives in various contexts—historical, cultural, literary, geographical, political. Though this biography draws on those contexts as needed, I have as much as possible structured the book in chronological order.

Crockett Johnson died when I was six years old, by which time I had already read (and loved) *Harold and the Purple Crayon*. I have often wished that I had persuaded my parents to drive me from our home in Lynnfield, Massachusetts, to the Johnson-Krauss home in Westport, Connecticut, but the idea never occurred to me at the time. And although Ruth Krauss lived for nearly two decades longer, I never met her either. She died just as I was finishing my first year of graduate school, before I became a scholar of children's literature. Though I am on a first-name basis with Ruth and Dave and I know them intimately, that knowledge derives solely from my research. I wish I had had the chance to know them during their lives.

1

RUTH KRAUSS'S CHARMED CHILDHOOD

There should be a parade when a baby is born.
—RUTH KRAUSS, *Open House for Butterflies* (1960)

During a midnight storm on 25 July 1901, Ruth Ida Krauss was born. She emerged with a full head of long black hair and her thumb in her mouth. According to Ruth's birth certificate, twenty-one-year-old Blanche Krauss gave birth at 1025 North Calvert Street, a Baltimore address that did not exist. This future writer of fiction was born in a fictional place. Or so her birth certificate alleges. But it was filed in 1933, at which time the attending physician did live at the above address. Presumably, she was born at 1012 McCulloh, which in 1901 was the doctor's address and a little over a mile from the Krauss home. Her father, twenty-eight-year-old Julius Leopold Krauss, was in the unusual position of being able to afford to have a doctor attend to his child's birth—at the turn of the twentieth century, 95 percent of children were born at home, and physicians were present at only 50 percent of births.[1]

Ruth came home to the three-story frame house at 2137 Linden Avenue, where she lived with her doting mother, father, and paternal grandfather, Leopold Krauss, who had been born in Budapest, Hungary, about 1839. His wife, Elsie, had been born in Frankfurt in about 1848. After the failed European revolutions of 1848 and the German wars of unification in the 1860s, Leopold joined the great wave of U.S.-bound immigrants, and by 1863, he had settled in downtown Baltimore, where he operated a furrier's business. In 1869 and 1872, his furs won gold medals from the Maryland Institute for the Promotion of the Mechanic Arts.[2]

Elsie emigrated to the United States at around the same time and soon met and married Leopold Krauss. They and their two children, Carrie (born 1871) and Julius (born 1872), lived a comfortably middle-class life. Both children attended school, Elsie kept house, and Leopold ran a thriving business in a rising clothing industry center. Although Ruth recalled that Julius "liked to draw & paint," he followed his father into the furrier's trade. By 1893, he was

Ruth Krauss at six months. Image courtesy of Betty Hahn.

working for Leopold as a salesman, and five years later, Julius had become manager. In 1899, the business changed its name from "Leopold Krauss" to "L. Krauss & Son," but within two years, Leopold Krauss dropped "& Son," and in 1902, Julius Krauss opened his own furrier shop, though he returned to his father's firm a year later and remained there for the rest of his working life. He may have had to cede his creative ambitions to his father, but his daughter would be able to pursue her dreams. Julius would see to that.[3]

Just before the turn of the twentieth century, Julius Krauss met Blanche Rosenfeld. Born in about 1879 in St. Louis, Blanche had moved to Baltimore as a child. She, too, was the daughter of an immigrant—Australian-born Carrie Mayer—and her husband, Henry Rosenfeld.[4]

On Sunday, 14 October 1900, Blanche and Julius married at Baltimore's beautiful new Eutaw Place Temple. The young couple soon moved with Ruth's father and grandfather into the Linden Avenue house. (Grandmother Elsie died before she could meet her daughter-in-law.) Like many other affluent Baltimore Jews, the Krausses migrated northwest through the city into the neighborhoods just south of Druid Hill Park. Although the Krauss family moved frequently during Ruth's childhood, they never resided more than half a dozen blocks south the park. Established in 1860, Druid Hill was part of the same urban parks movement that inspired Central Park. By the turn of the twentieth century, it was Baltimore's largest park, with fountains, a duck

Advertisement from Baltimore City Directory, 1893: Leopold Krauss, Ruth's grandfather.

pond, gardens, stables, a greenhouse, a zoo, tennis courts, swimming pools, and a lake for summer boating and winter ice skating. Because Baltimore was a segregated city, the park also had separate facilities for use by black visitors, an injustice that left an impression on young Ruth. An active child, Ruth made frequent use of the park—when she was well.[5]

As an infant, Ruth developed a severe earache, and doctors discovered that her ear was infected and filled with fluid. She underwent an operation to drain the ear and had to wear a bandage around her head for the next year. Ruth also suffered from many childhood diseases that were common in the days before vaccinations, including diphtheria, two kinds of measles, chicken pox, and whooping cough. She later recalled, "I nearly died a lot." Nevertheless, she recovered and grew into an energetic and inquisitive little girl. At three years old, she stood in her house's bay window and lifted her dress so that two passing women could see her. At five, she and two boys played show and tell behind a couch.[6]

Ruth Krauss, ca. 1916. Image
courtesy of Betty Hahn.

Ruth's parents catered to their only child's needs. When she grew old enough to go to school, she cried so much that her family relented and let her stay home. The following year, when she began attending school, she returned home each day to find a piece of chocolate on her dresser, a reward from her grandfather.[7]

Ruth's earliest ambition was to be an acrobat. She later recalled having spent "eight years of my life walking on my hands in the backyard." There were many different backyards. In 1903, the Krausses moved a block and a half north to a three-story frame house at 826 Newington Avenue. In 1904, they moved three blocks south, to another three-story frame house at 1904 Linden Avenue. In February 1904, the Great Baltimore Fire destroyed more than fifteen hundred buildings in the city's downtown business district, but the Druid Hill Park neighborhood and the Krausses' shop at 228–230 North Eutaw Street were far enough north that they escaped the flames. Memories of the conflagration stayed with Ruth, who had a lifelong fear of house fires.[8]

By 1907, the family had moved yet again, this time taking their servant and cook five blocks northwest to a brand-new, stone-front, three-story house at 2529 Madison Avenue, where they would remain for the next eight years. According to Gilbert Sandler, Jews in the area, known as the Eutaw Place–Lake neighborhood, "founded their own separate society, with an in-town club (the Phoenix Club), a country club (the Suburban Club), and their own funeral home (the Sondheim Funeral Home)."[9]

Health problems continued to plague Ruth. At age eleven, she developed appendicitis and had an appendectomy. The next year, she came down with pemphigus, a rare autoimmune disorder that results in blistering of the skin and mucous membranes. Despite the efforts of five excellent doctors, including a skin specialist from Johns Hopkins, she spent two months in bed, becoming so weak that she could no longer speak and could ask for a glass of water only by wiggling the little finger on her left hand. To lift the girl's spirits, Blanche Krauss and her three sisters took turns reading to her—all of H. Irving Hancock's *Dick Prescott* stories. As Ruth recalled, "They took Dick from the time he was a little squirt and finished him off at Westpoint [*sic*] when he got engaged. I can remember my Aunt Edna giggling as she read to me how Dick got himself engaged." Only later, after her recovery, did Ruth learn that pemphigus was usually fatal: Doctors told her that only one other person had survived, and he "had to live in a bathtub of ice for a year"—or at least that was her "impression of the story."[10]

While she was convalescing, Ruth received a bicycle from her family. Not yet permitted to leave the house, she learned to ride in the hallway so that "the first time I was able to go outside after being sick, I could ride it."[11]

Ruth remained close to her grandfather, Leopold, who would read her the Twenty-Third Psalm ("The Lord is my shepherd") and letters his wife had written him when they were engaged, an experience she found "very touching." As the fall of 1913 turned to winter, Leopold's health declined, and one day Ruth returned from school to find her dresser without its usual piece of chocolate. On 8 December 1913, Leopold Krauss died at the age of seventy-six.[12]

Ruth found some consolation in stories. She enjoyed listening when her father told her about his childhood and read to her from *David Copperfield*. On her own, she read fairy stories and reread the *Dick Prescott* stories. She also began writing and illustrating her own stories. When she finished a story, she created a binding by sewing the pages together along one edge. As a teenager, she wrote in a secret language a book that she hid from her parents.[13]

In 1915, Ruth enrolled at Baltimore's Western Female High School, and the family moved to the Marlborough, a new luxury apartment building at the corner of Eutaw Place and Wilson Street whose other residents included several prominent Baltimoreans, notably Claribel and Etta Cone, major patrons of Impressionist and post-Impressionist art. The Cone sisters' eighth-floor apartment became a private museum, featuring works by Picasso, Matisse, and Renoir. If the building's double-thick fireproof walls and concrete floors truly did ensure "absolute immunity from noisy neighbors," as management claimed, the Krausses' neighbors were probably grateful. During her teenage years, Ruth took up the violin. She was a creative if not technically accomplished player. Holding the violin between her chin and neck gave her a chronic boil, so she began practicing with the far end of the violin against a wall, delighted by the different sounds that resulted: "A plaster wall gave one sound. Wall-board another, quite sepulchral. A wooden door gave another. The bathroom tile, still another." Ruth imagined herself performing on a concert stage, running around and pressing the violin against different objects to get different sounds.[14]

Ruth studied violin with the Peabody Conservatory's Franz C. Bornschein, a teacher, composer, and arranger who was also giving lessons at Western Female High School. Unlike some girls' schools of the time, Western was no mere finishing school. Ruth attended twice-weekly physical education classes and studied both science (botany or physiology for freshmen and zoology or biology for sophomores) and foreign languages (Latin, French, German, or Spanish).[15]

In 1917, after her sophomore year, Ruth left Western to become an artist. She later noted that because her "formal education stopped after two years of public high school," she was "naturally illiterate in my language and I sometimes wonder if this isn't simply a continuation of the way I talked as a child." Ruth enrolled as a day student in the new costume design program at the Maryland Institute for the Promotion of the Mechanic Arts (now the Maryland Institute College of Art). Ruth's interest in exploring her creativity collided with the school's pragmatic emphasis on subjects such as interior decoration, which would, according to the institute's director, Charles Y. Turner, "offer a medium of making the young artist self-supporting in a far shorter space of time than the painting of abstract subjects or portrait work." In addition to making inexpensive goods for domestic consumption, graduates also made clothes and other items for American troops abroad.[16]

Free of the need to earn a wage, Ruth did not participate in war industries. By 1918, she and her parents had moved to the Rochester, another upscale apartment building, located just over a mile from the Maryland Institute. Most of Ruth's costume design classmates were female, in keeping with prevailing views about pursuits for which women were suited. In the words of costume design instructor Elsie R. Brown, "Mother Eve herself ranked clothes only second in her scheme of things, curiosity about apples being her first and consuming interest." Similarly, an article on the costume design program noted that "women naturally have an instinctive interest in clothes." But Ruth's interests were pulling her away from costume design, and in mid-1919, she left the Maryland Institute and began thinking about resuming her study of the violin.[17]

First, however, she went to Camp Walden, deep in the woods of Denmark, Maine. Her five weeks there were transformative. Though her family had moved six times in eighteen years, she had always lived in the same neighborhood. Far away from Baltimore for the first time, Ruth rediscovered writing.[18]

2

BECOMING CROCKETT JOHNSON

"Have you been doing any thinking about what you're going to be
when you grow up?" asked Ellen.
  "No," said the lion. "Have you?"
—CROCKETT JOHNSON, *Ellen's Lion* (1959)

Crockett Johnson was born David Johnson Leisk (pronounced *Lisk*), in New
York City, on 20 October 1906. His grandfather, David Leask, was a carpenter
in Lerwick, in Scotland's Shetland Islands. He and his wife, Jane, ultimately
had ten children, all of whom attended school until they were old enough to
learn a trade. Their third child and second son, named for his father, was born
on 3 August 1865, and by age fifteen, he was an apprentice stationer. By 1890,
after a brief career as a journalist, young David had left what he called the
"treeless isles" and emigrated to New York, where he found work as a book-
keeper at the Johnson Lumber Company.[1]

In a department store on Fifty-Ninth Street, David Leisk met Mary Burg,
a twenty-eight-year-old saleswoman who as a teenager had emigrated from
Hamburg, Germany, to Brooklyn with her parents, tinsmith William Burg, and
his wife, Johanna. In October 1905, David and Mary married and moved into
a six-story apartment building at 444 East Fifty-Eighth Street in Manhattan,
a block west of the East River and a block south of where the Queensboro
Bridge (the Fifty-Ninth Street Bridge) was under construction. A year later,
Mary gave birth at home to the couple's first child. The new parents named
their son after his father and his place of employment: David Johnson Leisk.
When daughter Else joined the family on 27 May 1910, her literature-loving
father gave her the middle name George in honor of novelist George Eliot.
By 1912, the Leisks had moved out of their Manhattan apartment and into the
suburbs—Queens.[2]

A new borough of New York City, Queens had unpaved streets, no sew-
ers, and more chicken owners than any other borough, though the Board
of Health was beginning to crack down on unlicensed livestock. The Leisks

David Johnson Leisk and his mother, Mary, n.d. Image courtesy of Smithsonian Institution. Reprinted with the permission of the Estate of Ruth Krauss, Stewart I. Edelstein, Executor. All Rights Reserved.

lived in Corona on the second floor of a two-story wood-frame house at 2 Ferguson Street (today, 104-11 39th Avenue, next door to the Corona Branch of the Queens Public Library). Young David and Else Leisk loved pets, and their big, gentle father indulged them with cats, dogs, and a bird. The boy often brought home lame animals, many of them rescued from the Leverich Woods, a block west of their home. Dave attended Public School 16, two blocks south of the Leisk home and directly across the street from Linden Park, a 3.5-acre oasis in increasingly urban Corona. In the summer, the park hosted band concerts, and boys fished in Linden Lake; in the winters, the lake offered ice skating.[3]

Dave's father retained the affinity for the sea that dated back to his childhood in the Shetlands. He built a sailboat in the family's backyard and took his son sailing on Long Island Sound. On Sundays during Dave's childhood, his father would frequently row a small boat out into the water, and Dave and Else would swim and play. By 1915, however, sewage emptying into Flushing Bay led the Board of Health to advise against swimming there.[4]

During the summers—and especially when the winds blew from the east—the Leisks and their neighbors inhaled the pungent smell of garbage, rotting

David Leisk, "Kuku Karl and Hesa Nutt Visit the Museum," *Newtown High School Lantern*, May 1921.

in the heat. They lived four blocks west of the Corona dumps, famously described by F. Scott Fitzgerald's *The Great Gatsby* (1925) as "a valley of ashes." Thinking the former Corona Meadows an ideal location for an industrial park, real estate developer Michael Degnon bought them, employing laborers to fill them in with ashes from Manhattan. When the railway cars full of ash came to a stop at the meadows, Fitzgerald wrote, "the ash-grey men swarm[ed] up with leaden spades" to unload them. Although Degnon's Borough Development Company was supposed to be dumping only clean ashes and "street sweepings" (a euphemism for horse manure), people threw out all kinds of garbage along with their ashes.[5]

In September 1915, nine-year-old Dave saw his first strike when the ashgrey men walked out to protest the wages and hours demanded by the

Borough Development Company. In October, the company fired the men and hired a new group of workers, but the incident left an impression on young Leisk. In "Kuku Karl and Hesa Nutt Visit the Museum," one of the first cartoons he drew for his high school newspaper a few years later, one character "saw how big a pyramid is" and "asked where they would have buried the king in case of a brick-layer's strike!"

To distinguish himself from the other boys named David in the neighborhood, Leisk borrowed a name from a comic strip about frontiersman Davy Crockett, and some friends began to call him Crockett. In 1934, he started signing his work Crockett Johnson, and by 1942, the phone book listed him under that name. After his childhood nickname became his professional name, however, he began using Dave privately. But private and public were closer than he was willing to acknowledge. Crockett Johnson's works were always a reflection of Dave Leisk. It's no coincidence that his most famous character, Harold, is also an artist.[6]

Dave was relentlessly creative. At the Methodist church the Leisks attended, he drew pictures in the margins of the hymnals. At home, he made clay models and sketched famous people both past and present. One summer, when his sister was away, Dave drew a cartoon in which he imagined her adventures, presenting it to her when she returned. He also wrote stories.[7]

In these and other respects, Dave took after his father. In addition to his weekly pinochle game with the guys from the neighborhood, the elder David Leisk enjoyed reading and writing. His interests ranged widely and included history and poetry, which he wrote as well as read. He also enjoyed singing—at church and at home, with company or without—and composed a few hymns. He submitted a full news story about the 1920 America's Cup race to his hometown newspaper, the *Lerwick Times*. Young Dave also inherited his father's slow, deliberate manner of speaking.[8]

Mary Leisk was less easygoing than her husband and was stricter with her children, particularly Else. Reflecting the beliefs of the time, she considered her son more important than her daughter. Resentment at such favoritism sometimes strained relations between the children, though at other times, Else and Dave got on well. They played checkers and chess and tossed a football. However, in addition to being a boy and nearly four years Else's senior, Dave also had a much sharper mind. Asked a simple question, Dave understood the problem so thoroughly that he might not give a straight answer but instead express himself whimsically, wryly, or even sarcastically. When he did, Else thought that he was being condescending. Believing that her mother

D. J. Leisk, "An Off Day," *Newtown High School Lantern*, March 1921.

encouraged such behavior, Else frequently spent time with one of her father's Johnson Lumber coworkers and his wife, who lived below the Leisk family and had no children of their own.[9]

Dave was intrigued by people who could make things, including his father, who built boats in the backyard, and craftsmen in a borough perpetually under construction. In October 1915, workers began constructing what would be the largest station on the Corona Elevated Railway (now New York City's Number 7 Train). Opening ceremonies for the two-block-long 104th Street Corona Station, located a block south of the Leisks' house, were held on 21 April 1917 and featured a band, five hundred girls from Public School 16, two hundred Boy Scouts, and members of the Junior American Guard. The Corona El made the trip from Grand Central Station in just sixteen minutes, bringing Queens closer to Manhattan than ever before.[10]

For German natives like Mary Leisk, this celebratory moment cloaked the shame and fear inspired by the U.S. declaration of war on Germany two weeks earlier and by increasing anti-German sentiment. In October 1915, former

David Leisk, "Newtown H.S. . . .," *Newtown High School Lantern*, May 1921.

President Theodore Roosevelt had said, "There is no room in this country for hyphenated Americanism. . . . There is no such thing as a hyphenated American who is a good American. The only man who is a good American is the man who is an American and nothing else." Although Queens had other immigrant groups (notably Italians and Swedes), prejudice against "hyphenated Americans" was directed largely at Germans. Reflecting the tenor of the times, in the 1915 New York State Census, Mary Leisk listed her birthplace as the United States.[11]

With war raging in Europe, some Leisk cousins visited the United States, staying with Mary, David, and their children. When U.S. soldiers bound for Europe visited the young women, the elder David bought them cigarettes. Else remembered her father as "patriotic," though he generally "didn't voice any opinion." On another occasion, the nieces played piano and David sang along, carrying the bass part on "Mother Machree" and "My Bonnie Lies over the Ocean."[12]

In the fall of 1920, Dave Leisk, then nearly fourteen, moved on to Newtown High School, where he soon became an artist for the school magazine, the *Lantern*. The publication's second issue, which appeared in March 1921, included "An Off Day," by D. J. Leisk, chronicling the exploits of a round-headed schoolboy identified as "you." The bottom right corner of the final panel

David Leisk, cover for the *Newtown High School Lantern*, May 1923. Image courtesy of the Queens Borough Public Library, Long Island History Division. Reprinted with the permission of the Estate of Ruth Krauss, Stewart I. Edelstein, Executor. All Rights Reserved.

Newtown High School, Class of 1924. Reproduced Courtesy of the Queens Borough Public Library, Long Island History Division, Frederick J. Weber Photographs.

features an overlapping cursive *D* and *L*, the sigil that would become his signature for his high school work.

The cartoon offers a glance at the high expectations faced by Newtown students. A student arriving after 8:45 A.M., as the one in the cartoon does, needed to get a late slip and bring it home for a parent's signature. Each night, students were expected to spend two to three hours on homework: Those who did not would "probably fail in some subjects." Newtown offered a general four-year course, a three-year commercial course, a three-year salesmanship course, and four-year courses in both agriculture and music, among other avenues of study. The school encouraged all students to "decide early upon your vocation and choose your college" so that they would meet the entrance requirements: "Don't make the mistake of supposing that a high-school diploma will admit you to any course in college." The school offered classes in history (both American and European), economics, mathematics (including algebra and plane geometry), natural and physical science, and German, French, and Spanish. English classes featured works by Wordsworth, Stevenson, Tennyson, Emerson, Shakespeare, Milton, Coleridge, Abraham Lincoln, and George Eliot as well as Canadian poet John McCrae's "In Flanders Fields" (1915), a patriotic call to arms that had become popular among Allied troops during World War I.[13]

Dave contributed to the *Lantern* as both a writer and an illustrator. He drew his first cover for its May 1922 issue: Framed by tree branches, a laughing boy's head rises above the surface of what may be Linden Lake. His cover for the May 1923 *Lantern* features a similar drawing, showing a young man who has fallen asleep while fishing by the lake's edge. If his cartoons are

David Johnson Leisk at age seventeen. Reproduced Courtesy of the Queens Borough Public Library, Long Island History Division, Frederick J. Weber Photographs.

any guide, Dave knew that he was a dreamer but was less sure where those dreams might lead.[14]

Though he took up smoking at a young age, Dave was a natural athlete, with a particular interest in swimming, running, baseball, and football. In his senior year, Dave was a member of Newtown High's undefeated baseball team, though he seldom took the field. Dave also was a shot-putter on the school's excellent track team, coming in third in the Queens championships. He played tackle on a football team, but since Newtown High School banned football "for fear of safety of the players," Dave had to play beyond school grounds.[15]

On 26 June 1924, David Johnson Leisk joined 148 classmates in graduating from Newtown High School. Though not an ambitious student, he had done well enough on New York State's Regents exams to earn a scholarship to Cooper Union, in Lower Manhattan. He commuted there for two semesters, taking classes in art, typography, and drawing from plaster casts. By the spring of 1925, however, Dave's father had died, and at the age of eighteen, he dropped out of school to get a job and support his family.[16]

3

PORTRAIT OF THE ARTIST AS A YOUNG WOMAN

Hands are to make things.
—RUTH KRAUSS, *A Hole Is to Dig* (1952)

In the summer of 1919, eighteen-year-old Ruth Krauss was one of Camp Walden's oldest campers. Founded three years earlier by New York City principal Blanche Hirsch and teacher Clara Altschul, Camp Walden sought to promote democratic cooperation, to foster a love of nature, and to give girls "a happy and vigorous summer, and ample opportunity for all forms of athletic activity," including archery, swimming, diving, hiking, basketball, baseball, and tennis.[1]

Ruth took part, displaying more exuberance than skill and earning the nickname Doggie. In an account of "The First Counselor-Girl Basket-Ball Game" in the summer of 1920, fellow camper Ruth Loebenstein wrote, "Doggie got her periods mixed up, and thought she was in dancing class. She did the wilted flower stunt several times, and Miss King even had to blow the whistle to remind her that she was one of the guards and not one of the garden." That same summer, Ruth captained one of the teams in a friendly weekend camp sports tournament, leading her team to victory. Though they did keep score, Walden was careful to make its competition as noncompetitive as possible: The teams had to cheer for each other. As Ruth would write in *Open House for Butterflies* (1960), "I think a race looks prettier when everybody comes in even."[2]

Walden's noncompetitive approach derived from Hirsch and Altschul's allegiance to the principles of Ethical Culture, a movement that sought to create a more humane society by recognizing that each person is unique and by trying to nurture the development of each person's talents. Parodying the camp's ethical philosophy, however, Ruth and her best friend invented a "'lie cheat and steal' society based on a whole new set of morals." The young women also resisted their counselor's insistence that the campers speak only French in their bunks, and the campers combined care packages from home into secret midnight feasts.[3]

At three hundred dollars for five weeks, the camp attracted girls from well-to-do families, mostly of German-Jewish backgrounds. Walden offered Ruth many outlets for her creativity. Campers took art classes and wrote and staged plays. At a 1920 Backward Party, participants wore their camp uniforms backward. The 1919 issue of the camp yearbook, *Splash*, contains the earliest surviving piece of Ruth's creative work, "The Climb up Washington as Told to Me by Ham." In it, she relates her conversation with a fellow camper who describes the dangers of climbing Mount Washington while Ruth serves as an attentive audience:

HAM: And, Ruth, if you made one mistake you would have gone over. Imagine!! And every second we saw a sign saying THIS MAN DIED HERE. Oh, it was terrible!! They say the scenery was marvelous, but if I had looked down, I would've gone right over. And then we'd see another sign saying: THIS GIRL DIED HERE. Oh, it was terrible! You would have died!!

ME: Ye Gods!

HAM: I wish you could have been there. It was a wonderful experience. Look at my shoes.—and Mr. Hale slipped once on Suicide Path. We had to crawl along on our hands and knees there and test every stone before we tread on it. And you should have seen the falls.

Ruth's narrative finds the comedy in ordinary language, picking up on Ham's frequent repetition of "You would have died" and tendency to describe the experience as simultaneously terrifying and wonderful.[4]

The following summer, Ruth served as entertainment editor for *Splash*, which featured a chart offering a glimpse of her personality:

Name	Nickname	Favorite Expressions	Ambition	Ultimate Result
R. Krauss	Doggie	I don' wan' to	Be a fortune teller	Wears a shoe lace for a tie.[5]

In the fall of 1919, after her first summer at Walden, Ruth decided to return to the violin. Her Western High violin teacher, Franz Bornschein, taught at Baltimore's Peabody Conservatory of Music, which was located only two miles from her home—and she applied to study there. Peabody informed her that she was not yet advanced enough to enroll but was welcome to join the

Ruth Krauss at Camp Walden, Maine, 1920. Image courtesy of Betty Hahn.

conservatory's Preparatory Department. After a year of studying harmony, music history, and the violin, Bornschein described her as industrious, intelligent, and musically gifted though with an "odd make up" and "not a systematical worker." By the end of her second year, he had lost confidence in her. While he still thought she was "instinctively" gifted musically, her work habits were "harum-scarum," and he wondered if her intelligence might not be "sub-normal." In her 1920–21 student record, he labeled her as having "an over abundance of temperament; this wildness is difficult to mold into an obedient condition."[6]

Ruth was nonetheless serious about her musical pursuits, and the following year, she chose a different violin teacher, Frank Gittelson. He was younger and a better violinist than Bornschein, had a sense of humor, and was more sympathetic to Ruth's efforts. Although he found her intelligence "very erratic," he thought her industrious and more musically gifted "than her performance shows." That said, he described Ruth as "a hard but undisciplined worker" who "practices a great deal but [is] blind to her defects."[7]

In November 1921, fifty-year-old Julius Krauss died of leukemia. Ruth had been very close to her father, and after he died, she gave up the violin. The following year, she left the Peabody Conservatory for good. Having dropped out of high school, abandoned art school, and failed at the conservatory, Ruth was adrift. She shared an apartment with her mother and wondered what to do with herself. She went to work as a cashier in 1923, becoming a clerk in 1926 and a manager the following year. At some point during these years—possibly during 1924 and 1925—they lived with Blanche's sister, Edna Hahn; her husband, Charles; and their son, Richard. Though Dick was twelve years Ruth's junior, he became like a younger brother to her, and their close friendship endured throughout their lives.[8]

In 1927, Blanche's mother, Carrie Rosenfeld, died, prompting Ruth to make a decision about her future and giving her the money she needed to act. She would leave home and become an "artiste": As she later wrote, "Naturally one cannot become an artiste if one remains at home." Fur designer John Gray recommended that she apply to New York's School of Fine and Applied Art, popularly known as the Parsons School. For the first time, she would move away from Baltimore, where she had lived in for twenty-six years. She would be going not to a small, supervised camp in Maine but to the largest city in North America. In the late summer of 1927, with renewed determination and sense of purpose, Ruth packed her bags and boarded the train for New York.[9]

She enrolled full time, paying a hefty tuition of $250 for her first year and living in one of New York City's many "girls' clubs"—likely either the Three Arts Club or the Parnassus Club, which were recommended in the school's 1927–28 *Prospectus*. Receiving credit for her costume design coursework at the Maryland Institute of Art, Ruth enrolled as an "honor student" in costume design and illustration, a popular new major introduced the previous decade by school president Frank Parsons. According to Ruth, being an "honor student" meant "that I skipped the part where you had to work in materials themselves, and stuck only to the drawing and painting part, the part I was interested in."[10]

Though Ruth preferred the aesthetic pleasures of drawing and painting, she could not avoid the Parsons School's emphasis on the practical. Frank Parsons wanted students to become good artists, but he also wanted them to be able to get a job. Influenced by Bauhaus founder Walter Gropius's belief in "the basic unity of all design in its relation to life," Parsons taught its pupils to extend aesthetic judgment into the everyday, an idea that resonated with Ruth's interest in colloquial language. Parsons students learned to see beauty in ordinary things. Designing a chair should be as important as designing a building; an advertisement should be designed with as much care as a mural. Frank Parsons believed that teaching students to develop good taste would democratize art. Furthermore, as he told students in 1927, "If you can produce taste in advertising, costumes, interiors, you can get the job."[11]

In her first term at Parsons, Ruth faced one required class that nearly made her quit: dynamic symmetry. Based on his study of Greek art and design, Jay Hambidge concluded that beauty was based on symmetry. Naming the Greeks' lost principle "dynamic symmetry," he devised a mathematical formula—known as the Golden Ratio, 1.6180 (also rendered as $1:\sqrt{5}$)—to express the relationship between elements of a particular object. That object could be anything: a drinking cup, a chair, a building, a book layout, or architectural decoration. Putting Hambidge's principle into practice, Parsons instructors had students use geometry to map the symmetry of an object before sketching it. The idea was that the mathematical calculations would gradually become second nature to students who practiced dynamic symmetry, thereby bringing the "craft inheritance" of the Greeks to modern design.[12]

Ruth began her battle with the subject in July 1927, when she took life drawing. Determined to follow her instructor's guidance to the letter, Ruth so obsessed over each detail that she lost sight of her larger aims. As she recalled with more than a little irony many years later, "Since my meticulousness and literal following of teaching was, to put it politely, naïve, my first year's output—giving say Life drawings as an example—resembled architectural floor plans for labyrinths. The human figure was found to have more variety by me than by all the other artists of the ages thrown together. I did finally 'master' the art of 'seeing' and I became very adept at drawing by discernment of rhythms alone—a sort of transmission of 'tactile perceptions,' a form of abstracting essentials to represent the whole, the abstraction itself on a ruggedly individual level of feeling. Is level the right word? Oh well." Her tenacity helped her master the subject, even if she never fully understood the theory.[13]

Parsons required Ruth to work hard, and she rose to the challenge, pursuing her homework with single-minded intensity:

They were fiends at Parson's [sic] for exact matching of color and many other details. On one painting I remember spending days mixing tones of "rose." I mixed in actual fact three hundred different tones of rose trying to get a background color combining "a sense of brightness and doom." I was living at a girls' Club at the time and locked myself in my room for several days, having my meals sent up (for a quarter extra) trying to get the "rose." Finally I was set. I put it on. It turned out entirely different-looking over the large background area than in my sample, of course—but anyway they were pretty exacting in certain ways at Parson's. What I am driving at is that I spent an awful lot of time, thought and feeling, on "Art."

29

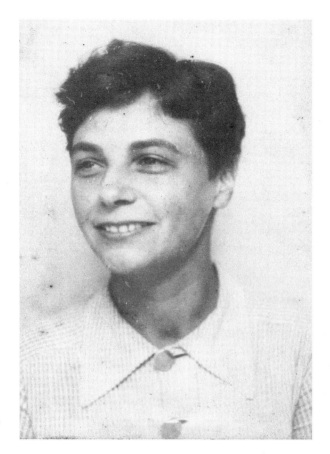

Ruth Krauss, n.d. Image
courtesy of Betty Hahn.

If confining herself to her room for a few days might yield results, Ruth was willing to try.[14]

To prepare for the working world, Parsons required costume design students to draw up and create various types of costumes, including personal clothes. In 1928–29, she received critiques from art deco illustrator Georges Lepape, whose fashion designs pioneered greater physical freedom in women's clothes. Ruth was very much in favor of that idea, as was fellow costume design major Claire McCardell, who was a year ahead of Ruth at Parsons and who would revolutionize American women's fashion by making clothes that were stylish, comfortable, and affordable—putting the school's principles into practice.[15]

After two years of study and a bout with the measles, Ruth graduated from Parsons in June 1929. While seeking work, she moved in with an Italian man she later identified only as Guido, with whom she had her "first physical 'affair.'" Fifty years later, Ruth recalled her younger self as always having been "boy-crazy" and described sex as "a paramount feature in my feeling & thinking." Also in the late 1920s, she had a brief affair with sculptor Isamu Noguchi, who had just returned to New York from Paris.[16]

With her Parsons education, Ruth Krauss felt poised for success: "I left Parsons able to work in all mediums, from pencil and charcoal through water color, 'gouache,' and oils, to finger-paint." Her confidence soon crashed, along with the stock market: As an art school graduate during the Great Depression, Ruth "found a few jobs, but I had to walk my feet off and sit humiliated for hours in offices waiting and hang around three months between jobs for which I was then paid thirty to fifty dollars—or on one big haul, not at all. Because the magazine itself folded up. Among other things I did the first picture-jacket ever used by the Modern Library. It was for *Alice in Wonderland*" (1932). She also did the book jacket for the Modern Library's edition of *Gulliver's Travels* (1932).[17]

With jobs few and far between, Ruth survived the depression in part thanks to the financial support of her mother, who continued to run the Krauss family's furrier business until March 1930, when she married Albert A. Brager, a wealthy widower and founder of the Brager-Eisenberg department store.[18]

In the early 1930s, Ruth met Lionel White, a journalist and writer of detective stories, who was working on an edition of Lewis Carroll's *Logical Nonsense: Works, Now, for the First Time, Complete*. According to Ruth, she and Lionel met at an "Arts Ball," where they danced and laughed together. Both were in costume: "I think I was dressed like a boy—Lionel was dressed I can't remember how but *not* like a girl." After the party, the two walked hand in hand through Greenwich Village. Ruth was in love.[19]

31

4

PUNCHING THE CLOCK AND TURNING LEFT

The ramifications of a financial panic are—SAY! . . . That never occurred to me! . . . Your dad fired! Denied access to means of producing
the necessities of life! You and your mother in rags! The icebox bare—
Cushlamochree! The icebox bare!
—MR. O'MALLEY, in Crockett Johnson, *Barnaby*, 5 April 1945

In 1926, unable to afford their home of a dozen years, the Leisks moved about
two miles west into a house at 53 North Prince Street (now 33-43 Prince
Street) in Flushing, Queens. The new house was only ten feet wide, especially
cramped for a family that included Dave's cousin, Bert Leisk, and his friend,
Jim McKinney, who had fled Britain's postwar economic slump in 1923. Glad
for a temporary escape from these close quarters, Dave sought work.[1]

Department stores were thriving in the 1910s and 1920s—Marshall Fields
in Chicago, Filene's in Boston, and Macy's in New York. In the winter of 1926,
on the strength of his Cooper Union art courses, Dave became the assistant
art director in Macy's advertising department, a position he described as "a
glorified office boy." Macy's had strict rules for its more than five thousand
workers: As at Newtown High School, those who arrived at work after 8:45
needed to obtain a special pass, without which they could neither enter the
locker rooms nor go to their jobs. Working in the advertising department gave
Dave a chance to develop skills in typesetting and illustration but few opportunities to express his creative side. Department managers requested ads, staff
members drew items to be advertised, and other staff created advertisements
that conformed to Macy's style, using the company's distinctive typefaces and
trademark red star. Artists had no control over the final layout.[2]

If these rigid conditions clashed with Dave's creativity, the culture of advertising could not have increased his job satisfaction. As copywriter Helen
Woodward wrote in 1926, "To be a really good copywriter requires a passion
for converting the other fellow, even if it is to something you don't believe in

yourself." Naturally skeptical, Dave did not stay at Macy's for very long, quitting just before he was fired for wearing a soft collar instead of a regulation stiff one.[3]

Dave next found employment hefting ice in an icehouse. He may also have played semi-professional football for the Flushing Packers. He enjoyed the game because it wasn't much of a "passing game. It was mostly just a bumping-down-on-the-ground game." All Dave, a big offensive lineman, had to do was lean. Dave and the other linemen would mock the alleged arrogance of the quarterback. "The slick quarterback thinks he's the team," Dave would say. After a pause, he would add, "*We* are."[4]

Just two weeks after his twenty-first birthday, Dave returned to publishing, becoming the first art editor of *Aviation*, which eventually evolved into *Aviation Week*. The cover of the 7 November 1927 *Aviation*, the first issue on which Johnson worked, displays a photo of Charles Lindbergh's *Spirit of St. Louis* flying back to New York. Just a few months after his historic solo flight from New York to Paris, Lindbergh had undertaken an aerial tour of all forty-eight states to promote aviation, appearing before huge crowds and receiving accolades. Moreover, the latter half of 1927 saw four other successful transatlantic flights as well as the first flight from the continental United States to Hawaii, events that *Aviation* covered with enthusiasm.[5] On the strength of his new income, Dave and his mother and sister moved to more comfortable quarters at Hyacinth Court, a new four-story apartment building in Flushing.

During his years at *Aviation*, Dave began taking typography and graphic design classes at New York University's School of Fine Arts, where one of his teachers was Frederic Goudy, a master of print design who invented more than a hundred typefaces. Goudy described his work as "simple[;] that is, it presents the simplicity that takes account of the essentials, that eliminates unnecessary lines and parts," articulating an aesthetic that finds echoes in Johnson's later view of his illustrations as "simplified, almost diagrammatic, for clear storytelling, avoiding all arbitrary decoration."[6]

Dave was also receiving an on-the-job education in layout and design. In early 1929, publisher James McGraw added *Aviation* to his portfolio of business periodicals. During the corporate reshuffling that followed, Dave became art editor of a half dozen McGraw-Hill trade publications, apparently including *American Machinist* and *Bus Transportation*. However, the stock market crashed less than eight months after Dave joined the McGraw-Hill payroll. The company's fortunes declined along with the economy as circulations

David Johnson Leisk, ca. 1930s. Photograph by Eliot Elisofon. Image courtesy of Smithsonian Institution. Used by permission of the Harry Ransom Research Center, University of Texas at Austin.

dropped and some magazines disappeared entirely. McGraw-Hill laid off large numbers of editorial and business personnel, and Dave and the others who remained received significantly reduced salaries.[7]

Like many members of his generation, Dave turned left. He joined the Book and Magazine Writers Union. He read Communist publications such as

"HARRIET HERE IS PRACTICALLY AN *AUTHORITY* ON COMMUNISTS. SHE WRITES PIECES ABOUT THEM IN THE NEW YORKER."

Crockett Johnson, "Harriet Here Is Practically an Authority on Communists. She Writes Pieces about Them in the New Yorker," *New Masses*, 17 April 1934. Image courtesy of Tamiment Library, New York University. Used by permission of International Publishers, New York.

the *Daily Worker* and *New Masses* and befriended others in the movement, including Charlotte Rosswaag. He also fell in love with her.

Like Dave's mother, Charlotte was a strong-willed German. Born in 1908, Charlotte emigrated to the United States with her family in 1915. Her father, Adolph, worked as a diamond cutter for a jewelry factory, while her Polish-born mother, Veronica, both kept house and cleaned others' houses. According to Mary Elting Folsom, who knew Dave and Charlotte during the 1930s, Charlotte had a "rather plain, very lively face" and "was always laughing." She was free-thinking and plain-spoken and shared Dave's progressive politics. Charlotte could be blunt, but her sense of humor softened the edges of her frankness. All in all, Charlotte was "a very pleasant, laughing person, but a tough lady." By the mid-1930s, Dave and Charlotte were married and living with their two dogs in a garden apartment on or near Bank Street in Greenwich Village. She was a city social worker, and Dave continued to do magazine layout for McGraw-Hill.[8]

Dave met Mary Elting; her future husband, Franklin "Dank" Folsom; and other radicals through the Book and Magazine Writers Union. Elting, a magazine editor and later prolific a children's author, cofounded the union with Viking editor David Zablodowsky, McBride editor Elizabeth Morrow "Betty"

"Aw, be a sport. Tell the newsreel audience you still have faith in the Lawd and good old Franklin D."
CROCKETT JOHNSON

"Aw, Be a Sport. Tell the Newsreel Audience You Still Have Faith in the Lawd and Good Old Franklin D.," *New Masses*, 28 August 1934; reprinted in Robert Forsythe, *Redder Than the Rose* (New York: Covici, Friede, 1935). Used by permission of International Publishers, New York.

Bacon, editor Alex Taylor, and others. Through the union, Dave also befriend-ed *Daily Worker* journalist Sender Garlin and *TASS* editor Joe Freeman.[9]

Freeman also served on the editorial board for *New Masses*, and Crockett Johnson began to contribute to the Communist publication, which had just begun appearing weekly. His first cartoon appeared in the magazine on 17 April 1934 and mocks self-professed experts on communists. Three months later, *New Masses* printed another cartoon in which Johnson skewers President Franklin D. Roosevelt for his concern with the well-being of the rich. Billionaire industrialist J. P. Morgan reclines on a deck chair on a luxury liner, the *Corsair*, a name that connects Morgan to piracy. A young man deliv-ers a message: "Radiogram, Mr. Morgan. The White House wants to know are you better off than you were last year?"

In 1932 and 1933, 24 percent of Americans were unemployed, up from 3.2 percent in 1929. Though the unemployment rate would drop to 21 percent in 1934, the nascent New Deal had yet to produce major results. It was a time when people went on hunger marches, when police shot strikers, and when general work stoppages shut down major U.S. cities. As Michael Denning writes, "The year of the general strikes—1934—was also the year young poets and writers proclaimed themselves 'proletarians' and 'revolutionaries.'"[10] Johnson announced his sympathy with the proletarians and revolutionaries. In another cartoon commenting on the wave of strikes that swept the United States during 1934, a young lady at a cocktail party asks a young man, "Was it Marx, Lenin, or Gen. [Hugh] Johnson [a supposedly neutral mediator in a walkout by San Francisco longshoremen] who said: 'The general strike is quite another matter'?" Johnson mocks a bourgeoisie that in its ignorance confuses revolutionary thinkers with the general whose comments aided the suppression of the strikers. Taking on the Hearst press, a May 1935 cartoon has a secretary from Hearst's International News Service hand an article back to its author, saying, "Mr. Hearst says he'll buy your farm articles if you'll just change 'Arkansas,' 'Louisiana,' and 'California' and so on, to Soviet Russia."

He signed his first cartoons simply "Johnson." By August 1934, he began signing them "C. Johnson," sometimes reverting to "Johnson" and once to "C. J. Johnson." Whatever name appeared on the image itself, *New Masses* nearly always printed his byline as "Crockett Johnson," the public debut of his pseudonym. The first cartoon to bear that name was published on 7 August 1934 and showed a wealthy capitalist wife complaining, "Just because your greedy workmen decide to go on strike I can't have a new Mercedes. Somehow it doesn't seem *fair*." Thoughtful, soft-spoken art editor Dave Leisk had become radical cartoonist Crockett Johnson.

5

FIRST DRAFT

wits
stars
tough and terrible times
two boiled potatoes
and you in my bed
—RUTH KRAUSS, "Poem for the Depression" (1960)

While Dave and Charlotte were making friends with leftists in Greenwich Village, Ruth and Lionel were living nearby, in the West Village. She was at 325 West Twelfth Street (between Greenwich and Hudson), and he was two blocks north, at 78 Horatio Street (between Washington and Greenwich). At least, those were the addresses they gave to the Coast Guard in November 1934.

In 1934, Lionel and Ruth decided to travel down to Baltimore by boat for Thanksgiving. They joined writer and artist Richard Barry, who was taking his forty-foot cabin cruiser, the *Henry S.*, to Florida and would stop in Baltimore along the way. The trio embarked on the evening of 24 November but got only as far as Long Branch, New Jersey, before the *Henry S.* ran out of gas and began to drift south toward Asbury Park. Barry took a gasoline tank and set off in the cruiser's dory in search of fuel. But rough surf overturned his little boat, and "Mr. Barry was so exhausted by his efforts to reach shore that he was taken to hospital." The Coast Guard ultimately rescued Ruth and Lionel.[1]

Ruth's years with Lionel were exciting and difficult. Born in July 1905 on a Los Angeles farm, Lionel White moved east with his family as a child. His father worked for automobile manufacturers in Cleveland and later in Buffalo, where Lionel grew up with his twin brother, Harold, and sister, Betty. At eighteen, Lionel fell in love with and married a beautiful, volatile young Russian émigré named Julie. After a couple of years as a police reporter for newspapers in Ohio, he and Julie moved to New York, where he worked as a rewrite man and sports editor for several different papers. He was a gifted storyteller as well as a self-described drunk. Julie, too, was a heavy drinker, prone to leaving home for a few days on drinking binges. After taking off on one of these episodes, she simply failed to return. When Ruth came into his life, Lionel was writing and editing stories for pulp magazines. Following Lionel's lead, Ruth began to write pulp adventure as well as detective stories, although she apparently published these works under a pseudonym, probably because pulps were considered a sensational venue not suitable for women writers. In the mid-1930s, the number of pulp magazines peaked at more than two hundred, and many writers tried their hand at the genre.[2]

It was a precarious existence, and Ruth and Lionel moved frequently, living in Dutchess County, New York; Bernardsville and Pittstown, New Jersey; and in small towns along the Delaware River in Bucks County, Pennsylvania. But the two were in love and decided to marry in the fall of 1935. Her mother, her aunt, and possibly her stepfather drove up to Philadelphia for the wedding on 25 November. In anticipation of meeting Ruth's well-to-do relatives, Ruth and Lionel polished their car with bacon fat and bought a hat for Lionel and a four-dollar ring for Ruth. Donning the best clothes they could gather, Ruth and Lionel drove to Philadelphia, married, and immediately drove back to return her wedding band. They needed the four dollars more.[3]

Their early married life was difficult. Ruth later wrote, "We were literally 'broke'—we'd get up some mornings—nothing in the house—no coffee, no salt, no soap, no eggs, no nothing." The winter of 1935–36 was bitterly cold, and "we had 3 fires going in 1 room—a fireplace, a pot-bellied stove, and a 'cook-stove.'" Ruth's mother had no idea of her daughter's financial circumstances and sent the young couple oriental rugs, which they hung on the ceiling and walls to keep the cold out. They slept huddled together in their clothes. The cottage lacked indoor plumbing, so Ruth and Lionel bathed in the river. To comb her hair in the mornings, Ruth first had to "unfreeze the water-container"; her newly combed hair would quickly freeze, "stand[ing] up stiff with ice like spikes." They washed their clothes with water hauled from the river with a bucket on a rope. In March 1936, rising temperatures, melting snow, and an abundance of rain combined to cause flooding along the Delaware River that killed more than a hundred people and injured four thousand. The water topped the cabin's roof, but Ruth and Lionel had already fled to higher ground.[4]

Despite the tribulations, Ruth enjoyed her bohemian years. When her mother sent packages of coffee and tins of caviar, Lionel and Ruth would host gatherings of their neighbors, all of whom were in similar financial straits. And as Ruth later wrote in her "Poem for the Depression" (1960), she may have had only "two boiled potatoes," but she did have someone to share her bed.[5]

In 1938, however, Ruth discovered that Lionel had never divorced his first wife and was already seeing another woman, Anna Maher. Then living in New Jersey at "a small store house on a great Estate belonging to a man I had once had an affair with," Ruth learned that Lionel "had 'committed bigamy' with me." Heartbroken but hanging on to her marriage, Ruth went with Lionel back to New York City, where they checked into Greenwich Village's Marlton Hotel. Determined to drive Ruth away from him, Lionel came up with a convincing lie. Walking east along Eighth Street, he told her that Maher was carrying his child. Ruth became so upset that she literally fell into the gutter. Only then did she decide to divorce Lionel.[6]

Ruth moved into a fourth-floor apartment at 36 West Tenth Street and slowly began to regain her bearings. The building's owner, an older woman, lived on the second floor and frequently visited Ruth to chat. The landlady gradually furnished the room with a "small but comfortable compact arm-chair" with a "tiny diamond-shaped patch" on its upholstery, an "old-fash-ioned" green wing chair, and a new lamp with a chipped china base. When the room was relatively empty, Ruth felt empty, but as it filled, she grew comfort-able and found solace in her new home: "I came to cherish its calm. If I had been out, I would look forward as I came along the street, to the awareness of entering it." Eventually, "just sitting in my room became an affirmation to me. The coffee table and the two armchairs before the black fireplace were particularly good to look at. . . . I enjoyed so much sitting in the small yellow armchair with a cup of coffee before me on the table and a book or paper to read."[7]

A few months later, Ruth boarded a ship for England, though she had no specific plans for what she would do when she arrived there. Another pas-senger, a "dopey guy" named Elwyn, suggested that she stay in London with a friend of his. Joan, a twenty-something teacher at the University of London, had a flat off of Trafalgar Square in St. Martin's Mews that became Ruth's home base during her stay in England.[8]

Ruth and her "newly acquired rucksack" joined two sixteen-year-old Cockney lads, one couple, and a German refugee who was studying at the University of London and "spent a week wandering . . . from hostel to hostel" around southern England. The episode later reminded Ruth of J. B. Priestley's *The Good Companions* (1929), in which a group of people from diverse back-grounds meet and form a traveling theater troupe. Ruth subsequently set off

Ruth Krauss and unidentified person, ca. 1939. Image courtesy of HarperCollins Archives. Reprinted with the permission of the Estate of Ruth Krauss, Stewart I. Edelstein, Executor. All Rights Reserved.

on her own, traveling by bicycle, on foot, or by bus when she was "sick or it was too cold and raining or [she] was too tired to go on."⁹

In Kent, she spent a weekend with the Newnham family in "a wonderful and a slightly crazy" cottage. The family's five children included a college girl who brought "the 'intelligentsia' and the Artistic and journalistic crowd" to the house. Ruth arrived at night and was shown to a room with two beds. A girl was asleep in one bed, so Ruth climbed into the other. When she awoke, her bed had three people in it, and the other bed had four. "It turned out this was the girl's side [of the hall]. Across the hall was the boy's side." A pup tent in the yard housed another five people. Though Ruth spent "a pleasant dizzy week-end" with the Newnhams, she was also keenly aware of the hardships they faced. The family raised chickens and vegetables, bought milk from local farms, and ate red meat only "when guests bought it." Mr. Newnham had not held a regular job since World War I. The weekend that Ruth was there, the Newnhams had a job picking hops for beer, for which they were paid a shilling a bin, "the bin being a rather huge affair and hops pretty frail things with which to fill it. I doubt if they made a shilling a day." Twelve-year-old Mary worked "in a florist shop in Tunbridge Wells to which she traveled daily by bicycle and bus, several miles by bike before the bus. Her weekly salary was something like twelve shillings." Mary "could not continue her schooling because she fainted each time she took the tests into what would be our equivalent of public high-school." To attend a nearby vocational school, where she could learn the more lucrative skills of stenography and typing, Mary would have needed to pay a guinea per year, which her family could not afford. After leaving Kent, Ruth sent the Newnhams the money to send Mary to school.[10]

Returning to London, Ruth befriended artists living in a houseboat on the Thames. She was enjoying the trip, but her mother and aunt were worried. Adolf Hitler had come to power in Germany, and the country had taken over Austria and Czechoslovakia. Though British prime minister Neville Chamberlain had predicted "peace in our time" the previous fall, war seemed to be on the horizon. While Germany's invasion of Poland was yet months away, it was not a great time to be a Jew traveling abroad. Blanche Krauss Brager wanted her daughter to come home. In the spring of 1939, Ruth sailed back to New York.[11]

6

CROCKETT AND THE RED CRAYON

I Am a Real Red!
—slogan on sign carried by radical child on Crockett Johnson's cover
for *New Masses*, 27 July 1937

New Masses appealed to Crockett Johnson because, as cartoonist and contributor Mischa Richter noted, the magazine was "the only place where you could
be published regularly with ideas that attacked the fascists." In a December
1934 cartoon, Johnson likened fascism to a racket run by a gang of thugs.
As they sit around a card table, one gangster cleaning his gun and a second
having a drink, a third contends, "But regimentation won't hamper your individuality, Eustace; this Fascism racket will give real freedom to our artistic
souls." With the repeal of Prohibition the previous year having dried up the
profitable black market in alcohol, Johnson suggests that fascism is the new
organized crime.[1]

The threat of fascism was growing. Benito Mussolini had been Italy's leader
since 1922, and Adolf Hitler became German chancellor in 1933. In America,
MGM explored fascism's appeal in its film *Gabriel over the White House*
(1933), starring Walter Huston as a fictional new U.S. president: After a near-
death experience, a visit from the Angel Gabriel converts this weak president
into a decisive dictator. Father Charles E. Coughlin, the popular Catholic
priest whose radio programs reached virtually all of the American East and
Midwest, was beginning to preach anti-Semitic fascism to his listeners.[2]

Against the rise of fascism and police harassment of striking workers,
Americans banded together to fight back, forming the Popular Front, a loose
alliance of communists, socialists, Democrats, and other liberals. According
to Michael Denning, the culture born from this front "took three political
forms: a social democratic electoral politics; a politics of anti-fascist and an-
ti-imperialist solidarity; and a civil liberties campaign against lynching and
labor repression." In the 1930s, prominent artists aligned with this "cultural

front" included Orson Welles, Archibald MacLeish, Langston Hughes, John Dos Passos, Duke Ellington, and Crockett Johnson.[3]

Signaling his commitment to the cause, Johnson in March 1936 redesigned a radical monthly publication with close ties to the Communist Party, *Fight against War and Fascism*. In its two and a half years of existence, *Fight*'s circulation had grown to nearly thirty thousand, a promising start. *Fight*'s editors hoped that having Johnson transform it into "a big, colorful magazine" would help it become "the magazine of all people, worker, professional, farmer, teacher, student, housewife." The April *Fight* featured cover art by Hugo Gellert and contributions from journalist George Seldes, writer Kenneth Fearing, and artists William Gropper and Art Young as well as the editors' gratitude to Johnson: "THANKS to Crockett Johnson, who in his quiet and persistent way worked night in, night out. This magazine was his in the evenings after working in the daytime on other publications. Who said the profit makers' press has no role in life?"[4]

In June 1936, Johnson joined the staff of *New Masses*, earning between twenty and twenty-five dollars per week. As the publication's art editor, Johnson would redesign the weekly with the aim of increasing circulation beyond its radical readership. As editor Joe Freeman noted, the staff had "met hundreds of readers in New York at small gatherings held in private houses" before deciding that "a change in format [was] necessary." Seeking advice, the staff invited twenty artists, among them Rockwell Kent, the best-known and most successful American printmaker, to a 30 July meeting at the Bancroft Hotel. Kent could not attend but invited Johnson to visit his home in Ausable Forks, New York.[5]

In early August, Dave traveled the three hundred miles north, where the two men planned an easier-to-read layout and design for *New Masses*, adding more artwork and pictorial covers. Johnson explained, "The idea now is to go in for decorative covers that are not too blatant (and often non-committal) about our editorial viewpoint. Titles, when we use them, will pose a question rather than dogmatically state a fact. The intention is of course not to deceive the prospective reader, but to try to avoid having him react unfavorably to our position as stated by headlines or an unpleasant or too strong political cartoon before he's bought the magazine and read all the facts we present." The first redesigned *New Masses* appeared on 15 September: Instead of listing article titles, as previous issues had, the cover bore a bold Kent illustration of a woman's profile, facing right. Her right hand holds a pole, with a blank flag waving just over her head. Left hand cupped to her open mouth, she calls out.

Her expression is hard to read: The eye is open, and the eyebrow is slightly raised. Her gaze and the angle of her hand point to the right side of the page, inviting the reader to open the magazine and discover what has made her so animated.[6]

Inside, readers found news with a distinct Communist Party flavor. Two articles support the Spanish Republican Army, while two others discuss the 1936 U.S. election, praising the Communists and lauding the formation of a committee (chaired by Kent) to support the party's presidential ticket of Earl Browder and James W. Ford. A full-page piece devoted to photos of Isamu Noguchi's sculptured wall in Mexico City's Mercado Rodriguez quotes the sculptor: "Capitalism everywhere struggles with inevitable death—the machinery of war, coercion, and bigotry are as smoke from that fire. Labor awakens with the red flag." Johnson expanded the "Between Ourselves" segment, which provided bios of contributors and other news, and moved it to the inside of the front cover, inviting readers to have a more intimate relationship with the magazine's editors, writers, and artists. He also increased the number of cartoons. During his tenure, *New Masses* featured the work of the best cartoonists in the business: Gropper, Gellert, Maurice Becker, Adolf Dehn, Charles Martin, Gardner Rea, Art Young, Syd Hoff, Abe Ajay, Ad Reinhardt, and Mischa Richter.[7]

Reinhardt and Richter became Johnson's lifelong friends and likely began contributing to *New Masses* because of that relationship. Ajay, who had sent his first cartoon to the magazine while he was still a Pennsylvania high school student, moved to New York in 1937 and became friends with all three men as well as with George Annand, a left-leaning advertising man and gifted raconteur.[8]

Although Dave was seven years older than Reinhardt, the two had much in common. Both were sons of working-class immigrants, had German-born mothers, and had served as the art editor of Newtown High School's magazine. They also shared a sardonic sense of humor and a keen eye for detail, traits that served them well when they collaborated on *New Masses*. Reinhardt created the small spot drawings that Dave used to enliven the magazine's layout, compact, sharp-angled, witty illustrations that break up the space either at the top of or in the middle of columns. Johnson did not know where these illustrations would be needed until the final stages of layout, requiring quick work from Reinhardt.[9]

In early May 1937, Dave attended a *New Masses* party hosted by interior decorator Muriel Draper, who had traveled to the Soviet Union in 1934–35 and

Crockett Johnson,
"I Am a Real Red!,"
New Masses, 27 July
1937. Image courtesy
of Tamiment Library,
New York University.
Used by permission of
International Publishers,
New York.

became sympathetic to communism. At the party, playwright and screenwrit-er Donald Ogden Stewart, who would win an Academy Award for adapting his friend Philip Barry's *The Philadelphia Story* (1940), gave a talk on behalf of *New Masses*. On another occasion, the Cartoonists Guild had a field day in Van Cortlandt Park, in the northwest Bronx, where they played baseball. Hoff recalled, "When Dave got up at bat, he was the greatest of us all. He kept hit-ting balls at least as far as Yonkers."[10]

Johnson's *New Masses* cartoons figure children's imaginations as power-ful, evincing an interest in what Julia Mickenberg has called the "Pedagogy of the Popular Front," a movement in progressive parenting designed to pro-duce open-minded children unfettered by their parents' prejudices. The child who appears on the cover of the 27 July 1937 issue holds a sign reading, "I Am a Real Red!" and looks like Harold's radical cousin. A full-page illustration from the 4 January 1938 *New Masses* promotes the Popular Front by having children from around the world leading the fight: The French child shoulders a "People's Front" banner, the American child wields the power of unions (a CIO sign), the Chinese child brandishes a sword, the Spanish child grips a rifle, and the Soviet child carries a hammer and sickle. All charge into battle together, conveying the power of children to effect social change.[11]

In February 1938, the Communist Party grew concerned that *New Masses* lacked firm political leadership. Wanting to put a trusted party member in a position of power, general secretary Browder asked A. B. Magil to move from the *Daily Worker*'s editorial board to the *New Masses* board. A frequent contributor to *New Masses* and the author of a popular pamphlet, *The Truth about Father Coughlin*, Magil brought a more explicitly communist tone to the publication. He and Johnson worked closely together, and Magil remembered "a very quiet man. He worked, he devoted his time to work and not to conversation. He was an efficient worker who really did what was needed by the magazine in the way of the artwork and fitting in things into the pages of the magazine and so on."[12]

Did Johnson ever join the Communist Party? Magil later recalled, "I always assumed that Dave was a party member. . . . I may be wrong about that, but I think he was considered a party member, as were most of the people who were working then on the magazine." Though Johnson may or may not have been a Communist (with a capital *C*), he was surely a communist (with a lowercase *c*). Whether formal or informal, such affiliations with the communists were typical for artists of Johnson's generation. Many people committed to social justice saw the Communist Party as a legitimate means of promoting their cause. In 1931, when nine young African American men were falsely accused of raping two white women on an Alabama train, the first organization to hire a lawyer to defend the Scottsboro Boys was the Communist Party; the National Association for the Advancement of Colored People did not act until later. The Communists, too, had begun speaking out against fascism more forcefully and earlier than any other major political group. In the latter half of the 1930s, the U.S. Communist Party was at its most powerful, and 40 percent of its members lived in New York City. *Redder Than the Rose* (1935), a collection of *New Masses* columns by Robert Forsythe (pseudonym of Kyle Crichton), featured illustrations by Johnson as well as Gropper, Rea, and Ned Hilton and had sold ten thousand copies by October 1936.[13]

As the Popular Front version of communism began to warm to FDR later in the 1930s, so did Johnson. A May 1938 cartoon, "The Primary Candidate

The Primary Candidate Who Tried to Make a Mountain Out of a Mole-Hill

Crockett Johnson, "The Primary Candidate Who Tried to Make a Mountain Out of a Mole-Hill," *New Masses*, 17 May 1938. Image courtesy of Tamiment Library, New York University. Used by permission of International Publishers, New York.

Who Tried to Make a Mountain Out of a Mole-Hill," displays Johnson's changed attitude toward the New Deal and shows the clean, minimalist style that would become the hallmark of the artist's work. In the *New Masses* cartoons and in all of his subsequent work, Johnson practiced what Scott McCloud calls "amplification through simplification." He strips images down to their essential components—a curved line for a man's open mouth, three short lines for a mole's whiskers, an oval for a rock. As McCloud observes, "If who I am matters *less*, maybe what I *say* will matter *more*."[14]

In April 1939, Crockett Johnson gave a talk on "the art of composing leaflets" at Commonwealth College, a radical labor school near Mena, Arkansas. Indicative of his increased prominence on the left, Johnson joined a distinguished roster of visiting lecturers that included Jack Conroy, socialist (and Commonwealth cofounder) Kate Richards O'Hare, and communist Ella Reeve "Mother" Bloor. In 1935, the Arkansas House of Representatives had attempted to shut the college down because it was "being used for the teaching of atheism, free love, and communism"; supported "complete social equality of blacks and whites"; and was promoting "revolutionary changes in our form of government." The attacks not only did not succeed but made Commonwealth a leftist cause célèbre, at least for a few years. By the time of Johnson's visit, however, the school had become openly communist, alienating both its financial backers and organized labor, and it closed the following year.[15]

Back in New York that summer, Johnson drew a cartoon for the 18 July 1939 issue of *New Masses*, "News Item Chamberlain Warns Hitler," that mocks British prime minister Neville Chamberlain's ineffectual attempts to secure peace with the German leader. A month later, many on the U.S. Left were shocked when the Soviet Union signed a pact with Nazi Germany in which the two countries agreed to stop war preparations against one another. Literary critic Granville Hicks, a *New Masses* contributor since 1932, quit the Communist Party and resigned from the magazine's editorial board in response. Some younger staff members followed, but Johnson remained committed to the cause. In November, Johnson spoke with Hoff about an idea for a cartoon based on Marx's idea (and Lenin's claim) that revolution is the locomotive of history. Published in the *New Masses* on 28 November 1939 under the pseudonym A. Redfield, Hoff's drawing shows the locomotive's relentless progress over obstacles. A group of former supporters marches away from the train tracks, with leaders bearing a sign announcing themselves as "The 'Russia Was Okay Until . . .' Society" and followed by smaller groups carrying smaller signs such as "Until Trotsky Left," "Until Kerensky Left," and "Until

Crockett Johnson at *New Masses*, ca. 1939. Unlike later photographs of Johnson "drawing" Barnaby, this one does not appear to be staged. Photo by Phil Stern. Image courtesy of the Smithsonian Institution. Reproduced courtesy of Phil Stern/CPi Syndication.

that Pact." Despite the optimism of Johnson, Hoff, and others, the pact marked the beginning of the end for *New Masses*, and its support, both financial and otherwise, dwindled until it finally ceased publication in 1948.[16]

As Dave's politics entered a rocky time, so did his marriage to Charlotte. The reasons for their problems are not clear, but they decided to divorce. And Ruth had returned to New York.

7

"WE MET, AND THAT WAS IT!"

Two little people on a long winding road and they meet in the middle.
—RUTH KRAUSS, *A Moon or a Button* (1959)

By about June 1939, Ruth returned to America and moved back into her 36 West Tenth Street apartment. But she did not stay there for long. She "felt a definite need for a broadening of information and a deepening of insight in general—'education'—so, when I met Maggie who was at that time just starting her postgraduate work in anthropology at Columbia, I went along."[1]

"Maggie" was Maggie Parry, and in the summer of 1939, she participated in an expedition, led by Columbia University anthropologist Ruth Benedict, to the Blackfeet Indian nation in Montana. Others on the expedition included psychologist Abraham Maslow; his brother-in-law, Oscar Lewis, a graduate student who would go on to do important work on the culture of poverty; Gitel Poznanski, a blues singer and later a noted anthropologist; painter Robert Steed, whom Poznanski subsequently married; and Ruth Krauss.[2]

Krauss and Parry "lived in a tent full of flies" with their Blackfeet host family. As during her days with Lionel, Ruth did not mind roughing it. They bathed in Two Medicine River, even though "local health authorities" had "pronounced [it] polluted." Drinking water was hauled from the river and then boiled. Ruth had neglected to take "any typhoid or Rocky Mountain fever injections before coming" and was regularly exposed to tuberculosis and typhoid as well as trachoma, a type of conjunctivitis: Group members "had to be careful not to get our hands near our eyes for fear of trachoma which nearly all the Blackfeet had or had had, many of the older ones being blind from it."[3]

Krauss embraced the experience as both keen observer and active participant. She and Parry traveled "everywhere [their] Indian family went." Ruth rode horses "to get around the Plains, riding through the river and up hillsides and down other hillsides," although she never felt "at home" on horseback. At other times, Krauss and Parry spent "days sitting on the Plains of Montana watching the Blackfoot races and rodeo and gambling games." They joined in, with Parry and Poznanski playing blackjack and Krauss playing "the 'hand game'" and blithely losing her last quarter.[4]

Krauss's anthropological interests focused on language. She was intrigued that all of the Blackfeet she met "had 'European' first names," like Joe Yellow Owl and Louie Littleplume. At "an owl-dance," Ruth danced "with a studious looking Blackfoot," Samuel Chicken Fast Buffalo Horse. She noted that her accent and inability to speak their language marked her as different, sometimes to her disadvantage: "I even got my first and last dog bite out on the reservation. Louie Littleplume and his family were going by and their dog was going along with them, and all I said was 'hello doggie,' and he rushed over and bit me in the calf. Possibly he was not accustomed to my Eastern voice, as most of the Blackfeet have some sort of 'accent,' that is those who speak English at all. There are varying degrees of both English-speaking and of accent." The trip and work in anthropology broadened Krauss's perceptions.[5]

If Marxism lay at the root of Crockett Johnson's political awakening, anthropology did the same for Ruth Krauss. The trip and the anthropology courses she took at Columbia showed her the ways in which social structures push people around and pressed her to consider more equitable ways of organizing a society. As Benedict wrote in a 1942 *Atlantic Monthly* article, the Blackfeet shared their resources with one another not out of charity for the less fortunate but as a consequence of a belief that sharing is mutually beneficial. In the Blackfeet nation, according to Benedict, "no man goes hungry while there is food in the community, and he exercises this right to subsistence not as a claim on charity but as a civil liberty which all tribesmen share." Leaders took care of their followers, and an individual with ability could enter any profession. This distribution of power and opportunity, Benedict said, gave them true freedom: "They have been able to unite the whole society into a kind of joint-stock company where any denial of rights is a threat to each and every member. It is the basis upon which strong and zestful societies are built and the basis for the individual's sense of inner freedom." In the 1940s, her progressive views would make Benedict a target of anticommunist zealots, but the 1939 summer expedition attracted no such attention.[6]

When the expedition ended in August, Krauss returned to New York, where she considered which anthropology courses to take in the fall. Four weeks before the term began, Germany invaded Poland, beginning World War II. Four blocks east of Ruth's apartment, *New Masses* editors were in their new offices at 461 Fourth Avenue, trying to explain why the nonaggression pact

Crockett Johnson, Ruth Krauss, and their dogs, Sean and Gonsel, Darien, Connecticut, 1944. This is the first photograph in which Johnson and Krauss appear together. Photo by Frank Gerratana, from the *Bridgeport Sunday Herald*, 1 October 1944. Image courtesy of the Smithsonian Institution.

between the Nazis and the Soviets did not mean that communists supported fascism: The USSR had signed the pact out of necessity. The Soviets lacked European allies, and British prime minister Neville Chamberlain and French prime minister Édouard Daladier had been tacitly encouraging Hitler to take his war east. If and when Germany attacked, the Soviet Union would defend itself. A nearly wordless Crockett Johnson cartoon from 5 September 1939 dramatizes the editors' point of view. In the first three scenes, Chamberlain and Daladier point Hitler's attention to the east. In the fourth and fifth panels, Hitler encounters a mighty Soviet soldier and thinks better of fighting what would be a losing battle. Instead, Hitler chases after Chamberlain and Daladier. In the final scene, the British and French leaders flee, shouting, "That dirty Russian deserted us!"[7]

While Johnson defended Soviet foreign policy, Krauss was beginning her formal study of anthropology. As when struggling with dynamic symmetry

Alarm Clock

at Parsons, Krauss was both confused by this new subject and determined to master it. Some of the discipline's "technical lingo" initially baffled her. She did not know about acculturation, or about the difference between matrilineal and patrilineal, or what gestalt psychology was. So she "spent a lot of time learning and, in order to translate it so I could understand it, unlearning anthropological terminology."[8]

That fall, at a party in Greenwich Village or on Fire Island, the outgoing, energetic Ruth met the wry, laconic Dave. He was tall and taciturn. Seven inches shorter, she was slim, exuberant, and ready to speak her mind. Her exuberance drew him out of his natural reticence and into conversation. His calm, grounded personality balanced her turbulent energy. They were complementary opposites who felt an immediate attraction toward one another. As Ruth liked to say, "We met and that was it!"[9]

When they began dating, Dave was considering leaving *New Masses* and pursuing a career as a cartoonist. In late 1939, he invented a nearly wordless strip starring a little man who offered comic observations on life's daily absurdities through the movement of his eyes. He submitted it to *Collier's*. While Dave waited for a response, he continued to work at *New Masses*. His 2 January 1940 cartoon, "Wonderfullums Inc.," criticized the racist assumptions of *Gone with the Wind* (1939), imagining a rather different Civil War story in which a Union Army soldier is the hero and an abolitionist is the heroine.[10]

Later in the month, Gurney Williams, the soft-spoken man who bought cartoons for *Collier's*, offered to run Johnson's new strip every week. With the obligation to turn out a weekly comic, Johnson decided to step down as the

Liberal at the Crossroads   CROCKET JOHNSON

Crockett Johnson, "A Liberal at the Crossroads," *New Masses*, 14 May 1940; reprinted in Joseph North, *New Masses: An Anthology of the Rebel Thirties* (New York: International, 1969). Used by permission of International Publishers, New York.

art editor for *New Masses* and asked his friend Mischa Richter if he would like the job. Richter took over in February.[11]

Johnson's *Little Man with the Eyes* comic strip debuted in *Collier's* on 9 March 1940.[12] Recalling Otto Soglow's *The Little King* in both its economy of line and gently humorous tone, *Little Man* was largely apolitical. Because the strip has no words other than the caption, the joke is delivered entirely through slight shifts in perspective. In the first strip, "Table Tennis," panels show the little man's eyes alternating between looking left and right. "Alarm Clock" makes its joke a bit more obvious: The little man goes from sleep to wakefulness to determined sleep to eyes open and finally to a last act of resistance, placing the pillow over his head.

With only small changes between panels, the strip was ideal for a man who professed to dislike drawing. To save himself labor, Johnson made one "key drawing" for each strip that contained all the necessary elements he needed for his narrative. Then he made multiple photostats and used ink and white-out to alter the images before pasting together the final sequence. For a strip in which the little man is startled awake and then resumes sleep when he realizes it was "Only the Cat," Johnson drew a single panel of the man's head on his pillow, covers pulled up to his chin, one eye wide open and the other closed. With minute alterations to copies of the image, the little man's eyes stay closed in the first panel, pop wide open in the second, and relax at half-open in the third before returning to closed in the fourth panel. In the nearly three years that he drew the strip, Johnson created 134 *Little Man* cartoons, and they were popular enough that Ford used them in an advertising campaign later in the decade.[13]

Work on *Little Man* kept Johnson from doing much for *New Masses* in 1940, but he did what he could. In April, he helped raise money for the financially strapped magazine by donating original artwork to an auction, which also featured work by William Gropper and Rockwell Kent. Auctioneers included *New Masses* contributors and editors Ruth McKenney, author of the best-selling *My Sister Eileen* (1938); and her husband, Richard Bransten, who wrote under the pen name Bruce Minton. In May, *New Masses* printed Johnson's final cartoon as a regular contributor: "A Liberal at the Crossroads" announced that war was coming and that liberals needed to face facts before it was too late.[14]

President Franklin Delano Roosevelt had reached the same conclusion. In September 1940, he signed the Selective Training and Service Act, the first peacetime conscription in American history. At thirty-three years old, Dave

Crockett Johnson, self-portrait, The accompanying note begins, "Crockett Johnson did this caricature of himself to prove that he doesn't look like the Little Man who has delighted Collier's readers for the past two years. Besides, he's six feet tall, weighs two hundred and ten and has several hairs on his head." *Collier's*, 16 November 1940. Reprinted with the permission of the Estate of Ruth Krauss, Stewart I. Edelstein, Executor. All Rights Reserved.

was not required to register, but he did. The military recorded that he was employed by McGraw-Hill; was five feet, eleven inches tall, and weighed 215 pounds; and had blue eyes and blond hair that was "thin in front," a feature he comically exaggerated in a self-caricature he did the following month.[15]

The *Collier's* profile makes no mention of Ruth, but she and Dave had become quite smitten. He was steady, easygoing, reliable. Ruth could count on him. She was passionate, spontaneous, original. Dave enjoyed her verve, her energy. They made each other laugh. In late 1940, Ruth moved into Dave's apartment at 36 Grove Street, in the West Village. Though they did not legally wed for several more years, both later claimed 1940 as the date of their marriage; for them, sharing the same address confirmed their mutual commitment. Soon after she moved in, Dave was looking for a rag to clean up a mess he had made. He asked Ruth, "Where are your rags?" Ruth replied, "You mean, where are *our* rags?" Dave quickly learned to correct his assumption that only the woman knew where the cleaning materials were.[16]

While Ruth studied anthropology, Dave continued his fight against fascism, especially after the Japanese attack on Pearl Harbor brought the United States into the war. The military rejected Dave for service, but in January 1942, he helped found the American Society of Magazine Cartoonists' Committee on War Cartoons, which included J. A. Blackmer and Mel Casson and was chaired by Greg d'Alessio. Making its debut at the Art Students League the following month, the committee's *Artists against the Axis* show featured some of the best cartoonists then working in the United States: Charles Addams, Peter Arno, Maurice Becker, William Gropper, John Groth, Syd Hoff, Charles Martin, Garret Price, Gardner Rea, Ad Reinhardt, Carl Rose, Saul Steinberg, Arthur Szyk, and Barney Tobey as well as Casson and Johnson.[17]

Addams drew hungry wolves pursuing a car full of Nazis, one of whom looks back in alarm. Hoff showed a child standing in his crib and asking his mother, "The Three Bears nertz—when are we gonna beat the Axis?" One of Johnson's contributions showed Hideki Tojo marching behind Benito Mussolini, who is carrying a sign reading "Follow the Leader," while Hitler sprints in the opposite direction. Another Johnson cartoon depicts a worried Hitler, shifting his glance between a ticking clock and a globe with flags marking Axis victories. To counter his fear that time is running out, he reaches up and stops the clock's pendulum. *Artists against the Axis* subsequently moved to the Metropolitan Museum of Art and then toured the country, helping raise money for the war effort.[18]

Dave was well positioned to coordinate cartoonists' contributions because he knew and mixed socially with so many artists. He and Ruth were among the select few guests at a birthday party for the great political cartoonist Art Young. After a delicious dinner of ham and baked acorn squash, Ruth fell forward into her plate, asleep. This after-dinner narcolepsy afflicted Ruth throughout her life. Dave initially worried that their friends would be insulted, but he came to understand that Ruth could not stay awake and accepted her evening naps.[19]

Crockett Johnson, "Follow the Leader," from *Artists Against the Axis*, February 1942. Image courtesy of the Terry-D'Alessio Collection, Museum of Comic and Cartoon Art. Reprinted with the permission of the Estate of Ruth Krauss, Stewart I. Edelstein, Executor. All Rights Reserved.

Johnson began to conceive of a new strip with a wider scope than the *Little Man with the Eyes*. In May 1941, he and George Annand formed Colored Continuities with the goal of syndicating Dave's new comic and Annand's *Ripley's Believe It or Not*–style strip. When that plan failed, Johnson resumed seeking a syndicate for his strip. He believed that a move to the country would help him concentrate on this new project, so he and Ruth decided to relocate. Though a convenient one-hour commute from the city, Darien, Connecticut, was smaller, with far fewer distractions. In addition, he could escape New York City's dust and pollution, which triggered his allergies. Dave and Ruth rented a small house at 122 Five Mile River Road from Judson H. Williamson, a bandy-legged seaman and avid Republican. Dave, able to get along with anyone, avoided discussing politics with his landlord and stuck to their mutual love of boats.[20]

Dave soon discovered that he found it no easier to concentrate outside the city and was no less allergic to country dust. He told an interviewer in late 1942, "In New York, I used to go out in the park and watch the kids play. I'd wander around the streets watching people. I'd spend hours washing my paint brushes. But now I go down to the beach and watch the tide come in or I watch the grass grow—in season. And I spend a lot of time coddling the furnace." He also spent time visiting friends in Darien, including Annand and his daughter, Alice, and Richter and his wife, Helen (Alice's sister), and their son, Dan.[21]

While still in New York, Johnson had decided to build his new comic strip around a precocious five-year-old boy living in a proper suburban home, and he eventually discovered that he had begun to think of the boy as "Barnaby." As he worked on the comic in Connecticut, however, he realized that the boy alone was not enough to sustain the strip. So he added Mr. O'Malley, Barnaby's pink-winged, cigar-champing fairy godfather, a character seen by the strip's children but almost never by the adults. He later recalled, "I fumbled around, just like O'Malley, and O'Malley came in by himself."[22]

8

BARNABY

Cushlamochree! Broke my magic wand! You wished for a Godparent
who could grant wishes? Lucky boy! Your wish is granted! I'm your
Fairy Godfather.
—MR. O'MALLEY, *Barnaby*, 21 April 1942

Crockett Johnson tried for more than two years to find a home for *Barnaby*. In addition to the abortive effort at self-syndication, Johnson's idea was rejected by *Collier's*. But shortly after the move to Darien, Charles Martin, Johnson's friend and the art editor of the new *PM*, came to visit and saw a half-page color Sunday *Barnaby* strip. He offered the strip to King Features, which rejected it. But *PM's* comics editor, Hannah Baker, loved it.[1]

Founded in 1940 by former *Time* editor Ralph Ingersoll, *PM* was a Popular Front newspaper. Original plans for the publication did not include comics, but Dante Quinterno's *Patoruzu* began running in August 1941, followed in December by the antifascist adventure strip *Vic Jordan* by Paine (the pseudonym of Kermit Jaediker and Charles Zerner). The progressive paper's readers included Franklin Delano Roosevelt and Eleanor Roosevelt, Vice President Henry Wallace, bandleader Duke Ellington, and writer Dorothy Parker. It printed writings by future Speaker of the House Thomas P. "Tip" O'Neill, Ernest Hemingway, and Erskine Caldwell; photographs by Margaret Bourke-White and Weegee (Arthur Fellig); maps by George Annand; and cartoons by Carl Rose, Don Freeman, and Theodor Geisel (Dr. Seuss).[2]

PM was pro–New Deal, anti–poll tax, and antifascist. When the newspaper received criticism for its leftist politics or its failure to gain a wider circulation, Geisel rose to its defense, praising it as a courageous voice amid an otherwise docile domestic news media. In March 1942, he wrote, "Give this paper a break—remember that for almost a year it was a lone voice in American journalism sounding the alarm that America would be attacked." To avoid compromising its editorial judgment, the paper refused to run ads, relying

Crockett Johnson, *Barnaby*, 20 April 1942. Image courtesy of Rosebud Archives. Reprinted with the permission of the Estate of Ruth Krauss, Stewart I. Edelstein, Executor. All Rights Reserved.

Crockett Johnson, *Barnaby*, 21 April 1942. Image courtesy of Rosebud Archives. Reprinted with the permission of the Estate of Ruth Krauss, Stewart I. Edelstein, Executor. All Rights Reserved.

instead on subscriptions and on department store heir Marshall Field III and other progressive investors to pay the bills.[3]

PM's readers met Barnaby Baxter on 14 April 1942 in an advertisement that shows him walking, looking up, and calling "Mr. O'Malley!" Several more ads followed before the strip made its debut on 20 April.

Johnson always claimed that O'Malley was not based on any particular person. Eight months after the strip's debut, Johnson said, "None of my friends, in spite of what *their* friends have been saying, is Mr. O'Malley." He continued, "O'Malley is at least a hundred different people. A lot of people think he's W. C. Fields, but he isn't. Still you couldn't live in America and not put some of Fields into O'Malley. O'Malley is partly [New York] Mayor [Fiorello] La Guardia and his cigar and eyes are occasionally borrowed from Jimmy Savo," a vaudeville comic and singer.[4]

For all the attention that Mr. O'Malley would ultimately receive, Johnson always considered Barnaby the star: "Even if Mr. O'Malley gets all the notice, it's still Barnaby who is the hero. We're all looking at Mr. O'Malley through Barnaby. He couldn't exist without The Kid." In late 1943, he answered the question of who had inspired Barnaby: "I don't get anything much from kids. How can you? They are all different. And I don't draw or write Barnaby for children. People who write for children usually write down to them. I don't

Crockett Johnson, "Don't Blab," cartoon for the Office of War Information, ca. 1942. Image courtesy of the National Archives II, College Park, Maryland. Reprinted with the permission of the Estate of Ruth Krauss, Stewart I. Edelstein, Executor. All Rights Reserved.

believe in that. . . . [W]hen it comes to knowing about children, it's a terribly old thing to say, but everyone was once a child himself."[5]

In the earliest strips, Johnson was still working out his style, the characters, and the boundaries between O'Malley's world and the world of the grown-ups. In addition to *Barnaby*, Dave continued to write the *Little Man with the Eyes* for *Collier's* and served as liaison between the U.S. Treasury Department and American Society of Magazine Cartoonists, helping to promote the War Bond campaign. He wrote the script for a War Bond strip drawn by Ellison Hoover that ran "in house organs of big companies."[6]

Ruth Krauss continued to commute into New York to take anthropology courses at Columbia. Her instructors included Gene Weltfish, whom she

considered "a friend," and Ruth Benedict, whom Krauss "used to go and hear
... lecture the way some people go to plays." She also sought to contribute to
the war effort by "fighting 'Fascism,' on the home front as well as abroad. Also
seeing the disappearance of all attitudes involving cruelty to others or denial
of the rights of others; and having these attitudes supplanted by those based
on scientific research and a sense of fairness," as she wrote in March 1944.
When the idea of distributing an antiracist pamphlet among the members of
the U.S. armed forces came up, Krauss and about a dozen others connected to
Columbia's anthropology program drafted ideas that would inspire Benedict
and Weltfish's best-selling *The Races of Mankind* (1943).[7]

A thirty-two-page booklet illustrated by Ad Reinhardt, *The Races of
Mankind* used science to show that we are all "one human race" and that
culture, not nature, explains differences between peoples. In the 1940s, this
idea was controversial. Among those who objected, Kentucky congressman
Andrew May was upset by Benedict and Weltfish's use of data from World
War I army intelligence tests in which southern whites scored lower than
northern blacks and by the authors' contention that "the differences did not
arise because people were from the North or the South, or because they were
white or black, but because of differences in income, education, cultural ad-
vantages, and other opportunities." May persuaded the army not to distribute
The Races of Mankind, thereby inspiring public protests, garnering media coverage, and boosting sales. The pamphlet sold nearly a million copies in its first
ten years and was translated into French, German, and Japanese.[8]

Barnaby rapidly built a devoted following among culturally influential
people, including Dorothy Parker, W. C. Fields, *Terry and the Pirates* creator
Milt Caniff, and Duke Ellington. When O'Malley and Barnaby visited a radio
station in a November 1942 strip, O'Malley said, "Give ear to the strains of this
Duke Ellington opus, m'boy . . . Sizzling but solid—as we cognizant felidae
say." Ellington subsequently wrote in to *PM*, "Please tell Crockett Johnson to
thank Mr. O'Malley on my behalf for coming out as an Ellington fan. That
makes the admiration mutual." He concluded, "Tell Barnaby that I believe in
Mr. O'Malley—solidly." When the first *Barnaby* collection was published in
September of the following year, Parker wrote, "I think, and I am trying to talk
calmly, that Barnaby and his friends and oppressors are the most important
additions to American arts and letters in Lord knows how many years. I know
that they are the most important additions to my heart."[9]

Despite its prominent fans, the comic's circulation grew slowly. In late 1943,
Barnaby was in 16 American newspapers, and by the following October, that

Chapter XXIV

YOU PAY TAXES, TOO!

Millionaire Cadwalader and thirty-dollar-a-week Tom Kent pay the same indirect taxes

Crockett Johnson, illustration from Constance Foster, *This Rich World: The Story of Money* (New York: McBride, 1943). Reprinted with the permission of the Estate of Ruth Krauss, Stewart I. Edelstein, Executor. All Rights Reserved.

number had grown to 33. At its height, *Barnaby* was syndicated in only 52 papers. (By contrast, Chic Young's *Blondie*, the strip with perhaps the largest circulation, was appearing in as many as 850 papers at that time.) As Johnson observed in late 1942, "If *Dick Tracy* were dropped from the *News*, 300,000 readers would say, 'Oh dear!' But if Barnaby went from *PM*, his 300 readers would write indignant letters." Though it never had a mass following, *Barnaby* was by 1943 already earning Johnson five thousand dollars per year.[10]

In the spring of 1943, Johnson's career branched in another direction when he illustrated his first children's book, Constance J. Foster's *This Rich World: The Story of Money*. Along with Ruth Brindze's *Johnny Get Your Money's Worth*

(1938), *This Rich World* is one of the first wave of children's books inspired by the consumer movement, designed to educate children about money and the marketplace. Expressing Foster's understanding that "many of our problems are economic at root," *This Rich World* is also the sole children's book to display any hint that Johnson was once a *New Masses* editor. One illustration notes that "Millionaire Cadwalader and thirty-dollar-a-week Tom Kent pay the same indirect taxes," a not-so-subtle criticism of the flat nature of the sales tax. Another suggests the precariousness of an economic system built on borrowing. One man in a suit gives a thousand-dollar deposit to another man in a suit, identified as banker. The banker then gives a thousand-dollar loan to another man in a suit, who gives a thousand-dollar check to the first man.[11]

For her part, Krauss soon became annoyed that when a student did research, the professor's name went on the publication. Moreover, her anthropological work made her acutely aware that children quickly absorb the values of their culture; effecting change would require reaching children early in life. When she discussed this idea with one of her friends, the friend responded, "You should be writing for children and not doing this." Inspired, Krauss started writing a book that she hoped would give children progressive ideas. She undertook an anthropological examination of prejudice that would teach children about the dangers of fascism and anti-Semitism.[12]

She took her manuscript to Harper and Brothers, riding the elevator up to the office of Ursula Nordstrom. Nearly a decade younger than Krauss, Nordstrom had joined Harper in 1931 and had become director of the Department of Books for Boys and Girls in 1940. When Krauss stepped off the elevator, she met Nordstrom's assistant, Charlotte Zolotow, who was supposed to screen visitors. Zolotow remembered a young woman with "disheveled hair," an "off-beat" sense of humor and "perspective about life," and obviously strong "feelings for children." After a few minutes, Zolotow went into Nordstrom's office and said, "You've got to see her, you've *got* to see her!" Nordstrom and Krauss then talked for a long while. After Krauss left, Nordstrom told Zolotow, "She's wonderful, and she's going to write a book for us." But it would not be the manuscript Krauss had brought with her: "That was a life of Hitler, and I didn't think that would do for the children's book world."[13]

Before the end of World War II, children's books that tackle prejudice are rare. In the wake of the war, Ernest Crichlow's illustrations for Jerrold and Lorraine Beim's *Two Is a Team* (1945) show black and white children who are best friends. H. A. and Margret Rey, the creators of *Curious George* and acquaintances of Krauss and Johnson, created *Spotty* (1945), in which spotted bunnies and white bunnies learn to get along. Ruth's manuscript was still a couple years ahead of the curve.[14]

Johnson, too, was working on what would become his first published book, revising and redrawing the best episodes of *Barnaby*'s first ten months for publication in a single volume in the fall of 1943. He also continued to work on new daily *Barnaby* strips, usually at night. Sitting at his desk and smoking a cigarette, Johnson would write and draw from 11:00 at night until 5:00 the next morning. He usually spent two nights writing the week's script, followed by two nights drawing the strips. Sometimes he was running so late that at 6:00 in the morning, he would bring his strips, ink still wet, to his neighbor Bob McNell, who would drop them off at the PM Syndicate on the way to his job in New York City. Like his character, Harold, Johnson relied on his ability to improvise under pressure. Just as, when falling off a cliff, Harold keeps "his wits and his purple crayon" and draws himself a balloon, so the approaching deadline focused Johnson's wit, igniting his imagination at night.[15]

9

A GOOD MAN AND HIS GOOD WIFE

Then, the man and the girl get married.
They hold hands
and they ride home
—galoop galoop galoop galoop
galoop galoop galoop galoop—
together.
—RUTH KRAUSS, *Somebody Else's Nut Tree and Other Tales from Children* (1958)

Dave's working methods meant that he and Ruth kept very different hours. Ruth rose at seven in the morning, after which she would take their two dogs for a walk along the Five Mile River. While he slept, Ruth began working on story ideas in her upstairs studio. Dave rose at noon, and Ruth fixed his breakfast and her lunch shortly thereafter. Then he would read for about two hours before working in their Victory Garden or going sailing while she swam. At 5:30, they had dinner, prepared by Ruth. Dave would start work on *Barnaby* at 8:00 but found that he only really got under way after the 11:00 news. Despite living in different personal time zones, they were a very close couple—so close that, on 25 June 1943, they got married in New London, Connecticut.[1]

Harper gave Krauss a three-hundred-dollar advance and a contract for her first children's book in October 1943. Influenced by her work on Ruth Benedict's anthropological project on south Italian farming families, *A Good Man and His Good Wife* offers a novel twist on folktales that mock a husband's failed attempts to copy his wife. In contrast, Krauss has mimicry supporting the husband's efforts to teach a lesson to the wife. Nonetheless, as Krauss admitted four years later, *A Good Man and His Good Wife* "made some mistakes" because "the characters are cast in the conventional roles." The "good man" can never find anything because his good wife keeps moving things around, explaining, "My dear, I get so tired of the same things in the same place." Frustrated, he puts his shoe on his head, his garters around his neck, his tie around his knee, his pants on his arms, his coat on his legs, his spectacles

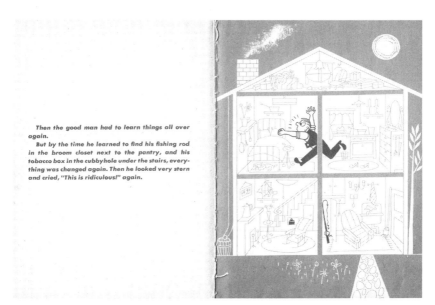

Then the good man had to learn things all over again.

But by the time he learned to find his fishing rod in the broom closet next to the pantry, and his tobacco box in the cubbyhole under the stairs, everything was changed again. Then he looked very stern and cried, "This is ridiculous!" again.

Ad Reinhardt, two-page spread from Ruth Krauss, *A Good Man and His Good Wife* (New York: Harper, 1944). Reproduced courtesy of Anna Reinhardt. Copyright © Anna Reinhardt.

on his elbow, and his socks on his ears. He then sits on the breakfast table, eating his napkin and wiping his face with a biscuit. When his wife exclaims, "My dear, this is ridiculous!," he replies, "My dear, I get so tired of the same things in the same place." The tactic cures "his good woman of a bad habit": she stops moving things around.[2]

Ad Reinhardt received the same advance and worked up a rough dummy of the book while Krauss pondered her next project, an anti-ageist children's book, *I'm Tired of Being a Grandma*. Ursula Nordstrom found parts of the beginning amusing but considered the manuscript "forced" and "not a really good follow-up to *A Good Man and His Good Wife*." Krauss persisted, sending Nordstrom two new versions of the story because "our concepts of how people think, feel, and behave at certain ages, are socially conditioned," and these concepts were "practically as bad as race-prejudice, prejudice against women, immigrants, etc." Krauss pointed to "the Northwest Coast Indians of the United States and Canada" as holding "entirely different concepts about old people": "Among these Indians, the high point of romantic sex is old-age, about seventy to ninety. You're supposed to be romantic then; so, consequently, you

Crockett Johnson with the cover drawing for *Barnaby* (New York: Holt, 1943). Image courtesy of the Smithsonian Institution. Reprinted with the permission of the Estate of Ruth Krauss, Stewart I. Edelstein, Executor. All Rights Reserved.

are romantic then." Though sympathetic, Nordstrom did not think the idea worked as a story.[3]

Also in October 1943, Henry Holt published *Barnaby*, bringing the darling of the smart set to a wider audience. Rockwell Kent praised "Crockett Johnson's profound understanding of the psychology of the child, of grownups and of fairy godfathers." William Rose Benét, who won the 1942 Pulitzer Prize for poetry, called *Barnaby* "a classic of humor" and declared Mr. O'Malley "a character to live with the Mad Hatter, the White Rabbit, Ferdinand, and all great creatures of fantasy." Ruth McKenney, whose *My Sister Eileen* had been nominated for an Oscar earlier that year, took delight in "that evil intentioned, vain, pompous, wonderful little man with the wings." She "suppose[d] Mr. O'Malley has fewer morals than any other character in literature which is, of course, what makes him so fascinating." Dorothy Parker began her "Mash

Note to Crockett Johnson" by confessing that she had tried and failed to write a review of his work: "It never comes out a book review. It is always a valentine for Mr. Johnson."[4]

The first printing of ten thousand copies sold out in just a week, and sales reached forty thousand copies by the end of the year. The 4 October issues of both *Life* and *Newsweek* ran features on *Barnaby*. Reprinting the ten-strip sequence in which Gorgon, the dog, begins to talk, *Life* described *Barnaby* "as a breath of sweet cool air" and thought the comic "written and drawn with the intelligent innocence of a Lewis Carroll classic." *Newsweek*'s profile reprinted some of the positive press, noting that, although "only seven papers" run *Barnaby*, "the intense enthusiasm of their small audience more than offsets the lack of numbers." Indeed, if *PM* were "to cease publication tomorrow, the first question asked by a large bloc of its 140,000-odd readers would be: 'Where is Barnaby going?'" On 9 November, New York's Norlyst Gallery began a four-week exhibition of original *Barnaby* strips. For two hours on opening night, Crockett Johnson sat at a table between two mounted displays of his *Barnaby* comics. With cigarette in his left hand and pen in his right, he signed copies of *Barnaby* for fans, including Broadway actress Paula Laurence and painter Jimmy Ernst.[5]

Of all the *Barnaby* characters, only O'Malley truly captured the public's imagination. When *Barnaby* fan clubs began to form, they inevitably named themselves after the club to which O'Malley belongs, the Elves, Leprechauns, Gnomes, and Little Men's Chowder and Marching Society. Such societies formed not only in New York, New Jersey, and Connecticut but also in Colorado and in Italy (founded by a serviceman). One fan urged the postmaster general to issue an O'Malley stamp, and another nominated him as *Time*'s Man of the Year. In 1944, O'Malley inspired both a song ("Mr. O'Malley's March") and an ad campaign for Crown Zippers. To capitalize further on the strip's success, *PM*'s Hannah Baker licensed the manufacture of dolls based on the *Barnaby* characters, although war shortages delayed production and Baker eventually abandoned the project.[6]

Krauss continued to envision other ideas for books, none of them successful. In January 1944, she sent Nordstrom *Elizabeth Hears the Story of Our Flood*, based on her experience of the 1936 Bucks County flood. In February, Krauss sent Nordstrom a rough dummy for what she called "a 'culture' book for older children: i.e. putting across the idea that behavior taken by us for granted as natural is actually conditioned." Nordstrom was not interested in either book but encouraged Krauss to keep trying.[7]

Krauss's next idea came after she found herself imagining a conversation with the five-year-old boy who lived next door. The result was a one-hundred-word story, *The Carrot Seed*, about a little boy who believes his carrot will come up even though everyone tells him that it won't. Johnson created an illustrated dummy for the book, and Nordstrom loved it. In late May 1944, Johnson and Krauss received book contracts and advances of three hundred dollars each. Krauss joked that on a per-word basis, she had become "the highest paid author of the printed word." Ruth was proud of herself. For the first time, she seemed to be succeeding in her chosen occupation.[8]

Because *Barnaby* had given Crockett Johnson name recognition and Ruth Krauss lacked it, Harper's marketing department initially promoted *The Carrot Seed* to bookstores as illustrated by Crockett Johnson and "written by his wife." Angry, Krauss wrote to her publisher that the phrase was "embarrassing because I'm made to trade on another person's reputation." The wording implied that the "artist with reputation illustrates this book, *not* because it is a good book and one that he's interested in illustrating, by a writer named Ruth Krauss, but because he's being nice to his wife, Ruth Krauss, who's [*sic*] book probably stinks except that he's probably touched it up here and there." Nordstrom found Krauss's attitude "incredible" but nevertheless told her, "OK—we'll never mention your marital connections again."[9]

With two-color cartoon illustrations by Reinhardt, *A Good Man and His Good Wife* was published in the fall of 1944. Although it now seems somewhat sexist, reviewers at the time found it funny and offered praise. The *Magazine of Art* named it one of the year's best children's books, "infused . . . with real wit" that would be "enjoyed by people of all ages." Three decades later, critic Barbara Bader wrote that "nonsense" is key to the tale's appeal. The man's tactic of taking his wife's words at face value is "not unlike the way kids confound their elders, sometimes innocently, sometimes not, by taking their words literally too."[10]

Once *Barnaby* became moderately successful, Johnson found that creating a finely tuned daily strip required a lot of work: "There's nothing worse than the obligation to be funny." He realized that he needed help. Fresh out of the army, Howard Sparber got a job at *PM*, thinking that he would be a staff artist. When he reported for work, however, he learned that Johnson had seen Sparber's portfolio and wanted to hire him as an assistant to do inking on *Barnaby*.[11]

Meeting Johnson's exacting standards was a challenge. According to Sparber, "I could never quite grasp the tightness of his line. I learned a great deal from him, but I didn't draw that way." Sparber saw Johnson as more than a perfectionist: "Perfectionist is sort of ordinary. He was way beyond that." Johnson's background in layout and in typography inspired him to set his dialogue in type. *Barnaby* was the first strip to always use typeset dialogue, with Johnson using *italicized Futura medium*. Designed by German typographer Paul Renner in the 1920s, Futura embodies the Crockett Johnson aesthetic: it excises needless detail, rendering its simple geometric forms in precise lines of uniform width. This devotion to precision informs Johnson's diction, too. As Sparber explained, the type "wasn't just sort of dashed in. Dave would be writing the text as if he was counting characters in his head, because he knew he had to do five lines to fit into a balloon that would be over Mr. O'Malley's head."[12]

Once a week, Sparber went to the type shop at *PM* and picked up the type to be pasted into the *Barnaby* speech balloons, along with galleys of completed but wordless strips, and brought the materials to Darien. Sparber would stay with Krauss and Johnson for two or three days while Johnson wrote a week's worth of new *Barnaby* dailies and pasted the words into the galleys of the earlier strips. Because Johnson worked at night, Sparber saw little of him, although "once in a great while, he'd come down and we'd have breakfast together. Then he'd get back upstairs because he was tired—he had to get to sleep in the day."[13]

Johnson was also working on a new *Barnaby* book. As with the first collection, he selected only the best strips, revising and redrawing seven months' worth of work for inclusion in *Barnaby and Mr. O'Malley*. Probably aided by his friend Joseph Skelly, a Du Pont Chemical engineer who may have been a model for Atlas, the strip's slide-rule-carrying "mental giant," Johnson revised the math formulae in the 26 May 1943 strip, when Atlas meets Barnaby's fairy godfather but forgets his name. In the original strip, Atlas speaks a mathematically meaningless formula that serves as a mnemonic for *O'Malley*; in the revised version, however, the formula has meaning:

$$(e^{ni} + 1) + M \int_0^A dx + \begin{vmatrix} \log N & y \\ -1n^{-1} 1 & L^2 \end{vmatrix}$$

$$N \to 10$$

As J. B. Stroud shows, Euler's equation demonstrates "that $e^{ni}+1=0$." Simplifying the next component, $M \int_0^A dx = MA$. Thus far, Atlas's formula spells out "0 + MA." Unscrambling the rest of the equation, Stroud proves that

$$\begin{vmatrix} \log N & y \\ -1n^{-1}\,1 & L^2 \end{vmatrix} = (\log N)L^2 + (1n^{-1}\,1)y \text{ as } N \to 10$$

$$= (\log 10)L^2 + e^1 y$$

$$= LL + ey$$

The equation thus spells *O'Malley*, a complex joke comprehensible only to mathematicians. The math professors not only got the joke but used *Barnaby* strips in their lectures. In late 1948, when Engineering Research Associates got the go-ahead to build a code-breaking computer for the U.S. government, the engineers named the machine Atlas.[14]

The sophistication was too much for some. In late June 1944, the *Baltimore Evening Sun* dropped *Barnaby* because managing editor Miles H. Wolff thought it "had not held up and was getting rather boresome." The *Sun* soon found itself flooded by letters demanding the return of Barnaby and his fairy godfather: "A dastardly attack has been made upon the most subtly sophisticated character of our time," wrote Mary E. O'Malley (who described herself as "no relation!"). "Here at last we have a comic that captures completely the magical world of childhood," she continued, "where . . . the adult world is revealed in all its cynical dullness." Fans signed a petition to restore *Barnaby*, insisting that the "strip has a genuinely subtle humor which surpasses that of all others found in your publication." If some readers don't "appreciate this humor," that is "insufficient reason for withdrawing it from a newspaper whose aim, we presume, is to please those of all intellectual levels." A week later, *Barnaby* returned, with Wolff's apologies.[15]

The strip's subtle political humor gave it a wider appeal than Johnson's *New Masses* work. For example, in the fall of 1944, O'Malley expresses his support for Thomas E. Dewey, the Republican nominee in the upcoming presidential election, because "a lot of generals got to be presidents, but, so far, not any ADMIRALS." Johnson also depicts three ghosts as strong Dewey supporters: One of the ghosts, Colonel Wurst, is named for two anti-Roosevelt and isolationist newspaper owners, Colonel Robert McCormick of the *Chicago Tribune* and William Randolph Hearst of the *New York Journal-American* and several other papers. Wurst introduces another ghost, A.A., as "able to give us the direct, uncolored view of a 'Man in the Street,'" but when A.A. advises Barnaby, "Sell short, young fellow, sell short," it becomes clear that he is not a "Man in the Street" but an investor. Implying that Dewey's supporters are deluded by nostalgia, Johnson has Colonel Wurst printing progressively

Crockett Johnson, page from *Barnaby and Mr. O'Malley* (New York: Holt, 1944). Reprinted with the permission of the Estate of Ruth Krauss, Stewart I. Edelstein, Executor. All Rights Reserved.

Crockett Johnson, *Barnaby*, 8 September 1944. Image courtesy of Rosebud Archives. Reprinted with the permission of the Estate of Ruth Krauss, Stewart I. Edelstein, Executor. All Rights Reserved.

Crockett Johnson, *Barnaby*, 29 September 1944. Image courtesy of Rosebud Archives. Reprinted with the permission of the Estate of Ruth Krauss, Stewart I. Edelstein, Executor. All Rights Reserved.

earlier newspapers. One from 31 October proclaims "Peace in Our Time" (Chamberlain's defense of the Munich agreement, September 1938), and by 7 November 1944, the clock has been turned back to before the 1929 stock market crash: The ghosts stroll off, singing "Happy Days Are Here Again." Johnson thus mocks without offending: As the *Bridgeport Sunday Herald*'s Ethel Beckwith observed in October 1944, "Nobody gets mad. Readers of both parties think they are slyer than the cartoonist in making it out for their side."[16]

Johnson, however, remained a supporter of Franklin Roosevelt's reelection, lending both his name and his artwork to the Artists Committee for the President's Birthday and to the Independent Voters Committee of the Arts and Sciences for Roosevelt (IVCASR). To promote FDR's campaign, IVCASR published a twenty-two-page booklet containing the text of FDR's 23 September 1944 speech to the Teamsters Union with illustrations by nineteen progressive artists. In the address, Roosevelt commented about recent Republican criticism, "Well, of course, I don't resent attacks and my family don't resent attacks, but Fala does resent them." Fala was the president's Scotch terrier, and when he learned that "the Republican fiction writers in Congress" had alleged that Roosevelt had sent a destroyer to fetch the dog, "his Scotch soul was furious. He has not been the same dog since." Hugo Gellert drew a

Crockett Johnson, illustrations from "Sister, You Need the Union! . . . And the Union Needs You!" (United Auto Workers–CIO pamphlet, 1944). Images courtesy of the Smithsonian Institution. Reprinted with the permission of the Estate of Ruth Krauss, Stewart I. Edelstein, Executor. All Rights Reserved.

heroic portrait of FDR, William Gropper caricatured Republican opponents of the New Deal, Lynd Ward offered a heroic image of the American factory worker making airplanes, and Syd Hoff showed the common man donating a dollar to FDR while a fat capitalist gives a big sack of money to Dewey. Crockett Johnson drew a portrait of an indignant Fala.[17]

Earlier in 1944, Johnson illustrated a United Auto Workers–CIO pamphlet, "Sister, You Need the Union! . . . *And the Union Needs You!*," that reminded women to get involved with their union and to help themselves by helping the union "make a better world." It concluded by advising, "Get Busy in the CIO Political Action Campaign. *Register and Vote!*" Enlisting O'Malley in support of the war effort, Johnson also devised slogans for a War Bond display window in Lewis and Conger, a New York department store.[18]

Holt published *Barnaby and Mr. O'Malley* in September 1944 to mixed response. Even reviewers who praised the first volume now struggled to classify Johnson's comic strip. Isabelle Mallet of the *New York Times*, who had called *Barnaby* "a series of comic strips which, laid end to end, reach from here to wherever you want to go before you die" and who found the new book engaging, could not find the right words to "pay suitable tribute. We might just as well try to fasten the Nobel Prize on a rainbow." In *Booklist*, proletarian novelist Jack Conroy, whose first children's book, a collaboration with Arna Bontemps, had appeared in 1942, concluded that *Barnaby and Mr. O'Malley* had "adult and adolescent appeal, rather than juvenile, but the book might be

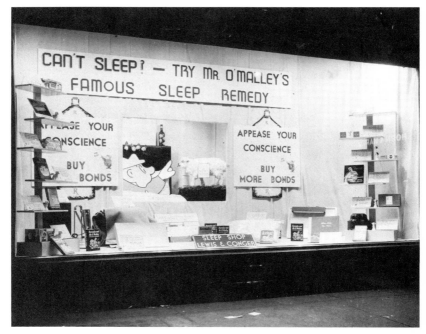

"Can't Sleep?—Try Mr. O'Malley's Famous Sleep Remedy. Appease Your Conscience. Buy More Bonds." Window display at Lewis and Conger, New York, October 1944. Image courtesy of the Smithsonian Institution. Reprinted with the permission of the Estate of Ruth Krauss, Stewart I. Edelstein, Executor. All Rights Reserved.

used with older children as a substitute for comic books." *Commonweal* reviewed the book in a section devoted to works for "the very young." Its review was equally confused: "Appeals to readers of all ages, though it is a rather special taste. Some like it and some do not."[19]

Johnson was also working on the final artwork for *The Carrot Seed*. Nordstrom thought the little boy "perfect in most of the pictures" but felt he "shouldn't look surprised or doubtful in any of" them because he needs a "sense of sublime assurance throughout." Johnson agreed with the suggestion and "fixed . . . up" the boy's expression. He gave precise instructions to the printers to ensure that the book's colors were exactly right: brown, red, green, and light cream, though he was not completely sure about the last one. "Omit Light Cream?," he wrote on the chart. The printers did, and yellow appeared in the final book.[20]

A week after he sent in the final changes to the *Carrot Seed* illustrations, Dave and Ruth took the train into New York City, where, at the Hotel Commodore Ballroom, they attended a dinner honoring Johnson's *New Masses* colleague William Gropper on his forty-seventh birthday. Sponsored by the Joint Anti-Fascist Refugee Committee, the dinner featured remarks from Dorothy Parker, Carl Sandburg, and radio broadcaster Norman Corwin. In addition to Johnson, the sixty-five sponsors listed on the program included conductor-composer Leonard Bernstein; composers Aaron Copeland and Earl Robinson; lyricist E. Y. Harburg; artists Alexander Calder, Marc Chagall, Rockwell Kent, Boardman Robinson, Louis Slobodkin, and William Steig; novelists W. Somerset Maugham and Howard Fast; screenwriter John Howard Lawson; and Paul Robeson.[21]

At around the same time, a coalition including some of Johnson's *New Masses* friends formed the Committee for Equal Justice for Mrs. Recy Taylor, and by February 1945, Johnson had joined the group. Taylor was a black Alabama woman who had been gang-raped by six white men in September 1944. Although local law enforcement could identify the men, they were not charged with the crime. Though much less famous than the Scottsboro Boys case thirteen years earlier, Taylor's plight highlighted persistent racial injustice in Alabama, an issue that Johnson also took up in *Barnaby*. In November 1943, O'Malley had been elected to Congress, and a March 1944 strip had him telling Barnaby about Representative Rumpelstilskin, a blowhard who supports the poll tax, offering "incoherent shrieks about states' rights" as a result of his "neurosis." According to O'Malley, Representative "Rump" is "elected by only 2½ per cent of the people in his district. Other congressmen get eleven times his vote. Representing a minority group, he feels he doesn't amount to very much." The National Committee to Abolish the Poll Tax subsequently used this *Barnaby* strip in its campaign.[22]

Barnaby was poised for greater success. In March 1944, George Pal, creator of the Puppetoons animated movies, sought to adapt the comic strip for a short film. Johnson had already begun collaborating on a musical version of *Barnaby* with Ted and Matilda Ferro, residents of Cos Cob, Connecticut, who were also writing the radio serial *Lorenzo Jones*. For the music, they enlisted Harold J. Rome, author of the music and lyrics for *Pins and Needles*, a Popular Front Broadway musical about love and labor in the garment industry. Neither project came to fruition, but by the middle of 1944, a new creative team began adapting *Barnaby* for the stage.[23]

The producer behind the new venture was Barney Josephson, proprietor of Café Society, a progressive and integrated New York nightclub where the bartenders were Abraham Lincoln Brigade veterans and where Billie Holiday first sang "Strange Fruit." For the book, Josephson brought in Michael Kanin, who had won an Academy Award in 1942 for *Woman of the Year*, which starred Katharine Hepburn and Spencer Tracy. When Kanin's Hollywood career prevented him from working on *Barnaby*, Josephson sought *New Yorker* humorist S. J. Perelman. For the lyrics, Josephson enlisted John LaTouche, lyricist for "Ballad for Americans" (1940), the unofficial anthem of the Popular Front. Jimmy Savo, one of the inspirations for Mr. O'Malley, signed on to play Barnaby's fairy godfather.[24]

This success gave Dave enough income to buy a home, and in February 1945, he purchased a house in Rowayton, directly across the Five Mile River from the Darien house he and Ruth had been renting. Located at 74 Rowayton Avenue, on the corner of Crockett Street, the house faced the water. He also bought the land on the other side of Rowayton Avenue so that he could moor his boat at the dock across the street.[25]

That spring, Harper published *The Carrot Seed*, which Ruth privately called *The Toinip Top*. The book was an immediate hit. *Kirkus* called it a "good humored tale" and noted that "the publishers, in choosing Crockett Johnson, creator of Barnaby and Mr. O'Malley, as illustrator, have picked the ideal person for the job." The *New York Times Book Review*'s Ellen Lewis Buell thought it a "parable" that would appeal to old and young alike, "portrayed in pictures that are economical of line as the text is with words." It quickly became a phenomenon.[26]

One admirer sent a copy of *The Carrot Seed* to the United Nations Conference on International Organization in San Francisco, where representatives from fifty countries would sign the United Nations charter that June. In August, the president of an engineering firm sent out one hundred copies to executives in many fields, who in turn sought copies to send to their colleagues and employees. The Catholic Church put *The Carrot Seed* on its list of recommended reading, conveying the message, "Have faith and you'll get results." A neighbor of Ruth and Dave's thought it a "swell book" with a great moral: "Never trust anybody, not even your parents." The book's openness to a range of interpretations was key to its success.[27]

In the fall, Dave and Ruth moved into their own home, where they would reside for the next twenty-seven years, creating many more classic books. First, however, they would need to learn to cope with their own success.

10

THE ATHENS OF SOUTH NORWALK

I'll admit, Barnaby, at times I nourish misgivings about the entire venture.
—MR. O'MALLEY, in Crockett Johnson, *Barnaby*, 9 April 1945

Crockett Johnson's success brought financial security—and more work. People wrote to request original strips, ask him to donate artwork to various causes, and inquire if they might reprint *Barnaby* comics. Editors found *Barnaby* very useful for illustrating concepts.

To highlight the need to educate the public about statistics, the *American Statistical Association Bulletin* chose a *Barnaby* in which O'Malley misuses statistical methods, "fitting the data to the curve" instead of using the data to plot the curve. For a report on the wartime scarcity of cigarettes, a December 1944 *Advertising Age* uses a strip in which O'Malley suggests that "advertising writers" are responsible for the tobacco shortage: "They never write about anything but the FINEST tobaccos. And the superlatives can be applied to only about one percent of the crop," leaving "ninety-nine percent of the tobacco . . . utterly wasted!" To accompany an article on daytime radio serials illustrated by Saul Steinberg, the March 1946 *Fortune* ran Dave's 30 January 1945 comic, in which Barnaby points to a radio broadcasting the words "Sob. Sob. Sob." He observes, "This lady sounds just like the ones on all the other programs, Mr. O'Malley." His godfather explains that this is "a very stylized art form," but the "tiny nuances writers and actors are permitted to inject" serve as "the basis of the devotee's esthetic enjoyment." To display the best of the nation's popular culture, the U.S. Office of War Information asked for six *Barnaby* cartoons to feature in a spring 1945 exhibition of American cartoons in Paris. Johnson sent six original strips.[1]

Adapting *Barnaby* for the stage was proving trickier than anticipated, and changes in script, writers, and cast threatened to delay production. *Barnaby* did, however, make its radio debut on 12 June 1945. On the second half of that day's *Frank Morgan Show*, Morgan (best known for portraying the title character in MGM's *Wizard of Oz*) played O'Malley, and seven-year-old Norma

Crockett Johnson posing with the Barnaby strip of 22 April 1944. Image courtesy of the Smithsonian Institution. Reprinted with the permission of the Estate of Ruth Krauss, Stewart I. Edelstein, Executor. All Rights Reserved.

Jean Nilsson played Barnaby. No further episodes aired. At the same time, Johnson was cranking out six *Barnaby* strips each week, imprisoned by his own perfectionism: "I never feel that I can let down. If I did, the stuff wouldn't get to be just mediocre; it would be terrible." Thinking that quarterly deadlines might allow him to take some time off, he sought "to do strips that were syndicated only in quarterlies." The first issue of the *Barnaby Quarterly* made its debut in July 1945, reprinting Barnaby's adventures from the first five months of the year.[2]

Ruth Krauss had more time to think but was out of ideas. Even before *The Carrot Seed* was published, she had begun contemplating next her book but found herself uninspired. She rummaged through "some cartons full of old manuscripts" that she kept "in honor of an occasion like this" and pulled out on story about a boy who imagines that he's a superhero. But "the story was around ten thousand words long," far too long for a picture book, and although "the idea seemed clear, . . . it needed a lot of rewriting."[3]

Krauss rewrote the story over and over but was not satisfied. She noticed that when she told the story to friends, they laughed. To try to capture that

Crockett Johnson, cover of *Barnaby Quarterly*, July 1945. Reprinted with the permission of the Estate of Ruth Krauss, Stewart I. Edelstein, Executor. All Rights Reserved.

comic tone, she decided to write the story the same way that she spoke it. Pleased with her inspiration, she took the manuscript to Ursula Nordstrom at Harper, who laughed and immediately said, "I'll take it." She wanted some changes, though. She thought it should be "built up" here and there, and although it was now only fifteen hundred words, Nordstrom thought it was still too long.[4]

For assistance in revising the story, Krauss brought the manuscript to the Bank Street Writers Laboratory in July 1945. Established by Lucy Sprague Mitchell in 1938, the laboratory helped authors create books that recognized that young children's speech reflects their "immersion in the here-and-now world of the sensory realm," that children learn language not to communicate but because it is fun to play with words, and above all, that adults must trust the child's imagination.[5]

Ursula Nordstrom, n.d. From Leonard Marcus, *Margaret Wise Brown: Awakened by the Moon* (1992; New York: Quill/ Morrow, 1999). Reprinted by permission of HarperCollins Publishers.

That trust came naturally to Krauss because she took children's ideas seriously. According to Mischa Richter's son, Dan, "She just talked to children as though they were just other people." She saw him as a friend, not as a seven-year-old, and took him to see the original theatrical release of *The Razor's Edge* (1946). Recalled Richter, "Most adults are like these faces that are bending over, talking to you in sort of abridged English," but Ruth "didn't talk down to me or baby me at all." Her treatment of children as equals made the Bank Street Writers group a good fit for her.[6]

She met with the Bank Street group and "let the whole bunch go to town on" her manuscript. Krauss was "wary of the general prejudice against comic-books," and Nordstrom had suggested that the boy's superhero costume be changed because "the American Library Association will object. And many parents will object." To avoid this problem, Krauss decided on a "mixed-hero costume"—the boy would wear aspects of different heroic costumes, such as "an Indian Chief's hat," a "football suit with big padded shoulders," and "cowboy boots with spurs."[7]

The Bank Street writers had different ideas. One person said, "If I were a child and someone gave me an Indian hat and didn't finish up the Indian

THE ATHENS OF SOUTH NORWALK

costume, but gave me something else instead, I'd be awful mad." Another said, "He ought to be a sort of glorified policeman." After three hours' discussion, Krauss got the sense that "the suit should be like a supersuit, but not the supersuit; that is, it should be generally glorious and symbolic of ability—but nothing specific. This was very helpful." She went home to revise some more.[8]

The mid-1940s also saw the beginning of Ruth and Dave's long and close relationship with Phyllis Rowand, her husband, Gene Wallace, and their daughter, Nina, who was born in New York City in November 1945. The following March, four-month-old Nina took her first trip to "the country"— Connecticut. The members of the Rowand-Wallace family piled into a car with Simon and Schuster vice president Jack Goodman; his wife, Agnes, an editor; and their Great Dane, Sam, and drove up to Rowayton. That June, Gene, Phyllis, and Nina moved up to Rowayton, renting the Goodmans' cottage at 89 Rowayton Avenue, just four houses up the street from Ruth and Dave.[9]

Wallace, a World War II veteran and naval architect, shared many of Dave's interests: Both men liked to sail, enjoyed making things with their hands, and played a good game of chess. They spent many an afternoon working on their boats or smoking their pipes and chatting over the chess board. Rowand, who wrote for *Woman's Day* and created ads for Houbigant Perfume and other clients, had been thinking about branching out into children's books. Even before moving to Rowayton, she had begun collaborating with Ruth on *The Growing Story*, a tale of a little boy who notices that the grass, flowers, and trees are growing. After learning that chicks and a puppy will also grow, he asks, "Will I grow, too?" As the year passes, he notices that the plants and animals are growing but cannot see any changes in himself. When he puts on his winter clothes, however, they have become too small. He runs out into the yard to tell the chickens, "I'm growing too."[10]

Though Ruth and Dave did not raise chickens, their new home definitely felt like the country. Located in South Norwalk, Rowayton was a nineteenth-century oystering community that had become a popular summer destination for vacationers, artists, and progressives. Dave liked to call the tiny village "the Athens of South Norwalk." Ruth and Dave soon became close to other neighbors in addition to Wallace and Rowand. Actor Stefan Schnabel and his wife, singer/actress Marion Schnabel, and their children became good friends. Sculptor Harry Marinsky and his partner, Paul Bernard, moved in just across Crockett Street from the Johnson-Krauss house. The presence of an openly gay couple did not bother Ruth and Dave or anyone else in the neighborhood.

Fred Schwed Jr., Harriet Schwed, and Crockett Johnson, n.d. Image courtesy of the Smithsonian Institution. Reprinted with the permission of the Estate of Ruth Krauss, Stewart I. Edelstein, Executor. All Rights Reserved.

However, as an out gay couple, Marinsky and Bernard were atypical. Johnson and Krauss's other gay friends—Ursula Nordstrom and Maurice Sendak—did not make their sexuality public knowledge. In contrast, Marinsky and Bernard were living as a married couple some sixty years before Connecticut recognized gay marriage.[11]

Dave and Ruth also became particularly close to neighbors Fred Schwed Jr., a magazine writer and former stockbroker, and his wife, Harriet. Fred Schwed was the author of the satirical *Where Are the Customers' Yachts?; or, A Good Hard Look at Wall Street* (1940), which expressed the same sort of sentiments present in the brilliant satire of Wall Street that Johnson presented in *Barnaby* from February to May 1945. O'Malley becomes a Wall Street tycoon not through shrewd investing but because of the speculative nature of market economics. By having a character whom adults regard as imaginary use purely imaginary assets to become a wealthy financier, Johnson blurs the line between real and imagined to suggest that free-market capitalism is inherently precarious and that Wall Streeters' romantic view of the marketplace ill equips them to differentiate between profitable fantasies and market realities. As Schwed wrote, "The notion that the financial future is not predictable is just too unpleasant to be given any room at all in the Wall Streeter's consciousness." Those who work on Wall Street "are all romantics, whether they be villains or philanthropists. Else they would never have chosen this business which is a business of dreams."[12]

The *Barnaby* episode begins when O'Malley phones stockbrokers to ask about purchasing 51 percent of Hunos-Wattall Ltd. (pronounced *Who-knows-what-all*) but unknowingly talks only to an office boy. He thinks O'Malley is a "bigshot" and word gets out that "international financier" O'Malley is starting a new company. Since no one wants to admit that they have never heard of O'Malley, investors back his company, real people begin running it, and the stock soars. But speculation becomes O'Malley Enterprises' undoing: When O'Malley offers to pay cash to tailors Cuttaway and Sons for his trousers, they are insulted that he does not charge the purchase to his account. Word spreads that his credit is no longer good, and the stock plummets, bringing down the company with it. Only a few years after the end of the Great Depression and with many people worried that the conclusion of World War II might end wartime prosperity, Johnson was making a very serious point about the instability of capitalist economies. As O'Malley says about a week prior to O'Malley Enterprises' collapse, "I'll admit, Barnaby, at times I nourish misgivings about the entire venture."[13]

As the country drifted to the right, the popularity of market-driven economics revived. The death of President Franklin Roosevelt in April 1945 and the end of the war four months later marked the beginning of the end of the Popular Front. Its decline did not change Johnson, who continued to support progressive ideals. When the Independent Voters Committee of the Arts and Sciences for Roosevelt became the Independent Citizens Committee of the Arts, Sciences, and Professions (ICCASP) in December 1944, Johnson remained an active member, regularly attending meetings of the group's Norwalk chapter and winning election to the branch's executive committee in January 1946. At the national ICCASP's annual meeting in New York the following month, he was elected one of thirty-two members of the group's board of directors, along with Leonard Bernstein, Duke Ellington, Gene Kelly, Langston Hughes, Howard Fast, Moss Hart, Lillian Hellman, John Hersey, Bill Mauldin, Hazel Scott, and Orson Wells. One of the ICCASP's goals was passage of the Wagner-Murray-Dingell Bill, which promised national health insurance and money devoted to building more hospitals. To aid that cause, Johnson illustrated the Physicians Forum's *For the People's Health*, a pamphlet supporting the measure.[14]

Crockett Johnson, cover of *For the People's Health* (New York: Physicians Forum, 1946). Image courtesy of Toby Holtzman. Reprinted with the permission of the Estate of Ruth Krauss, Stewart I. Edelstein, Executor. All Rights Reserved.

That bill met defeat, but some of Johnson's causes thrived. In 1945, he signed on to the Committee for the Reelection of Benjamin J. Davis, a Communist serving on the New York City Council who won reelection by a wide margin. That same year, Johnson joined Davis in supporting the End Jim Crow in Baseball Committee, whose members also included Rockwell Kent, Paul Robeson, and Langston Hughes. In August 1945, at Stamford's Russian Relief Headquarters, both Johnson and Krauss served as sponsors and participants in the Books for Russia Committee of the American Society for Russian Relief. Krauss's involvement was unusual: She rarely expressed her political convictions by joining organizations.[15]

The story about the boy dreaming of being a superhero acquired a title, *The Great Duffy*, and Krauss hoped that Johnson would provide illustrations, as he had for *The Carrot Seed*. When his other commitments prevented him from doing so, Krauss turned to Mischa Richter, now a successful *New Yorker* cartoonist. Johnson, however, did the layout, chose the type (fourteen-point Bodoni bold), and created some sample drawings.[16]

88

Mischa Richter, cover of Ruth Krauss, *The Great Duffy* (New York: Harper, 1946). Image courtesy of the Northeast Children's Literature Collection, Dodd Research Center, University of Connecticut, Storrs. Used by permission of the Estate of Mischa Richter.

Perhaps inspired by Johnson's efforts to bring *Barnaby* to the stage, Krauss drafted a movie treatment for *The Great Duffy*. The film would have "the usual blacks and greys to symbolize reality" and "Technicolor to symbolize imagination." Each time six-year-old Duffy (renamed Buzzie in the movie version) encounters a major disappointment, he launches into a fantasy. Just before each daydream, the film dramatizes his feelings of "being very little in a very big world" by making everything larger: "Adults would enlarge to giants, ordinary furniture would take on architectural and engineering qualities." As the film switches to Technicolor, objects return to their normal size and Buzzie drifts into his fantasy world. After several such episodes, the movie concludes with him facing the challenge of crossing the street by himself but not retreating into daydreaming: To Buzzie, dealing with traffic was "as adventurous as his daydreams." He succeeds and feels "a little surer of himself."[17]

Krauss's adaptation of *The Great Duffy* expresses a deep understanding of young people's relative powerlessness in the world, a theme that remained on her mind in the fall of 1945. On 31 October, she visited Nordstrom to discuss several ideas for future books, including a short chapter book "on being small" and a picture book on the same subject. Krauss also proposed a collaboration with child psychologist Stephanie Barnhardt to edit a series of books covering "common problems," such as "fear of the dark, first day at school, refusal to eat, the new baby in the family, temper tantrums, etc." Nordstrom demurred, saying that Margaret Wise Brown's books already "did this sort of thing subtly and artistically": Brown's *Night and Day* (1942) addressed the fear of the dark; *Little Chicken* (1943) concerned the first day of school; and *The Runaway Bunny* (1942) offered the "reassurance of mother's love." Krauss pressed her idea, arguing that a series "sponsored by well-known educators would sell well," and Nordstrom acquiesced. Krauss also proposed a book inspired by her husband's tendency to let his dogs be themselves that Nordstrom thought "could be extremely funny and good." The tale about "Why the Dog Is Man's Best Friend" shows a puppy gradually "taking over a human's entire life, home, time, money."[18]

While Krauss was gearing up to write more stories, *Barnaby* was wearing Johnson out. In early November 1945, he met with Ted Ferro and Jack Morley to see if they would take over the strip. Johnson would sit in on story conferences and share in the strip's profits, but he wanted Ferro to take over writing and Morley to take over drawing. They agreed. Johnson was earning 50 percent of the net receipts of *Barnaby* reprints, with the other half going to *PM*. Johnson reduced his share to 20 percent, giving Ferro and Morley 15 percent each. Beginning on 31 December 1945, Crockett Johnson's name no longer appeared on *Barnaby*.[19]

11

ART AND POLITICS

Who ever would think a Fairy Godfather could be a nuisance?
—BARNABY, in Crockett Johnson, *Barnaby*, 28 April 1942

Freed from the daily obligation of writing and drawing *Barnaby* strips, Crockett Johnson at last had some time for all his other *Barnaby*-related projects. The second issue of the *Barnaby Quarterly* appeared in November 1945, with the third issue following three months later. Johnson was working on a third *Barnaby* book, not a collection of redrawn daily strips but "an illustrated story." Having already illustrated two children's books and drawn a comic strip that appealed to young people, Johnson was considering writing for children. The new book never appeared, likely because the *Barnaby* play needed extensive revisions. The idea of making it a musical fell by the wayside, and Jerome Chodorov, cowriter of the successful stage adaptation of *My Sister Eileen*, began working on it.[1]

Though Johnson remained active on the left, the Popular Front coalition unraveled, and its members began to attract suspicion. In March 1946, former British prime minister Winston Churchill gave what would become known as his Iron Curtain speech, warning the United States that the Soviets sought the "indefinite expansion of their power and doctrines." American conservatives took note. A month later, when the *Philadelphia Record* wanted to claim that the Independent Citizens Committee of the Arts, Sciences, and Professions had communist influence, the paper pointed to Johnson: "Suppose we look at the directors of the ICASP. Among them are the following, all closely tied with the Communist Party and/or *Daily Worker*: Howard Fast, Henrietta Buckmaster, Jose Ferrer, Crockett Johnson, Lillian Hellman (whose trip to Russia was paid for by the U.S.S.R.), and Paul Robeson." Further arousing the *Record*'s suspicion was the fact that Johnson supported New York's 1946 May Day parade, as did William Gropper, Rockwell Kent, Edward Chodorov (Jerome's brother), Fast, Clifford Odets, and Jerome Robbins.[2]

Though Johnson was not secretly working for Soviet Russia, the *Record*'s claims had some merit. Like many in the communist and peace movements, Johnson hoped that the wartime alliance between the United States and the Soviet Union could be extended into the postwar period, marking a new era of peaceful cooperation. On 14 May, he donated one hundred dollars and attended a New Haven "Peace and Security Rally" sponsored by the Communist Party of Connecticut. He joined the National Committee to Win the Peace, which sponsored the Win the Peace Conference at New York's Manhattan Center near the end of June 1946. As the group's ad in the *Daily Worker* noted, its members hoped "to carry forward F.D.R.'s policies of peace based on Big Three unity." Insinuating that Win the Peace was a communist-front group, *Time* magazine reported that at the conference, "in a strong Russian accent, delegates clamored for destruction of all atom bombs, [and] acceptance of the Soviet plan for 'outlawing' atomic war."[3]

Reflecting Johnson's activism, *Barnaby* both grew more politically engaged and conveyed wariness about political engagement. Although Johnson was no longer drawing and writing the daily strips, he remained involved in their planning. He was influential in developing a plot line that began in July 1946 about O'Malley persuading the mayor and town council to solve the postwar housing crisis with tent cities. That month and the next, Barnaby's father, Mr. Baxter, initiated petitions and organized protests, rallying citizens against the tent cities and in favor of proper housing. By the end of the month, Baxter's efforts had persuaded the council to build low-cost housing, though he received no credit for the idea. Baxter says he is satisfied with the results, but the many meetings tire him: "I'm through with politics. You make friends. But you also make enemies. Life's too short."[4]

While Johnson was attending lots of meetings, Jerome Chodorov's draft of *Barnaby and Mr. O'Malley* had become a hot Hollywood property. For the film rights, Columbia Pictures bid one hundred thousand dollars plus 5 percent of the film's profits if the play ran for five weeks, with an additional 1 percent for each week up to 30 percent. The authors would receive 60 percent of that money—half to Johnson and half to Chodorov. RKO then outbid Columbia, with a down payment of one hundred thousand dollars and a final amount that might rise as high twice that, depending on the play's success. Having created *Barnaby* in hopes of gaining a steady income, Johnson was now poised to become quite wealthy.[5]

Producers Barney Josephson and James D. Proctor likewise thought they would do very well with their first venture. To direct, they secured Charles

Friedman, director of the hit Broadway musicals *Pins and Needles* (1937–40) and *Carmen Jones* (1943–45). Offering to help Friedman stage *Barnaby and Mr. O'Malley* was playwright Moss Hart, author of *You Can't Take It With You* (1936–38) and *The Man Who Came to Dinner* (1939–41), both of which became successful films. Director Elia Kazan read Chodorov's draft and thought the play would be great. Chodorov had focused the story on two main narratives. First, the Baxters' concern about their son's "imaginary" fairy godfather prompts them to consult a child psychiatrist. The doctor advises the boy's father to make himself "more glamorous in the child's eyes," so he runs for the New York State Assembly. In a variation on O'Malley's campaign for Congress in Johnson's strip, Baxter competes against the well-funded Homer Mintleaf, whom O'Malley criticizes for wasting "thousands of dollars on cheap exhibitionism like that sky writing campaign. . . . The voters are being asked to support a businessman—well, if this wholesale waste of money is Mintleaf's idea of *business* give me a starry-eyed idealist every time!" Barnaby repeats these remarks to reporters, drumming up support for John Baxter. The play ends with O'Malley flying off to Albany to assist Baxter in his new political career. Much of Johnson's dialogue appears intact, but Chodorov also invents material to stitch together the narrative strands. In mid-August 1946, rehearsals for *Barnaby and Mr. O'Malley* began, with Irish-born Broadway veteran J. M. Kerrigan in the role of O'Malley. More than six hundred boys tried out to play Barnaby, with the part going to seven-year-old Tommy Hamilton, whom Johnson said looked "more like Barnaby than any real child I ever expected to meet." To prepare for its arrival on Broadway in early October, *Barnaby and Mr. O'Malley* would open in Wilmington, Delaware, on 6 September, moving to Baltimore on 9 September and to Boston a week later.[6]

As *Barnaby* headed for the stage and possibly the screen, Ruth Krauss worked on a children's book that would use anthropology to debunk stereotypes, echoing the approach of *The Races of Mankind*, which United Productions of America had adapted into a successful cartoon, *The Brotherhood of Man*, the preceding year. Ruth's first chapter, "On Women," noted that for Africa's Dahomey people, "Women form one third of standing army"; among the Bathonga, "Women are the great story-tellers." The second chapter, "On Men," reported that in Manus society, "men tend the babies," while the Tchambuli see men as having "the flighty character." Her fourth chapter was explicitly anti-ageist. Chapters 3 and 5 countered dominant assumptions about humanity. Hoping to prove that killing was not a "natural" part of human behavior, she pointed out that among the Todas, "there no

Barnaby Goes Broadway

Gee, Barnaby, didn't you ever see a diplodocus? They don't have much brains.

Gosh, Barnaby, I'll have to ask Mr. O'Malley. It sounds like one of his friends.

Thomas Hamilton, one of the two boys who will play the role of Barnaby on Broadway, talks things over with Barnaby himself. *Story and Barnaby in Picture News, Pages 4, 18*

Tommy Hamilton meets the character he portrays on stage. *PM*, 1946. Image courtesy of Thomas Hamilton.

record of any murder" and that certain Australian peoples had never had war. Having just seen the second world war in three decades, Krauss was drawn to the idea that a better future began with the next generation. With proper education, these children might grow into adults less inclined to pursue war as a means of resolving differences.[7]

The fall of 1946 saw the publication of *The Great Duffy* to generally good reviews. The *San Francisco Chronicle*'s Florence Little thought that the book would entertain children, citing one young reader who judged it as good as Dr. Seuss's *And to Think That I Saw It on Mulberry Street* (1937). Marjorie Fischer's *New York Times* review called the book "the child's equivalent of 'The Secret Life of Walter Mitty.'" *Kirkus* agreed that the book's "adventures . . . catch the 'Walter Mitty touch.'" Praising the book's "imaginative understanding of real small boy psychology," the review considered *The Great Duffy* a

94

"delectable book for the distracted parent who wants to wean small sons from too constant demand for comics." However, the book was "'banned' by the Child Study Association, who even refused to take ads from Harper."[8]

The production of *Barnaby and Mr. O'Malley* continued to be plagued by problems, many of them related to its costly special effects, which included making O'Malley fly out over the audience. The play was late opening in Wilmington and was staged only twice there before moving on to Baltimore; the planned weeklong run there ended when the production closed for re-pairs after just two shows. Josephson and Proctor remained convinced that *Barnaby and Mr. O'Malley* was "a potential hit" but conceded that it "needs revision." A lot of money had already been invested in the show—forty-four backers had contributed more than eighty thousand dollars. The producers dismissed the director and spent twelve weeks to reworking the play, hoping to open in New York before Christmas. Johnson had been only minimally involved in adapting *Barnaby* for the stage, and though he was not happy about being left out, had held his tongue, wanting to give the producers some "aesthetic autonomy." Now that the show had flopped, however, he offered his assistance. Josephson accepted, assuring Johnson that he would work closely with Chodorov on the revised version.[9]

With *Barnaby and Mr. O'Malley* in limbo, Dave and Ruth took a vaca-tion, driving to New Orleans and then flying to Mexico. They spent a few days in a "little jungle" in the Yucatán, enjoying the warm weather, fresh fruit, and spicy food. Back home, Johnson continued his political activities. At the end of December 1946, he had been a delegate to the joint convention of the Independent Citizens Committee of the Arts, Sciences, and Professions and the National Citizens Political Action Committee. The two groups vot-ed to merge, creating the Progressive Citizens of America (PCA). In June 1947, he and Mischa Richter organized a PCA-sponsored reception for sec-retary of commerce and former vice president Henry Wallace in Westport, Connecticut.[10]

While her husband was preparing for Wallace's visit, Krauss was work-ing on another book, "Mr. Littleguy and the Laundry." Ursula Nordstrom at Harper had turned down a draft, and Krauss again sought help from the Bank Street Writers Laboratory. The group generally liked the tale, which involved a laundryman who prefers to "paint little pictures on clothes instead of just con-ventional laundry marks." Some customers complain, but others like the pic-tures, and his shirts eventually cause a sensation in the art world. Though the members of the Bank Street group "thought the writing was *not too* rough,"

Krauss disagreed: "I know they're wrong." Krauss pushed her doubts aside and sent the new version to Simon and Schuster, which replied that the story would not suit the Little Golden Books series. The editors encouraged her to send in a revised version, and Krauss worked on it some more and again sent it to Nordstrom. Yet another rejection followed: Nordstrom declared the story too "noisy" and suggested that Krauss write another story featuring the central character. A discouraged Krauss abandoned Mr. Littleguy and resurrected "The Last of the Mad Waffles," a chapter of a novel about the Depression that she thought might be adaptable into a story for children.[11]

Johnson turned his attention to *Barnaby and Mr. O'Malley*, working in Rowayton on plot, staging, and production ideas and lining up a Manhattan apartment so that he could come down to New York and work on the play with Chodorov. However, Chodorov had arranged with Josephson and Proctor to turn the project over to Kay Van Riper, screenwriter for Busby Berkeley's *Babes in Arms* (1939) and a half dozen Andy Hardy movies. Johnson did not learn of the change until he received a note requesting his signature on some legal documents during the first half of 1947. He sent an irate telegram to the producers and hopped on a train to New York. He obtained a copy of the script just an hour before meeting with the producers and Van Riper. Van Riper stuck with the project for only a few months before dropping it, and the producers gave up. Again, however, they neglected to tell Johnson. Although Johnson's involvement with the play had been minimal, some investors blamed him for its failure. He asked Josephson to correct this impression and in a rare display of anger told him that the producers and Jerome Chodorov had managed "the most offensive personal and professional insult ever callously and deliberately inflicted on a writer" and the most "fantastically irresponsible treatment ever accorded a literary creation."[12]

As *Barnaby and Mr. O'Malley* slowly imploded, Johnson began to think about other projects. He dropped in to see William Sloane, former vice president of Henry Holt and Company, publisher of the first two *Barnaby* books, who in 1946 had founded a new publishing house, William Sloane Associates. While waiting to see Sloane, Johnson began to read one of the company's latest novels, Ward Moore's *Greener Than You Think* (1947), a gonzo satire of public apathy, bureaucratic incompetence, government hypocrisy, and media appetite for disaster. Johnson told Sloane, "Say, this is the kind of book I like," and that fall, those words appeared at the top of a full-page advertisement in the *New York Times Book Review*. Johnson's name still carried a certain cultural cache. As Coulton Waugh wrote in *The Comics*, published the same year,

Barnaby's "very discriminating audience" would likely "influence the course of American humor for years to come." "Underlying [Barnaby's] fantasy" was a "sharp, razor-edge of social satire," and the strip provided "a patch of cheerful, sunny green in the scorched-dust color of our times."[13]

Dave and Ruth were now living comfortably in Rowayton. By the summer of 1947, they had purchased the first TV in town, and Fred Schwed, George Annand, and other friends frequently dropped in to watch tennis, boxing, baseball, and football. With martinis and snacks at their fingertips, the blinds pulled down to keep out the sun, and the TV showing their favorite games, it was, according to Schwed, "a good way to spend the summer in the big outdoors."[14]

That summer, the daily *Barnaby* strip created by Jack Morley and Ted Ferro began to drift from its original premise. The topical satire became less sharp, and O'Malley's diction lost some of its lexicographical exuberance. Following a misunderstanding during which Mr. Baxter threatens to shoot Mr. O'Malley, Barnaby's fairy godfather leaves the narrative from 24 May through 1 July, by far his longest absence from the series. Much of *Barnaby*'s particular style had come from Johnson, and Ferro was simply not Johnson. Johnson returned to writing the strip in September 1947, though Morley stayed on to do the art, and the two men worked jointly on the strip until 1952. Johnson wrote the dialogue, planned the layout, and often provided Morley with rough sketches to use as guides. For the remainder of *Barnaby*'s run, Johnson remained actively involved in the strip's creation.[15]

Harper released Krauss's *The Growing Story*, illustrated by Phyllis Rowand, in 1947 to complimentary reviews predicting that child readers would identify with the protagonist. Writing for the *New York Herald Tribune*, May Lamberton Becker said, "If the five-year-old for whom you are choosing a story is like others of his age he finds the rate of his own growth a matter of warm interest." The *New York Times*'s Lillian Gerard wrote, "The phenomenon of growth, combined with a child's interest in himself, makes this a fascinating story, easy to read aloud and discuss." *Kirkus* noted that the "author of some of our very favorite juveniles . . . has again given us a satisfying, lovely text that will get repeated reading from four to six year olds" and described Rowand's drawings as "modern and stylized without sacrifice of a certain tenderness."[16]

Frequently asked why she never had children, Ruth often answered that she knew that she was not responsible enough to be a parent. This may be true: Ruth found it easy to talk to children because she was so like a child; her emotional receptiveness to young people's experiences made her a good friend to children but might not have made her a successful mother. In any case, Ruth and Dave did not need to have a child of their own. They had Nina Rowand Wallace, who was like a daughter to them. And they had the children of their imaginations. Dave had Barnaby. Ruth had Duffy and the unnamed protagonists of *The Carrot Seed* and *The Growing Story*. Many of the greatest creators of children's literature—Beatrix Potter, Lewis Carroll, Edward Lear, Margaret Wise Brown, Dr. Seuss, Maurice Sendak, and James Marshall—had no biological children. In a practical sense, time not spent on raising children could instead be devoted to writing for children; however, childlessness meant that these authors had to find inspiration elsewhere. Crockett Johnson drew on his memories of his childhood. Ruth Krauss looked to folklore, to imagined conversations with neighbors, and to unpublished work for adults. Though all three methods brought her success, she had not yet found a reliable muse. She had not yet realized that her best source of ideas might be children themselves.

12

AT HOME WITH RUTH AND DAVE

On a piece of paper
I write it

On my looking-glass
And on snow
I write it
—RUTH KRAUSS, *I Write It* (1970)

For Ruth Krauss, the harsh 1947–48 winter brought writer's block. Through the middle of December, the temperature had been a bit warmer than usu-al, but on the 26th, two feet of snow blanketed Rowayton, the beginning of a three-month stretch when New England received twice as much snow as usual. By February, Krauss found it difficult to write, a situation for which she blamed William James, although she mixed him up with Henry: "It must have been Henry because according to my present figuring William is the fictionist (I know I should know which is who and all but the fact remains that except for this figuring out loud, I off hand do not)." William James (not the fiction-ist) disliked being interrupted when inspiration struck, anxious that he would lose his creative spark. She took his words to heart, and since then, Krauss ex-plained, "I've spent a lot of time seizing on the impulse divine. I have stopped all and sundry—in fact, I stop everything still. I hide, I seek, I lure, I pretend I'm alone . . . to insulate myself, in order to carry out the creative urge because this James guy told me off at an early age." As a result, "I have got so I really find I write best only when 'inspired,' in fact that [I] otherwise cannot write at all." In the winter doldrums, sitting around waiting for inspiration was a poor strategy.[1]

To get started, Krauss borrowed an idea from a friend, possibly Nancy Goldsmith, who "planned to write three pages a day, in this way getting her 'novel' done." From late February to late March, Krauss sat at her Remette typewriter nearly every day and wrote a few pages. If she kept typing, she reasoned, she would eventually come up with something she could publish—she could do "a lot of cutting and then a lot of building up the places where interesting subject matter comes in." If that plan failed, then "maybe it can be of value just as a historical document." The resulting 123-page manuscript is precisely that, providing a glimpse into Ruth and Dave's daily lives, their relationship, and Krauss's aspirations.[2]

Krauss titled the piece "Where Am I Going?," reflecting her uncertainty about the direction her professional life was taking. She was not earning a living from writing children's books, and Ursula Nordstrom had rejected Krauss's most recent efforts. Hoping to publish an old novel manuscript, Krauss sent it off to be retyped. Thinking that she might publish her work in magazines, she composed an article about the writing of *The Great Duffy*. She worried that her life lacked focus.[3]

Movies provided her with welcome distraction. When reading a novel, Krauss tended to get bored by the details about a quarter of the way in, skip to the ending, and then put the book aside. But movies were her "own special form of almost (infantile) secret pleasure": "I . . . like to just slump in the dark with my feet propped up on the back of the seat in front." Krauss had recently overcome her fears and learned to drive, though she did so only during daylight hours and close to home. Either alone or with Phyllis Rowand, Krauss would drive to Stamford, do some shopping, and see a movie. She described Red Skelton's *Merton of the Movies* as "very funny and also pathetic in parts," but on a weekend trip to New York City, Georges Rouquier's *Farrebique; ou, Les Quatre Saisons*, a symbolic film about rural post–World War II France, sent her straight to sleep.[4]

In New York, she and Dave had "a sublet of a sublet." On winter Fridays, they would take the train into the city for the weekend. There, they would see publishers, go to parties, and visit friends such as Herman and Nina Schneider, left-leaning authors of many science books for children, and anthropologist Gitel Poznanski and painter Bob Steed, both of whom had traveled with Ruth on the Blackfeet expedition nine years earlier. Ruth could not stay awake through all these visits. After dinner one night with Dave, Poznanski, Steed, and psychologist Al Leighton, the author of *The Navajo Door*, which Ruth was reading, narcolepsy began to overtake her. Poznanski led Ruth to a bed in the next room, where she slept for an hour. The next night, at a party on Riverside Drive, Ruth fell asleep in a comfortable chair and dreamed of eating with chopsticks and then pulling paper toweling from a roll over her head. She found her dreams interesting but baffling: "If there is any significance anyone can find in these things, kindly communicate and the finder will be rewarded by I don't know what."[5]

Back in Rowayton, Ruth's mind veered toward her fear of fire, which had resurfaced just after she and Dave moved to Connecticut. One afternoon, looking across the Five Mile River at the street where she and Dave had lived a few years earlier, Ruth saw Bob and Helen McNell's house on fire and immediately phoned to tell them. During the winter of 1947–48, two more houses in the neighborhood caught fire, both "on nights of great snow around three thirty a.m." The sirens woke Ruth, and looking out an upstairs window, she saw "the fires flaming up and coloring everything, and the sparks flying in the wind out over all the other houses and the weeds." She and Dave dressed and went outside to join other neighbors. They could do little except "keep watch on the sparks" to see that the fire did not spread. These fires stirred memories of the Great Baltimore Fire of her youth, but Ruth tried to reassure herself that her anxieties were irrational: She did not worry about fire while staying in New York, and they had already had the Rowayton house's furnace inspected and cleaned.[6]

But another night, Ruth woke up at 4:00 in the morning to a strange smell. She "thought immediately of fire, and specifically of the furnace." Not wanting to wake Dave, who had come to bed only two hours earlier, she went to investigate. The smell, "pungent, . . . like strong urine, and slightly smoky," led her to the basement door. When she opened it, the odor hit her "full blast," but she saw no smoke. She pondered what to do before walking slowly down the stairs. Despite the absence of smoke, she turned off the furnace, and she subsequently determined that the smell seemed to be coming from the boiler. Nothing appeared amiss, but she woke Dave anyway, and the two of them "sniffed all around" their cellar. Dave concluded, "It must be a skunk," but Ruth remained worried. Ruth went back to bed and Dave offered to "sit up and finish some work and 'keep watch'" so that she could finish her night's sleep.[7]

Ruth appreciated Dave's thoughtfulness and willingness to assuage her fears. Because she sometimes got the idea that "people are about to attack me in the middle of the night," Dave got in the habit of "locking the front door when he goes to bed" and was quite "conscientious about this." However, he never thought to lock the house's other doors. When fire became her main phobia, she began to feel that she would prefer to have the door unlocked, but she believed that she could not "simply turn around and claim on the same grounds—fear—that I want it open." So she said nothing.[8]

Because they kept such different hours, Ruth and Dave slept in separate beds, both of which Dave designed and built, customizing them to suit their individual needs. Dave slept easily and never made his bed unless company were coming to visit. Ruth, however, could only sleep if she had first made her bed. In the mornings, she lacked the energy to make the bed properly, instead arranging the bedspread so it resembled a made- up bed. At the end of the same day, exhausted, she would, as she put it, "have to start all over again and make my bed, first kind of tossing up the mattress to see that it isn't too harsh or lumpy. By the time I get through I am usually very much awake again."⁹

One day each week, however, Ruth simply went upstairs and straight to sleep: the day Ethel Lerner cleaned the house and made the beds. Lerner be- gan working for Dave and Ruth when they first moved to Connecticut, but even six years later, Lerner's presence made Ruth feel self-conscious and even slightly guilty, especially if she were "sitting idly doing nothing like lying in the sun on the grass in summer, or even sitting thinking which to me is an es- sential." To counter any impression of laziness, Ruth would "clatter away at the typewriter" or do some washing, a compulsion she recognized as "rather silly." One source of Ruth's anxiety was race: Lerner was black. Ruth consciously sought to treat the cleaning woman the same way she treated everyone else: "I always introduce her to my friends as Mrs. Lerner or, if I use her first name, I use theirs too. I always call myself by my first name when writing a note or phoning or anything, and the same with my husband. But she still calls me Mrs.—and I'm such a sissy that I've never got around to asking her not to." In March 1948, an accusation leveled at a different black maid brought Ruth's ra- cial consciousness into sharper relief. One of Ruth's white neighbors accused her maid of stealing two cups and two forks. Ruth believed that the white woman should have overlooked the theft because the accusation would make it difficult for the maid to find work and could damage race relations in the area: "If I personally were in a situation where I absolutely knew that a Negro had taken something from me, I wouldn't mention it. Too much else is at stake in attempting to build up and keep good relations between peoples of all skin- colors, nationalities, religions, etc. Nothing is accomplished by accusation."¹⁰

Another unfolding drama that winter starred their dog, Gonsul, named for a character (usually spelled *gunsel*) in the detective novels and true crime sto- ries that Dave enjoyed. Gonsul enjoyed visiting his old friends, jogging across the iced-over Five Mile River to Darien, heedless of the fact that the ice was starting to melt. One day, after pacing up and down on a cake of ice, he made a jump for the next slab of ice and missed. He managed to scramble out of the icy waters and swam safely to shore but drew no lesson from his narrow escape and continued his perilous journeys. Worried that Gonsul might drown, Ruth told Dave. Dave replied, "He's such a goof. He probably doesn't know what's going on but just saw a lot of dogs standing around there one day and he started to stand there too. He probably thinks they're all standing in line to get samples of horsemeat." Another day, a neighbor, Mr. Bates, phoned to report that Gonsul had fallen through the ice and was trying to reach the Darien side. Dave dashed to his car and drove over the bridge and around to the Darien side, where he found Gonsul playing his dog friends. Gonsul's ill judgment amused Dave but worried Ruth and distracted her from writing.[11]

If slightly bemused by Ruth's creative approach, Dave fully supported her experiment. One morning, Ruth mentioned that she was writing a book. He asked, "What is it about?" Ruth replied, "Oh, you just sit down and write." Dave paused before asking, "No idea?" Ruth answered, "No. No idea." Ruth and Dave both laughed.[12]

In another instance, when Ruth wondered aloud how she might end her narrative, Dave told her that Mark Twain, having got stuck at a certain point in *Puddn'head Wilson and Those Extraordinary Twins* (1894), just "finished off his characters by something like the following: 'Rowena went out in the back yard after supper to see the fireworks and fell in the well and was drowned.'" Deciding that this "seemed a prompt good way of weeding out people that had got stalled," Twain drowned several other characters. Dave used this plot device in a December 1948 *Barnaby* sequence: Reciting some allegedly magic words learned from phony exorcists, the curmudgeonly Mr. Merrie makes himself disappear rather than ridding his house of Gus the ghost. Mr. O'Malley then observes, "Mark Twain had a method for getting rid of characters he no longer had a use for. They all happened to fall in the well and drown." O'Malley adds, "That exit of Mr. Merrie's isn't as plausible from a literary point of view, perhaps."[13]

In late February 1948, Johnson and Krauss signed a petition supporting Henry Wallace's 1948 presidential bid. The preceding November, Johnson had joined five hundred others who signed "A Message of Greeting and Support" for Wallace when he arrived at LaGuardia Airport after two-week tour of Palestine. The document praised Wallace as the "true spokesman for the millions of liberals who are now uniting to demand a return to the program of the late Franklin D. Roosevelt." On 23 December, Johnson, Mischa Richter, and other Connecticut progressives met with Wallace, urging him to run for president as an independent candidate. Wallace formally declared his candidacy six days later. He attracted strong support from Popular Front liberals, including many who wrote for children (Eve Merriam, Louis Slobodkin, and Lynd Ward) and current and former *New Masses* contributors (Richter, Adolf Dehn, William Gropper, Rockwell Kent). Wallace sought to create a "people's peace [that] will usher in the century of the common man," declaring, "I have fought and shall continue to fight programs which give guns to people when they want plows." He also called for a fight "to end racial discrimination" and for "free labor unions, for jobs, and for homes in which we can decently live."[14]

Though Krauss was less politically active, she too worked on behalf of social justice. In March 1948, she and Phyllis Rowand attended a Bank Street subcommittee conference in preparation the National Conference on Family Life to be held the following May. The conference sought to address some of the problems families were facing, among them housing, divorce, juvenile delinquency, education, health, medical care, recreation, home management, and social and economic welfare. Attendees included nine hundred delegates from twenty-nine professions and representing all forty-eight states, plus observers from thirty other countries.[15]

At a Bank Street Laboratory meeting earlier that winter, Krauss, Rowand, and several others had volunteered to analyze sexism in magazines for young people. Krauss offered to read through issues *Boy's Life* and soon regretted having done so, fearing that the task would prevent her from finishing the book she was writing. However, she became both engrossed in the task and appalled by the sexism she discovered: The stories never showed men as involved in child rearing, always depicted boys at a distance from the family, and emphasized danger as manly. In contrast, the rare depictions of girls showed them as petty, foolish, or cruel. Krauss also found the magazine's colonial politics distasteful—for example, its depictions of "simpler societies" as "savages"—and its glorification of capitalism. She concluded, "There needs to be an almost complete changing of ideal goals, goals that are strongly defined by our culture and in to which we are all born and in which brought up." "Better general education for all" and mass media could help create change, she concluded, "because these are a great means of the perpetuation of traditional themes."[16]

The coming of spring brought another stage adaptation of *Barnaby*, this time at Indiana's Terre Haute Children's Theatre. Adapted and directed by Robert and Lillian Masters, the production had Barnaby's father running for mayor against the corrupt Boss Snagg. The play borrows dialogue from Johnson's comic and focuses on characters rather than special effects or

Phyllis Rowand, 1946 or
1947. Image courtesy of
Nina Landau Stagakis.

scenery. The *Terre Haute Tribune* predicted that the two-act adaptation "bids fair to be a favorite with Children's Theatre producers all over the country." Johnson had sold the rights to the Masterses for one dollar plus the promise of 50 percent of any profits from sales or performances of the play.[17]

Radio also took another stab at *Barnaby* in 1948, with Lew Amster, Sidney Rumin, and Helen Mack in charge and veteran radio actor John Brown as Mr. O'Malley. Making his radio debut as Barnaby was John Brown's son, Jared. The first episode of the half-hour program was performed and broadcast twice before a live Hollywood audience, once for the East Coast and once for the West Coast. Brown-Elliott Productions recorded the episode in hopes of finding a sponsor for the program, but although the project generated enough interest to record a second episode, no sponsor came forward, and the project fizzled.[18]

The color Sunday *Barnaby* strip, which had begun in 1946, came to an end on 30 May 1948. Drawn by Jack Morley and written by Johnson, the Sunday comic, which followed a narrative independent of the daily strips, disappeared because its distributor, *PM*, was foundering. Having lost more than four million dollars on his investment, the paper's backer, Marshall Field III, sold *PM* to liberal San Francisco lawyer Bartley Crum. On 23 June, the former New Deal tabloid reemerged as the *New York Star*, with Walt Kelly as its new art director. Kelly also contributed editorial cartoons, and in October, his comic strip *Pogo* made its debut, running right next to *Barnaby*.[19]

The daily strip continued to register Johnson's dissatisfaction with the country's turn to the right and away from the concerns of working people. In late May 1948, Mrs. Baxter complains about rising prices, and O'Malley tells Barnaby, "Your Fairy Godfather will take over the management of the household in person! I'm moving in with you!" To economize, he proposes "buying the less expensive cuts of filet mignon" and slightly cheaper bottles of fine wine; firing Barnaby's dog; and letting go of the butler, secretary, chef, chauffeur, footman, gardener, and caretaker (none of which the Baxters actually employed). O'Malley's cost-cutting plans are ludicrous, but the narrative underscores the difficulties people face when prices rise faster than wages and alludes to Wallace's proposal for price controls on the basic necessities. Most of *Barnaby*'s commentary is subtle, but Johnson occasionally was more direct. Just before proposing to run the household, O'Malley returns from a planned job as a research scientist, having "given up science" because it has become politicized. "Army and Navy investigators! State troopers! Loyalty oath administrators! City police! FBI men!," he says. Finally, "when a visiting congressman saw my pinkish wings and subpoenaed me to Washington, I left science to its own resources."[20]

Such comments reflect Johnson's opposition to U.S. policy toward communism at home and abroad. In the same month that those strips appeared, Johnson, along with Aaron Copland, W. E. B. Du Bois, Howard Fast, E. Y. Harburg, Rockwell Kent, John Howard Lawson, Donald Ogden Stewart, Dalton Trumbo, and others, signed a statement praising Wallace's open letter to Stalin, which called for an end to the Cold War, a "reduction of armaments" on both sides, "free movement" of citizens "within and between the two countries," "unrestricted trade (except for goods related to war)," and the "free exchange of scientific information." Wallace argued that "there is no difference" between the United States and the Soviet Union that could not "be settled by peaceful, hopeful negotiation." Wallace's proposal gained no traction with the

Truman administration and met criticism from the press. For those on the left, the open letter was but a minor setback compared to what they would soon face.[21]

13

THE BIG WORLD AND THE LITTLE HOUSE

"Home" is a way people feel about a place. These people felt that way
about the little house.
Some people feel that way about room, which is just part of a house.
Some people feel that way about a corner—
—which is just part of a room that is part of a house.
Some people feel that way about the whole world
—RUTH KRAUSS, *The Big World and the Little House* (1949)

On 20 July 1948, a federal grand jury indicted twelve Communist Party leaders under the Smith Act (the Alien and Registration Act of 1940). Crockett Johnson personally knew at least one of the "New York Twelve," having campaigned for New York City councilman Ben Davis. The Smith Act imposed fines and/or up to twenty years imprisonment on anyone who "advocates, abets, advises, or teaches the duty, necessity, desirability or propriety of overthrowing" the U.S. government. As Michael Steven Smith notes, this was "the first statute since the Alien and Sedition Acts of 1798 to make mere advocacy of ideas a federal crime." In endorsing Federal Bureau of Investigation director J. Edgar Hoover's suggestion that the Smith Act be deployed against communists, President Harry S. Truman hoped to challenge Republicans who accused Democrats of being soft on communism.[1]

Unlike four years earlier, *Barnaby* in 1948 offers no direct commentary on the presidential candidates. Indeed, at least one sequence focuses on the limitations of art as a means of social critique. Johnson's comic comes closest to social critique in its advocacy of better schools. Henry Wallace's Progressive Party platform proposed a "Federal grant-in-aid program to build new schools, libraries, raise teachers' and librarians' salaries, improve primary and secondary schools." From 21 September through 10 November, the need to build more classroom space motivated the plot of *Barnaby*. Mrs. Baxter joins the PTA, whose leader discusses the need "to arouse community interest and force the city to build the proposed annex to this school. There just isn't any other solution to this overcrowdedness." Mrs. Baxter agrees, but O'Malley has loopier solutions to the problem: "Adopt the efficient and budget-cutting O'Malley Plan of 'round-the-clock education! Little nippers who hate to go to bed at night can attend school on the graveyard shift." When O'Malley pushes a button that turns out to be the fire alarm, he leads the kids safely out of the school, but the incident raises concerns that if the fire had been real, over-crowding would have been a problem, and the "wonderful publicity" helps the town realize that it needs to buy land for an annex. This strip's narrative advances Wallace's platform but presses its message subtly, never mentioning the Progressive Party or its candidate.[2]

The press and the polls predicted a victory for the 1948 Republican presi-dential candidate, Thomas Dewey, but Truman won reelection. Wallace came in fourth, just behind Dixiecrat Strom Thurmond. Johnson nevertheless re-mained unwavering in his support of Wallace's vision, sharing the candidate's belief that the United States should seek peace with the Soviet Union and op-posing Truman's crackdown on "subversives." The same day that Truman won, Johnson signed a statement "protesting the New York indictment of the twelve Communist Party functionaries by a Federal Grand Jury, claiming such as 'an attack on the civil and political liberties of all Americans.'"[3]

In the wake of the Progressives' defeat at the polls, *Barnaby* steered toward lighter subjects. When O'Malley accidentally makes himself vanish, Johnson brings in Sergeant Ausdauer, a fairy-godfather-sized policeman. The sequence gives Johnson a chance to poke fun at detective fiction, a genre he loved. Explaining why it has taken him so long to find O'Malley, Ausdauer says, "No well-read person expects the police to solve a case so quick." He explains, "It's a handicap, not having a tough shamus who drives 90 miles an hour, drinks several quarts of Arak for breakfast, moves all the bodies, slugs everybody, hides the clues." After Ausdauer departs, the strip offers a more child-focused narrative, centering on Barnaby's wish for snow. O'Malley brings in Jack Frost as a consultant because, as the fairy godfather says, "I don't want to over do it, you know, like last year. . . . And there was 1888 too, when I intended to bring on a flurry or so, and, er—But never mind."[4]

That winter brought better weather as well as good news for Ruth Krauss's career when strong reviews greeted *Bears*, her second book illustrated by Phyllis Rowand. In *Bears*, Krauss returned to a child's perspective she had in *The Growing Story*, *The Great Duffy*, and *The Carrot Seed*. This time, however, she strived not only to see the world as a child might but also to emulate chil-dren's language. In its entirety, the text reads,

Bears, bears, bears, bears, bears
on the stairs
under chairs
washing hairs
giving stares
collecting fares
stepping in squares
millionaires
everywheres.

The playful verse, rhyming *bears* with *millionaires*, and the neologism *everywheres* exemplify the Bank Street notion that, to children, the sound of words is often more important than their meaning.

Reviewers praised the book. In the *New York Herald Tribune*, Louise Seaman Bechtel thought *Bears* "very funny and surprising," a "merry little book which I find delights small children." The *Christian Science Monitor*'s Anne Thaxter Eaton concurred: "The pleasant absurdity of the idea and the rhyming words . . . will please children from three to seven. An amusing picture book made in a spirit of gayety and frolic." Only the *Horn Book*'s Alice M. Jordan was less than enthusiastic, describing Krauss's text as "slight" and crediting Rowand's "funny pictures [as] the main feature of this nonsense book for the youngest."[5]

Late in 1948, Krauss got involved in one of the Bank Street Writers Laboratory's projects, a series of Golden Books. The series had begun with Lucy Sprague Mitchell's *The New House in the Forest* (1946, illustrated by Eloise Wilkin) and *The Taxi That Hurried* (1946), cowritten by Mitchell, Irma Simonton Black, and Bank Street nursery school director Jessie Stanton and illustrated by Tibor Gergely. To draw the pictures for Krauss's new book, *I Can Fly*, Golden enlisted Mary Blair, then best known for her Disney work: the conceptual paintings for *The Three Caballeros* (1945) and the sets and costumes for *Song of the South* (1949). *I Can Fly* (1950) recalls *Bears* in its emphasis on sounds and imaginative play with language, as Krauss creates a series of scenes in which an unnamed little girl pretends to be animals: "A bird can fly. So can I" and "Swish! I'm a fish," and "Bump bump bump I'm a camel with a hump." The book concludes in an exuberant burst of neologisms: "Gubble gubble gubble I'm a mubble in a pubble. I can play I'm anything that's anything. That's MY way."[6]

Krauss was quite excited about both the quality of the book and the fact that it would have a large print run: "We get royalties. . . . Printings are enormous . . . and apparently writers get around two thousand or so within a two year span. . . . Writer and Bank St. share fifty-fifty. No other writers except Brownie get royalties from Golden Books. Mine, I think, is a pretty good book, and I feel good about it considering it's the first time I've ever worked to order." "Brownie" was Margaret Wise Brown, whose classic *Goodnight Moon* had been published the previous year. Bank Street's most famous graduate, Brown and Krauss were acquainted but did not get along. They rarely saw each other socially, although they not only shared the Bank Street connection but also both worked with Ursula Nordstrom at Harper.[7]

Ruth's *I Can Fly* is one of the best-known and best-regarded books in the Bank Street Golden Books series, and in 1951, it "became the first Little Golden Book to receive an Honor distinction at the prestigious Herald Tribune Children's Spring Book Festival." Encouraging wider recognition of the character if not the book, Blair used a version of the book's little girl protagonist in advertisements for Meadow Gold cottage cheese and Baker's Instant chocolate milk mix.[8]

In December 1948, Krauss finally got her chance to write a socially conscious children's book. Henry Schuman commissioned her to write "a book for children" with "a 'one world' idea incorporated in it." Earlier that year, Schuman had published *In Henry's Backyard: The Races of Mankind* (1948), a children's book version of the successful United Productions of America cartoon adapted from Ruth Benedict and Gene Weltfish's 1943 pamphlet. Krauss was excited by this project, both because it would be "worthwhile financially" and because she believed in this message, although she worried about delivering that moral without being overly didactic: "This will be a tough job . . . to do it well without having the preaching stuff show. I don't know if I can but am trying."[9]

The result was *The Big World and the Little House* (1949), in which one family's restoration of a little house serves as a metaphor for rebuilding the world. As the family moves into and repairs the formerly abandoned house, Ruth weaves in several allusions to other countries: The house has a rug "made by a lady in Canada"; if you dial "the right number" on the telephone, "you could talk with somebody in China"; the radio and television enable "other parts of the world [to] come into the house; the big world could be a part of the little house, as well as the little house being a part of the big world." After the family

Marc Simont, cover of Ruth Krauss, *The Big World and the Little House* (New York: Schuman, 1949). Image courtesy of the Northeast Children's Literature Collection, Dodd Research Center, University of Connecticut, Storrs. Reproduced courtesy of Marc Simont.

has turned the broken shell of a house into a warm and inviting home, the narrator notes, "Home is a way people feel about a place. These people feel that way about the little house. Some people feel that way about the whole world."

Krauss asked Marc Simont to illustrate the story. Born in Paris in 1915, Simont settled in the United States in the mid-1930s and gained success illustrating children's books. Krauss likely knew his work from several works he illustrated for Nordstrom: Leclaire Alger's *Dougal's Wish* (1942), Meindert DeJong's *Billy and the Unhappy Bull* (1946), and Margaret Wise Brown's *The First Story* (1947). According to Simont, Nordstrom was not pleased that "one of her authors [was] picking out one of her illustrators to do a book for . . . 'that other publisher.'" But Harper had turned down all of Krauss's political books, and she admired Simont's work.[10]

Though they let go of their sublet in March 1948, Ruth and Dave made frequent visits to Manhattan, often staying for the weekend and sometimes longer. When Dave's friend Adolf Dehn traveled to Haiti in mid-January 1949, Dave and Ruth made his 230 East Fifteenth Street apartment their primary residence until he returned on 1 April. While staying at Dehn's apartment, Dave attended the Scientific and Cultural Conference for World Peace at the Waldorf-Astoria Hotel. The more than eighteen thousand others in attendance included Henry Wallace, Mary McCarthy, John Howard Lawson, Robert Lowell, I. F. Stone, Gene Weltfish, W. E. B. Du Bois, Aaron Copland, and Dmitri Shostakovich. The conference generated hostile press coverage, protests, and censure from the U.S. government, which labeled the forum part of the communist "peace offensive" and denied visas to attendees it suspected of being communists. More than two thousand people picketed the Waldorf-Astoria, carrying placards and shouting, "Down with the Russian skunks" and "Go back to Russia where you belong." The newly formed Americans for Intellectual Freedom staged a rival meeting to condemn the Red Menace and to highlight the danger that the conference posed to the United States. As historian Robbie Lieberman writes, Popular Front liberals who hoped "for a lasting peace built on U.S.–Soviet cooperation" had their hopes dashed by the Cold War's "very different view of peace and freedom—centered on anticommunism and military preparedness." As a result, by the late 1940s and into the 1950s, members of the U.S. peace movement were often accused of being communists.[11]

The House Un-American Activities Committee was also interested. The committee had already cited Lawson for contempt, and in January 1949, Johnson was one of more than a thousand people who signed a letter condemning Congress for abusing its authority in making "'investigations' . . . into the religious and political beliefs of private citizens." In April, Johnson's name appeared a dozen times in a committee report on the peace conference, which noted his backing of Henry Wallace, "open support" for "Communist candidates," opposition to the Smith Act trials, participation in the 1946 May Day Parade, work for *New Masses*, praise of Wallace's open letter to Stalin, and membership in the National Council of the Arts, Sciences, and Professions.[12]

At the end of January 1949, the *New York Star* folded, and *Barnaby* moved to the city's *Daily Mirror*. With Johnson's politics under attack, he moved the strip further away from advocacy of particular causes and toward fantasy. A few strips in January and February make a case for national health care, but by early March, *Barnaby* begins an exploration of the themes that Johnson

They sniff. They run. They stop.

They stop. They laugh.
They laugh. They dance.

Marc Simont, two-page spread from Ruth Krauss, *The Happy Day* (New York: Harper, 1949).
Illustrations copyright © 1949 by Marc Simont. Copyright © renewed 1977 by Marc Simont. Used
by permission of HarperCollins Publishers. Reprinted with the permission of the Estate of Ruth Krauss,
Stewart I. Edelstein, Executor. All Rights Reserved.

would later develop in his books. During an after-hours visit to the art museum, O'Malley and Barnaby witness a dissolution of the boundary between art and life. Myron's *Discobolus* throws his discus, Rodin's *Thinker* stops thinking to unwind with a murder mystery, Thomas Gainsborough's *Blue Boy* and Barnaby swap hats, Whistler's mother resumes her knitting, and a piece of abstract art complains that "NOBODY understands me." Prefiguring Harold and his purple crayon, this *Barnaby* sequence finds power in the imagination, suggesting a permeable boundary between representation and reality.[13]

Krauss's ideas for children's books were again finding favor with publishers. About ten days before the World Peace Conference, she received a contract for *Flower in the Snow*, which would ultimately be published as *The Happy Day*. The story certainly embodies the Bank Street idea that young children do not need fantasy because the everyday world is fantastic enough to them, but the combination of Bank Street's influence and Nordstrom's editorial judgment made the book work. Krauss's original text for *The Happy Day* occasionally used "See?" at the end of a series of short sentences ("They sniff. They run.

See?" and "They sniff. They run. They stop. See?). Nordstrom said, "Ruth, I don't think you need the word *see*. The children will be looking, and they will see the pictures." Krauss replied, "But I like the word *see*." Nordstrom said, "But you don't need it." Krauss responded, "But I like it." After further back-and-forth, Nordstrom finally said, "Ruth, for heaven's sake. Give me the word *see* for Christmas!" Krauss said, "But Ursula, I was going to give you a pair of red galoshes." And Nordstrom replied, "I would rather have the word *see*." That's how the word *see* left *The Happy Day*, published in the fall of 1949.[14]

Simont's illustrations for the book won him his first Caldecott Honor, but Krauss was very particular about where the pictures were placed. She sent him a copy of the manuscript on which she had marked the side of the page on which the text should be placed and in some cases was even more specific about wanting type to go near drawings of certain animals. Simont generally did not like sharing his work in progress, but Krauss insisted that she have the opportunity to comment on every rough drawing. Although unaccustomed to such authorial "interference," Simont thought that her "remarks were very good." The process resulted in a classic.[15]

Susan Carr Hirschman, who ultimately had a half-century career in children's book publishing, considers *The Happy Day* "one of the few perfect books for children that have ever been written." Contemporary reviewers agreed. The *Atlantic Monthly* called it "far and away the best of this year's picture books." The *New York Herald Tribune Book Review*'s Louise S. Bechtel thought it "a lovely winter picture book for the nursery age." And even Anne Carroll Moore, the New York Public Library's children's librarian, who disdained the Bank Street school of picture-book writing, was positive: "I think it a picture book children will love to own as a welcome change from activities to nature itself."[16]

Reviews of *The Big World and the Little House*, however, were mixed. Although Simont's illustrations consistently won praise, reviewers disliked Krauss delivery of the text's well-intentioned message and disagreed about what was appropriate for inclusion in a children's book. Marcia Winn in the *Chicago Tribune* embraced the book's innovations, suggesting that "everything about it is a departure from accepted methods of writing and drawing for children" and that "when the prize-winning awards for juveniles are handed out this year, *The Big World and the Little House* unquestionably will be a candidate." But *Library Journal* "object[ed] to children being referred to as 'kids,'" and the *San Francisco Chronicle* considered the book "slangy, ungrammatical," and likely to lend "encouragement to such generally frowned upon habits as

Nina Wallace, ca. 1949. Photo by Agnes Goodman. Courtesy of Nina Landau Stagakis.

writing on the walls, putting feet in chairs, and rude yelling"—precisely the qualities that Winn cited as key to the book's success.[17]

Such hits and misses continued to characterize Krauss's professional endeavors. In March 1949, Nordstrom turned down Krauss's suggestion of "a 'nonsense collection'" in which she "would write all the nonsense." At around the same time, Golden offered Krauss $450 but no royalties (as was customary for Golden) for a revision of "Mr. Littleguy and the Laundry" that editors believed would work well for slightly older readers. Krauss considered the offer insulting and rejected it.[18]

But Krauss had a creative breakthrough with *The Bundle Book*, her first work based directly on her observations of children. Previously, she had been imagining herself in the place of children and drawing on memories of her childhood. *The Bundle Book*, in contrast, was inspired by friends of Krauss's, Nina Schneider and her daughter, Lucy, and Phyllis Rowand and her daughter, Nina. Each mother played a game in which she pretended that she did not recognize her child hiding under a blanket, and Krauss was fascinated by the little girls' reactions, telling Nordstrom that they "seemed a little frightened." Drawing on her study of psychology, Krauss believed that the game represented "one of a child's first experiences playing with the excitement of danger—the danger being in this case the baby's thinking maybe the parent won't recognize him or her as him-or-her-self." Krauss took the game and put it on paper, complete with reassuring ending:

> "Can it be a bundle of laundry? I don't think I need any laundry."
> "No," the bundle replied. "I'm not a bundle of laundry."
> "Can it be a bundle of carrots? I don't think I need any carrots."
> "No, no," the bundle replied. "I'm not a bundle of carrots."
> "Let me think again," the mother said to herself. She stopped to think again. "Maybe it's a monkey? I think I'm sure I don't need a monkey."

The guessing game goes on until the child reveals itself: "It's ME!" The mother says, "You! Well, so it is! so you are. It's you. And—you're just what I need."[19] The book was not released until 1951 and then generated only tepid reviews and sales, but Krauss had hit on the formula that would bring her acclaim. When she saw the world from the perspective of a child, Krauss produced her best children's books.

Still hoping that *Barnaby* would find mainstream success, Johnson had buried the failed and abandoned adaptations, regained control of the rights to the strip, and again sought to make a movie. He talked with successful screenwriter Sidney Buchman, who declined to become involved. Johnson turned to his friends Lew Amster, who had worked on the radio version, and Lou Bunin, an artist, puppeteer, and animation pioneer. In their darker vision of *Barnaby*, the topical satire centers on the stock market, with Mr. Baxter preoccupied with Wall Street finance, "a world in which any myth if it is big enough is believed in." According to a two-page outline for the movie, "It is not too surprising that Barnaby, exposed to his father's glib financial jargon, entertains a fantastic creature with the attitudes and vocabulary of O'Malley." The fairy godfather creates a financial crash that both shatters Mr. Baxter's dream and ends "O'Malley's own reason for being." O'Malley's departure draws Barnaby and his dad closer but effectively ends the fantasy.[20]

This conclusion may have reflected Johnson's declining interest in writing the comic strip and hints at his broader disillusionment. In October 1949, eleven of the New York Twelve were convicted of conspiring to violate the

Smith Act. By that time, *Barnaby* was largely avoiding current events in favor of lampooning the growing world of television entertainment. But Johnson was not ignoring the increasingly oppressive political environment, and it was not ignoring him.

14

ARTISTS ARE TO WATCH

When a thing *seems* to be so, kangaroos usually hop to the conclusion
that it *is* so.
—CROCKETT JOHNSON, *Who's Upside Down?* (1952)

On 6 February 1950, Crockett Johnson signed a friend of the court brief supporting the American Communist Party in *United States v. William Z. Foster et al.*, the trial of the final member of the New York Twelve. Three days later, Senator Joseph R. McCarthy claimed to have a list of fifty-seven State Department employees who were members of the American Communist Party. By the end of April, the FBI's New York Division identified Crockett Johnson as one of "400 concealed Communists" and began compiling a file on him.[1]

According to FBI director J. Edgar Hoover, communists sought to influence the United States through "five principal areas" of "thought control": "open" party members, concealed party members, fellow travelers, opportunists (who supported the party for personal gain), and dupes. A concealed party member such as Crockett Johnson was as dangerous as an open party member, "if not more so." The "concealed communist, because he is not known as a communist, can often advance the Party's cause among people and in organizations where an open member would be scorned."[2]

Though Crockett Johnson was not a "concealed communist" in the 1950s, his FBI file noted his work for *New Masses* and his support for both Ben Davis and radical politician Vito Marcantonio, who represented East Harlem in the U.S. Congress for fourteen years between 1935 and 1951. But Johnson had drifted away from his close communist ties of the 1930s and had become more of a socialist. The FBI file mentioned that Johnson had spoken at a February 1944 program sponsored by the National Council of American-Soviet Friendship but neglected the fact that the two countries were allies at the time. Other "subversive" activities included supporting civil rights for African Americans and the veterans of the Abraham Lincoln Brigade during the Spanish Civil

War. On 4 August, an FBI agent knocked on Krauss and Johnson's front door. When Johnson opened it and began talking to the man, a second agent covertly took Johnson's photograph.[3]

Dave Johnson and Ruth Krauss's social circle included several people targeted for their alleged political beliefs. Dr. Shelley Trubowitz, who became a friend and neighbor when he moved to Rowayton in 1951, recalled seeing the couple at parties with John Howard Lawson, who along with the other members of the Hollywood Ten served a one-year prison sentence in 1950–51 for refusing to cooperate with the House Un-American Activities Committee (HUAC). Howard Fast, an unapologetically leftist writer, was another acquaintance of Dave and Ruth's who served three months in prison for contempt of Congress.[4]

Though Johnson was of a satirical turn of mind, his published work during the early 1950s makes almost no references to the FBI, HUAC, or Senator McCarthy. In contrast, in the 1940s, Johnson made fun of the Red-hunting activities of the Dies Committee, as HUAC was known at the time. In *Barnaby* strips from November and December 1943, the O'Malley Committee, run by Barnaby's fairy godfather, launches an investigation into that notorious Red, Santa Claus. In one of *Barnaby*'s few allusions to McCarthy, in a May 1950 strip, O'Malley, concerned that the U.S. Census is overlooking his fellow pixies, undertakes his own count. When McSnoyd, the invisible leprechaun, objects, "That's a phony G-man badge," O'Malley responds that it is "genuine plastic." But McSnoyd still will not cooperate, saying, "You can't pump me, O'Malley."[5]

Whether or not readers of *Barnaby* perceived Johnson's subtext here, McCarthy was certainly on people's minds. On 8 May, Ursula Nordstrom wrote to Krauss, "From behind the Iron Curtain comes the Czech edition of *The Growing Story*. I think it looks darling. We're sending you a couple of copies right away. No doubt McCarthy will check up on you shortly." By 28 July, the FBI was indeed checking up on Krauss. One report noted that in 1945, she and Johnson had attended the American Society for Russian Relief's "tea party to launch the 'Books for Russia' campaign." Agents investigated whether Johnson and Krauss had applied for passports and checked up on her correspondence with an "L. Krauss" in Baltimore—her mother.[6]

Though less inclined to sign petitions, Krauss was every bit as progressive as Johnson. In late 1949 or early 1950, she was visiting Baltimore and went to lunch at Nate's and Leon's Delicatessen with Georgia Hahn, the wife of her cousin, Richard; their daughter, Linda; and their maid, Gertrude. The waitress

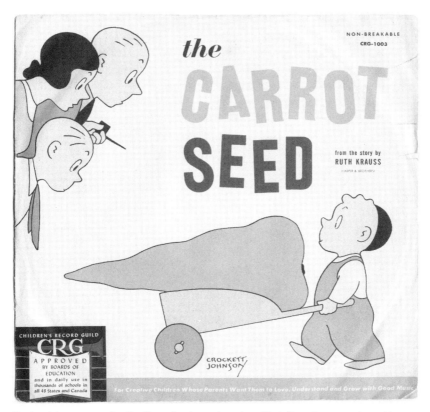

Crockett Johnson, cover for *The Carrot Seed*, an adaptation of Ruth Krauss's story performed by Norman Rose. Children's Record Guild, ca. 1950. Reprinted with the permission of the Estate of Ruth Krauss, Stewart I. Edelstein, Executor. All Rights Reserved.

took one look at Gertrude and said, "We don't serve colored." Incensed, Ruth insisted that they be served and refused to leave. The waitress relented. For the duration of their lunch, they integrated Nate's and Leon's.[7]

Published in the fall of 1950, Krauss's *The Backward Day* is quietly subversive, though not in an obviously political sense. Illustrated by Marc Simont and inspired by Krauss's memory of Camp Walden's Backward Party, *The Backward Day* offers a nonsensical challenge to proper behavior. The book's protagonist, a young boy, announces, "Today is backward day," and then puts on his coat, his pants and shirt, and finally his underwear. He walks backward down the stairs, turns around his father's chair, sits down, and tucks his napkin in at the back of his collar. When his father appears, the little boy says, "Goodnight, Pa." His father replies, "Goodnight," and the rest of the family joins in the experiment. At the end of the book, the boy puts his clothes properly and announces the end of Backward Day. Reviews ran from mixed to enthusiastic. In the *New York Herald Tribune*, Louise S. Bechtel felt that the book had "an amusing conception," but "somehow it doesn't quite 'come off,' even with the undoubted brilliance of the Simont pictures." In contrast, the *New York Times*'s Ellen Lewis Buell thought *The Backward Day* "written out of a true appreciation of a child's imagination and humor" and predicted that it would inspire an "immediate performance" from its child readers.[8]

In 1950 and 1951, Krauss also began gathering material for her next book, tentatively titled *Definitions*. The germ of the idea came from child psychologist Arnold Gesell, who observed that a five-year-old "is a pragmatist. His definitions are in terms of use: *A horse is to ride; a fork to eat.*" Gesell's observation reminded Krauss of the Bank Street School's game of Definitions, in which children offered their own meanings for words.[9]

Visiting Harriet S. Sherman's kindergarten class in Rowayton, Krauss talked with children and recorded their phrases and words. Krauss also had Eleanor Reich, head of Bank Street's Harriet Johnson Nursery School, ask teachers to collect definitions from four-year-olds and five-year-olds there. By January 1951, Krauss found herself "getting so much wonderful material in the schools that I'm afraid I'll have a good book in spite of myself." She provided Nordstrom with some examples: "Stars are not only to twinkle, but also when you make your bed you get a star"; "a face is something on your head"; "you put a house in a *hole* and a floor is to keep you from falling in the hole your house is in." Krauss also asked questions to children on the beach. When she asked one boy, "What is a hole for?," "he looked at me like I was nuts, frowned, and walked away from me. Another child, however, said 'A hole? A hole is to dig.' And that's how the title was born."[10]

Although Nordstrom loved Krauss's ideas, potential illustrators did not. Nicolas Mordvinoff, who would win the 1952 Caldecott Medal for *Finders Keepers*, said that no book or illustrations could be made for "so fragmentary and elusive a text." Nordstrom turned to Maurice Sendak, a twenty-three-year-old F. A. O. Schwarz window display artist who had already illustrated two books for Harper. After he had turned in the illustrations for the second, she asked to see his sketchbook. He left it with her, hoping that she might like what she saw. According to Nordstrom, "We needed something very special, and Maurice's sketchbook made me think he would be perfect for it." He was

Maurice Sendak in his twenties. Photo courtesy of Maurice Sendak. Used by permission
of Maurice Sendak.

enthusiastic about Krauss's manuscript; she took one look at Sendak's sketches
of Brooklyn children playing in the street and said, "That's it." Sendak was nervous about meeting Krauss, but she immediately put him at ease, and he soon
"adored her. She had this little girl's laugh, this uncontrollable giggle." When
she told him that his tiny figures were just what she wanted for the book, he
was thrilled. Moreover, she invited him to spend time with her and Dave in
Rowayton. At the time, Sendak was still living with his parents, and he was
"not very happy" with them, "nor were they happy with me especially. So, here
I was, free invitation to work with the famous Ruth Krauss, married to the famous Crockett Johnson, in Rowayton, in an old-fashioned white house with
a porch, with the water there, and Dave had a sailboat. Well, you can imagine
how I felt. Like the luckiest kid on the block." Throughout the 1950s, Sendak
would spend as many as two weekends a month with Ruth and Dave.[11]

Sendak began working on sketches for *A Hole Is to Dig* during the summer
of 1951, and by the fall, he was spending weekends in Rowayton. Johnson and

Ruth Krauss, sketches for *A Hole Is to Dig*. Image courtesy of the Northeast Children's Literature Collection, Dodd Research Center, University of Connecticut, Storrs. Reprinted with the permission of the Estate of Ruth Krauss, Stewart I. Edelstein, Executor. All Rights Reserved.

Krauss "became my weekend parents and took on the job of shaping me into an artist. . . . Ruth and I would arrange and rearrange and paste and unpaste and Ruth would sing and Ruth would holler and I'd quail and sulk and Dave would referee. . . . His name should be on all our books for the technical savvy and cool consideration he brought to them." A page in Johnson's block capitals, with Sendak's doodles of a cat in the margins, shows detailed instructions for the book's binding and format: "Area for Front and Back Cover Will Be within 5¼" x 6¾"." It was Johnson's idea that the book be in the small size.[12]

Johnson also drew up plans for five-inch-wide interlocking bookshelves, each one designed to hold "a series of Tiny Golden Books . . . , stressing a 'Five-Inch Shelf of Classics' theme." When purchased, the shelves would contain books organized around "a 'classic' theme," such as "Simple Science (big oaks from little acorns, etc.), Disney Characters, Lear Jingles, Sleep Songs, Counting Stories and Chants (one, two, buckle my shoe, etc.), Nursery Rhymes, First Books of Industry (cow to bottle, sheep to coat, etc.), Holiday Classics, Stories of the Seasons, Game Street Songs (farmer in the dell, etc.)." For any given theme, the color of the shelf would match the color of the books' spines. Parents could buy one shelf at a time, adding a new shelves to form a

Maurice Sendak, sketches for Ruth Krauss, *A Hole Is to Dig*. Image courtesy of the Northeast Children's Literature Collection, Dodd Research Center, University of Connecticut, Storrs. Reprinted with the permission of the Estate of Ruth Krauss, Stewart I. Edelstein, Executor. All Rights Reserved.

bookcase. The promotional material should emphasize that "primarily these are worthwhile and entertaining books for younger children; secondarily they are toys or novelties." It is not clear whether Johnson ever pitched his idea to Simon and Schuster, the publishers of Golden Books, but it never reached fruition.[13]

While Sendak and Krauss worked on *A Hole Is to Dig* and Johnson tinkered with his ideas, federal investigations proceeded. HUAC's *Report on the Communist "Peace" Offensive: A Campaign to Disarm and Defeat the United States* (April 1951) named Crockett Johnson three times, a fact picked up by local newspapers. On 19 June, professional informant Louis Budenz told the FBI that "Crockett Johnson was a member of the Communist Party. He was very active in the *PM* unit." Budenz also claimed that author Kay Boyle had been a communist. These claims were untrue, though both Johnson and his old friend Boyle had signed many petitions on behalf of groups now classified as "Communist front" organizations. Budenz was eventually discredited, but in the interim, a cloud of suspicion hung over Johnson, Boyle, and many others.[14]

Krauss continued to find rich material for her children's books. Before she and Sendak had finished *A Hole Is to Dig*, she visited fellow Bank Streeter Norma Simon's class at New York's Downtown Community School, a progressive coeducational elementary school whose board of trustees included many Johnson-Krauss friends: Lucy Sprague Mitchell, Mary Elting Folsom, progressive publisher William R. Scott, and civil liberties lawyer Leonard Boudin. Krauss observed as Simon's students took packing boxes and made them into houses, and she came up with an idea for a new book, *Crazy Crauss Hauss*. In October 1951, she sent Ursula Nordstrom a draft of the text that began,

> O dum dum deedle
> dum dum doodle doodle
> dum dum deedle deedle dum dum dum
>
> I have a house—
> it's not a squirrel house
> it's not a house for bears
> —it's not any house you'd see—
> and it's not in any street
> and it's not in any road. Oh
> it's just the house for me Me ME.

The book became *A Very Special House*, with illustrations by Sendak. In his view, this book "most perfectly simulates Ruth's voice—her laughing, crooning, chanting, singing voice." Nordstrom loved Krauss's proposal. "Honestly, Ruth," she wrote, "I howled with pleasure over so much of it, and I think it is going to make a wonderful book." The "Crazy Crauss House brightened up a whole dreary day for me. Don't ever change. Don't get sane." Nordstrom immediately embraced the book's mischievous message to children, encouraging their impulses to think independently. Pointing to Krauss's line "NOBODY ever says stop stop stop," Nordstrom added, "Quelle purge! I know some of the influential ladies will want to put you in jail for writing such a book, and me in the stocks for loving it. But oh, the happy happy little kids!"[15]

Before turning to *A Very Special House*, Krauss and Sendak had to finish struggling with the *Definitions* book, which Krauss would consider calling *Toes Are to Wiggle* and then *Stars and Mashed Potatoes* before settling on *A Hole Is to Dig*. One weekend, when she and Sendak were, in his words, "worn thin with the whole messy business of pasting, doing, and undoing," Krauss noticed something in Sendak's pictures that upset her. She accused him "of assigning the kids middle-class roles: boys doing boy things, and girls (even worse!) doing girl things. 'God forbid, a boy should jump rope!' screamed Ruth." Sendak made some last-minute changes to the illustrations, resulting in "some suspiciously hermaphroditic-looking kids." On the last page, he had drawn a little boy sleeping on a book. At Krauss's request, Sendak changed him to a little girl.[16]

Krauss and Sendak's collaboration on *A Very Special House* proceeded much more smoothly because, according to Sendak, "we had then tuned in on each other. There was much less her having to schlep me up intellectually. I was ready for her on that one." Each page of the book shows the two of them in cahoots, Sendak's drawings cavorting around her words, her text rubbing shoulders (and sometimes feet) with his pictures. The book is his favorite from their creative partnership: "Those words and images are Ruth and me at our best."[17]

That fall brought reviews for *The Bundle Book*, Krauss's first based entirely on her observations of children. In what must have seemed ominous news for her second such book (*A Hole Is to Dig*), *The Bundle Book* (1951) received only fair sales and mixed notices. *Kirkus* thought the illustrations "may appeal more to Mother than to the toddler," but the story had "a gleeful humor the toddler will recognize and appreciate." In contrast, the *Horn Book* thought the book had "just the right amount of suspense for the nursery age." The *New York Times*'s Lois Palmer was more enthusiastic: "All those who enjoyed *The Carrot Seed* and other books by Miss Krauss will respond to the excitement of the author's latest story." However, as Nordstrom said in November 1951, "I thought reviews would be ecstatic and they have certainly been less than that," and "sales so far of *The Bundle Book* haven't come up to my loving expectations."[18]

Books influenced by progressive educational philosophies still faced an uphill struggle for success. Both Anne Carroll Moore, the children's librarian at New York Public Library, and her successor, Frances Clarke Sayers, took a dim view of children's books inspired by Bank Street's "here-and-now" method, and the two women wielded considerable influence in the children's book world. Much to Nordstrom's annoyance, the New York Public Library had consistently failed to include Margaret Wise Brown's books on its recommended list, which influenced the purchasing habits of libraries around the nation. During Children's Book Week that November, when Brown and Nordstrom arrived at the New York Public Library for "the annual celebratory

Crockett Johnson, *Barnaby*, 31 January 1952. Image courtesy of the Smithsonian Institution.
Reprinted with the permission of the Estate of Ruth Krauss, Stewart I. Edelstein, Executor. All Rights
Reserved.

Crockett Johnson, *Barnaby*, 2 February 1952. Image courtesy of the Smithsonian Institution.
Reprinted with the permission of the Estate of Ruth Krauss, Stewart I. Edelstein, Executor. All Rights
Reserved.

tea," a staff member met them at the door checking for invitations. Nordstrom
produced hers, but Brown searched through her handbag and came up empty.
According to Leonard Marcus, "As there was no reason to doubt that Margaret
had been sent one, the door-keeper's adamancy was ludicrous in the extreme."
Nordstrom refused to enter without Brown and instead, Nordstrom told
Krauss, they sat on the library's Fifth Avenue steps "and jeered at children's
book editors who came rushing along to go to the meeting." Annoyed that
The Bundle Book also did not make the list, Nordstrom observed, "The New
York Public Library doesn't like *any* of Margaret's books either, so the *Bundle
Book* is in good company." She criticized the "meetings of all the ladies in their
new hats" who take a "precious 100%-adult approach to children's books" and
predicted that *A Hole Is to Dig* "will put them all on their ears."[19]

For his part, Johnson was finishing one phase of his career and starting on
the next. Barnaby learns that his fairy godfather must leave "on or about" the
boy's sixth birthday, although O'Malley explains that he can stay if Barnaby
decides not to grow up—after all, "lots of people never grow up." At Barnaby's

sixth birthday party, Gus, McSnoyd, and O'Malley stop by to say good-bye. With that, *Barnaby* ended its ten-year run.[20]

Johnson told journalist Charles Fisher, "I had to let the strip go. I think the last year or so hit a peak for quality but sales continued to slough off steadily. I decided that while I continued writing it I would never be able to start anything else. Now I have to." Declining sales may have been a result of blacklisting, or readers may have simply grown less interested in *Barnaby*. Nevertheless, the strip still had its devoted fans: *Troy Record* editor Dwight Marvin wrote that *Barnaby* "has the smallest reader percentage of any of our comics, but those who read it read no other comic." Indeed, he noted, some people from beyond the *Record*'s usual delivery area subscribed solely to get *Barnaby*. Knowing that its *Barnaby* readers would call and write to complain, the *Philadelphia Inquirer* altered the final strip: Instead of panels depicting O'Malley's arrival in another little boy's bedroom, the paper's readers saw a notice announcing that the strip had ended. One Pennsylvania reader responded, "There have been deaths in my family that have hurt me much less."[21]

Barnaby's fans paid tribute in other ways, too. In 1953, Brown University's Pembroke College dedicated its yearbook to Johnson and adapted his characters to comment on Pembroke. Johnson supported this effort, providing the editors with "encouraging letters, . . . sincere interest, [and] incomparable help." The editors noted, "Perhaps Crockett Johnson did not foresee Mr. O'Malley in the role of mentor to eight hundred college women, but he is just that."[22]

Johnson had already begun exploring other vocations, one of which was inventing. In 1951 and 1952, he was working on a four-way adjustable mattress. At home, he kept a board beneath his mattress to provide the right degree of firmness. When traveling, he slept poorly, uncomfortable on soft mattresses. Krauss, too, often had back trouble. Such difficulties helped inspire Johnson's invention: two mattresses strapped together, with a board in one. By turning the mattresses to reposition the board, the sleeper could adjust the mattress's firmness from extra hard to medium hard, medium soft, or soft. Johnson submitted a patent application for the device in May 1952.[23]

Johnson also began to explore writing for children. He had witnessed Krauss's success as a children's author, and he decided to try his hand at it. The job of children's book creator would surely be less demanding than turning out a daily comic strip, right? In 1952, William R. Scott published the first children's book written and illustrated by Crockett Johnson: *Who's Upside Down?* The story is a parable of perception in which a kangaroo picks up a geography book, sees herself in Australia, and exclaims, "I'm down underneath and upside down! . . . It certainly seems to be so!" Johnson's narrator explains, "When a thing *seems* to be so, kangaroos usually hop to the conclusion that it *is* so." Although the book contains no explicit reference to McCarthyism, Johnson gently debunks the kangaroo's tendency to jump to conclusions. Contemporary reviewers detected no such subtext and praised the book. In the words of the *New York Times Book Review*'s Lois Palmer, Johnson "tackles the question of gravity and . . . gives an easy-to-grasp answer. . . . Children will be delighted with the mother kangaroo who gets all mixed up on the subject and with the baby kangaroo's proof that she is always right side up."[24]

Despite such favorable reviews, *Who's Upside Down?* was not a big commercial hit. In contrast, Krauss and Sendak's *A Hole Is to Dig* generated both strong reviews and brisk sales. The *New York Times Book Review*'s Ellen Lewis Buell thought it "a unique book" that would "set children thinking" and found Sendak's drawings "bouncing with action and good humor." The *Horn Book* praised *A Hole Is to Dig* as "original in approach and content" and thought its illustrations "perfect." The *San Francisco Chronicle* called it "that rare and wonderful [children's book] that is genuinely original and imaginative."[25]

The book's success launched Maurice Sendak's career. Krauss had insisted that rather than being paid a flat fee for his illustrations, Sendak receive half her royalties for the book. The resulting income enabled him to quit his day job and become a full-time freelance illustrator. By the end of the decade, he would illustrate seven more of Krauss's books.[26]

Krauss's pleasure at the success of *A Hole Is to Dig* was tempered by Blanche Krauss Brager's death in August 1952, on the eve of the book's publication. Ruth and Dave spent most of a week Baltimore, attending her mother's funeral and dealing with other matters. Less than a year and a half later, in December 1953, Dave's mother, Mary Leisk, died.[27]

Ruth returned home to more enthusiastic reviews for *A Hole Is to Dig*, a book that soon became a cultural phenomenon, in part because of the baby boom. Higher birth rates not only created a market for children's books but also pushed children to the fore of public consciousness. The book's freshness and humor as well as the misperception that it is sweet and sentimental may also have played some role in its success. More important, however, *A Hole Is to Dig* is in its own small way fairly radical. As Julia Mickenberg notes, Krauss is heir to the imaginative vision of the Lyrical Leftists of the 1920s— Carl Sandburg, Wanda Gág, and Alfred Kreymborg—"who wished to preserve rather than tame the child's 'uncivilized' impulses." A two-page spread depicting "Mud is to jump in and slide in and yell doodleedoodleedoo" may not be

politically radical, but it does authorize the child's right to dream and to question adult authority. To be a child is to be on the receiving end of power, to
have one's voice denied, one's language corrected, one's will thwarted. *A Hole Is
to Dig* grants children agency by showing their particular voices and allowing
them to define the world on their own terms. As Sendak said, Krauss was "the
first to turn children's language, concepts, and tough little pragmatic thinking
into art."[28]

If contemporary readers perceived any subversive sentiments in Krauss's
work, their responses have not survived. The FBI certainly never viewed
the children's books by either Krauss or Johnson as subversive. But the FBI,
HUAC, and McCarthy mostly left children's authors alone. As Mickenberg
has documented, many on the left found work in the field of children's books
because during the Cold War, "there was no blacklist per se in children's publishing." Seeing children's books as a field dominated by women, Red-hunters
deemed it less important and so did not watch it closely. By the middle of 1952,
the FBI had backed off on its surveillance of Johnson and Krauss as well. The
agency decided not to open a file on Krauss, finding "no information available
that [she] has been affiliated with any subversive organizations." On 11 June,
the FBI also closed its case on Johnson, at least temporarily.[29]

15

THE ART OF COLLABORATION

They and I are making secrets
and we're falling over laughing
and we're running in and out
—RUTH KRAUSS, *A Very Special House* (1953)

Neither Crockett Johnson and Ruth Krauss nor their friends and neighbors knew that the FBI had turned its attentions elsewhere. At least some Rowayton residents believed in the early 1950s that when the couple gave a party, the FBI would record the license plate numbers of those who attended. With the blacklist shrinking his American acting jobs, friend and neighbor Stefan Schnabel left to work in the West German film business until the early 1960s. Other old friends were testifying before McCarthy's Senate Permanent Subcommittee on Investigations. On 1 July 1953, the subcommittee called Rockwell Kent, who refused to cooperate and began to read a statement. McCarthy rushed him off the stand before he could finish, but Kent handed reporters printed copies of his prepared remarks, accusing McCarthy of "conspiracy . . . to overthrow our form of government . . . by force and violence"— precisely the charge that McCarthy was leveling at alleged communists. On the same day, another of Johnson's *New Masses* colleagues, Joe Freeman, testified. Johnson must have wondered if he, too, would be called.[1]

Krauss and Johnson were living among like-minded people. The section of Norwalk, Connecticut, directly east of Rowayton was Village Creek, which was and is a fully integrated community. In 1948, city planner Roger Willcox and about thirty others, most of whom were veterans who met through Henry Wallace's presidential campaign, wanted waterfront property where they could raise their families and go sailing. They decided that "one of the basic principles" of their cooperative neighborhood should be "no discrimination." In July 1949, they drew up a covenant prohibiting discrimination "on account of race, color, religious creed, age, sex, national origin, ancestry or physical disability."[2]

Although Dave and Ruth had friends in Village Creek and might well have bought there if it had existed when they moved to Connecticut in 1942, some Norwalk residents were suspicious. Calling it "Commie Creek," detractors claimed that the houses' modern roofs, when viewed from an airplane, pointed straight to New York City—clearly designed to guide Soviet bombers there. They also alleged that the big glass windows of the houses facing Long Island Sound enabled residents to signal Soviet submarines. But Village Creekers united against adversity. When local banks refused to underwrite mortgages, Village Creek property owners either built their houses themselves or sought mortgages from New York banks. When real estate agents would not show Village Creek houses to white families, Village Creekers helped keep the neighborhood integrated by selling houses via word of mouth.[3]

When some of the parents in Village Creek wanted to set up a cooperative preschool, they turned to Norma Simon, whose students had inspired Krauss's *A Very Special House*. In 1953, the basement of Martin and Sylvia Garment's Village Creek house became the Community Cooperative Nursery School, providing Krauss with another venue in which to talk with children, listen to children, and transform their ideas into children's books. Within a few years, the school moved out of the Garments' basement and into a larger building off of Rowayton's Witch Lane that local conservatives dubbed the "Little Red Schoolhouse."[4]

Krauss's association with the Little Red Schoolhouse escaped the FBI's notice, but the bureau was watching others in the neighborhood, including some of Johnson and Krauss's friends. Mischa Richter's wife, Helen, chased FBI agents off of her front porch with a broom. The agents shouted at her, "We're gonna see you in court!" She shouted back, "I'll be there, and I'll be wearing my black dress!" Two blocks from Johnson and Krauss's house, physician Abe Levine and his wife, Frume, who ran the Jewish School for the Blind's nursery school, hid their political books behind other books on the shelf. In 1953, when one of their daughters hummed a union song, "Solidarity Forever," in front of a friend, Frume Levine panicked even though the song shares a tune with "The Battle Hymn of the Republic."[5]

That year, another longtime Johnson friend, Kay Boyle, moved with her husband, Joseph Franckenstein, and their children from Europe to Rowayton after Franckenstein was suspended from his job with the U.S. Foreign Service as a security risk and Boyle found herself unable to sell her stories. Both Boyle and Franckenstein found jobs at Miss Thomas's School.[6]

"Have you considered using Kimberly-Clark coated papers?"

Crockett Johnson, advertisement for Kimberly-Clark. Used with the consent of Neenah Paper, Inc.

Not all of Rowayton's residents were candidates for political persecution, however. Jack Goodman, now a director of Simon and Schuster, and his wife, Aggie, continued to spend their summers there, occasionally throwing large parties attended by such theatrical luminaries as Marlon Brando and Loretta Young, notable people from the literary world, low-ranking people from the publishing house, and neighbors—Gene Wallace and Phyllis Rowand, Abe and Frume Levine, Fred and Harriet Schwed, Harry Marinsky, Shelley Trubowitz, and Ruth and Dave. Dave was never the center of attention at parties but was more likely to observe the conversation, slightly bemused. When he did speak, his timing was excellent. In his soft voice, Dave would offer wry, well-phrased observations that made people chuckle. Often, you had to be a friend of his to appreciate his subtle humor. Filmmaker Gene Searchinger recalled a story Dave told about his sailboat. One friend had a small yacht, and the other a fairly large yacht. These two friends and Dave decided to swap boats and pay each other the difference in the values of the boats: in other words, the two people who got larger boats would pay the difference between it and the values of their original boats. At the end of the year, all three said, "Ahh, I'd rather go back to the boat I had." So each boat went back to its original owner. At this point, Dave paused, looked at Gene very seriously, and said, "And we all made a fine profit on the deal." Laughing as he thought about this story, Gene observed, "If you weren't attuned, it just went right by you—you would think, 'Well, that was kind of a silly remark.' But it was hysterical. It was a comment about capitalism and the mythology of Americans and so on and everything else. It's a very profound little joke."[7]

Johnson was avoiding the political spotlight and pondering his future after *Barnaby*. Even after the publication of *Who's Upside Down?*, he had not made up his mind to pursue the children's book business. He did advertisements for the Kimberly-Clark Corporation, *Ladies' Home Journal*, and the American Cancer Society. He and Jules Feiffer collaborated on a comic strip, with Johnson providing the dialogue and Feiffer creating the pictures. Feiffer had just finished a two-year stint in the U.S. Army and wanted to break into children's books. Ursula Nordstrom introduced him to Maurice Sendak, who in turn introduced him to Krauss and Johnson. Feiffer was thrilled when Johnson suggested that they collaborate on a new comic: "I thought this was my chance to get into the big time, which I had up till then taken several shots at and was in despair that nothing was happening." They created two weeks of strips about a private eye named Herkimer and his assistant, Matson, a small

Crockett Johnson and Jules Feiffer, untitled comic strip, 1953. Image courtesy of the Smithsonian Institution. Reprinted with the permission of the Estate of Ruth Krauss, Stewart I. Edelstein, Executor. All Rights Reserved.

Maurice Sendak, two-page spread from Ruth Krauss, *A Very Special House* (New York: Harper, 1953). Pictures copyright © 1953 by Maurice Sendak. Copyright © renewed 1981 by Maurice Sendak. Used by permission of HarperCollins Publishers. Reprinted with the permission of the Estate of Ruth Krauss, Stewart I. Edelstein, Executor. All Rights Reserved.

boy. Feiffer and Johnson never settled on a name for the comic, and no syndicate was interested.[8]

Reviewers and readers, however, were very interested in Krauss and Sendak's second collaboration, *A Very Special House*, published in November 1953. The book offers an even stronger endorsement of children's ideas than did its predecessor and is more radical in the freedoms it grants children. Its protagonist draws on walls, jumps on the bed, and brings home a lion (who eats the stuffing from the cushions) and a monkey (who leaves "little feetprints on the ceiling"), but "NOBODY ever says stop stop stop stop." The book completely disregards adult authority, encouraging children to think and act independently. Reviewers embraced the idea. The *Horn Book*'s Virginia Haviland thought *A Very Special House* "as full of bounce as *A Hole is to Dig* and even richer in ideas fascinating to small children." Writing in the *Atlantic Monthly*, Margaret Ford Kieran praised the book's "unorthodox" qualities, suggesting that it would "win the approval of fond uncles and aunts more than parents." While it is "no handbook for deportment," "in the blowing-off-steam department, it deserves an award." It won a Caldecott Honor in March 1954.[9]

Crockett Johnson, illustration from the dummy of Ruth Krauss and Crockett Johnson, *Is This You?* Image courtesy of the Northeast Children's Literature Collection, Dodd Research Center, University of Connecticut, Storrs. Reprinted with the permission of the Estate of Ruth Krauss, Stewart I. Edelstein, Executor. All Rights Reserved.

Krauss and Sendak had already begun work on their next project, *I'll Be You and You Be Me.* As with *A Very Special House,* the author and illustrator were very much in sync, and Sendak found the process "great fun because every page was an experiment, every page we changed our minds. And yet the book hangs together in a way that's fascinating because it's the two of us." In the wake of the strong reviews and sales for their first two books and with their third collaboration under contract, Krauss thought that she and Sendak deserved more than their customary five-hundred-dollar advance for their next project, *I Want to Paint My Bathroom Blue,* a color chosen because it was Krauss's favorite. He agreed but was apprehensive about raising the issue because "anything relating to money with Ursula was a nightmare." In the early spring of 1954, he and Krauss were in Nordstrom's office and Krauss brought up the subject of how much she and Sendak were being paid: Given their success, they should get a larger advance. Her voice rising, Nordstrom suddenly "became the House of Harper" and accused Krauss and Sendak of being ungrateful. Nordstrom had given Krauss the freedom to create *A Hole Is to Dig* and to choose Sendak as her artist—an artist, she reminded Krauss, who had no experience. "Who else in the whole world would do that?," Nordstrom asked. Krauss replied, "OK. It happened already. We've done it, and we're a

138

Crockett Johnson, "Is This How You Take a Bath?," from Ruth Krauss and Crockett Johnson, *Is This You?* (New York: Scott, 1955). Reprinted with the permission of the Estate of Ruth Krauss, Stewart I. Edelstein, Executor. All Rights Reserved.

successful team." The tension between the two women made Sendak uneasy. He shrank deeper into his chair, no longer caring whether they received more money. He just wanted the fight to be over. But Nordstrom was angry. She cleared her desk with her hands, sending papers, books, and pencils flying, with some landing on Krauss and Sendak. They hastily pushed back their chairs. Nordstrom began screaming, "Get out! Get out!" Krauss and Sendak fled to the elevator and began their descent from the sixth floor to the lobby. He was thinking, "This is the end. I'm through at age twenty-six! Why has Ruth blown it all for money?" Krauss tried to console him. When they reached the lobby, the elevator doors opened to reveal Nordstrom, who. She had run down six flights of stairs to continue her tirade. "I never want to see you again! Get the hell out of my sight!," she shouted. Sendak thought his career was finished. Instead, a few weeks later, he and Krauss each received a one-thousand-dollar advance for *I Want to Paint My Bathroom Blue.*[10]

Krauss was working on other books in addition to those with Sendak, including two that Johnson illustrated, *How to Make an Earthquake* (1954) and *Is This You?* (1955). He also provided drawings for Margaret Wise Brown's *Willie's Adventures*, published in 1954, after her death. *Is This You?*, credited to Johnson and Krauss as coauthors, provides a sense of how they worked together. The book, which was her idea, teaches children how to write a book. Krauss was inspired by her childhood and by her friendship with seven-year-old Nina Rowand Wallace, who then lived right across the street. Wallace recalled, "Sometimes Ruth would take me off on adventures, . . . and she'd say, 'Let's get lost. It's so much fun to get lost.'" The pair would go "driving around the back roads of Darien and Westport and Norwalk," and the girl learned the "wonderful thing . . . that it's okay to be lost, and that it's always an adventure and you never know where things will turn." Krauss used the same method when creating a book.[11]

Is This You? poses a simple question, offers preposterous answers, and then asks the question again. For the question "Is this how you take a bath?," Krauss suggested a series of accompanying illustrations: a child in a "bird-bath—with birds & big brush," a child with "bathing-cap and towel" placing a "finger in [a] soup-bowl," a child in a "tank with [a] big rhino," and a child "asleep in bed." The series ends with the reader prompted to draw a picture of how he or she takes a bath. Johnson suggested replacing the illustration of the sleeping child "because of bedwetters and their shame. How about in shower with umbrella, raincoat & rubber boots?" Krauss agreed with Johnson's concerns, writing "Yes" next to his suggestion. She crossed out "asleep in own bed" as well as his suggestion of "in shower with umbrella, raincoat & rubber boots" and added some of her own ideas: "day-dreaming," "grapefruit in the eye," "elephant-trunk," and "in very-very elaborate set-up" with "butlers, towels galore," and "bubbles." Next to "elephant-trunk," Dave wrote, "No—too trite." In the final book, Dave illustrated the bird bath and the soup bowl; the child bathing with a large animal, although a hippo has replaced the rhino; and a child in a shower with a raincoat, hat, and boots. The drafts show a couple talking to one another and taking one another seriously.[12]

"Is this what you eat for breakfast?" shows a girl eating grass and another with a hat in her mouth; boys are shown taking a bite out of a piano leg and digging up worms. Some of Johnson's unpublished sketches, including "Is This Your Pet?," display a darker sense of humor that recalls the *New Yorker* cartoons of Charles Addams, which Johnson knew, and the books of Edward Gorey, first published in 1953 and 1954.[13]

Published by William R. Scott in the spring of 1955, *Is This You?* garnered positive reviews, with the *New York Times Book Review*'s Ellen Lewis Buell hailing this "very funny" and "daffiest of do-it-yourself books" as saying "more than it means to" and the *Bulletin of the Children's Book Center* praising the book's "rollicking type of humor in the combination of picture and text." A

140

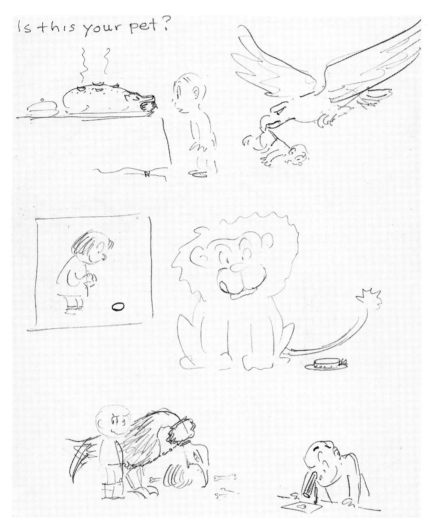

Crockett Johnson, sketches for "Is This Your Pet?," a sequence not included in *Is This You?* Image courtesy of the Northeast Children's Literature Collection, Dodd Research Center, University of Connecticut, Storrs. Reprinted with the permission of the Estate of Ruth Krauss, Stewart I. Edelstein, Executor. All Rights Reserved.

few months earlier, *I'll Be You and You Be Me* had been released to glowing reviews. The *New York Herald Tribune*'s Louise Seaman Bechtel called it "probably the best combination thus far of the Krauss selective reporting on the talk of small children, with the Sendak genius of carrying out their ideas or carrying them further, in hundreds of tiny figures." Buell was struck by the range of emotional experience Krauss captured and thought that Sendak's "small, delicately drawn" illustrations had "a force and an ebullience out of all proportion to their size."[14]

The Krauss-Johnson collaboration, *How to Make an Earthquake*, released in the fall of 1954, received mixed reviews. The book features games invented and explained by children, including Nina Rowand Wallace and Emily Levine. Krauss had watched her young neighborhood friends play and thought that rather than make another activity book *for* children, she would make one *by* children. The resulting book offers advice on "how to make sitting interesting" ("lie on your back in a big chair and put your legs up the back of the chair"), "how to balance a peanut on your nose" (place a sticky raisin on your nose and stick the peanut on top of the raisin), and "a good way to entertain telephone callers":

When the phone rings, answer it.

First, you should ask who it is. And then, ask if they'd like to hear some entertainment because maybe they wouldn't. But if they do, you should tell them, "Hold the line a minute, please." Then sing a little bit, or recite a little, or if you know a piano piece you could play a little of that. Just do a little at first. This is testing. Then go back to the phone and ask, "Did you hear me?" If they answer yes, say, "Hold the line a minute, please," again. And then you can play your whole piece for them, or whatever is your talent.[15]

Some reviewers saw the humor: The *Christian Science Monitor*'s Rae Emerson Donlon found "just the right blend of sense and nonsense," and the *New York Times*'s Lois Palmer enjoyed Krauss's "close understanding of what tickles young children, of how they like to mix reality with make-believe." But others saw the book as "written in the tone of an adult laughing at children" and as lacking "the childlike qualities of language and humor that have made Miss Krauss' earlier books so popular with children and adults alike." At least one reader wrote to Harper to claim that the book was not for children but "for adults to enjoy after three or four cocktails"; the book's ideas ran "contrary to any parent or teacher trying to teach a youngster good manners." Johnson and Krauss believed that such critics had missed the point, and he was particularly amused by librarians who cataloged the book "with other how-to books such as how to collect stamps and how to sew a seam."[16]

Ruth and Dave had little time to dwell on reviews that fall. In August, Ruth had "a bad back attack," and she was still bedridden in September. Afraid of needing an operation, she coped with the pain by having her doctor (likely her neighbor, Abe Levine) give her a shot before bedtime. Immediately after Ruth had her nightly shot, Dave raced downstairs, dished up a bowl of chocolate ice cream, and then raced back upstairs so that Ruth could have a few spoonfuls before the drugs sent her off to dreamland.[17]

While Ruth was lying in her upstairs bedroom, Phyllis Rowand was mourning. On 3 September 1954, Gene Wallace's car collided with a truck on Noroton Hill in Stamford. He was killed instantly. Wallace was thirty-six. His daughter was not yet nine. Dave and Ruth grew even closer to Nina and Phyllis. Later that month, after Ruth was upright again, daughter and mother began joining her and Dave for dinner at least once a week. As an appetizer, they had graham crackers and V8. For dinner, Ruth might prepare spaghetti with sauce, accompanied by artichokes and sour cream. After they had eaten, Ruth would lie down on the living room rug and go to sleep. Dave, Phyllis, and Ruth (while awake) would talk, including Nina in the conversation as an equal. Sometimes, George Annand would join them. Nina did not always understand all of the talk of noteworthy books or the latest news in *I. F. Stone's Weekly*. But she was glad to be included.[18]

Dave became a surrogate father and mentor to Nina. He built her a Nina-sized table and chair and set them up near his own. His workspace, in the front room, faced the house's front windows, looking out onto the porch and to the sea beyond. Behind and to the left of his table sat Nina at her table, looking out onto the side porch and Crockett Street, where she and her parents had moved just before her father's death. She spent many hours drawing at her desk while Dave smoked cigarettes and drew at his desk, which "was always free of clutter," with "sharp pencils and paper at hand—ready for action." Behind her sat the bulky television set with its small screen. Sitting there, drawing, Nina felt fortunate and "in the center of the action" but able to concentrate on her work, just as Dave concentrated on his.[19]

Upstairs, Krauss was creating art for *I Want to Paint My Bathroom Blue* and text for *Charlotte and the White Horse*. She also had three new projects in mind. One was on children's dreams and ideas about dreaming. Another was a book of songs. Her third would be "'natural' as a follow up" to *A Hole Is to Dig*.

New Words for Old would feature children's "word-inventions"—used either "when they don't know the correct ones" or invented "for fun" when "they *do* know the correct word." As she explained, a child might use *biggie* to refer to a grown-up or *not-turtle* to refer to any animal that isn't a turtle. Krauss also overheard three children discussing trikes and bikes:

> A: "I have a two-wheeler."
> B: "I have a three-wheeler."
> C: "I have a broken-wheeler."

Nordstrom was skeptical: Some of these "new words" sounded like "just plain baby-talk" to her. "It isn't that I don't trust you, dear," she wrote, "But couldn't you carry it out just a bit more before we, you and I, come to final conclusions about how inevitable it would be as a follow-up to the sacred *Hole*????" Krauss disagreed: "They are real *word-inventions* . . . & they are the child's *direct observation*. . . . A complete collection will take me 6 months to a year's play with the idea, that's all." The book, *Open House for Butterflies*, did not appear until 1960.[20]

Johnson wrote more swiftly and with a sharper focus than Krauss did. Within a couple of months of acquiring his new officemate and becoming a surrogate father, he began writing a children's book about a boy and his crayon. This book would garner the sort of acclaim Dave had not seen since *Barnaby*'s heyday, and it would firmly establish him as Crockett Johnson, author of children's books, the career for which he is best known today.

16

HAROLD

But, luckily, he kept his wits and his purple crayon.
—CROCKETT JOHNSON, *Harold and the Purple Crayon* (1955)

In November 1954, Dave finished dummies for *Harold and the Purple Crayon*. The previous year, his sister, Else Leisk Frank, and her husband, Leonard Frank, had adopted a boy, whom they named Harold David, after Harold Gold, the attorney who helped with the adoption, and her father. Though Dave was not especially close to his sister, their mother's death eleven months earlier had brought them together, and he named his character after his nephew. The week before Thanksgiving, he sent the manuscript to Ursula Nordstrom.[1]

Had she known that the FBI was investigating Johnson, Nordstrom would not have cared. After learning that Howard Selsam, the husband of Harper author Millicent Selsam, was being called before McCarthy's committee, Nordstrom replied, "I don't care, as long as he's not a Republican."[2]

Though politically sympathetic to Johnson, Nordstrom was not initially enthusiastic about *Harold and the Purple Crayon*: "It doesn't seem to be a good children's book to me but I'm often wrong—and this post–Children's Book Week Monday finds me dead in the head. I'd probably pass up *Tom Sawyer* today." She offered to reread the manuscript when she was "more caught up" and passed it along to reader Ann Powers, whom she described as "young . . . and less tired than I am." Powers was confused: "I don't think it is anything sensational, but it is a little different" and "even bears rereadings." She liked "falling into the sea, the sailboat" but also doubted "came up thinking fast (pun?)" and the "1st picture drawing a sail." She thought children would enjoy "the buildings" but also wondered "why he should look for his room in both a small house and a large apt. building." By the end of her report, she conceded, "the more I look at the book, the more I like it," concluding, "This is undoubtedly one of those books which are indescribable in copy."[3]

Three weeks later, after making a few minor changes in accordance with suggestions from Nordstrom, Johnson returned the revised *Harold* to Harper.

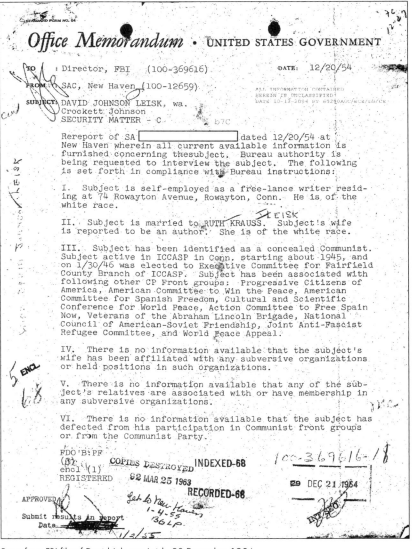

STANDARD FORM NO. 64

Office Memorandum • UNITED STATES GOVERNMENT

TO : Director, FBI (100-369616)   DATE: 12/20/54

FROM : SAC, New Haven (100-12659)

SUBJECT: DAVID JOHNSON LEISK, wa.
Crockett Johnson
SECURITY MATTER - C

b7C

ALL INFORMATION CONTAINED
HEREIN IS UNCLASSIFIED
DATE 10-13-2004 BY 60240AUC/BCR/LR/CR

Rereport of SA [   ] dated 12/20/54 at
New Haven wherein all current available information is
furnished concerning the subject. Bureau authority is
being requested to interview the subject. The following
is set forth in compliance with Bureau instructions:

I. Subject is self-employed as a free-lance writer resid-
ing at 74 Rowayton Avenue, Rowayton, Conn. He is of the
white race.

II. Subject is married to RUTH KRAUSS. Subject's wife
is reported to be an author. She is of the white race.

III. Subject has been identified as a concealed Communist.
Subject active in ICCASP in Conn. starting about 1945, and
on 1/30/46 was elected to Executive Committee for Fairfield
County Branch of ICCASP. Subject has been associated with
following other CP Front groups: Progressive Citizens of
America, American Committee to Win the Peace, American
Committee for Spanish Freedom, Cultural and Scientific
Conference for World Peace, Action Committee to Free Spain
Now, Veterans of the Abraham Lincoln Brigade, National
Council of American-Soviet Friendship, Joint Anti-Fascist
Refugee Committee, and World Peace Appeal.

IV. There is no information available that the subject's
wife has been affiliated with any subversive organizations
or held positions in such organizations.

V. There is no information available that any of the subject's relatives are associated with or have membership in
any subversive organizations.

VI. There is no information available that the subject has
defected from his participation in Communist front groups
or from the Communist Party.

FDO B PF
(3)
encl (1)
REGISTERED

COPIES DESTROYED

02 MAR 25 1963

INDEXED-68

RECORDED-68

100-369616-18

29 DEC 21 1954

APPROVED
Submit results in report
Date

Let to new Haven
1-4-55
BGLP.
1/3/55

Page from FBI file of David Johnson Leisk, 20 December 1954.

Nordstrom apologized for her "lukewarm and unenthusiastic" initial reaction: "I really think it is going to make a darling book, and I certainly was wrong at first." Her recent successes had made her overconfident in first impressions: "The Harper children's books have had such a good fall, on so many lists, etc. etc., and I was feeling a little good—not *satisfied*, you understand, but I thought gosh I'm really catching on to things, I bet, and pretty soon it ought to get easier. And then I stubbed my toe on Harold and his damned purple crayon."[4]

On 20 December 1954, Harper sent Johnson a $750 advance and a contract for *Harold and the Purple Crayon*. The same day, the FBI's New Haven office asked J. Edgar Hoover for "Bureau authority" to interview Johnson. The New Haven agents cited their uncertainty about whether Johnson "has defected from his participation in Communist front groups or from the Communist Party." Their "informants [are] negative re current CP activity," but the G-men wanted to be sure. They hoped that he would become an informant, which meant that the communists would have to believe that he remained loyal to them. So the FBI had to tread carefully.[5]

On 4 January 1955, Hoover authorized an interview with Johnson but cautioned, "Due to his employment and the extent of his activity in [Communist] front groups he should be interviewed only within the restrictions laid down by the Security Informant Program." In January and February, the FBI's New Haven office again had Johnson under surveillance; agents discovered that he worked mostly at home, leaving only to go to the post office, "at which time it was not appropriate to contact him." When asked if agents might interview Johnson at home, Hoover said no: "Due to his former high position in Communist circles and due to his occupation as a writer it is not believed advisable to accede to your request. Subject should only be interviewed away from his home by experienced agents and the utmost discretion should be used in the conduct of the interview."[6]

On 5 April, a federal agent visited the Rowayton house of Kay Boyle and Joseph Franckenstein and attempted to confiscate her passport on the grounds that she was then a Communist. Boyle refused and told the agent to see her lawyer. Agents had even less success with Johnson: On 22 April, the New Haven FBI office reported that attempts to interview him "have not been successful. It has required that agents stay outside of subject's home in order to contact him. It has been noted that on the days attempts have been made to interview him, he confined himself to his home entirely. He has been observed working at a desk in his home." In other words, they could see Johnson, he could see them, and he would not come out.[7]

In May, Hoover suggested that interviewing Johnson might not be worthwhile "in the light of the difficulties involved." Fearing adverse publicity, the FBI gave up: "It is possible that if the interview were conducted under any type of adverse circumstances that it may become embarrassing to the Bureau at a later date, therefore this case is being placed in a Closed Status in the New Haven Division." Case closed, four months before Harold's debut.[8]

Though disappointed by the mixed response to *How to Make an Earthquake*, Krauss was looking forward to the fall publication of *Charlotte and the White Horse* and working on her next book. For three years, she had been collecting paintings by Rowayton schoolchildren for a visual version of *A Hole Is to Dig*. Where *A Hole* used children's words, this new book would use their art.[9]

As summer approached, Ruth spent less time visiting children in the Rowayton and Norwalk schools and instead swam or sailed with Dave. Children, however, kept coming to her. As a May 1955 newspaper profile noted, "The neighborhood small fry are in and out of [Johnson and Krauss's] comfortable house. The Johnsons are known as likely customers for Girl Scout cookies and always have a cookie available for young visitors." Krauss explained, "I like to listen to children talking. Certain things come out that I could not catch any other way."[10]

While Krauss's busy mind gathered new material, yet another adaptation of *Barnaby* was in the works—this time, a weekly television show. Johnson was also contemplating other ideas for children's books. That February, he began to consider a book about children's imaginary friends, such as those outlined in his mock-scholarly essay "Fantastic Companions," which appeared in the June 1955 issue of *Harper's*. Though Mr. O'Malley was "a purely fictional creation," parents had written to him about "the astonishing creatures that visited *their* homes." Johnson introduced readers to six different companions, among them Bivvy, who "knocks things over and breaks things," immediately fleeing the scene of the accident, leaving only young Mildred "by herself amidst the debris," and Henry M.'s friend the Gumgaw, "who 'is big, with a face like an elephant' and who 'talks all the time' in a voice that surprisingly, considering his bulk, is pitched high enough to be mistaken through a closed door for Henry's own." Johnson asked Nordstrom about making the concept into a book, but the imminent publication of *Harold and the Purple Crayon* drove the idea from their minds. The book also eclipsed Johnson's receipt of a patent for his four-way adjustable mattress, though he was optimistic about the invention's success and told the *New York Times*, "I'd love to go into a motel and be asked how I'd like my bed."[11]

Published in the fall of 1955, *Harold and the Purple Crayon* was a runaway hit. The first print run of ten thousand sold so quickly that Harper ordered a new print run of seventy-five hundred by November. The book encourages reflection on the relationship between representation and reality. Like the *New Yorker* cartoons of Saul Steinberg, Johnson's drawings are metapictures, with meanings that shift as they develop. What seems to be a curve becomes a balloon, as a line of *U*s morphs into an ocean, and all drawings become as real as the artist character creating them.[12]

Harold and the Purple Crayon is also about Crockett Johnson. Where Ruth Krauss based her characters on children she observed, her husband created his child characters from his own experiences. As a child, Dave loved to draw, just as Harold does. Like Harold, Dave was a bald artist who worked mostly at night. (Of his tendency to draw bald characters, Dave said, "I draw people without hair because it's so much *easier!* Besides, to me, people *with* hair look funny.") Though the crayon is purple, the cover of the book is brown, Johnson's favorite color. He lived in a brown house, furnished with comfortable brown leather chairs, and drove a brown 1948 Austin Tudor sedan. He wore chocolate-colored pants and T-shirts, often ordered from the Sears catalog. When the weather was cooler, he wore brown cardigan sweaters. If he needed to be more formal, he wore one of his brown suits. In the morning, there was no question about how to dress: brown goes with brown. The clean, unadorned style of his art, identical to Harold's artistic style, echoes Johnson's sartorial minimalism. That Harold should greet the viewer from a brown cover is apt because both Harold and his purple crayon are imaginative extensions of Johnson.[13]

Nordstrom immediately began encouraging Johnson to write a sequel: "I know you don't want to do *Harold and His Green Crayon* or *Harold and His Orange Crayon*, but I honestly think further adventures of Harold would sell and not be a cheap idea, either." Johnson had begun a new comic strip about a dog, *Barkis*, in May 1955, but it had not caught on. Brad Anderson's *Marmaduke* had made its debut the summer before and cornered the market for single-panel dog-related strips, so the syndicate dropped *Barkis* in early November. In response to Nordstrom's suggestion, therefore, Johnson was free to get right to work on *Harold's Fairy Tale*, finishing a dummy by mid-December. From that point onward, writing and illustrating children's books became

Crockett Johnson, *Barkis*, 1955. Reprinted with the permission of the Estate of Ruth Krauss, Stewart I. Edelstein, Executor. All Rights Reserved.

Johnson's primary occupation: Over the next ten years, he would create five more *Harold* books and a dozen others.[14]

It is tempting to read *Harold and the Purple Crayon* and its sequels as radical political commentary. The books suggest that the real world can be transformed by the imagination and encourage impulses to explore alternatives to that world, bringing to mind 1960s French student radicals' slogan, "All power to the imagination." The imagination, however, is neither radical nor conservative. It is amoral. By allowing us to step outside of morality, the imagination can show us that what does exist is not necessarily what ought to exist or what might exist. Echoing Percy Bysshe Shelley's notion of the imagination as "the greatest instrument of moral good," Harold uses his imagination with a sense

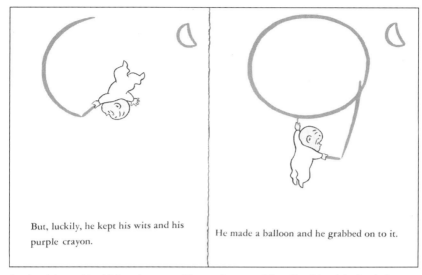

But, luckily, he kept his wits and his purple crayon.

He made a balloon and he grabbed on to it.

Crockett Johnson, Harold "kept his wits and his purple crayon," from *Harold and the Purple Crayon* (New York: Harper, 1955). Text copyright © 1955 by Crockett Johnson. Copyright © renewed 1983 by Ruth Krauss. Used by permission of HarperCollins Publishers. Reprinted with the permission of the Estate of Ruth Krauss, Stewart I. Edelstein, Executor. All Rights Reserved.

of moral responsibility. In *A Picture for Harold's Room*, Harold needs "rocks to step on" to climb "out of the sea and on to the hill." Realizing that the ship he drew "was too near the rocks," Harold "put up a lighthouse to warn the sailors." When, in *Harold and the Purple Crayon*, the boy creates more pie than he can eat, he leaves "a very hungry moose and a deserving porcupine to finish" the leftovers. Harold uses his imagination to create new worlds but does so without causing harm. If the purple crayon is radical, it proposes a velvet revolution, not a violent one.[15]

Reviewers did not see the book as radical but noted its emphasis on the imagination. Considering *Harold* "an ingenious and original little picture story," the *Horn Book*'s Virginia Haviland wrote, "This is a little book that will be loved, for Crockett Johnson's wide-eyed little boy and his simple lines in purple crayon are the kind of illustration to stimulate the imagination. They will suggest similar drawing adventures." The *New York Times*'s Ellen Lewis Buell thought the book would "probably start youngsters off on odysseys of their own."[16]

It did. Future poet laureate Rita Dove, who was three years old at the time of the book's publication, has cited *Harold* as her first favorite book because "it showed me the possibilities of traveling along the line of one's imagination," an idea that made "a powerful impression" on her. It was the most memorable childhood book for Chris Van Allsburg, author of *The Polar Express* (1985) and six when *Harold* was published, because of both its "theme, which has to do with the power of imagination, the ability to create things with your imagination," and its succinct presentation of "a fairly elusive idea."[17]

When Harold draws a mountain to help him see his bedroom window, he climbs to the top and slips: "And there wasn't any other side of the mountain. He was falling, in thin air." As always, his skill at responding to an ever-changing situation saves him: "But, luckily, he kept his wits and his purple crayon. He made a balloon and he grabbed on to it. And he made a basket under the balloon big enough to stand in." And off he goes again. Just as Harold adapts to shifting power dynamics, so did Crockett Johnson. Out of work and under surveillance, he kept his wits and began to imagine—new comic strips, a better mattress, children's books. The purple crayon is an imaginative extension of Johnson, who had by then distanced himself from the Communist Party and had worked on Democrat Adlai Stevenson's 1952 presidential campaign. No matter what the FBI might have thought, Harold's crayon is definitely purple, not red. In December 1955, Johnson was asked why the crayon was purple. He replied, "Purple is the color of adventure."[18]

17

STRIKING OUT INTO NEW AREAS OF EXPERIMENTATION

You can write books about anything.
—RUTH KRAUSS, "How to Write a Book," in *How to Make an Earthquake* (1954)

Though pleased by the swift sales and strong reviews of *Harold and the Purple Crayon*, Crockett Johnson viewed his success from a gently sardonic perspective. In November 1955, his clipping service sent him the *Winston-Salem Journal and Sentinel*'s single-sentence review by Dave Marion, age four: "Harold can draw whatever he wants with his purple crayon, and then it really is." Bemused, he passed the clipping along to his editor: "Dear Ursula," he wrote. "Just in case you missed this—It's a very good review."[1]

Ruth Krauss's work was getting good reviews, too. An eight-page article in *Elementary English* proclaimed that she "has probably gone further than any other author in experimenting with the form and content of picture books." Hailing her as at the vanguard of the "realistic 'here and now' type of story," the piece attempted to define the Krauss aesthetic: "Children are neither cute darlings to be patronized, nor miniature adults to be civilized, but rather lively, well-organized people with . . . ambitions of their own" who "are fascinated by language" and "have an exuberance and joy in daily living, and an irrepressible sense of the ridiculous which may differ radically from an adult's idea of what's funny." Singling out Krauss's gifts as a poet, the essay's author, Anne Martin, said that in *A Very Special House*, Krauss "has successfully depicted a world of riot, chaos, and confusion by employing a strictly disciplined, rhythmical, almost lyrical style in symmetrical form." Martin wondered whether Krauss would "continue to work along the lines of *I'll Be You and You'll Be Me*, or perhaps strike out into completely new areas of experimentation." For children, "a Ruth Krauss book 'is to look at' over and over again, to quote from and laugh at and talk about, and even (going along with Sendak's illustrations) to hug lovingly and to drop off to sleep with."[2]

Krauss continued to experiment. *Charlotte and the White Horse*, published in the fall of 1955, leaves behind the humor of her earlier child-authored stories. Unlike the playful nonsense of *Bears*, *Charlotte*'s verse is lyrical, with pictures that Maurice Sendak described as "my first attempt to unite poetry with William Blake." As the seasons change

> the wind and the rains are gone
> the grass is coming out of the ground
> the leaves are coming out of the trees
> the people are coming out of doors.

Though Krauss makes the poetic cadences visible, she also signals that the words come from one of her child acquaintances: the entire text is in quotation marks, with the opening mark appearing before the first word on the first page and the closing mark after the last word on the final page. There is a touch of sadness when the father suggests that Charlotte's colt "won't make a good race horse so we will sell him." Krauss repeats twice, "Now just sorrow is coming in," and Sendak shows the sad little girl, turning away, looking down. Her father relents, and girl and horse share a tearful embrace.[3]

Sustained by Sendak's delicate watercolors, this tale of Charlotte and her colt, Milky Way, is one of the best-reviewed Krauss books. The *Horn Book* called it a "little book of unusual beauty," the *New York Times Book Review*'s Lois Palmer thought that Krauss "has shown again how clearly she understands how children feel and what is important to them," and the *New Yorker*'s Katharine T. Kinkead found "a guilelessness and spontaneity" reminiscent of "the actual conversation of an imaginative child." Sendak's "exquisite pictures" (as the *Chicago Tribune* described them) won critical approval, too. The *Times* thought the "soft tone" of his art apt, and Kinkead believed that "the softly colored illustrations" had "exactly caught" the "tenderness and exultation" of "the girl's love song to her pet." The *New York Herald Tribune* went even further, saying that Sendak's "pictures match and surpass the tenderness of the text, giving it all a dreamlike fairy tale quality."[4]

Both Nordstrom and Susan Carr liked the dummy for *Harold's Fairy Tale* but suggested revisions. Nordstrom asked Johnson to change "(page 12) that business of making himself smaller and (page 16) making himself bigger," when he draws the mouse hole into the castle and later draws stairs to measure his height. Telling rather than showing, Johnson had written, "Harold made himself smaller" next to the illustration of Harold drawing the hole and a mouse larger than himself, and "Harold made himself bigger" next to the illustration of him drawing the steps. Nordstrom and Carr thought this "too intricate," with Nordstrom adding, "I started to say 'too intricate for children,' but I have to admit that it missed me entirely and I am in my late 'teens, as you very well know." Johnson took Nordstrom's advice, allowing images rather than words to convey most of the meaning in the book. According to Johnson, "Without telling readers over seven Harold 'made himself small' (a flat statement of a magical act) we let them get the 'joke' by themselves. Readers under seven, who can't be expected to understand relativity, will know perfectly well that Harold made himself small (and by magic) without being told. Readers who are exactly seven let's not sell any books to." On Christmas Eve, he sent out the revised dummy along with a promise to create the finished drawings by early January.[5]

As 1955 drew to a close, both Johnson and Krauss had become successful children's authors. However, as a newspaper profile noted, they never competed with one another. Instead, they worked—usually separately but sometimes together—on books "that enchant adults as well as children." Krauss continued to work during the daytime, but Johnson was now more flexible, drawing in the day and "writing at night, away from the interruption of meter man and telephone." When he needed a break, he liked to step out and watch the boats go by or go sailing. Krauss enjoyed swimming at the Norwalk Y. And both maintained professional interests beyond the world of juvenile publishing. Johnson was optimistic that his adjustable mattress would find a market, and Krauss still harbored ambitions of writing for an adult audience.[6]

Some prominent adults were reading her children's books. In the fall of the following year, Henry Miller, author of *The Tropic of Cancer* (at the time banned in the United States), wrote to Harper that he thought *A Hole Is to Dig* "a wonderful little book" and asked for a copy for his son, Tony, plus another half dozen to give away as gifts. Nordstrom passed along Miller's comments to Krauss. The notion of a Henry Miller blurb for *A Hole Is to Dig* must have amused both women.[7]

Johnson moved on to the jacket design for *Harold's Fairy Tale*, feeling both modest about the first *Harold* book's success and keen to repeat it. Given that reviewers of children's books "are so extravagantly kind to all the books they review," the *Horn Book*'s praise indicated "no more than that the reviewer accepted the book as run of the mill." He wondered, "If quotes sell at all, wouldn't an adjective or two from *The New York Times*, *The New Yorker*, or even *The Chicago Tribune* mean more to a purchaser?" Moreover, although

"About spring," she said, and she hesitated, wondering how to tell the snowman that when spring came he wouldn't be there. "I mean, I'm not worried about it." "Why should you be?" said the snowman. "Spring won't come, while I'm here." "What?" Irene stared at him.

6

"While I'm here, spring won't come." The snowman picked up the rope that had dropped from Irene's hand and, with a happy grunt, he flung himself on the sled and went coasting down the hill. "Wait!" Irene slid down the hill after him.

Crockett Johnson, illustration from *Time for Spring* (New York: Harper, 1957). Reprinted with the permission of the Estate of Ruth Krauss, Stewart I. Edelstein, Executor. All Rights Reserved.

he had "discouraged the use of the word 'Barnaby' in the past," "recently in two public ventures it has been made plain to me that 'Barnaby' is much better known than my own name." Perhaps the cover of the new book should mention his most famous creation. Carr agreed about referring to *Barnaby* but assured Johnson that the *Horn Book* would have "a far better chance" of influencing libraries than would any of the other publications.[8]

Harold's first adventures had done so well that by April 1956, two animated cartoon companies were proposing Harold series for short-subject release in movie theaters. Constable sought rights for the United Kingdom edition of *Harold and the Purple Crayon*. In Denmark, Skrifola wanted to publish it. And Johnson was already contemplating a third Harold book for release in the fall of 1957.[9]

Inspiration for another book came from Johnson's dog, Gonsul, the fourteen-year-old son of the dog who had inspired Barnaby's talking terrier, Gorgon. As Dave liked to point out, Gonsul "neither talks nor sings. But his pantomime is excellent." In the spring of 1956, Dave sent Ursula a dummy for *Terrible Terrifying Toby*, in which Toby the puppy encounters "terrible and terrifying" things in his backyard—a squirrel, a frog, and a sparrow. He discovers that if he growls, they leave, making him feel more "terrible and terrifying." But when he enters the house and encounters a mirror, he frightens himself.

That same spring, Johnson also sent Nordstrom a dummy for a very different book, *Time for Spring*, in which he balanced melancholy with humor. In clean, elegant prose and gray watercolors, the book tells the story of Irene, who is very ready for winter to end, and of her O'Malley-esque snowman, who is not. Irene reluctantly makes "a very little snowman" because she has "very little interest left in things that had to do with winter." He comes to life, and, though he proves a rather obnoxious playmate, Irene remains concerned that spring threatens his existence. When she tries to tell him about his impending demise, he brushes off her concern: "Spring won't come, while I'm here." The two of them go back and forth, debating the incompatibility of his presence and that of spring. When the snow melts and she sees the snowman's hat lying on the grass, Irene says, "He went away, but he left his hat," adding, "I'll save it for him for next year." Nordstrom found the tale "rather sad, as well as funny, I think. And I like it." Harper reader Bunny Aleshire also approved: "The recognition that you must lose something to gain something is not something to be expected in a children's book."[10]

This sense of loss, atypical for a Crockett Johnson story, may have many emotional roots. His niece, Bonnie Frank, who had been born in 1947 with a form of mental retardation, died in 1955. As in Irene's response to the snowman, Bonnie's siblings Harold (born 1953) and Tony (born 1948) may not have fully understood the meaning of their sister's death. Dave's father had died when he was a teenager, and his mother died a little over two years before he sent in this manuscript. His good friend Gene Wallace also had died eighteen months earlier, leaving a behind an eight-year-old daughter, who, like Irene, had dark hair. Nina is the first of more than two dozen children thanked at the beginning of Ruth's *I'll Be You and You Be Me* (1954).

The last of the "children" thanked is "Ursie," aka Ursula Nordstrom, who accepted both *Time for Spring* and *Terrible, Terrifying Toby*, paying Johnson a thousand-dollar advance for each book. With William R. Scott allowing *Who's Upside Down?* to go out of print, Johnson hoped that Harper would reissue the book, which he called "a supplementary text book in elementary cosmology," but Nordstrom declined.[11]

When he visited the Harper offices, Johnson's reserved, quiet demeanor sometimes puzzled people. His characters were adventurous and outgoing, but he seemed shy. Occasionally, however, close friends would glimpse of another side of him. On one occasion, he commented to Maurice Sendak that one of the young women working at Harper had "a fantastic ass." Though they were well out of earshot, Sendak was shocked: "I didn't even know he knew the word 'ass.' It was a glimpse into 'Wow, this is a hot patootie, this guy.'" Laughing at the memory, Sendak added, "And that was the only mad expression I ever heard coming out of Dave Johnson. And he was right: she had a great ass." Similarly, although Ruth and Dave rarely publicly displayed their affection for each other, they were very loving in private and around their closest friends. Nina Rowand Wallace remembered seeing Ruth "come up from behind and hug" Dave, "cuddl[ing] that wonderful bald head of his very affectionately." The two slept in separate beds and bedrooms not because they lacked passion for each other but because Dave was nocturnal and Ruth was not. Both were awake in the afternoons and evenings.[12]

Acutely aware that different people need different beds, Johnson pursued his plan of marketing the four-way-adjustable mattress. In late May or early June 1956, he met with Conrad Hilton to see if his chain of hotels might be interested in buying the four-way adjustable mattress. Johnson also contacted mattress manufacturers, hoping to entice them to produce his invention. In June, Johnson wrote to Nordstrom that he wanted to do a "definitive" *Barnaby* book "soon, but this week and next I have to spend tome time founding a vast industrial empire with my lawyer and a rubber tycoon and a mattress mogul. I will be around to bother you the week after that." By July, the Sealy mattress company was considering producing Johnson's invention. Johnson worked on other projects as well, illustrating William H. Whyte Jr.'s "Budgetism: Opiate of the Middle Class" for the May 1956 issue of *Fortune*, Bernadine Cook's *The Little Fish That Got Away* (1956), and Franklyn M. Branley and Eleanor K. Vaughn's *Mickey's Magnet* (1956).[13]

On weekends, Sendak continued to visit Johnson and Krauss, working on her books—in 1956, *The Birthday Party*—and relishing his time with them. Typically, Krauss was energetic, unpredictable, and tiring, while Johnson was calm, steady, and laconic. With Johnson, Sendak would sit and talk quietly. In his early fifties, Johnson had the "big burly body" of an ex-football player, his chest and arms starting to go soft. He was a large man with a gentle demeanor. Though much smaller, Krauss was the "jumping jack," the "full-color stage performance," "this explosion of energy and laughter and rage." With her lustrous hair piled on her head, a few long strands falling down the sides of her face, Krauss would throw back her head and laugh when she was in a good mood. When she was in a bad mood, "she was a banshee!" Sendak "never

Ruth Krauss. Image courtesy of the Estate of Ruth Krauss. Reprinted with the permission of the Estate of Ruth Krauss, Stewart I. Edelstein, Executor. All Rights Reserved.

understood" Krauss and Johnson's marriage: "He was as quiet as she was noisy. He was as calm as she was like a hurricane. And yet it seemed to work."[14]

It worked well for Sendak, too: The Johnson-Krauss house continued provide him with a "place of total safety" where he could work and be with people who understood him. To Sendak, "Dave was the father I always wanted. And Ruth was a bit too much like the mother I already had." Yet where Maurice's mother seemed consumed by her darker moods, Krauss "somehow . . . was stronger and fiercer and fought that depression."[15]

Despite her bubbly, outgoing nature, Ruth remained plagued by anxieties. During the 1940s, she discussed her problems with her physician; by 1956, she

Crockett Johnson, last page from and front cover for Merry Go Round (New York: Harper, 1958). Reprinted with the permission of the Estate of Ruth Krauss, Stewart I. Edelstein, Executor. All Rights Reserved.

was seeing a psychiatrist, traveling into New York City for her weekly session at least until the mid-1960s. Her therapist was Dr. Daniel E. Schneider, whom another former patient described as "like a sledgehammer." A strict Freudian, Schneider saw many creative people, including novelist Tom Wolfe. Schneider liked and respected Ruth, admiring her creativity and success as an artist. He believed that art was not the product of neurosis. Instead, liberation from neuroses left artists "free to develop . . . technical creative mastery" of their art. He considered writer's block "the neurotic fear and separation of intuition and cognition," and his counseling apparently helped Ruth overcome that hurdle, because she published prolifically during this period. Ruth found Schneider's ideas so persuasive that she referred to them in conversation. Moving her hands as she spoke, Ruth would mention his opinion and then giggle to cover her embarrassment.[16]

By October 1956, Johnson had completed his third children's book of the year; like *Time for Spring*, it charted new territory. *Merry Go Round: A Story That Doesn't End*, was precisely that. With pages to be lifted up rather than turned from right to left and illustrated only on the front side, *Merry Go Round* invites endless page turning, and Johnson proposed binding it with rings to encourage this activity. The center of every page features the boy on the merry-go-round, but the background shifts, recording the child's motion. Beneath each picture is a single line of text, minimally punctuated, with the sentence continuing on the next page. The last page ("on he rode, past the yellow sign and on") does not end with a period, leading the reader directly back to the first page (the front cover), which has the words "and round and round and round and round and round" at the bottom. This experimental work presented several design challenges. When rings proved too expensive, Harper opted for spiral binding. However, since spirals tear pages more easily, they used larger, heavier paper stock. Agreeing to a cover, that did not bear the author's name, Harper wrapped the book in a thin paper band with Johnson's name and the book's subtitle, publisher, and price.[17]

As the year came to an end, Johnson prepared to send Nordstrom the final version of yet another book, *Harold's Trip to the Sky*. Again breaking with picture book conventions, he wanted black pages. More than half the book would follow Harold through the darkness of outer space. To achieve this effect, Johnson proposed that he make his "own photographic negatives, . . . laying in the color by my own hand." Overall, this process would be cheaper for Harper than having the printer and engraver make the black pages, but it would increase Johnson's out-of-pocket costs, and he asked the publisher to reimburse him. He did not mind spending his own money, but "I find that many people nowadays like to receive such bills because they can take them off their corporate income tax, thereby cutting down on the number of atomic bombs the government can make." Harper agreed to the reimbursement.[18]

As Johnson's comment about atomic bombs reflected, the political atmosphere had shifted. By 1956–57, McCarthyism had lost some of its hold on the popular imagination, and people on the left were speaking out. The Supreme Court's decision in *Brown v. Board of Education* (1954), the Montgomery Bus Boycott (1955), and the integration of Little Rock's Central High School (1957) had begun "to reshape the national and political agenda." Registering this change in the national mood, *Harold's Trip to the Sky* contains some topical satire, marking Johnson's first venture into political commentary since *Barnaby* ended its run. After drawing himself into a desert, Harold thinks that "there isn't much else to do . . . except play in the sand." Then, however, "he remembered how the government has fun on the desert. It shoots off rockets."[19]

Though topical, the specific target of this wry observation is trickier to pin down. In the context of the 1956 presidential contest, Johnson may be mocking Eisenhower's push for guided missiles, Stevenson's call for more missile spending, or both ideas. Whatever its target, Dave's sly, politically ambiguous reference would likely escape the notice of reviewers, the following fall. Or would it?[20]

That fall, most reviewers saw in Ruth and Maurice's latest—*I Want to Paint My Bathroom Blue*—another beautiful trip into the "innermost feelings of little children," as the *New York Times*'s Lois Palmer wrote. "Maurice Sendak's pictures show the happiness and activity of the little boy in his pretend world," and children will want to "pretend along with him." The *Christian Science Monitor* thought the book "a charming bit of fantasy for imaginative small children, the kind that sets them to dreaming and satisfies something that wants expression deep down inside." Like Krauss, the little boy in the book likes open windows and believes in racial equality. Sendak drew the child's friends in a rainbow of colors (orange, blue, brown, purple, yellow, pink), standing side by side, smiling and waving. Krauss considered this depiction "a definite statement in 'race' integration," and although reviewers overlooked this theme, Krauss had at last written a antiracist children's book.[21]

After completing a "child-language brochure" for the American Friends Service Committee, Krauss moved on to another project that would reunite her with Phyllis Rowand. Dedicated to Rowand's daughter, Nina, "when she was a monkey," *Monkey Day* marks the first time Krauss recycled an earlier story. The version that had appeared in *I'll Be You and You Be Me* presents "a new holiday and a good song / if you have a monkey for a friend friend friend." A little girl explains the holiday, sings the song (a version of "Happy Birthday"), and concludes with some "special talk / for talking to monkeys": "Cheep cheep cheep." Losing the gentle whimsy of the original, *Monkey Day* is filled with unnecessary details—presents, a wedding, and several dozen little monkeys.[22]

The decision to rework an earlier tale signaled Krauss's creative restlessness. In a dozen years, she had published seventeen children's books, had several other completed manuscripts, and was working on even more. Though she had done well as a writer for children, she never let go of her ambition to write for adults, and in the fall of 1957, she took Kay Boyle's ten-week course in the history and analysis of the short story. Johnson, too, was seeking new outlets. He considered new types of children's books and pushed the boundaries of his popular Harold series. Both authors were in the midst of a period of bold experimentation.

18

NEW ADVENTURES ON PAGE AND SCREEN

And, if they weren't exactly in their right order, none of them complained.
—CROCKETT JOHNSON, *Harold at the North Pole* (1958)

As she considered pursuing new directions, Ruth Krauss still had to earn a living. To find ideas for her children's books, she continued to do what had worked in the past—visiting the Rowayton Kindergarten and the Community Cooperative Nursery School. Even though they knew she was older, children accepted her as one of them. If Krauss wondered what the children were discussing, she would ask. They were happy to answer and to let her take notes.[1]

By the first few months of 1957, Krauss had gathered enough of their stories to show Ursula Nordstrom. In April, the two women began debating which ones to include in a new book. Nordstrom liked "The Happy Egg" so much that she thought it "could make a tiny little book by itself! . . . 2 year olds would love it." However, "The Mish-Mosh Family," a story about a "whole family inside of a child," should go. They eventually settled on seventeen tales, and Maurice Sendak began creating drawings for each. Marking a change in Sendak and Krauss's collaborative style, the layout was uncharacteristically straightforward—the text on each left-hand page, the illustrations on each right-hand page. By late July, Sendak had finished his pictures, and he and Krauss had had settled on a title, *Somebody Else's Nut Tree*, after the book's final story, in which a child finds and adopts a pretty little nut tree, only to learn that it is not hers. That tale's sudden shift in perspective underscores the book's major theme—transformations.[2]

During the summer and fall of 1957, two major changes came to Ruth and Dave's social circle. First, on 21 July, Simon and Schuster editor Jack Goodman died of a cerebral hemorrhage at the age of forty-eight. Once central to the social life of Rowayton's artistic community, the Goodmans' parties came to an end. Then, Phyllis Rowand remarried. Her new husband was Sidney Landau, the cofounder of Mayles Textiles, and he legally adopted Nina Rowand

Wallace, joining his new family as a regular dinner guest at the Johnson-Krauss house.[3]

Published in the fall of 1957, Krauss and Rowand's *Monkey Day* met a mixed reception. *Library Journal* thought it "cluttered" and "in poor taste" and marked it "Not recommended." The *New York Times Book Review*'s George Woods called it "a silly, excessive story of monkey-cult devotion." Other reviewers, however, thought *Monkey Day* classic Krauss. "Again it seems that Ruth Krauss has built a simple little phrase into a series of happenings that very little children will savor with delight," wrote the *New York Herald Tribune Book Review*'s Margaret Libby.[4]

The fall of 1957 also saw the publication of *Harold's Trip to the Sky*, in which Harold rides a rocket, overshoots the moon, and meets an alien "thing." As Barbara Bader suggests, *Harold's Trip to the Sky* can be read as a dramatization of the "fears of the Fifties": "To Jung and others, the widespread sighting of UFO's at the time stemmed from fear of nuclear destruction, and the whole of *Harold's Trip to the Sky* can be seen as an expression of [these] anxieties, absorbed and transformed." Contemporary reviewers, however, noted no political subtext and praised *Harold's Trip to the Sky* as "just as funny and unexpected as ever," in the words of the *New York Times*'s Ellen Lewis Buell. *Booklist* alleged that "some of the concepts may be too advanced for the youngest of Harold's usual audience" but ultimately praised *Harold's Trip to the Sky* as "good *fun* for kindergarten-age space travelers."[5]

October 1957 also saw Harold take a journey to the big screen in David Piel's film version of *Harold and the Purple Crayon*, narrated by Norman Rose. Johnson urged Harper to be prepared to capitalize on the movie's imminent release. For the past year, he had been concerned that the publisher was not keeping the Harold books in stores—half a dozen people had told him that they could not find *Purple Crayon*—and that sales were lost as a result. The movie was due in theaters before Christmas, and he thought Harold would "get quite a bit of attention, at least enough to move a lot of books." If *Harold and the Purple Crayon* "really is out of print," he asked Harper's Mary Russell to "please rush around the office for me, screaming." Johnson offered to "subsidize a 'vanity' printing of fifty or a hundred thousand of each of [the three Harold books], to be stored in sheets ready for quick binding when a demand is indicated."[6]

Harper had no intention of letting *Harold and the Purple Crayon* go out of print. The publisher was considering launching a line of paperback children's books and executives thought the Harold series would sell particularly well and "could rival Pogo if we had him in paper." Nordstrom pursued the idea, though no paperback version of *Harold* would be produced until Scholastic's 1966 edition.[7]

When Johnson, Krauss, and assorted Harper employees went to a screening of the film in late October 1957, they loved it. By December, Piel was in negotiations with British industrialist and producer J. Arthur Rank, who expressed interest in "a series of Harold pictures, to be made with Rank money (and British government subsidy) and using less expensive British production facilities." But the plan came to naught, and Piel had difficulty finding a distributor for his *Harold*. A member of the family that made Piels Beer, thirty-one-year-old David Piel was new to filmmaking: *Harold and the Purple Crayon* was his first. He had financed the production with a lien on the film itself, and when investors foreclosed, the animated *Harold and the Purple Crayon* fell into legal limbo. As with *Barnaby* a decade earlier, Johnson's potential profits evaporated.[8]

These near misses and Johnson's involvement in other projects may have dampened his enthusiasm for a new *Barnaby* book. In June 1957, a year after promising Nordstrom that he would work on it "soon," he wrote again to say he would be in touch about it "next week." Six months later, he had "made a start on a middle-of-the-book Barnaby sample. But I keep getting interrupted by more urgent little jobs. I still want to write it." He never did.[9]

As Johnson passed on developing *Barnaby*'s commercial potential and bet on *Harold*'s, Krauss discovered that other companies were attempting to profit from *A Hole Is to Dig* without her permission. In 1956 and 1957, *Tide*, a trade magazine, sold its business services by "borrowing" phrases from the book ("arms are to hug") and creating similar ones ("a faucet is to splash"). Extolling the benefits of advertising in *Tide*, one such ad announces, "A business paper is to serve." Krauss was upset, and Harper not only asked the magazine to stop but appealed to the Joint Ethics Committee of the Art Directors Club, the Artists Guild, and the Society of Illustrators.[10]

A Hole Is to Dig also inspired many imitators—notably Joan Walsh Anglund's *A Friend Is Someone Who Likes You* (1958), Phoebe Wilson Hoss's *Noses Are for Roses* (1960), Sandol Stoddard and Jacqueline Chwast's *I Like You* (1965), and Art Parsons and Leo Martin's *A Library Is to Know* (1961). Parsons and Martin's work was a tribute—an affectionate satire for librarians—but the others merely echo the Krauss-Sendak aesthetic. Advertisers embraced the child-centric definitions as adorable and sweet, and parodists mocked them out of distrust toward what they perceived as the book's rosy view of childhood. In September 1961, *Mad* magazine's "A Hole Is What You Need This Book Like in Your Head" featured cynical definitions: "A Mother is to hide behind when Daddy gets mad at you," "Tears are to get your own way," "A brother is to blame things on." Though Nordstrom was not amused, Krauss had begun referring to the book as *A Hole in the Head* even before the *Mad* parody.[11]

A bona fide success both critically and commercially, *A Hole Is to Dig* embodied the best of the relationship between Nordstrom and Krauss. In early December 1957, Nordstrom showed her appreciation for Krauss and Sendak by presenting them with commemorative editions of *A Hole Is to Dig*, which had sold well over eighty thousand copies and was generating two-thirds of Krauss's income. Sendak was so touched by the gesture that he promised to put it "on his table right next to the Bible and Shakespeare and Sophocles." Nordstrom told Krauss, "We're very glad you stepped off the Harper elevator that day so long ago with the anthropology material. And we hope you are glad too." Krauss was: "What an absolutely wonderful surprise! I am truly touched!" Since Sendak was keeping his copy in such august company, Ruth said she would put hers on her table "right next to Jimmy Joyce and *the* play written by Picasso."[12]

In August, Johnson turned in a new picture book, receiving the contract (with its thousand-dollar advance) in late October. *The Blue Ribbon Puppies* is Johnson's most gentle book. Though it retains his characteristic ironic humor, there is no edge to it. The tone is sympathetic and the story is sweet: A little boy and a little girl decide to award a blue ribbon to the best of their seven pups but discover that each one is so adorable that they must name it the best at something.

It was the last time he did a Harper book with such complicated color separations. Problems had previously arisen with *Terrible Terrifying Toby*, prompting a June 1957 telegram from the author to Nordstrom: "Hold up printing of Toby at all costs colors wrong very many flagrant errors." When he submitted detailed color art for *The Blue Ribbon Puppies* two months later, the work somehow was lost. Johnson had to redraw the entire book and redo the color separations, a prospect he did not relish. To achieve different colors, the offset-lithography printing process used screens to filter out a percentage of each of the inks then available—probably black, red, blue, and yellow. In this process, 40 percent blue would create light blue. To create other colors, printers combined inks by printing one layer on top of another: combining 40 percent blue with 40 percent yellow would result in a shade of green. He

Crockett Johnson, page from "Harold and the Big Day," *Good Housekeeping*, December 1957. The story read left to right across two pages. Reprinted with the permission of the Estate of Ruth Krauss, Stewart I. Edelstein, Executor. All Rights Reserved.

Ruth Krauss in the living room at 74 Rowayton Avenue, 1959. Image courtesy of the Smithsonian Institution. Reproduced courtesy of the *New Haven Register*.

vowed "that my next book will be in black and white, complete in one piece, and no trouble to anybody." Though Harper's insurance reimbursed him $480 for the lost artwork, his next book, *The Frowning Prince* (1959), was indeed in black and white.[13]

Harold of course continued to draw in purple. By September 1957, Johnson had written a fourth Harold story, "Harold and the Big Day," which would appear in the Christmas issue of *Good Housekeeping*. Harper then published a longer version, *Harold at the North Pole* in 1958. Since Johnson saved no drafts of the Harold books, comparing the thirty-page "Harold and the Big Day" to the forty-six-page *Harold at the North Pole* offers a rare glimpse into the mind of Crockett Johnson at work. The primary difference between the two tales is a fuller development of the narrative style characteristic of the Harold books: free indirect discourse, a third-person narrative closely aligned with a first-person point of view. In "Big Day," "The snow stopped falling, but there were drifts everywhere. It looked like the North Pole." In the book, "The snow stopped falling but it lay in big drifts everywhere. It covered everything." Extending the scene to a second page, the narrative adds, "From the looks of things, Harold thought, he might very well be at the North Pole." "It covered everything" both better conveys a child's sense of size (the vastness of "everything") and allows Harold to consider the scene before deciding where he is. Adding "From the looks of things" and "Harold thought" reminds us that we are seeing the world as Harold does. Johnson also delivers the insights and language of a more sophisticated, wry narrator—perhaps Johnson himself. "But Harold went speedily to work rounding up the reindeer" becomes "But Harold confidently went to work lining up the reindeer." *Lining up* plays on the fact that the lines of Harold's crayon literally create this line of reindeer. Juxtaposed with Santa's "doubtful" look, *confidently* better conveys Harold's resolve and optimism. These seemingly small differences illustrate Johnson's genius at creating Harold's universe—a place where every detail of the crayon's trail is important and where the imagination has the power to change the world.

In contrast, Krauss's method of composition focused much more on the process than on the final result. Where Johnson would write out a complete story and then modify it according to the suggestions of his editors, Krauss made many drafts. Where Johnson would send either a complete book or a selection of complete stories, Krauss often sketched out her ideas in a letter, using Nordstrom's interest (or lack of it) to determine whether to proceed. On one occasion, Krauss asked Nordstrom if she would be interested in "a sort of bastard form between a record & a book." The song would be something that children recognized, but adults might be unable to "finish its middle" or "to begin it right" and indeed might "get it all mixed up, instead of just not being able to remember it." However, she wondered, "Does the child *want* the song to be mixed up, revolutionary, or want to have it straight?" The implication of her idea, she said, would "be that kids know things adults have long forgotten."

In another instance, Krauss envisioned a conversation between a little boy and his mother in which he announces what he would like to be, and she responds: When he wants to be a "wee mousie" so he can "run over the table," she would be a "mother-mousie." Krauss held onto all of her ideas, whether or not Nordstrom liked them, and sometimes reworked them.[14]

Krauss also continued to dream of writing for adults, joining a writing group that included Kay Boyle, Doris Lund, Bet Hennefrund, Pat Brooks, Cay Skelly, and sometimes others. Boyle and Krauss were the most accomplished of the group, followed by Skelly, the author, under her maiden name, Cathleen Schurr, of a popular Little Golden Book, *The Shy Little Kitten* (1946). Such a group would help Krauss in three ways. First, it would compel her to write rather than wait for inspiration, as was her inclination. Second, uncertain of her own abilities, she relied on others' judgment in determining what worked and what did not. Third, apart from a few early pulp magazine stories, she had never succeeded at writing for adults.[15]

Krauss's work for children began receiving critical praise from unlikely quarters. In 1958, W. D. Snodgrass, whose *Heart's Needle* would win the Pulitzer Prize for poetry in 1960, compared the record version of *The Carrot Seed* (which Krauss apparently adapted) to Thomas Grey's "Elegy in a Country Churchyard" as well as to the writings of Philip Larkin, Rainer Maria Rilke, Randall Jarrell, and Robert Frost. All, Snodgrass said, exemplify the poet's tact, able to shape meaning "by crucial words or phrases which are never spoken." In this essay, Krauss's children's story appears not just as an interesting anecdote but as an expression of a core belief about aesthetic quality.[16]

Although reviewers and readers liked Krauss's new books, the sales figures did not approach those generated by the phenomenal *A Hole Is to Dig*. The Harold series remained a strong seller for Harper, and with Johnson producing a new volume each year, the potential income was substantial. Nordstrom made sure to let both authors know that Harper was doing its best to keep their works on the bookstore shelves. In December 1957, the F. A. O. Schwarz toy catalog featured *Terrible Terrifying Toby*, which could lead to big sales and was, Nordstrom explained, quite "an honor." Both Johnson and Krauss were also "well represented" in Harper's catalog, and the publisher was running ads for their books in the *New Yorker* and the *New York Times*. Nevertheless, fissures would soon develop in the author-editor relationship.[17]

19

"HITTING ON ALL 24 CYLINDERS"

So, before he went to bed, he drew another picture.
—CROCKETT JOHNSON, *A Picture for Harold's Room* (1960)

Creatively, 1958 began very well for Ruth Krauss and Crockett Johnson. She was working on a book based on the artwork she had collected from children at the Rowayton public schools over the past six years. One child had drawn "Girl with the Sun on a String," a bright round yellow circle with yellow lines radiating outward; one line ran all the way down into the grip of a little girl's hand. A drawing of a white circle against a darker background bore the caption "A Moon or a Button." Instead of *A Book of First Definitions* (the subtitle of *A Hole Is to Dig*), this would be *A Book of First Picture Ideas*.

As with *A Hole Is to Dig*, Krauss repeatedly arranged and rearranged her ideas. Over three pages of notes titled "Child's Eye Visual," she created a layout of the illustration as a narrative, with each scene loosely suggesting the next. Krauss's associative logic creates a story that unfolds like a dream.[1]

Though recovering from a sprained ankle in early 1958, Johnson wrote three new stories and rewrote another. As Ursula Nordstrom told him, "You certainly are hitting on all 24 cylinders these days." Joining the roster of classic Crockett Johnson characters were Ellen, an imaginative preschooler, and a stuffed lion, her best friend and confidant. The lion is skeptical, unsentimental; Ellen is relentlessly creative, inventing adventures for herself and her lion, often a reluctant participant. Similar to Bill Watterson's Hobbes nearly thirty years later, the lion's status as stuffed animal is never in question, but his ability to think independently varies. He appears to be both animated by Ellen's imagination and able to arrive at his own conclusions, which tend to contradict hers. When she thinks he is sad and tries to sympathize with him, he tells her, "All this talk of sympathy for my feelings is silly, Ellen. I'm a stuffed animal."[2]

What Harold achieves with his purple crayon, Ellen does with words and props—she imagines for herself a role as malleable as the universe she creates.

Ruth Krauss, "Child's Eye Visual," early layout for *A Moon or a Button* (New York: Harper, 1959). Image courtesy of the Northeast Children's Literature Collection, Dodd Research Center, University of Connecticut, Storrs. Reprinted with the permission of the Estate of Ruth Krauss, Stewart I. Edelstein, Executor. All Rights Reserved.

Like Barnaby's friend, Jane, Ellen does not limit herself to "girlish" activities but moves easily between feminine and masculine roles. When the story "Fairy Tale" begins, Ellen is the "fairy godmother"; a few paragraphs later, she has become "the invincible knight"; near the end, she turns into "the lovely princess"; and she ends up as Ellen. Johnson also playfully shifts the narrative voice back and forth between Ellen's perspective and the view of a slightly bemused observer—sometimes in the same sentence. "Fairy Tale" begins, "Once, twice, and thrice the beautiful fairy waved her wand and, before she spoke, she took another bite of muffin covered with raspberry jam." Later, "the knight" is "eating jam and muffin as she surveyed the besieging army across the wide moat." Though the shifts from Ellen to the mildly ironic narrator do invite a smile at her games, *Ellen's Lion* treats her wishes with sympathy. Unlike Russell Hoban's *Bedtime for Frances* (1960), in which Father uses the threat of "a spanking" to silence Frances's imagination, *Ellen's Lion* celebrates a little girl's inventive mind.

In February, Johnson sent the first four Ellen stories to Nordstrom "in the hope that you will have time in the next week or two to look at it and let me know if it seems to you to be anything for children (or anything for anybody)." If she liked these stories, he would write more. Both Nordstrom and Susan Carr loved them: Carr thought "these Ellen and lion stories are absolutely enchanting, and will make a marvelous book. I am most eager to see the rest of the ms, and have no criticism at this point." During March, he wrote another seven stories.[3]

Johnson was also rewriting *The Frowning Prince*, redoing the color separations for *The Blue Ribbon Puppies*, and sketching plans for *Harold's Circus*, the fifth purple crayon adventure. On 7 April, he wrote, "I haven't had anything to do for a month except make up things in my head," suggesting that creating stories came easily to him. He had spent that time "sketch[ing] out a another 'Harold' book that I think will work out pretty well. It can be called 'Harold's Circus' maybe." In a sentence, he then describes the entire plot of what would become *Harold's Circus*. Would Harper "want another 'Harold' book for 1959?" Dave asked. Nordstrom replied that *Harold's Circus* could "be one of the best" and suggested making it a spring 1959 book: "If we do *The Frowning Prince* in the same publishing season it can't make too much of a problem I am *sure* because they are both so different."[4]

The Frowning Prince is different. Readers accustomed to smiling (or at least benign) expressions on the faces of Crockett Johnson's characters may be surprised by the prince's determined frown. When a king begins reading a story ard, bowing low again. "For one, your father has just said so, and he is the king."

"Tell us one of the other reasons," said the prince.

The grand wizard took off his glasses and polished them carefully. When he spoke again it was to the king.

"Tell me, your majesty, just how did all this arise?"

"Yesterday I borrowed a book from you," said the king. "A fairy tale."

"Yes, I remember it was the last book-of-the-moon selection. One arrives every perigee," said the grand

Crockett Johnson, page from *The Frowning Prince* (New York: Harper, 1959). Reprinted with the permission of the Estate of Ruth Krauss, Stewart I. Edelstein, Executor. All Rights Reserved.

about a princess with "an irresistible smile," his son proclaims, "Nobody could make me smile." Determined to prove his son wrong, the king calls in jesters, jugglers, and even the grand wizard. The queen, however, understands that this battle of wills merely encourages the prince: She tells the king, "Try not to let it bother you" and tells the prince, "It will go away," patting his head. Johnson's story playfully pokes fun at its fairy tale status: When the wizard suggests summoning the smiling princess from the book, the king tells him not to bother because the "book said the princess lived once upon a time." The wizard reminds him, "This is once upon a time." When the king points out that "the princess also lived in a faraway land," the wizard reasons, "This kingdom of yours is a faraway land, your majesty. And if two lands are both far away, they must be close to each other." Subtly advancing a theme of peace, the king must "call off the wars" with the neighboring kingdom to invite the other king and queen and their daughter for a weekend visit. Sure enough, the prince does at last smile, though the tale never indicates whether the cause is the princess's smile or the court's concession that the prince's frown is "immovable." The royal couples find that they have "much in common and enjoyed each other's company immensely," and, with the two kingdoms at peace, the "happy subjects" go back and forth between countries as well.

Harper bought those books, but Johnson also wrote one that either he never submitted to Nordstrom or Harper turned down. *Will Spring Be Early? Or Will Spring Be Late?* won a contract from Thomas Y. Crowell, publishers of the Crockett Johnson–illustrated *Mickey's Magnet*. On 2 February, the conscientious Groundhog prepares to make his prediction and must verify that spring will be early. As he listens and smells for the sun, a passing Artificial Flower Co. truck interferes with his senses. When he finds an artificial flower that has fallen from the truck, he thinks it real and shouts, "*Spring!* It's here *now!*" He rushes off to tell the Badger, Dormouse, Rabbit, Skunk, Chipmunk, Squirrel, Raccoon, Bear, and Pig. Echoing Krauss's *The Happy Day*, the animals dance in a circle around the flower. The Pig does not join in but instead chomps the flower and then announces, "The leaves are paper. The stem is wire. The petals are plastic. And the lot of you will freeze out here." He makes his own prediction: "It's going to snow." In a reversal of *The Happy Day*, this flower growing in the snow is not a sign of spring. The snowstorm begins, the "Groundhog [begins] to creep quietly away," and the disappointed animals seek to assign fault:

"We were all so happy," the Dormouse said, "until the Pig came and chewed the flower."

"Precisely!" shouted the Bear. "And now we're cold and miserable and ridiculous! It's perfectly clear who's to blame!"

The book ends with the narrator's summation: "They blamed the Pig, of course." The Groundhog continues to make his predictions each February, and Johnson's comic twist evokes a laugh of recognition at the human tendency to blame the messenger.

While continuing to write, Johnson and Krauss also oversaw foreign editions of their earlier books and promoted their work at home. When Constable and Company printed *Harold and the Purple Crayon* in the United Kingdom, the publisher made some changes in color, which in turn changed the line of the drawing. Now that Constable was planning to publish *A Hole Is to Dig*, Krauss was wary. Maurice would check on the colors himself when in England in late August 1958. If the publisher felt that he and Krauss were "being overly precious about this book," she wrote, "well, we are. We love the book. We both feel that its physical appearance—which was experimental in form . . . —is important to its appeal as a book." She, Sendak, Nordstrom, Johnson, and Harper's production department had "worked hard on the physical make up of the book," and they wanted "the English edition to be a lasting one—if it ever comes about." Either Krauss and Sendak's demands deterred Constable, or the publisher was not able to meet them. *A Hole Is to Dig* was not published in the United Kingdom until Hamish Hamilton's 1963 edition.[5]

In the United States, Krauss and Johnson made appearances to promote their work. They celebrated National Library Week at the Rowayton Library on 18 March 1958, joining other local writers such as *New Yorker* cartoonist Carl Rose, magazine writer John Sharnick, and journalist Leonard Gross, whose *God and Freud* had just been published. Many of the authors on hand were Johnson-Krauss friends: Fred Schwed, Phyllis Rowand, Aggie Goodman, and Jim Flora, who had moved to Rowayton in 1952 with his wife, Jane, and their children. When rock-and-roll records' preference for photographic jackets pushed his bright, angular jacket art out of favor, Flora began creating colorfully offbeat children's books, among them *The Fabulous Fireworks Family* (1955) and *The Day the Cow Sneezed* (1957). He and Johnson shared a background in typography and magazine design plus interests in playing with language, boats, and humor.[6]

Johnson's subversive wit emerged in his response to critics who complained that Harold's decoration of blank white pages inspired young readers to draw in books. A librarian from Ontario's Niagara Falls Public Library wrote of "the havoc" Johnson had caused, submitting as evidence the final two pages from *Harold's Fairy Tale*, generously embellished by a young reader's crayon. She added, "We have been accused of becoming a passive audience, it must give you pleasure to have written books which inspire action." Johnson was indeed pleased to inspire creativity, but he had heard this particular complaint one too many times and drafted a long, satirical reply. Although he was very aware of "the scourge of crayon vandalism," she had "been taken in by the enemy":

> Your letter reveals that you have no grasp of the problem that faces us and that you know very little about our opponents. Their organization, on the surface, is so apparently loose-knit and casual that I daresay you have not recognized it as an organization at all. Its members are disarmingly young, which tends to lead a superficial observer to laugh at the assertion that it systematically has been destroying the world's literature for centuries. . . . The average crayon vandal seems childlike and innocent, and actually he is. But there are millions like him, each with his small urge for destruction developed and channeled by the efficient hard core of the organization, by its precocious and dedicated leaders.

In fact, the Harold books were part of Johnson's plan to stop crayon vandalism: "A 'Harold' book invites an average vandal to indulge himself vicariously, to sublimate his urge. Often the effect is so long-lasting that the next two or three books that fall into his hands are spared. When any such lapse occurs the organization [decides that it] can no longer depend on member and he, finding himself with few assignments, usually begins to lose interest, and often he drops out. The object of course is to decimate the enemy's ranks, ultimately to make the dread organization of crayon vandals a thing of the past." He concluded, "But it is much too soon to talk of total victory. . . . It will be a matter of years, probably, before world statistics on crayon marks per page, for the first time in history, show a noticeable downward trend. But the day will come!" Having vented his feelings, Johnson sent the letter to Nordstrom but not to the complaining librarian.[7]

The intensity of Johnson's response is noteworthy because he tended to be modest about his work. He frequently worried, for example, that his characters all looked the same, and his concerns were not unfounded: The boy from *The Carrot Seed* could be a brother of Barnaby or Harold. However, what Johnson saw as an aesthetic weakness is actually a strength. His clean, precise style depicts only the details the story requires, omitting all else. In the words of R. O. Blechman, "Simplicity shows respect for the viewer. You don't give more than what the mind needs, nor less than what the eye deserves." Johnson's effective, efficient mode of storytelling looks simple but is in fact the result of rigorous perfectionism. As Johnson once said, "Never overlook the art of the seemingly simple."[8]

But Johnson's art was often overlooked. Though the Harold series earned favorable reviews and sold well, Johnson's other children's books received little critical attention. One reason is that until recently, the Caldecott Committee has ignored cartoonists. In the 1950s, the award went to such beautiful watercolors as Ludwig Bemelmans's *Madeline's Rescue* (1954), Marcia Brown's *Cinderella* (1955), and Robert McCloskey's *Time of Wonder* (1958). Sendak's magnificent india ink illustrations for *Where the Wild Things Are* would win in 1964. Dr. Seuss got Caldecott Honors in 1948, 1950, and 1951 but never received the top prize. Not until 1970, when William Steig won for *Sylvester and the Magic Pebble*, did a cartoon artist win the Caldecott Medal. The following year, Sendak's *In the Night Kitchen* (1970), inspired by Winsor McCay's turn-of-the-century Sunday strip *Little Nemo in Slumberland*, won a Caldecott Honor, and the medal subsequently has gone to several artists who either use a comic style or deploy the narrative techniques of comics. Though the Caldecott eluded him, Crockett Johnson received some recognition in 1958 when the American Institute of Graphic Arts awarded him a Certificate of Excellence at its Children's Book Show. He designed the poster for the *New York Herald Tribune*'s spring 1958 Children's Book Festival, depicting Harold standing atop a stack of purple-crayon-created books and reaching up over his head to draw a moon.

Sendak remained a regular visitor to the Krauss-Johnson home. He so loved his weekends there that he considered his time in Rowayton his "precious life." That said, working with Krauss could be trying. He would paste an illustration in one place, and she would rip it off the page and place it in another. On many occasions, their fights brought him near tears. Johnson would step in to referee, quietly making a suggestion about the composition of the page over which Krauss and Sendak had been arguing. Sendak believes that "part of her fury was educating me, the dumb Brooklyn kid, into a more interesting human being. She was determined that I have more insight, that

I think higher." In contrast, Johnson was a welcoming, gentle presence who "looked just like everything he drew. The face was Barnaby. And yet it was a beautiful face. . . . He was not a beautiful man, but it was a beautiful face." The two men sat by the fireplace and talked about books, with Johnson offering reading suggestions. Since Sendak had been reading Tolstoy, Johnson suggested that he try Dostoevsky and Chekhov. There was no test; Johnson never checked to see that Sendak had read the recommended books. Rather, he simply wanted to give his friend an opportunity to expand his intellectual horizons.[9]

Arriving one Friday, Sendak headed upstairs to begin unpacking. Happy to be in his room, with windows that looked out onto the water, he was shocked to discover that he had not packed his work for Krauss's book. "It was one of those Freudian moments where clearly I just wanted to be with them," he recalled. Embarrassed and nervous, he went downstairs and to explain that he did not have his work. Krauss was furious. "What the hell are you here for?," she shouted. "What do you think this is, a hotel, for Chrissake?" Johnson swiftly intervened, saying, "Maury can come when he likes. And I think I'm going to take him for a sailboat ride." He understood Sendak and was happy to accept him as their guest and friend. Krauss also understood but was not going to let Sendak know that. As he and Johnson walked out of the house and down to the dock, Sendak was so grateful that he didn't mention his fear of water. He thought, "If I drown, at least I'm drowning with Crockett Johnson." Sendak was safe with Johnson, but his "precious life" in Rowayton was ending.[10]

Krauss loved mentoring young people, helping them get started in their careers. By the latter half of the 1950s, however, Sendak was doing well professionally and was much in demand as an illustrator. Between 1953 and 1958, he illustrated between three and six books a year and published two books of his own. Krauss was happy for him but felt that he no longer needed her help.[11]

She began cultivating a professional relationship with another young gay artist she admired, Remy Charlip. Krauss loved his illustrations for *David's Little Indian* (1956), a Margaret Wise Brown book, and wrote him a fan letter suggesting that he contact her. Charlip knew *A Hole Is to Dig* and especially liked *I'll Be You and You Be Me*. He telephoned Krauss, and she invited him to visit. When he arrived, she explained the concept for her *Book of First Picture Ideas*. She had by then abandoned her attempt at a linear narrative, instead structuring it as a series of scenes, the same format *A Hole Is to Dig* followed. Charlip liked her idea and set to work creating full-color illustrations.[12]

Enthusiastic about his pictures, Krauss brought Charlip to see Nordstrom and Carr at Harper. Charlip put his colorful paintings on Nordstrom's desk. Nordstrom was irritated by Krauss's insistence on working with another young, inexperienced artist, and the editor's first response was "No color! Anyway, it's black-and-white that separates the men from the boys." Losing her temper, Krauss leaned over Nordstrom's desk, gathered Charlip's artwork in her arms, and flung it into the trash. Crying, Krauss then ran out of the office toward the ladies' room. Nordstrom ran after her. In the end, Nordstrom agreed to have Charlip as illustrator, though he would have to work in black and white. But she was particularly irritated by Charlip's insistence that the book be in *A Hole Is to Dig* size: "It will look as though you are imitating Krauss and Sendak, and enough other publishers do that these days without Harper getting into the game." Nordstrom did not want *A Moon or a Button* to detract from *Philosophy Book*, the "companion book" to *A Hole Is to Dig* on which Krauss and Sendak were working. When Krauss had suggested that project four years earlier under the title *New Words for Old*, Nordstrom had been lukewarm, but she had now agreed to publish it, and it was slated for Harper's fall 1959 list.[13]

Delays on *Harold at the North Pole* almost made it miss Harper's fall 1958 list, but it came out in time for the holiday season. Reviews were again laudatory, with *Kirkus* calling it "a whimsical holiday treat" and the *Oakland Tribune* describing it as "just as funny" as earlier *Harold* books. Only the *New York Times Book Review* was critical, having "expect[ed] more ingenious of Harold." The positive reviews were welcome news to Johnson. His attempts to market the four-way adjustable mattress had failed, but his career as a children's author was going well.[14]

Harold at the North Pole did not prove as popular as the other books in the series and ultimately went out of print. Figuring out how to sell Crockett Johnson's books' sly humor was sometimes challenging. For all his concerns about how well Harper was marketing his work, Johnson was not always sure which age group would want to buy his stories. After Johnson finished the manuscript of *Ellen and the Lion*, Carr and Nordstrom asked for a better title. He offered *Talks with a Stuffed Lion* because it "is as direct and descriptive a title as I will come up with and, . . . I kind of like it." Although he recognized that such a title "may not sell," "that is not important." At least a few buyers, he thought, "will make a fond connection with 'Talks with the Reverend Davison' and the old inspirational and sex misinformation books of fifty years ago, which shall sufficiently delight us all." Carr found this title "direct" but "also flat" and asked him to do better. When he came up with only *Ellen and the Lion* and *Ellen's Lion*, Johnson proposed choosing the less ordinary of the two: "If there aren't quite as many books called *'s Lion* as there are *and the Lion* how about calling the fall book *Ellen's Lion* instead of *Ellen and the Lion*?" Though it is impossible to know whether the title *Talks with a Stuffed Lion* would have helped, sales of *Ellen's Lion* did not meet Harper's expectations.[15]

Krauss was pleased to find resonances between her work in children's books and "serious" art. Coming across James Thrall Soby's *Arp* (1958), she was struck by the similarities between Jean Arp's art—especially his *Moustache Hat* (ca. 1918), a visual combination of the two title items—and the art for *A Moon or a Button*. Her awareness of the continuities between the avant-garde and her own work not only speaks to her ambition to write for adults but also stems from her frustration with critical condescension toward children's literature.[16]

The persistence of this attitude in the Authors Guild annoyed the members of its Children's Division and had been irritating Krauss since she had joined the group in the 1940s. In 1948, recalling a guild discussion on this subject that nearly became a fight, Krauss wrote, "The whole field of books for children bears somewhat of the same status accorded children themselves in our culture. Even though they are felt to be greatly desirable, they are still look[ed] down upon." Children's writers were paid less, as were the staffs of each publisher's juvenile division. A possible reason, Krauss thought, was that "except for a very few men, the publishers [of children's books] are women, and this is also true in greatest measure the writers."[17]

A decade later, some of the guild's left-leaning children's writers began to discuss the less remunerative book contracts offered those who wrote for a young audience. In 1959, they formed an informal caucus called the Loose Enders. According to Julia Mickenberg, the group "began to meet periodically for dinner, whenever they felt at 'loose ends,' and collectively they became an important force in the field." Regular members included Krauss and Johnson's old friends Herman and Nina Schneider and Mary Elting Folsom and Franklin "Dank" Folsom. Other core members included William R. Scott editor May Garelick and Scholastic's Lilian Moore, Beatrice Schenk de Regniers, and Ann McGovern. These editors also wrote for children: de Regniers's *The Giant Story* (1953) and *What Can You Do with a Shoe?* (1955) featured illustrations by Maurice Sendak. Krauss attended the Loose Enders, but as group member Leone Adelson recalled, "not regularly, because Ruth never did anything regularly." Johnson attended only rarely.[18]

Though the members' politics varied, all leaned left. As Mary Elting Folsom explained, that some were "more radical than others" was not an issue: "We just took it for granted that each of us shared with the others what I can only call a sort of basic liberal code." Mickenberg notes that some Loose Enders turned to children's books because McCarthyist purges had forced them out of teaching or other jobs. Others, however, turned to the field "not because other avenues had closed to them but simply because they discovered they liked to write for children." But all Loose Enders "were opposed to the war in Korea and, later, the war in Vietnam. All were deeply concerned about the effects of racism upon children."[19]

The Schneiders were perhaps the most financially successful of the Loose Enders, thanks to the National Defense Education Act, which created a market for their science books. Underwritten by that money, parties at their 21 West Eleventh Street brownstone in New York attracted an elite crew of artists and intellectuals, including Krauss and Johnson; Jules Feiffer; poets Stanley Moss and Stanley Kunitz; novelist Philip Roth; abstract painters Giorgio Cavallon, Linda Lindeberg (Cavallon's wife), and Mark Rothko; illustrator Mary Alice "Mell" Beistle (Rothko's wife); and electronic music pioneer Vladimir Ussachevsky and his wife, Betty Kray, director of the Academy of Poets. Mingling with other culturally important people and friendship with Nina Schneider, who also wanted to write for adults, nurtured Krauss's dream of writing for older readers.[20]

In January 1959, *A Moon or a Button* was going to press, but Krauss was making no progress on *Philosophy Book*. "These damn books of this sort of feeling or essence-of-something-or-other are truly difficult," she wrote to Nordstrom. A book of this type "just has to develop by itself." More important, Krauss's mind was no longer focused on this project. She wanted to be a poet.[21]

20

POET IN THE NEWS, CARTOONIST ON TV

And me I am writing a poem
for you
look! No hands—
—RUTH KRAUSS, "Drunk Boat," *There's a Little Ambiguity over There*
among the Bluebells (1968)

In that same January 1959 letter, Ruth Krauss announced, "I have become a
Poetry Nut. I'm not kidding. It has become the major interest of my life—at
this point." She was reading and writing poetry for an adult audience and
wondered whether Nordstrom would be interested in a book of children's
verse. It would "have every kind of poem in it from strict ballad form to dramatic poems, looser narrative forms, little couplets just coupled (honeymoon-
ers), rhyme, unrhyme, assonance, alliteration, strict meters of every kind and
no meters of every kind too." She knew that it would "never sell like a Hole in
the Head, but it will probably amble along and gather its own moss."[1]

To pursue her new interest, Krauss began taking Kenneth Koch's poetry
courses at Columbia University in 1959. Though he joined the faculty only
that year, Koch was an up-and-coming poet of the literary avant-garde, a
founder (with John Ashbery and Frank O'Hara) of what would be known as
the New York School of poetry. Some of his students (and Krauss's classmates)
in the early 1960s included Ron Padgett, David Shapiro, Gerard Malanga, and
Daphne Merkin. As a teacher, Koch promoted the aesthetic sensibilities he
would later summarize in "The Art of Poetry" (1975): "Remember your obligation is to write, / And, in writing, to be serious without being solemn, fresh
without being cold, . . . Let your language be delectable always, and fresh and
true." While "poetry need not be an exclusive occupation," Koch wrote, "You
should read / A great deal, and be thinking of poetry all the time. / Total ab-
sorption in poetry is one of the finest things in existence." Krauss considered
dropping out of the children's book field so that she could immerse herself in
poetry.[2]

Krauss, who turned fifty-eight in 1959, was the oldest student in Koch's class but also one of the most active participants, poet and filmmaker Gerard Malanga remembered. She "spoke up" in class, unafraid to "put [her] two cents in." She was "really the best one in the class." Although Koch and other teachers knew of Krauss's successes in children's books, most students did not; they were impressed by her poetry.[3]

Crockett Johnson remained immersed in an impressive array of projects. Though earlier attempts to adapt *Barnaby* for a weekly television show never got off the ground, in March 1959 Johnson found that it was "so live a TV property that I am almost constantly involved with some packaging outfit, network, or sponsor claiming to be on the verge of bringing it to the idiot's lantern in a big way." He suggested that Harper add a reference to *Barnaby* on the dust jacket of the forthcoming *Ellen's Lion*, since a TV *Barnaby* "just might possibly happen about the time the book comes out." The jacket was already in production, but *Barnaby* kept making progress toward the small screen, and Johnson worked on a new, more philosophical book for children.[4]

In October 1958, Nordstrom had asked if Johnson would be interested in writing a Harold story for the I Can Read series, Harper's response to the *Why Johnny Can't Read* crisis. Nordstrom had been planning this series for years, but Random House beat Harper into the field of reading instruction with Dr. Seuss's *The Cat in the Hat* (1957), published four months before Harper's first I Can Read book, Else Holmelund Minarik and Maurice Sendak's *Little Bear* (1957). At the time that Nordstrom suggested that Johnson write an I Can Read book, Harper had just published Syd Hoff's *Danny and the Dinosaur* and was recruiting other authors: Both Esther Averill's *The Fire Cat* and Gene Zion and Margaret Bloy Graham's *Harry and the Lady Next Door* would be published in 1960.[5]

Johnson said he would be interested. Working to keep his vocabulary at a slightly lower reading level than he had for his other Harold tales, he began work on a Harold I Can Read book. Inspired by the legend of the Fisher King, however, Johnson found himself writing not about Harold but about loss and imagination in what would be his most beautiful, poetic, and abstract story yet, *Magic Beach*, which he sent to Nordstrom in early April 1959.

In the story, two children, Ann and Ben, walk along a beach. Ann says, "I wouldn't mind if we were in a story" because "interesting things happen." Ben replies, "Stories are just words. And words are just letters. And letters are just different kinds of marks." (As Maurice Sendak later observed, these are two "Beckett-like kids.") When Ann is hungry, Ben spells *JAM* in the sand. A wave washes over the letters, receding to reveal "a silver dish" full of jam. They have a snack. Ben observes that "things like this don't happen . . . except in stories." Ann agrees: "In stories about magic kingdoms, usually." After Ben draws the word *KING* and a wave washes over it, the king appears, sitting on a rock, fishing. The two children explain to the king how the beach works, and they summon a horse so he can ride to his castle. Then he gives them a seashell and orders them to "leave the kingdom." With the tide coming in, Ben and Ann rush back up the steep sandbank to safety. Watching the kingdom disappear beneath the ocean, they wonder whether there was time for "a happy ending" or if the "tide came in too soon." Ann concludes, "The story didn't have any ending at all! . . . When we left, it just stopped!" She then revises her claim: "The king is still there, in the story. . . . Hoping to get to his throne." Ben says nothing but puts his ear to the shell, listening to the sea.

When he sent the manuscript of *Magic Beach* to Nordstrom, Johnson acknowledged the Fisher King influence, adding, "I am happy to say that I have avoided adding to the confusion by making sociological analogies as [T. S.] Eliot did." He continued,

> I believe I have restored to the legend some of its pre-Christian purity by making the grail a mollusk shell. You will notice I have used no part of Mallory's or de Troyes' cloak and dagger crap. Perceval (or Parsifal) becomes in this version a couple of typical American kids and the wasteland is nothing but an ordinary old sandbar. I am just telling you all this in case you happen to publish the book and somebody writes in, say a librarian, asking what it is supposed to be about. It is a variation on a poetic theme, a lesson in physical geography, a Safety council message, and a spelling bee, all rolled into one.

Though he added an "'I Can Spell' gimmick" to the tale by having the children spell out words on the beach, Johnson noted that unless the series had "made considerable headway in stamping out illiteracy in the age group, this is not an 'I Can Read' book." While confident of the quality of his story, he worried about the "limitations" of his artistic style and whether the spelling device might remind people too much of *Harold's Fairy Tale* (1956), where he had "touched on the wasteland and a fisher king (albeit sans flyrod)."[6]

In her reader's report, Susan Carr thought that *Magic Beach* "misses all around. It is not funny, it is not serious, and it is not a lovely combination of the two. . . . I truly do not see any way to rewrite this story to make it successful." This "is no book with which to follow up *Ellen's Lion*. It is almost impossible to believe they are written by the same man." Nordstrom called Johnson later in April to break the news to him more gently. He conceded, "I know it is the kind of thing that has to hit somebody just right or it must go as a miss entirely." He asked her to send *Magic Beach* back, and she did.[7]

In July 1959, Johnson wrote the I Can Read book about Harold, *A Picture for Harold's Room*. As was typical, he was not sure whether the book worked, but Nordstrom and her editors thought it did. Ann Jorgensen wrote, "This would be an excellent Harold book. I like it even more than some of the already published ones." The editors made a few suggestions about the ending. Through a trick of perspective, Harold finds himself "half the size of a daisy" and "smaller than a bird," and Johnson originally had him walk home across the mountains and sea. Jorgensen wondered, "Is it enough to simply have Harold draw himself in his room?" If he did, then children would worry less about Harold's ability to return. Johnson agreed, and instead of walking, Harold says, "This is only a picture!" He then crosses out the picture and draws the door to his room and the mirror hanging on its back. After drawing himself in the mirror, he says, "Yes. . . . I am my usual size." In addition to more dynamic storytelling (moving forward is more compelling than backtracking), the new version grants Harold's imagination the power to change his world.[8]

A Picture for Harold's Room explores the boundary between art and life but does so without *Magic Beach*'s sadness and sense of loss. *Picture*'s title page alludes to René Magritte's *Human Condition 1* (1933), in which an easel depicts precisely what the viewer would see were the canvas not obscuring the view. Like Magritte's art, *A Picture for Harold's Room* challenges its audience to reconsider the relationship between experience and representations of experience. When Harold draws a picture on his wall and literally steps "up into the picture to draw the moon," Johnson blurs the border that separates real from imaginary worlds, an idea he again invokes when Harold crosses out his picture and steps onto a blank page to begin drawing himself home. Though the framed picture Harold draws on the final page reasserts that border, it does so only within the broad canvas of his imagination. Since Harold never steps out of the drawing and goes back to a bedroom that is the exclusive creation of his crayon, Johnson leaves these boundaries ambiguous. This open-endedness is part of what makes the Harold books so powerful: After the final page, the unsolved mysteries of Harold's universe linger.

Though he and his most famous character are artists, Johnson did not use that word to describe himself. Instead, he said, "I make diagrams." This

Crockett Johnson in the living room at 74 Rowayton Avenue, 1959. Image courtesy of the Smithsonian Institution. Reproduced courtesy of the *New Haven Register*.

comment on his minimalist style reflects his doubts about his abilities as well as his ambivalence toward the idea of becoming an *Artist*. Though Johnson and Krauss had the wall space for paintings, they hung only one, an ersatz Mondrian, positioning it above the telephone to serve as a message board. As Gene Searchinger said, "It was kind of a mock painting to show what he thought. And he expressed contempt . . . for paintings on walls—you know, you didn't do that."[9]

After Johnson reviewed the text with Nordstrom to check that the vocabulary was not too advanced, Harper put *A Picture for Harold's Room* into production while Dave and Ruth put their aging dog in a kennel and took a late August vacation to New England. They drove more than three hundred miles north, spending the night atop New Hampshire's Mount Washington, before heading to coast and taking a boat ten miles out to Monhegan Island. There, they relaxed, wrote letters, and swam together, enjoying the break from their daily routine. They had become "two of the most successful authors of

Crockett Johnson and Ruth Krauss in front of 74 Rowayton Avenue, 1959. Image courtesy of the Smithsonian Institution. Reproduced courtesy of the *New Haven Register*.

children's books in America," in the words of the *New Haven Register*, which ran a profile of the couple in July. Krauss had published twenty-one children's books in fifteen years, while Johnson had authored a dozen children's books in seven years. They were "not really competitors," however; as Krauss explained, "I use the children's material and return it to them in a way they will appreciate. I call it writing from the inside out. I guess you could say I've learned to speak children's language." In contrast, Johnson described himself as working "on the principle that small children and adults are amused by the same things." He elaborated, "Teen-agers are different, but as you get older you sort of revert to your childhood." Krauss pointed out that her husband was "lucky he can do everything himself. He writes and draws pictures, and even lays out the pages. He can work mostly from home and hardly has to consult anyone. But I have to work with so many different people and I have to take so many trips to New York." Poetry, however, was a solo pursuit, enabling Krauss to avoid the trials of collaboration.[10]

Back in Rowayton, Krauss resumed work on *Philosophy Book*, which she had begun to call *The Book from Outer Space* and which would be published in 1960 as *Open House for Butterflies*. Sendak had drawn some illustrations, and Krauss invited him up to the house to do some more work—a few tiny figures for the corners and some double spreads to give it "more 'fullness' in look." After spending a day in Connecticut, Sendak returned to New York unenthusiastic about the project. "I felt like this was *A Hole Is to Dig II*," he later said, "a non-spontaneous version" of the earlier book. As a result, his drawings of little people "had hardened. They had none of the evanescence and silliness and clumsiness of the drawings in *A Hole Is to Dig*." Sendak's feelings may have resulted in part from his perfectionism as well as from the fact that Krauss had turned her attentions more toward her poetry. As she wrote when the book came out, "I guess I like *Open House for Butterflies*. I'm not sure of course. Now that I've turned poet, I'm not sure of *anything*."[11]

Krauss's focus on poetry and Sendak's independent success ended their close relationship. "I'd been launched, and once I'd been launched, not only was our collaboration ceased but even the friendship did," he says. Sendak and Johnson would send each other signed copies of their latest books, but he felt that "that wonderful nest which lasted almost ten years was just gone. There was no discussion." Sendak thought that Ruth and Dave had grown to dislike him, but he was wrong. They saved every card or letter he sent, newspaper articles on him or his work, and copies of essays he wrote. Though they might never have told him so, they both cared about him and were proud of him.[12]

Krauss began to identify herself primarily as a poet, not a writer of children's books. She often signed her letters to Nordstrom with fanciful pseudonyms—"Ruthie Kraussie," "Ruthless K.," "La Krauss," "Ruth the 'Mad,'" "Kruth the Sauss," and "your dear friend, Ruthie Kruthie the last of the Lausses." In August 1959, she added "Onward Folly," describing it as her "poetry name" and using that alias regularly over the next few years. She was fashioning a new identify for herself—Ruth Krauss, poet.[13]

If the humor in *A Hole Is to Dig* or *Open House for Butterflies* offered a laugh of recognition at the perspective (and perceptiveness) of children, some humor in Krauss's poems addressed serious subjects. As David Lehman says of Frank O'Hara, "The prejudice against humor and lightheartedness in poetry has caused some readers to overlook ... the incisive way his work captures a world, a time, and a place" as well as the poems' "news and cultural commentary." This claim captures the sensibility of Krauss's "Poet in the News," a brief prose poem composed in 1959:

A crowd of twenty-three thousand coy mistresses is expected to turn out this morning for the forty-four day ruby-finding meet by the Indian Ganges' side. Eighth race on the card is scheduled for quaint honor to succumb to the tide at 4:35 P.M. and will be telecast. Thus while her willing soul transpires she who wins shall take her due except she come up with the same bruised thigh that put her out of action last week.

Couching commentary in comedy, Krauss combines the diction of the evening news with that of Andrew Marvell's "To His Coy Mistress." Transforming the carpe diem poem into the latest news, she underscores the absurdity of both genres. She mocks the news's insistence on quantifying everything by parodying its objective-sounding numbers. She highlights the ridiculousness of figuring love-making as a race against time. Alluding to Marvell's violent imagery in her line "the same bruised thigh," Krauss also pokes fun at the blunt, unromantic entreaties—"scheduled for her quaint honor to succumb at 4:35 P.M." makes sex sound more like keeping an appointment than an expression of passion.[14]

"Poet in the News" was the first of Krauss's news poems, all inspired by Koch's and O'Hara's "headline" method. Both men liked to sit down with the day's *New York Times* and create poems from the words they found there. Most of Krauss's headline poems are purely absurdist. One of her many prose poems called "News" reads, "'This measure,' the Attorney-General stated, 'This legislation—which I endorse—requires some thirty thousand skylarks to register for the first time with my office.' And he left the room." One of many poems titled "Weather" reports, "Drizzle tonight off the east coast of my head." These poems lack any definite political goal, focusing instead on startling the reader with their freshness. As Lehman says of Koch, Krauss writes "as if it were the first obligation of the poet to provide a continual sense of surprise."[15]

Krauss's "If Only," one version of which is dedicated to Koch and George Annand, developed from an assignment Koch gave his students. He brought in André Breton's poem "The Egret," which begins, "If only the sun were shining tonight / If only in the depths of the Opera two breasts dazzling clear / Would ornament the word love with the most marvelous living letter" and asks such questions as "Why doesn't it hail in the jewelry shops?" Koch used Breton's poem "as a model for an 'If only' poem" because "Breton's poem is full of wishes for the impossible." Krauss clearly enjoyed the exercise, writing her first iteration of "If Only" in 1959 and revising and publishing different versions of it for the next decade.[16]

"Poet in the News" first appeared, along with three of Krauss's other prose poems, in the December 1959 *Bards' Bugle*, a mimeographed publication that was, as its masthead noted, "dedicated to the great unpublished. So far, that is." In her first published poems as an "adult" poet, Krauss combines the spontaneous verve of a child's words with some of the diction of "grown-up" writing. One of the poems reads, in part, "Words cannot express me. But as someone said, they really don't have to. They are more like hands across the sea or toes under the table. What fun!" She saw herself as "becoming an avante-garde poetess."[17]

In early December 1959, Johnson and Krauss flew to Hollywood to attend rehearsals for *Barnaby and Mr. O'Malley*, a full-color pilot episode for a new *Barnaby* series starring Bert Lahr as Mr. O'Malley, five-year-old Ronny Howard as Barnaby, and Mel Blanc as the voice of McSnoyd. Johnson loved meeting Lahr and thought he was great as Mr. O'Malley. Filmed at CBS, this *Barnaby* had one big advantage over previous dramatizations: Since it was not live, director Sherman Marks had more room to manipulate the performance, including doing multiple takes and adding music and sound effects after the fact.[18]

Marks's fine-tuning paid off. Introduced by Ronald Reagan, the half-hour program aired on CBS's *General Electric Theater* on 20 December and received strong reviews. The *New York Times*'s Jack Gould called it "a charming and hilarious holiday spree" and thought Howard "the most engaging child performer in many a day." *Variety* predicted that Howard's agent would soon find his phone ringing "with enough offers to keep [Howard] busy until next Yule time." *Variety* was right: In 1960, Howard landed the role of Opie Taylor on the *Andy Griffith Show*.[19]

Back in Connecticut after *Barnaby and Mr. O'Malley*'s success, Ruth and Dave faced the final months of Gonsul's life. Though their seventeen-year-old

Crockett Johnson, draw-
ing of Bert Lahr as Mr.
O'Malley, 1959. Image
courtesy of the Estate of
Ruth Krauss. Reprinted
with the permission of
the Estate of Ruth Krauss,
Stewart I. Edelstein,
Executor. All Rights
Reserved.

dog had been ailing for the past couple of years, he had been their companion for nearly all of their life together. He was the inspiration for both Barkis
and Toby. In March 1960, as the winter's snow last began to yield to spring,
Gonsul died. However, as Dave said, "By the comparable longevity standard
for mammals, figuring his puberty period at less than a year and ours at less
than twenty, he lived 350 years. Quite a while."[20]

Krauss found herself wanting to focus solely on poetry but unable to leave
her children's books behind. Nordstrom suggested that Johnson or Sendak illustrate Krauss's next one, but she wanted someone new: "You know, Dave &
I really do *not* want to work together; after all we've been married some 20!!
years." She also did not "think Maury & I want to work together particularly
either, although we get along that way." Moreover, both men were busy with
other projects. Sendak was illustrating three books a year as well as writing
and illustrating *The Sign on Rosie's Door* (1960) and the four-volume set *The
Nutshell Library* (1962). Johnson published four books in 1959 alone.[21]

Early in the new decade, however, Johnson's pace slowed dramatically. He published only one book in 1960 and no more until 1963. The rejection of *Magic Beach* had been discouraging, and other commercial projects demanded his attention. By early 1958, he had begun doing some work for Punch Films, run by his old friend, Lou Bunin. When Dave Hilberman organized Film Designers in 1959, he invited Johnson to join his roster of artists. A cofounder of United Productions of America and leader of the 1941 Disney animators' strike, Hilberman had since 1946 been running the Tempo Productions commercial cartoon studio New York, where he would often meet Johnson for lunch. For Film Designers, Hilberman enlisted Johnson's friend, Antonio Frasconi, already acclaimed as a painter and woodcut artist; Tomi Ungerer, then the author of a new picture book about Crictor, a boa constrictor; and *Punch* illustrator Ronald Searle, cocreator of the four Molesworth books (1953–59). Johnson was in good company.[22]

In March 1959, taking advantage of a chance to explore his interest in math and science, Johnson worked on a series of animated films about Einstein's Theory of Relativity. Educational films intrigued Johnson, but films designed purely to sell products did not. In April 1959, when Bunin invited him to work on some ad campaigns, Johnson confessed, "It is my old trouble in dealing with these people. For the length of time it takes to do a job properly I find I can't keep myself pretending that advertising men and their problems are real." On another occasion, he sent Bunin a mock advertisement for Bosco chocolate syrup that was even more sarcastic than the parodies then running in *Mad* magazine.[23]

Under very narrow conditions, however, Krauss agreed to let her work be used for other purposes, including advertising. In April 1960, she wanted to sue Whittlesey House for publishing Phoebe Wilson Hoss's *Noses Are for Roses* (1960), which paraphrased her "Toes are for wiggling" and "Arms are for hugging" as "Toes are to wiggle" and "Arms are to hug with." However, when Merck offered to pay and give credit to *A Hole Is to Dig*, she and Sendak agreed to the book's use in a campaign for a drug. With Sendak's art and Krauss's text, each ad used three definitions from the book, concluding with the slogan "Redisol is so kids have better appetites." Krauss also granted dancer Margot Harley permission to adapt *A Hole Is to Dig* for a March 1960 Contemporary Dance Productions performance in New York.[24]

In late April, Krauss and Johnson walked up the street to bring some of their books to the new Rowayton Arts Center. A minute's walk from their home in what had previously been Nelson's Lobster House, the Arts Center recognized the town's growing community of artists and writers. The first board of directors included Jim and Jane Flora, and among the center's first programs were an exhibit by Jane Flora and a lecture by Kay Boyle. Krauss was amused by the location but pleased by the attention it was bringing to local artists. As she told Nordstrom, "The place is a 'shack' over the River (well, *not quite*), but the amazing number of people filing through it this weekend resembles the opening of the Guggenheim."[25]

One of the books Krauss brought to the Arts Center was *Open House for Butterflies*, which was receiving mixed reviews for her text but praise for Sendak's pictures. Echoing the artist's assessment, *Kirkus* felt that the new book "lacks the spontaneous charm of" *A Hole Is to Dig*, though the reviewer praised the "irresistible diminutive drawings"; the text was "charming, funny, sometimes wise." Not trusting his own judgment, the *New York Times*'s George Woods sought the opinions of children: "Not only does its point and purpose escape me, but it also baffled six children to whom it was carefully, hopefully read." However, the children "loved Maurice Sendak's abundant and enchanting miniatures." The *Saturday Review*'s Betty Miles offered a more thoughtful assessment, noting that, to "a young child the comment that 'grownup means to go to nursery school' is flatly logical. To an adult it has a poignancy no child could understand." Lamenting what she saw as Krauss's decision to talk over children's heads to adults, Miles hoped for "more of the children's books that Miss Krauss used to write with such verve and insight: *The Carrot Seed*, *The Growing Story*, *The Big World and the Little House* were real juveniles, the kind that real children beg to have read to them in real living rooms."[26]

On 5 May 1960, Dave and Ruth were having martinis and dinner in their living room with two other couples, Ken and Jackie Curtis and Jimmy and Dallas Ernst. After dinner, a news bulletin interrupted the game they were watching on TV. The Soviet Union had shot down an American U-2 plane, claiming that it was a spy plane. According to the U.S. government, the plane had been "studying meteorological conditions found at high altitude, had been missing since May 1," when the pilot reported difficulty with his oxygen equipment while flying over Turkey, near the Russian border. Dave immediately said, "Oh, what a cock-and-bull story." Though they were liberals, the Curtises and the Ernsts did not share his skepticism. Jackie Curtis asked, "Well, why would the U.S. government lie about such a thing?" Within a week, Soviet leader Nikita Khrushchev would produce the pilot, Francis Gary Powers, who had survived the crash, along with the film in the plane's surveillance camera. Dave's suspicions were warranted.[27]

As the news grew stranger, Krauss's "surrealist-type news-items," as she called them, were finding readers—in June 1960, the *Village Voice* agreed to publish a dozen. Krauss also thought that if Nordstrom would publish "If Only" in "picture-book form" but *not* for children," the result "could be pretty popular." Nordstrom disagreed but was willing to help reissue *A Good Man and His Good Wife* with new illustrations. They tossed some names back and forth. Jules Feiffer had drawn up a dummy for the book some years earlier, but "he's terribly popular" now and has "never done a children's book." Krauss added parenthetically, "probably never will now," not knowing that Feiffer was then illustrating Norton Juster's *The Phantom Tollbooth* (1961). She and Nordstrom also considered R. O. Blechman, author-illustrator of *The Juggler of Our Lady* (1952), and Marc Simont.[28]

The original illustrator of *A Good Man*, Ad Reinhardt, came up to Darien and Rowayton on 30 July to visit Jimmy and Dallas Ernst, Abe and Betty Ajay, and Johnson and Krauss. A few years had passed since they had seen Reinhardt, now a famous abstract painter. The visit reconnected the two men, and they began to correspond.[29]

Spending time with old friends who had become successful artists and with Abe Ajay, who was abandoning his commercial art career to become a painter and sculptor, prompted Johnson to ponder his own future path. He was creating fewer children's books and hoped *Barnaby* might yet prove an on-screen hit, but he was growing creatively restless. His wife also served as a role model: She was now submitting her poems for publication in both smaller venues and larger ones. The year 1961 would be the first since the start of her career without a new Ruth Krauss children's book.

21

LORCA VARIATIONS AND HAROLD'S ABC

Harold had to think of some other way to speed his trip. I is for Idea. He
went to work on the next letter with his purple crayon.
—CROCKETT JOHNSON, *Harold's ABC* (1963)

Ruth Krauss was so invested in her new career as a poet that at age fifty-nine, she decided to learn French. Having read Andre Breton, Paul Eluard, and Arthur Rimbaud in Kenneth Koch's class, she felt that she should learn the language in which they had written. She and Dave planned a summer 1960 vacation "for a week or so only—maybe Quebec so I can practice reciting French poetry."[1]

Before leaving for Canada, Crockett Johnson sent a dramatic adaptation of *Barnaby* to E. Y. Harburg. But Harburg was too busy to take on the project, and although he thought *Barnaby* "one of the classics of our day," he did not have enough "time and energy" for the project. "I am both flattered and sad," he wrote.[2]

The Hall Syndicate, however, was interested in a revival of the *Barnaby* comic strip. Enlisting Warren Sattler to do the artwork, Johnson updated the original plots for the 1960s—the Hot Coffee Ring became the Counterfeit Credit Card Ring, and the Victory Garden sequence became a story about Barnaby's attempts to start a garden. He also added some new story lines that focused on contemporary topics such as marketing and questionnaires. Looking back at his old comic strips as he prepared them for the new series, Johnson was "amazed and stand in awe as I see how the characters solved their problems, seemingly without any aid from me." Privately, however, he complained about breaking in a new assistant and because "the size of newspaper strips has shrunk so that I am having to rewrite and redraw everything." Still, initial sales to newspapers were promising, and on 12 September 1960, the new *Barnaby* appeared in papers. Johnson created some inspired new episodes, but he was much less emotionally invested in the strip. Despite the

196

year's close-fought presidential election, the updated strip largely remained a passive observer of the political scene.[3]

His energies may have been too divided to give the strip the attention it needed. After the anticipated theatrical release of David Piel's film version of *Harold and the Purple Crayon*, which still lacked a distributor, Johnson was planning to film five other Harold stories. He also had plans to adapt *Barnaby* strip material for a full-length feature film and for a series of 130 five-minute animated films to be shown on television. His collaborator on both projects would again be Lou Bunin. For a recent paper industry trade show, the two men had created an ad: Johnson drew the backgrounds, and Bunin used puppets to demonstrate why American Cyanamid's new "wet strength" paper processes made stronger napkins and paper towels.[4]

The new *Barnaby* may also have lacked the earlier incarnation's political focus because Johnson's political views had become more complex. By the early 1960s, he was skeptical of those on the left as well as those on the right and believed that all politics was corrupt. Although he had supported Democratic candidates since the early 1950s and probably voted for John F. Kennedy in 1960, at a party soon after the election, Johnson remarked, "Kennedy's just a thug." When the crowd of liberals reacted in surprise, he continued, "Oh, well, his father was a bootlegger." Johnson's impulse to puncture his liberal friends' optimism may have stemmed from his political disillusionment or from his distrust of Joseph Kennedy Sr., who supported British prime minister Neville Chamberlain's appeasement of Hitler in the 1930s and remained a friend of Senator Joseph McCarthy into the 1950s.[5]

Johnson rarely talked politics, and he had friends across the political spectrum because he was reluctant to impose his convictions on others. As Shelley Trubowitz put it, "You could be the most reactionary bastard and be at his house. It didn't make any difference to him. Whatever you thought, go ahead and talk. He didn't have anything against you unless you were a Hitlerite or something like that." Though Johnson had long since grown suspicious of the Communist Party, he continued to believe that the best solution to the world's problems would be to start over with international socialism. But he voiced that opinion only to his closest friends.[6]

Through the winter of 1960–61, Johnson oversaw the production of revised *Barnaby* strips, and Krauss worked on her poetry. Atypically, she did not involve herself in Marc Simont's reillustration of *A Good Man and His Good Wife*. She was busy writing a group of poems inspired by Federico García

Jacqueline Kennedy, Caroline Kennedy, and Ruth Krauss's *I Can Fly*, 1961. Image from Leonard Marcus, *Golden Legacy: How Golden Books Won Children's Hearts, Changed Publishing Forever, and Became an American Icon Along the Way* (New York: Golden Books, 2007). Used by permission of the Estate of Jacques Lowe.

Lorca. *Harper's Magazine* editor Kay Gauss Jackson had turned down Krauss's submissions to date but encouraged her to send more.[7]

Krauss and Johnson spent Easter weekend visiting the coastal town of Cohasset, Massachusetts, where they picked up one of the Boston Sunday papers. In the *Parade* magazine insert, Ruth read a story about Caroline Kennedy, "the little girl in the White House." In an accompanying photograph, First Lady Jacqueline Kennedy smiles down at her three-year-old daughter, who holds a copy of *I Can Fly*, Krauss's decade-old Little Golden Book. Despite her husband's skepticism toward the Kennedys, seeing her *I Can Fly* in Caroline's lap increased Krauss's warm feelings toward the new first family.[8]

Determined to make an impression as a poet, Krauss was submitting poems to many journals, including the *Evergreen Review* and *Locus Solus*. The latter's summer 1961 issue, edited by Kenneth Koch, would include works by Frank O'Hara, John Ashbery, William S. Burroughs, and Gregory Corso along with five of Krauss's "news" prose poems and her "Uri Gagarin & William Shakespeare." One of her more serious pieces, it alternates between Shakespeare's Sonnet 18 and the words of the cosmonaut who in April 1961 became the first person in outer space. It begins,

> compare thee
> more lovely
> and a single spin around the earth
> winds do shake
> withstanding well the state of weightlessness
> too short
> too hot
> and often could see the earth my native.

Mingling the words of the Soviet pioneer with the Renaissance playwright aligns space flight with classic verse, figuring technological advance as an enduring art. Noting the sublime achievement of the man who beat the Americans into space, Krauss's poem also takes a stand. Against those who reviled all communists, the verse suggests at least that scientific advances transcend national boundaries and at most that the Soviet space program is as powerful as one of the English language's greatest poets. The poem is a political statement, too.[9]

Keeping his politics mostly to himself, Johnson was busy with other projects—the new *Barnaby*, advertising work, and children's books. By December 1960, with Nordstrom clamoring for Johnson to do the seventh Harold book, he confessed that he would like to do one, but only if "had an idea or a subject." He suggested that if Susan Carr, who had just been made managing editor, could "write a jacket blurb in a spare moment," he was sure he would "be able to write the book for it."[10]

In April 1961, Carr sent jacket flap copy for *Harold's Republic*:

> "Here is the flap copy," said Harold, "and anyone knows that books have flap copy. Therefore, if there is flap copy, it stands to reason that there must be a book."

Harold, inimitable hero of purple crayon fame, once again proves his versatility (and the versatility of his creator). Starting with only the flap, this Lilliputian Aristotle weaves himself into one adventure and out of another in a story that is as lovable and logical as Harold's basic premise.

Crockett Johnson's many fans, as well as students of philosophy, will recognize the truth of the following syllogism:

Books are good.

When Crockett Johnson writes one, they're better.

This new book about Harold is Crockett Johnson's best.

Carr's blurb planted the seed for another Harold book, but Johnson would not find time to work on it for another year.[11]

Ladies' Home Journal asked him to write a monthly story about Ellen and her lion. He submitted three new tales, and the editors sent him a handsome advance and promised to publish a new story each month for a year; the stories could then be collected into a book for Harper. However, an October editorial shake-up at the magazine derailed the project. Hoping to give new life to the stories, Johnson asked whether Harper would want another Ellen book. His last statement for *Ellen's Lion* showed only eighty-nine copies sold at the regular trade price; however, the book "seems to have picked up a tiny hard core of unusually ardent fans and this is a kind of encouragement." Two of those fans were Susan Carr and Ursula Nordstrom. Nevertheless, when Johnson submitted eight new Ellen stories in June 1962, the Harper editors were not enthusiastic. Carr found "a sameness about all these stories that never came up in the first book," with "Ellen always goading the lion, and being sort of horrid." She passed the manuscript on to Ann Jorgensen Tobias for a second opinion: Tobias believed that Ellen and the lion were "battling" too much and that the new stories lacked the "lightness of touch" in the originals. Nordstrom agreed, breaking the news to Johnson as gently as she could: The editors liked some of the stories a lot but were "terribly puzzled by the general tone of crabbiness."[12]

While Johnson faced rejection, Krauss continued to mull over her book of experimental poetry for children. After asking again whether Nordstrom would be interested in the idea, Krauss expressed some ambivalence about her status as a writer of picture books, signing the letter "Wm. Shakespeare the 15th (anti-pictherbooks campaign in session here)." Nordstrom quickly expressed interest and advised Krauss not to worry. Krauss sent in more poems, but Nordstrom responded less than enthusiastically: Though "lots of things in them are marvelous," she was "dubious about a lot of the poems' appeal" for children. However, "do send anything that you may write or that you may find filed away in your refrigerator. We would dearly love another Ruth Krauss book, of course."[13]

Krauss then sent Nordstrom "Yuri Gagarin & William Shakespeare" and a duet between Winnie the Pooh and Shakespeare. Using the cut-up technique pioneered by the surrealists (and later adopted by William S. Burroughs), the poem creates a dialogue between the "When daisies pied and violets blue" song from the final scene of *Love Labour's Lost* (1598) and Pooh's "Cloud Song" from the first chapter of A. A. Milne's *Winnie-the-Pooh* (1926), bringing in the Latin translation of *Pooh* for added flavor. The short conversation begins,

WINNIE: How sweet to be a cloud
W.S.: when daisies pied and violets
WINNIE: floating in the blue
W.S.: and lady-smocks all silver-white
and cuckoo buds of yellow hue
WINNIE: Iniquum fatum fatu
W.S.: Cuckoo cuckoo cuckoo

Nordstrom was "delighted with" both poems, especially "Yuri Gagarin & William Shakespeare," and would be happy "to keep reading whatever you send." In October, Krauss received more poetic encouragement, as *Harper's* published her "Variations on a Lorca Form," marking both her first appearance as a poet in a mainstream magazine and the first time she had been paid for her poetry. Each of the poem's seven short stanzas begins with the phrase "When I live again," suggesting the possibility of reincarnation.[14]

After sending these back in July, Krauss had left for a ten-day writers' conference at Wagner College on Staten Island, where she met editors from magazines (*Mademoiselle*, *New World Writing*) and publishers (Fawcett, Lippincott, Dial, Bantam, Scribner's). She also met literary agents. Like many of their contemporaries, she and Johnson had dealt directly with publishers. However, because she was moving into a new field, she began to consider representation. At the conference, she also met and befriended poet and Wagner English professor Willard Maas and his wife, filmmaker Marie Menken, the couple who inspired the intense, fractious George and Martha of *Who's Afraid of Virginia Woolf?* (1962), the Pulitzer- and Tony-winning play by Edward Albee (himself a participant in that year's conference). If Krauss had not yet met O'Hara, then this conference introduced her to him, and he would soon become her teacher and poetic mentor.[15]

Krauss was also serving as mentor to younger writers. In 1961, Doris Orgel and her husband, Shelley, a psychiatrist, moved to Westport, Connecticut, and met Krauss and Johnson through Maurice Sendak. Doris Orgel was just getting into children's books, and Sendak illustrated her first, a translation of Wilhelm Hauff's *Dwarf Long-Nose* (1960). With Krauss presiding, Orgel, Mary Ann Hoberman, and another aspiring children's author began meeting at a little bar on South Norwalk beach. Over Bloody Marys, they talked about writing and publishing books for children. Krauss advised them to do as she had done: participate in the Bank Street Writers group and observe children on playgrounds. Back at the Johnson-Krauss house, Johnson advised them not to fret and wait for publishers to reject their manuscripts. "Why do you put up with it?" he said. "I submit a manuscript of mine, and if I haven't heard back in three weeks, I go there, and I pick it up and I leave. I'm not going to wait longer than that."[16]

Ruth and Dave also became friends with the Orgels. When they went out to dinner, Doris Orgel was struck by Dave's ability to hold his liquor: At nearly six feet tall and with an ex-football player's build, drinks did not seem to affect him. As Gene Searchinger recalled, at restaurants, Dave would ask for two martinis. When waitresses would ask if one was for Ruth, he would respond, "No, two," pointing to two places on the table in front of him—"Here, and here." Next to those spots, he would neatly arrange his cigarettes and a stack of matches. Out with the Orgels, Dave might start with a boilermaker, followed by several other drinks. But Doris Orgel never saw him drunk. Rather, two martinis for Dave was equal to one martini for any other person.[17]

During the summer of 1961, Dave and Ruth took another vacation, driving up through New Hampshire and into Maine. Ruth suggested they drive up to Denmark, Maine, where she had spent two formative summers at Camp Walden forty years earlier. Within a mile of the camp, however, memories overwhelmed her, and she could not go on. Dave turned the car around and they headed back south.[18]

Not encouraged by the new *Barnaby*'s performance, Johnson decided to walk away from the strip. In January 1962, he told syndicate head Robert Hall that *Barnaby* had been written through March, at which point Johnson wanted either to bring the strip to and end or have someone else carry on the writing. He had, he thought, "turned out a respectable year and half of strips" and "a few even brilliant episodes." However, sales were not strong, and readers did not seem to be paying attention: The new strips "haven't provoked the slightest murmur of reaction from anybody (not even a harsh word)." Children's books "and maybe old age" were slowing him down; a "young and energetic fellow" might be able to give the strip the "push it needs toward popular reception." No one took the job. Sattler drew the strip through March, at which point Johnson took over, writing and drawing the final sequence, which recycled the ending he had created ten years earlier. The new *Barnaby* concluded on 14 April 1962.[19]

Johnson then returned to *Magic Beach*. After rewriting and shortening it, he decided it was "much better than the old one" and sent the manuscript back to Nordstrom in May. Harper reader Ann Jorgensen Tobias thought the story too "depressing" and complex for children, and Nordstrom admitted, "As an adult I love the mood of the story, and the tone of sadness. But we're afraid that it just isn't a children's book."[20]

That May brought similar criticism of Krauss's latest book, *Mama, I Wish I Was Snow—Child, You'd Be Very Cold*, published not by Harper but by Atheneum. Instead of gathering ideas from children or inventing a story, Krauss adapted Federico Garcia Lorca's "Cancion Tonta" (Silly Song), and Ellen Raskin provided illustrations. *Kirkus* called the book a "disappointment from the usually dependable Ruth Krauss," and the *New York Times Book Review*'s George A. Woods predicted that the book would "leave children very cold indeed." The *Christian Science Monitor* thought it unlikely even "to strike responsive chords in even the more imaginative child. . . . Sorry. Will await more butterflies."[21]

Though Krauss was finding places to publish her poetry for adults, her verse yielded very little money. A couple of months before, *New World Writing* finally "'bought' some poetry" she had sent eight months earlier—for fourteen dollars. Still, she overlooked the reply's tardiness and cashed the check. Hoping for a better return on her children's books, Krauss sent a draft of her latest manuscript to literary agent Marilyn Marlow. Reminiscent of Margaret Wise Brown's *Goodnight Moon* (1947), the *Goodnight Book* followed a child saying goodnight to various items—eyes, nose, fingers, toes, windows, doors, even Bloomingdales. Wary of working through an agent, Nordstrom was glad when Krauss decided not to have Marlow represent this book, but the author-editor relationship was changing.[22]

In addition to finding a better title for the *Goodnight Book*, Krauss needed to find an illustrator. She admired Beni Montresor's work but did not know him. Erik Blegvad lived nearby, but she was not sure he would be a good fit. Visiting old friends Nina and Herman Schneider in their Greenwich Village apartment, Krauss saw some artwork by their daughter, Elizabeth Susan Schneider, and asked if she would be interested in illustrating the book. Schneider welcomed the chance to prove herself to a publisher and won the job.²³

At age nineteen, Schneider took the train up from New York up to Rowayton on her first professional assignment as an illustrator. Krauss picked her up at the station wearing "this little muumuu-ish kind of dress, which she always wore." It was a very hot day, and Krauss began fluffing herself, saying, "I can't stand having anything binding me. I just can't stand clothing that sticks close to my body." At 74 Rowayton Avenue, Schneider presented her ideas for the very spare text, Krauss liked what she saw, and they had no further in-person discussions about the book. This would not be another close working relationship, as Krauss had had with Sendak. These days, she was a poet first.²⁴

She again went to the Wagner conference in July. That year, Willard Maas directed the conference, and the writers in residence included Kay Boyle and Kenneth Koch. Ruth's poem "Duet" appeared in *XbyX*, "a one shot magazine put out by" Maas. Gerald Malanga published another Ruth Krauss poem in the *Wagner Literary Magazine*, which Allen Ginsberg called "the best college magazine in America."²⁵

Johnson returned to his most successful character, putting together *Harold's ABC*. He had fun working in King Uranus, "the pre-Olympian god of the universe," and Queen Urania, "the somewhat later muse of astronomy," doubting whether "many seven-year-old classic scholars will write in complaining about the royal marriage as a barbarism." Johnson was confident that Nordstrom and her editors would like his "nonsensical tour de force," and they did. Ann Jorgensen Tobias and Carr made a few suggestions: When Harold reached the letter *V*, he lost interest in finishing the alphabet but only wanted to go home. Carr wrote, "It bothers me that Harold gives up. He never has before, and I don't think he should. . . . The thing about Harold is that he is so invincible. I really think Dave should not let him get so depressed." They also found had questions about "Z is for Zigzag. Dragging his crayon behind him, Harold sleepily staggered off to bed." This seemed "anticlimactic." He received a contract and a two-thousand-dollar advance for the book in January 1963, reworked the end of the book, and finished the manuscript in February.²⁶

In *Harold's ABC*, the seventh and last book to feature Harold, each letter forms a part of the object it names: *A* is the house's attic, *B* a stack of two books, *C* a cake with one slice (called a "cut") removed for Harold to eat. Most letters name more than one item: *E* stands for an "enormous edifice" made out of the letter as well as for "Etcetera" and for the elevators that Harold avoids because "they made his stomach feel funny." Not the more common arbitrary collection of alphabet words, *Harold's ABC* forms a narrative of the boy's journey through the alphabet, with each letter leading to the next. As is true of the other Harold books, *Harold's ABC* looks simple but is not.

During the fall of 1962, Krauss met regularly with Jane Flora, who was illustrating *A Bouquet of Littles*, a verse ode to smallness that strives for but does not quite arrive at the pithiness of *A Hole Is to Dig* and *Open House for Butterflies*, featuring such lines as "A little rug best fits a little floor, / A little storeman best fits a little store, / As my small sea best fits my little roar" and "a little storm best fits a little thunder / a little Alice best fits a little wonder." Krauss was finding it "a 'lulu' to get a good picture-motif" going. A bit frustrated with the creative process, she joked to Nordstrom, "At this point, I've decided no more pic-books *and* no more poetry. Bibles, that's what I'll write."[27]

Krauss was now studying poetry with O'Hara, whom she affectionately called "my teach," which amused him because he was not then as accomplished as she was. A fall 1962 mimeographed collection, *New School Poets*, contains three Krauss poems: "My Dream with Its Solar-Pulse Gallop," "Andy Auto Body," and "Imitation," a single-line riff on T. S. Eliot's "Love Song of J. Alfred Prufrock" (1922): "In the womb the womb men come and go."[28]

At midnight on 23 November 1962, two hundred people filled New York's Living Theatre for a "Reading of Poetry of Wagner Poets." Maas moderated, and the fourteen featured poets included Jean Boudin, Malanga, David Shapiro, Frank Lima, and Krauss. Though she disliked giving public readings, she did so on this occasion because it was a benefit for the *Wagner Literary Magazine*, which had published her, and because she wanted to support the school where her friend Maas taught.[29]

When not receiving guests or accompanying Krauss to midnight poetry readings, Johnson returned to revising the new Ellen stories. He conceded that the charge of "a general tone of crabbiness" was "a well-taken criticism" and made changes, including a complete rewriting of one of the tales. He now thought that the stories were "really pretty good, good enough to publish somewhere," though he acknowledged, "my opinion of the seemliness of my works can be a bit off; it still seems to me that far and away the best small thing I have done is that *Magic Beach* opus you sent rapidly back and which, since, half a dozen editors enthusiastically have turned down." He asked Nordstrom to tell him whether these revised tales would make "a Harper *Ellen's Lion* sequel" or to "give [him] a definite rejection."[30]

In December 1962, Elizabeth Schneider brought her dummy for Krauss's latest book, now called *Eyes Nose Fingers Toes*, to Nordstrom and Dorothy Hagen, the director of operations for Harper's manufacturing department. The text for *Eyes Nose Fingers Toes* does not specify the protagonist's gender, and Schneider had drawn a little girl. Hagen suggested changing the child to a boy because girl characters did not sell as well as boy characters. Krauss's response was uncharacteristically practical: "People buy boy's books for girls but *not* visa versa. . . . I hate so much work to go into a book, & then to have it *not sell* because it's a girl." In any case, she added, "I feel I've done my share & still do it of campaigning against male chauvinism." Krauss's willingness to see her book as simply a marketable product signals a changed relationship to children's literature: It was where she made her living, but not where she was most emotionally invested. Schneider would have to redo the drawings.[31]

In May 1962, Harper and Brothers merged with a textbook publisher, Row, Peterson, and Company, and major changes soon followed. Nordstrom was optimistic that the merger would give her books an entry into the elementary school and high school markets, writing to Johnson, "We think their seventy (70) salesmen will be great helps in selling Harold to schools. We think all our children's books will benefit, but Harold (especially the drawing one) is an example of a trade children's book which can be used in schools by an imaginative teacher." She joked,

> I refer to the 70 salesmen as though I were an old Coney Island type producer—you know:
> 30 GIRLS 30!
> But I say: 70 SALESMEN 70! Step up for the next show, price two bits. Excuse me.

Though she took the changes with a sense of humor, as Leonard Marcus notes, the merger "prepared the ground for a historic change in the company's management culture," strengthening the publisher's business side. After 1967, when the chairmanship of Harper's executive committee passed from Harper's Cass Canfield Sr. to Row, Peterson's Gordon Jones, "the house was now in the hands of business-oriented people, while those who combined business with editorial creativity were out of control."[32]

The new business emphasis would push Krauss and Johnson away from Harper, and both began to publish more frequently with other presses. In middle age, they were not content to repeat themselves. Though they could have relied on proven formulae for success, they instead kept inventing, Krauss in verse and Johnson in his increasingly philosophical tales. As Krauss had done, Johnson also wanted to pursue interests beyond the field of children's books. His first successful career was as a cartoonist. His second, a picture book author. Maybe it was time to bring this second career to a close and to do something else. But what?

22

PROVOCATEUR AND PHILOSOPHER

What a fine day for
an act and a show
a cold and a snow
—RUTH KRAUSS, *What a Fine Day For . . .* (1967)

Now back in touch with Ad Reinhardt, Crockett Johnson was taking an interest in his old friend's career. In April 1963, noting that Reinhardt's paintings were on display "around the world," Johnson asked, "Have you thought of Rowayton?" Kidding Reinhardt, who was then being canonized as a major American painter, Johnson added, "We have a nice little Art Association here and I think if I played my cards right I could wangle you into a group show. Oils priced over thirty dollars don't sell very well of course, and it will cost you fifteen dollars to join, but the prestige is enormous." Reinhardt should come up to take a look: "Pack a pile of your representative (I mean representative of your work; don't go and paint a lot of representational pictures through any misunderstanding) canvases and your family in the car and take off."[1]

If Reinhardt could not make it up to Rowayton, Johnson said he would visit on 1 May, when he and Ruth would be in Brooklyn Heights for a party hosted by Willard Maas and Marie Menken. Their parties were a who's who of the culturally influential. Andy Warhol called Maas and Menken "the last of the great Bohemians. They wrote and filmed and drank (their friends called them 'scholarly drunks') and were involved with all the modern poets."[2]

In 1963, Ruth Krauss published one of her most important poems, "This Breast," in the *Wagner Literary Magazine*. Begun in Kenneth Koch's class the previous year, the poem's inspiration may be Koch's "Thank You" (1962), which gives thanks for a series of items unlikely to generate feelings of gratitude: "Thank you for the chance to run a small hotel / In an elephant stopover in Zambezi, / But I do not know how to take care of guests, certainly they would all leave soon." Generating her own absurdist repetitions, Krauss's recurring "This breast" takes the place of Koch's recurring "Thank you." Krauss's sense of epic repetition likely also derived from her readings of Walt Whitman and Allen Ginsberg.[3]

The most striking difference between Krauss's poem and Koch's is tone. Where Koch sustains irony throughout, Krauss goes directly for surrealist pastiche. One stanza begins,

> This breast as the Irish Statesman so shrewdly remarked most unabashed explorer of the crypts of the soul
> This breast—but we have nothing but the word of Mr. Snooks
> This breast a dove
> This breast the flower of Gum Swamp
> This breast a little confused by this possibility

Juxtaposing *this breast* with a wide array of unrelated items creates a series of associations, ranging from comic to serious, banal to baffling. Koch's poem renders *thank you* ironic, but Krauss's poem completely changes the meaning of *this breast*. Alignment with such disparate phrases as *Mexican poetry* and *Chinese history* and *I seen it in the papers* empties out the word's meaning, transforming *breast* into a universal signifier. It can be an Irish Statesman, "composed entirely of scraps of historic fact," or a "Dostoevskian masterpiece."

Krauss's collection of avant-garde poems for children, which did not include "This Breast," was now making the rounds, represented by Marilyn Marlow. Like Ursula Nordstrom at Harper, Atheneum editor Jean Karl wondered about audience. Though the work "could only be done as a picture book," it seemed not "really suitable for the picture book age." Atheneum had published Krauss's Lorca book the previous year, and it had received poor reviews, adding to Karl's skepticism. Nevertheless, Karl "would certainly be glad to read anything" Krauss sent. This was best-selling children's writer Ruth Krauss, author of *A Hole Is to Dig* and *A Very Special House*. Perhaps she would yet produce another hit?[4]

Writing would become his most famous book, Maurice Sendak got stuck and came to visit Krauss and Johnson. After his *Nutshell Library* (1962) sold one hundred thousand copies in its first year, Nordstrom, seeing the makings of a successful series, asked him to create more Nutshell books. Having illustrated fifty books in the preceding decade, Sendak did not want to repeat himself. He wanted to do something new. When she suggested that someone else create sequels instead, he was upset. The *Nutshell Library* was his idea. Nordstrom backed off, and Sendak returned to *Where the Wild Horses*

Are, a book he had begun in 1955, during his apprenticeship with Krauss and Johnson but had set aside in favor of other projects. In the first months of 1963, Sendak carried around a spiral notebook, rewriting the story every few days. By May, Sendak had finished drafting the text and had changed the book's title to *Where the Wild Things Are*. But he remained unsatisfied and began making trips to Rowayton in search of guidance. As Sendak struggled with what to call the series of three wordless two-page spreads where the main character, Max, and the Wild Things cavort in the forest, Johnson proposed the word *rumpus*. So right before this visual sequence, Max says, "Let the wild rumpus start!" Sendak later reflected, "Max was born in Rowayton and . . . was the love child of me, Ruth, and Dave." Krauss and Johnson had taught Sendak the need to have a "fierce honesty" in children's books. Though Max is a version of Sendak, he also "has his roots in Ruth Krauss"—specifically, in her belief that children "were allowed to be as cruel and maniacal as she knew they were."[5]

The love child of the New York School and the Bank Street School, the first of Krauss's poem plays made it to the stage on 10 June 1963 as part of *The Pocket Follies* at New York's Pocket Theater. In its entirety, *A Beautiful Day* has a girl walk on stage, announce, "What a beautiful day!" and then "the Sun falls down onto the stage." Remy Charlip staged four very different versions, which were interspersed throughout the production as a running gag.[6]

The play was warmly received, but Krauss probably did not see it. During the first week of June 1963, Phyllis Rowand began having severe headaches. Ruth drove her to the hospital, where doctors discovered a brain aneurysm. Ten days later, she was dead at the age of forty-seven. The loss of such a close friend caused Dave to face his own mortality but not the health risks of his smoking. Though it was three years before the surgeon general's warning would appear on cigarette packets, the opening scene in "Doctor's Orders," from *Ellen's Lion*, suggests that Dave knew the hazards. Pretending to be a doctor, Ellen says, "You're a mighty sick little lion. . . . You'll have to stop smoking." Dave did not stop smoking, but he did draw up a will. (Ruth postponed facing anything that reminded her of her mortality.) His will offers a clear sense of who was most important to him. He left Ruth everything. If she were to predecease him, half of his estate would go to his sister's children; a quarter would go to Linda and Nancy Hahn, the children of Ruth's cousin, Richard Hahn; one-eighth would go to close friends Abe and Frume Levine; and one-eighth would go to Nina Rowand Wallace, who began art school that fall.[7] In her absence, Dave and Ruth became closer to the Frasconis. Antonio, Leona, and their sons Pablo (age eleven) and Miguel (age six) began a tradition of

Maurice Sendak at Lake Mohonk, New York, October 1968. At photographer Nancy Crampton's suggestion, Maurice posed on this waterbike, which is right alongside the dock and firmly tethered to it. Copyright © Nancy Crampton.

having Spaghetti Night at 74 Rowayton Avenue each Wednesday. After dinner, the adults sat at the kitchen table, drinking wine, and talking about art. Observing the creative lives of their parents and their parents' friends, the boys started to create art of their own. Pablo wrote poetry in Ruth's style, "experimenting with absurd and surreal imagery." He showed his poems to Ruth, and she encouraged him to keep at it.[8]

In the fall of 1963, Krauss's writing for children was not receiving much encouragement or even notice. The only review of *Bouquet of Littles*, in the *Bulletin of the Center for Children's Books*, declared the catalogs of rhymes "appealing but repetitive." In contrast, *The Lion's Own Story* and *Harold's ABC* attracted plenty of attention, most of it positive. The *Los Angeles Times* thought the sequel to *Ellen's Lion* "dull," but the *Chicago Tribune* loved the "delightfully droll conversations" and considered it "a marvelous book for any child who has owned a stuffed animal, any adult who has had either, for all readers of the preceding *Ellen's Lion*, and for all fans of Crockett Johnson." In the *New York Times Book Review*, Ellen Lewis Buell wrote, "Those agile-witted readers and listeners who liked *Ellen's Lion* will be glad to know the unpredictable little girl is in fine form again." The reviews of *Harold's ABC* were also strong, though not all noted the ingenious way Johnson wove each letter into a narrative. When he turned in the manuscript, Johnson had fretted that readers would overlook the complexity of what he had accomplished. The book "looks easy but it is difficult to find a word for each letter in order and fit the letter into the visualization (however absurdly), meanwhile keeping up a narrative (however nutty)." Only the *Horn Book*'s Ethel Heins understood that this was "a unique kind of ABC book" with "each letter actually generating a picture from which the word becomes part of an uninterrupted story," though the *New York Times* did note that "some of the transitions are wonderfully logical," such as when Harold "cuts a large wedge out of" a cake, making "a perfect C!"[9]

Johnson and Krauss were irritated by what they saw as Harper's indifference toward reprinting *Is This You?*, originally published by Scott and now out of print. After more than six months of correspondence without a definite publication date, the authors learned that the contract would receive no advance. Johnson then told Nordstrom that he and Krauss had decided to withdraw the book and seek another home for it. That December, Nordstrom sent a letter of apology. But it was an unpleasant end to a year that had more darkness than usual—Rowand's death in June and President Kennedy's assassination in November. As Nordstrom noted on December 20, "the assassination happened 4 weeks ago today, almost to the minute. It gets more unbearable all the time, doesn't it."[10]

January 1964 started out on an upbeat note. Johnson was contemplating some new children's books, and Krauss was looking forward to the production of some of her plays in the spring. She enjoyed defying people's expectations, both regarding what she could do as a children's writer and regarding generic conventions for picture books, poetry, or theater. One three-line poem play being produced starred a narrator, a spy, and lots of pineapples. The entirety of the play reads,

> NARRATOR: in a poem you make your point with pineapples
> PINEAPPLES: fly onto the stage from all directions
> SPY: and it would be nice to have a spy going in and out

Describing its upcoming performance, Krauss told Nordstrom, "Everybody throws pineapples all over the theatre. (I just thought you'd like to know.)" Krauss relished the mischief of her work.[11]

However, neither she nor Johnson relished *Captain Kangaroo* broadcasting readings of their books without payment. Despite the free publicity that would have ensued, they, Maurice Sendak, and Marc Simont declined to let the popular children's television show read *The Carrot Seed*, *The Birthday Party*, or the new edition of *A Good Man and His Good Wife* on the air. In these authors' view, "The television rights to literary properties . . . ought to be paid for in the United States, as they are in Britain, Canada, Australia, and other countries." It was a laudable moral position but a poor business decision.[12]

Business likes a formula. When *A Hole Is to Dig* is a hit, it wants more books like that; when *Harold and the Purple Crayon* is a hit, it wants more Harold books. The creative mind, however, does not necessarily find inspiration in the formulaic and market-tested. Johnson's imagination increasingly wandered in more philosophical, less commercially successful directions. In early 1964, he sent Nordstrom *The Emperor's Gifts*, a parable he modestly described as a "small morality play or something." It introduces a young emperor, sitting on his throne, awaiting the rulers of his six kingdoms. Knowing that each king would "come bearing wondrous gifts," the boy emperor "pondered what to give them in return." King Drowse the Lazy arrives bearing a bottle of Contentment and lies down to sleep in a far corner of the throne room. Next, King Wot the Learned brings a "tall crystal phial" of Wisdom. The emperor sees that learning has saddened King Wot and gives him the bottle of Contentment. King Rash the Foolhardy enters with a beaker of Bravery in one hand and his head in the other. Seeing that he needs wisdom, the Emperor gives King Rash the previous visitor's gift. And so the story goes. An astute judge of each visitor's strengths and weaknesses, this Harold-sized emperor deftly matches each gift with the king who needs it most.[13]

The story is about maintaining an equilibrium among personal characteristics that are admirable in moderation but dangerous in excess. Like Antoine de Saint-Exupery's *The Little Prince* (1943), *The Emperor's Gifts* is a quietly profound book about human nature, a children's book with great resonance for adult readers. The editors at Harper were underwhelmed. Susan Carr thought it "totally adult," a book that "you'd have to keep explaining to anyone under 10—even the kings' names." Nordstrom confessed to being "slightly baffled as to what age child it would really interest—as the type of format would appeal to a younger child than could possibly enjoy the ideas." They returned the manuscript to Johnson, encouraging him to send along a book "that we can accept and send you a big blue contract and a big fat check."[14]

Though Johnson's work no longer found editorial favor there, Harper's books were winning awards. In 1964, Harper won its first Newbery and its first Caldecott, with the latter going to Sendak for *Where the Wild Things*

"I was about to vanquish him," the head continued. "But, unfortunately, at that moment I lost my head." King Rash thrust it back in place, a bit off plumb. "Here," said the Emperor, offering him King Wot's phial.

"It's only a scratch," said King Rash. But he took the phial of Wisdom and drank it down bravely, making merely a slight face at the taste. He left with his head level and firmly fixed on his shoulders.

Crockett Johnson, illustration from *The Emperor's Gifts* (New York: Holt, Rinehart, and Winston, 1965). Reprinted with the permission of the Estate of Ruth Krauss, Stewart I. Edelstein, Executor. All Rights Reserved.

Are. In his acceptance speech, Sendak spoke of his "delight in choreographing dances for picture-book characters," his "favorite" being "a bouncy ballet some Ruth Krauss children danced to a Haydn serenade." Before the ceremony, Nordstrom wrote to Krauss, asking for a few words. To help magazines prepare articles on him, she was collecting comments from those whose work he had illustrated: Meindert DeJong, Charlotte Zolotow, Else Holmelund Minarik. But "it would hardly be an article without something from Ruth the Krauss." Krauss promised to send a "genuine appreciation" just "as soon as possible." It is unlikely that she managed to write it.[15]

In the first half of March 1964, Ruth began having intense headaches. Only nine months earlier, what began as headaches killed her friend Phyllis Rowand. Dave took Ruth to Norwalk Hospital, where doctors initially diagnosed her with a severe allergic headache. Whew. Their initial relief gave way to concern when the headaches grew so severe that she had to check in to the hospital on 22 March. Dave visited daily, bringing mail and news and pressing the hospital staff to run the tests that, he thought, they should have run in the first place. Coping with "inadequate medical facilities and shortages of nurses and other personnel," Dave grew "convinced it is sheer madness for anybody except millionaires to get sick without first moving to England or some other civilized country." In early April, doctors ran the tests and identified her problem as viral encephalitis, a rare but potentially lethal inflammation of the brain. She eventually began to improve and was allowed to come home but soon suffered a relapse. This time, doctors suggested that her illness was spinal meningitis and ordered a spinal tap. Throughout April and into May, Ruth lay in the hospital, some days feeling better and other days feeling worse. To cheer her up, Frank O'Hara sent some collages he created with Joe Brainard. Her friend Norma Simon also visited daily, knitting Ruth a sweater. By late May, she was able to sit up for short periods and returned to work on the proofs for *Eyes Nose Fingers Toes*. She did not like them. The layout did not match what Krauss had seen at the dummy stage, and she insisted on seeing "a paste-up of the precise way the book is going to press."[16]

While she was ill, Krauss missed the debut of her four new plays as part of an evening of theater directed by Peter Levin at the Hardware Poets Playhouse. The one-acts were a hit. The *Village Voice*'s Sydney Schubert Walter wrote, "The richest experiences of the evening came in four very short plays (or poems for the stage) by Ruth Krauss. These amusing little pieces are pure gold, mined from an extraordinary imagination."[17]

By early August, Krauss had recovered fully and gotten back to her poetry. Ted Berrigan had published some of her plays in *C*, so she sent him more work for his consideration. She also corresponded with poet Michael Benedikt, who had published her work in *Locus Solus*. He admired her poems, telling her, "You are possibly the only writer I can think of for whom the idea of creating a new form, or something close to it, is a necessary premise for going ahead and writing." Her forms are "so perfect within the structure of [her] experimenting that they look classical even next to what people who use old forms are doing. It's funny. Stravinsky I think accomplishes this also." Ruth also had admirers at Caffe Cino, a pioneering Off-Off Broadway coffeehouse founded in 1959 that had staged work by J. D. Salinger, Lanford Wilson, and Harold Pinter. In August 1964, Krauss's *38 Haikus* made its debut there.[18]

That year also saw Krauss's debut as children's-book illustrator with an adaptation of her story, "The Little Queen," which had first appeared in *Somebody Else's Nut Tree* six years earlier. *The Little King, the Little Queen, the Little Monster, and Other Stories You Can Make Up Yourself*, published as a Scholastic paperback in 1964, reprints the original story verbatim, adding similar tales about a little king and a little monster. Hoping to inspire children, Krauss ends the book with suggestions for other "stories you can make up yourself": "The Little Elephant," "The Little Egg," and "The Little ? ? ?" The book received no reviews until its 1968 republication by Whitman, at which time *Library Journal* called it "disappointing at best."[19]

Not deterred by Harper's rejections, Johnson sought a different publisher for *The Emperor's Gifts* and *Magic Beach*. Though his inner perfectionist might cause him to doubt about his work, Johnson had a sanguine disposition. As Harold did, he always kept his wits and his purple crayon—a helpful approach for many things, especially boats.

Having enjoyed sailing with Dave, Gil Rose bought a sailboat of his own but was a bit apprehensive about using it. Suppose the mast came down or the boat filled with water? He would try out the boat with Dave, an experienced sailor. On a pleasant afternoon, the two men the new boat out into Long Island Sound. Suddenly, just as Rose had feared, the mast came crashing down. He and Dave quickly gathered it and the sail together. They started the motor and headed back to shore. At the dock, they discovered that the mast was on a hinge, held upright by a cable. One of the screws holding the cable in place had been loose, come unscrewed, and caused the mast's sudden descent. They fixed the problem and, just to prove to themselves that they could do it, set out again for a sail. This time, the boat functioned perfectly. When they returned to 74 Rowayton, Dave invited Rose in for martini. When Ruth asked how things had gone, Dave replied, with complete sincerity, "Fine." Rose was astounded: "What do you mean, 'Fine'? The mast fell down. It could have hurt us or toppled the boat. So much went wrong!" Perplexed, Dave calmly responded, "We went out, we had a problem, we solved it. That's a good day."[20]

The optimism of his daily life did not extend to national politics. There, Johnson was sharply critical of the increasingly conservative Cold War America. In July 1964, when Barry Goldwater won the Republican presidential nomination, Johnson wrote to Frank Boyle, a Runyonesque leftist who ran a newsstand next to the main branch of the New York Public Library before retiring to Florida (his home at the time of this correspondence): "I see our man Buggsy Goldwater made it last night. It makes you proud of America. Where else could a little old immigrant Jewish peddlar spawn a beloved ideological leader of the white Protestant fascist set?" Change the tone slightly, and one might imagine O'Malley explaining the Republican National Convention to a bewildered Barnaby. Johnson went on to compare Goldwater to the ex-Nazi scientist played by Peter Sellers in Stanley Kubrick's *Dr. Strangelove*, released the preceding January, and said that Goldwater's choice of a running mate was important because he will become "president of the United States when Buggsy blows himself up experimenting with small atomic bombs in the cellar of the White House." Although he found most politicians disappointing, Johnson found hope in the new generation of activists.[21]

One evening in the fall of 1964, he phoned Antonio Frasconi and excitedly said, "Come over and see something on TV." The Frasconis found Dave watching television, transfixed by the Free Speech protests at the University of California at Berkeley. In September, chancellor Edward Strong closed a free speech area of campus, where students had been advocating on behalf of various causes, including the civil rights movement. Berkeley's administration then threatened activist students with suspension. Led by Mario Savo, thousands of students organized rallies and occupied university buildings, and more than eight hundred served jail time. By the end of the fall term, the university's board of regents replaced the chancellor, and the students won back their right to free speech. Dave was thrilled.[22]

Krauss's poetry also resonated with a much younger generation of writers and artists, appearing alongside works by Charles Olson and Diane Wakoski in the September and October issues of the poetry journal *Wild Dog* (1963–66), coedited by Black Mountain poet Edward Dorn. The premiere issue of *Nadada* (1964–65) placed Krauss in more avant-garde company. With a frontispiece by Andy Warhol, the journal's inaugural "Contemporary American Poets Issue" opened with Allen Ginsberg's "May 22 Calcutta," followed by Krauss's "Poem" and "Song" and poems by Bill Berkson, Frank O'Hara, Willard Maas, Ted Berrigan, Gerard Malanga, and Charles Bukowski.[23]

Where Krauss's work was becoming increasingly experimental, Johnson's writings were moving toward the existential. In September, he sent Harper *Gordy and the Pirate and the Circus Ringmaster and the Knight and the Major League Manager and the Western Marshal and the Astronaut and a Remarkable Achievement,* a new book of what he described as "slightly sophisticated humor for eight- or ten-year-olds." Young Gordy is on his way home from school when he meets and helps Dead Eye Eddie find buried treasure. However, because he "promised to come straight home from school today," he cannot help dig up the loot. A series of nonadventures follows: Gordy meets someone interesting, has an opportunity for excitement, but remembers his promise and continues home. Carr confessed that though she wanted to like it, she did not: "After a while you know (and I think even 7–8–9 year olds would know) exactly what is going to happen." Further, instead of being "fun or funny," the story was "sort of defeating" and "almost unfair." She suggested that Johnson write one such adventure about Gordy in a book of other Gordy stories, something more along the lines of the Ellen books.[24]

Instead, Johnson began looking for another publisher for Gordy, as he had done for *We Wonder What Will Walter Be? When He Grows Up*, published late that fall by Holt, Rinehart, and Winston. Also focused on choices, the book strongly echoes a cartoon the fourteen-year-old Johnson had drawn in which a boy dreams of possible future careers. In the new book, "Walter wished somebody could decide for him. He was trying to think what to be when he grew up." Clad in gray trousers and a black T-shirt, Walter resembles a young existentialist learning to accept the burdens of his freedom. His dark attire aside, Walter is not somber but thoughtful, marked by that inquisitive spirit that characterizes nearly all of Johnson's protagonists. The "best thinkers in the kingdom"—Antelope, Mole, Flamingo, Giraffe, Elephant, and Turtle—convene to ponder Walter's dilemma. Each one advises Walter to be more like him. In the end, Lion offers Walter the wisest advice: "Whatever you decide, be sure to make your decision bravely, without fear. Think boldly!"

As Dave moved toward his brave decision, Ruth made a bold decision of her own. Though she and Nordstrom had been corresponding for five years about the book of experimental poetry for children, at the end of December, Ruth signed a contract with Pantheon to release the volume. She did not tell Nordstrom.[25]

23

PAINTING, PASSPORTS, AND PROTEST

If only France was in Connecticut
If only England was in Connecticut
If only Connecticut was in Turkey
—RUTH KRAUSS, "If Only," *There's a Little Ambiguity over There among the Bluebells* (1968)

With Ruth recovered from her bout with spinal meningitis, she and Dave decided to travel abroad, applying for new passports in the fall of 1964. She was sixty-three and he was fifty-eight: If they were going to see more of the world, now was the time to do it. Before departing, however, they began speaking out at home against the Vietnam War, which had begun to escalate with the passage of the Gulf of Tonkin Resolution in August. In late December 1964 or early January 1965, Johnson was among the seventy-five national initiating sponsors of the Assembly of Men and Women in the Arts, Concerned with Vietnam. Joining him were old friends Kay Boyle, Antonio Frasconi, and Ad Reinhardt; *New Masses*–era colleagues Maurice Becker and Rockwell Kent; and Ray Bradbury, Lawrence Ferlinghetti, Allen Ginsberg, E. Y. Harburg, and Tillie Olsen.[1]

In February, the U.S. bombing of North Vietnam galvanized the antiwar movement, and Krauss soon added her name to those calling for peace in Vietnam. This was an unusual step for her. She did not usually sign petitions, but she abhorred violence, even in cartoons. Along with four hundred others, Krauss signed a statement that ran in the *New York Times* on 18 April. Titled "End Your Silence" and subtitled "A Protest of Artists and Writers," the full-page ad called for "an immediate turning of the American policy in Vietnam to the methods of peace." In addition to Johnson and many of the others who had already joined the Assembly of Men and Women in the Arts, Concerned with Vietnam, other signatories included Johnson-and-Krauss friends Remy Charlip and Nina and Herman Schneider; poets Donald Hall, Stanley Kunitz, Muriel Rukeyser, and Louis Untermeyer; novelists Joseph Heller and Philip

Roth; artists Hugo Gellert, Roy Lichtenstein, Robert Motherwell, and Mark Rothko; and critics Leslie Fiedler and Susan Sontag.[2]

By the time the ad appeared, Ruth and Dave had embarked for Europe. They traveled by ship to Lisbon, Naples, Athens, and the Greek isles of Rhodes, Delos, Santorini, and Astypalea. Ruth loved the seals on Delos's shore, but the children of Astypalea impressed her most—so much so that she wrote two letters to Ursula Nordstrom describing the "children running down from the hills with flowers all kinds & colors known & unknown & putting them all over me." Even when they did not speak her language, children were drawn to Ruth and she to them.[3]

Dave had never been to Europe before and relished learning everything about each place. After their sea voyage, they moved on to the European mainland, visiting Venice, Lausanne, and Vallorbe before crossing the border into France and arriving in Paris in early June. Dave seemed so at home there that a lost Frenchman came to him for directions in a Paris Metro station. A month later, they were in London, where Dave "poked around on every street north of the Thames from London Bridge to Battersea Bridge as far inland as Oxford and Holborn Streets and the Wall." He was intent on absorbing as much of each new place as he could, walking the streets, looking at the architecture, visiting landmarks. Ruth was less thrilled, writing, "I hate London— noise, dirt, traffic, confusion etc. etc. Dave loves it."[4]

While in London, Dave provided some wry "travel advice" for Harper's Barbara Dicks, who had previously lived there. Knowing that Ruth had visited London before, Barbara asked in a letter "if you find London changed since you were last there." Dave, who had never visited the city before, replied, "Of course there are so many new things for *me* to notice. Right between The Strand and Pall Mall there is a tall monument (in a circle they call Trafalgar Square) to some guy who was the boyfriend of Lady Hamilton, I think. This and a number of other things were not here in the London I knew back in 1765." He was also amused by New England's appropriations of old England's architecture: "Near Waterloo Station I saw (from the train from Folkestone) a church that is an exact replica of a Wren church in Provincetown. It took me a moment to figure out I was looking at the original."[5]

On 2 July, Ruth and Dave boarded the ship for home. Traveling had been exciting but exhausting. As Ruth wrote in "If Only," "If only France was in Connecticut / If only England was in Connecticut / If only Connecticut was in Turkey." Arriving back in Rowayton by mid-July, they found that their cars would not start, the stove would not light, and humidity prevented the windows from shutting properly. Moreover, the change in climate gave Ruth what she called "lying-down pneumonia," though she was soon up and about and returned to her manuscripts, which she kept in the freezer in deference to her long-held fear of house fires.[6]

As she approached her sixty-fourth birthday, Krauss was thriving professionally. In March, nine of her poetry plays had been staged under the title *The Cantilever Rainbow* at Brooklyn's Spencer Memorial Church, along with a play by Lawrence Ferlinghetti. In April, *The Cantilever Rainbow* moved on to Café La MaMa, a hip Lower East Side venue for experimental plays. Krauss's work received strong reviews in the *Village Voice*, and there was talk of presenting the plays at the Guggenheim in the fall. Ten of her plays appeared in the June issue of *Kulchur* (1960–65) an influential magazine that published John Ashbery, Allen Ginsberg, Anne Waldman, and Ted Berrigan. She learned that her poem plays would appear in Michael Benedikt's anthology *Theatre Experiment*, alongside work by Kenneth Koch, e. e. cummings, Gertrude Stein, and Wallace Stevens, company that caused her to exclaim, "Oui! oo-la la!" She was being taken seriously as an Artist.[7]

However, she found bringing her new poetic sensibility into children's books challenging. As she wrote to Berrigan, "I'm trying to trying to transfer into the field of writing for children some of the things I've learned as a 'poet.'" By way of example, she enclosed the text for *Little Boat Lighter Than a Cork*, a planned "poem-picture-book." Before leaving for Europe, she had asked her agent, Marilyn Marlow, to shop *Little Boat* to publishers. Nordstrom was irritated by Krauss's decision to use an agent rather than offering the manuscript first to Harper, but Krauss explained, "I think you would *not* want it. It would probably not sell well." Nordstrom immediately phoned Marlow, only to learn that the book was under review at another publisher. Nordstrom then wrote to Krauss, "Of *course* we would like to see the new Ruth Krauss children's book, you dope, and why do *you* have to decide what we will or will not love?" However, when Nordstrom ultimately saw *Little Boat*, she declined. Though "an exquisite poem," Nordstrom thought it had "more appeal for adults than for children." The book would not be published for another decade.[8]

While in Europe, Krauss finally told Nordstrom about the book of poems that Pantheon would be publishing under the title *The Cantilever Rainbow* (which differs from her play by that name). Nordstrom did her best to be gracious, writing that she was "sure it is going to be beautiful.... I am not jealous, not much anyhow, of Pantheon having you *and* [Antonio] Frasconi," who had done the woodcut illustrations. Published in the fall of 1965, the book grappled more or less successfully with the question of audience. Though Krauss saw the book's poems and poem plays as "not for 'children,'" Pantheon's juvenile division published *The Cantilever Rainbow*, marketing the book to ages eleven and up. Reviewers praised *The Cantilever Rainbow* but worried that it might be too advanced for its intended audience. *Library Journal*'s Lillian Morrison thought the pieces "funny, clever, imaginative in a Dada way, and often quite lovely and lyrical" but believed that the book would appeal to primarily "the brighter and more sophisticated" teenager. *Kirkus* suggested two likely audiences: "youngsters" whose "talented teachers" introduce them to the book, and "college students with a taste for curiosity and the avant garde." In *Book Week*, Richard Howard called Krauss "determinedly original in everything she does" and considered the work "the first book for children in the idiom of the New York School."[9]

Johnson at last found a publisher for his most experimental works when Holt, Rinehart, and Winston accepted *Magic Beach* and *The Emperor's Gifts*. For the former, the publisher accepted the manuscript but not the illustrations. Perhaps feeling that such an abstract story needed more concrete pictures, Holt enlisted Betty Fraser, a young freelance illustrator whose work had appeared in trade and fashion magazines. Her elaborate artwork was quite different from Johnson's spare, minimalist aesthetic, and he did not collaborate with her on the art. Although Johnson discarded most of his manuscripts, he saved his *Magic Beach* dummy, suggesting that he still hoped to publish the original version with his illustrations.[10]

In the spring of 1965, Holt published the book as *Castles in the Sand*. Reviewers were less baffled than the readers at Harper who had twice rejected the manuscript but did wonder what children would make of it. The *New York Times Book Review*'s Barbara Novak O'Doherty admitted that the book was "perhaps a little too oblique for a child" but nonetheless felt that Johnson "lifts the standard in children's literature considerably with this attempt, and I'm all for it." The verdict on the illustrations was mixed. *Kirkus* found some "effective" but others "done in a style that suggests Coloring Book Modern." *Library Journal* thought "Betty Fraser's pictures have the delicacy to match the text" but also believed that "literal-minded small children may be confused by the blend of fantasy and real life without any definite delineation between the two." In the Harold stories, Johnson's style invites readers' imaginations to supply absent details, subtly emphasizing the theme; in *Castles in the Sand*, Fraser's accretion of images crowds the canvas, leaving less room for readers to participate in the creation of meaning.[11]

Also published in 1965, *The Emperor's Gifts* generated similarly mixed reviews. *Kirkus* thought it "catchy and re-tellable," but *Book Week* considered it "third rate" and "a classic example of how not to handle abstract concepts in a storybook for kids." *Library Journal* labeled it "one Crockett Johnson title libraries can do without." The same year, Putnam's published *Gordy and the Pirate*, but it, too, was less than a hit. *Kirkus* found it "genuinely funny," but the *Bulletin for the Center of Children's Books* thought it only "mildly amusing" and lacking "the flair of *Ellen's Lion* or the author's even better-known *Harold* stories."[12]

As 1965 ended, 74 Rowayton Avenue was full of activity. On 26 December, twenty-year-old Nina Rowand Wallace married Brett Taylor, with a reception and a spaghetti dinner held at Ruth and Dave's house. The young couple then left for Greece to found an art school, a bold decision that Dave noted.[13]

Earlier in the month, Krauss's *A Beautiful Day* shared a bill with Gertrude Stein's *Play I Play II Play III* at the Judson Poets' Theater. Directed by Remy Charlip with music by Al Carmines, *A Beautiful Day* collected seven of Ruth's gently surrealist plays. Those in attendance on opening night loved Krauss's work, rising to their feet, cheering, and applauding. Johnson and Krauss saw the second performance, after which the crowd cried out "Bravo! Bravo!" and "wild applause rang from the theatre's rafters," much to Johnson's delight. He turned to Krauss and said, "Isn't this wonderful?" Disappointment on her face, she looked at him. "I'm crushed!," she said. "This audience is not as enthusiastic as the one we had last night!"[14]

Plenty of critical enthusiasm greeted the show. Reviewing what he called "the miracle of 'A Beautiful Day,'" the *Village Voice*'s Michael Smith considered Krauss, Charlip, and Carmines "geniuses." Smith described Krauss's work as "insistently human, grounded in the reality of experience, and despite its lightness it never floats into the looser, more detached regions of fairy tale and fantasy. Its distinct and incisive bite produces the nourishment of astonishment and delight." He saw Krauss's writing as the key to the poem plays' success: "Their content is simple, charming, and often sentimental, but they are saved from sentimentality's traps by two characteristics in the writing. One is its range and specificity of reference, which by bringing together disparate fragments from the most widely separated fields places events in the context of the real wide world. Second is its pure verbal felicity, which occurs mainly in the variations of rhythm and sound patterns and by graceful irregularity keeps the ear and mind alert." Encouraged by the reception to her work, Krauss wrote to Ferlinghetti, enclosing a program for *The Cantilever Rainbow*,

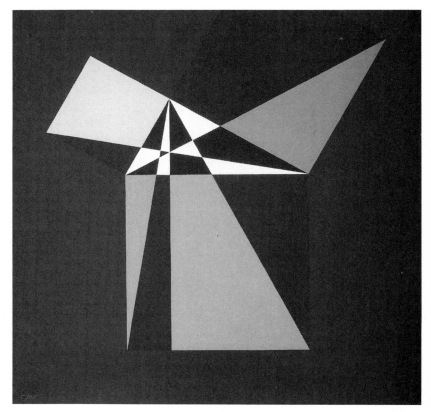

Crockett Johnson, *Proof of the Pythagorean Theorem (Euclid)* (1965). Image courtesy of the Smithsonian Institution. Reprinted with the permission of the Estate of Ruth Krauss, Stewart I. Edelstein, Executor. All Rights Reserved.

presented in March along with one of his plays and some of her other work. He was complimentary about her work but declined to publish it: "You certainly have a wild and beautiful imagination. I would like to see a lot of it on stage. Delightful. On the page, is another matter, however. I really don't see these pieces in print. For our purposes, for use in City Lights Journal or in the Pocket Poets Series for instance, I find the whole a little light."[15]

Ferlinghetti's was a minority view. Most contemporary critics praised Krauss's verse, and culturally important journals and anthologies published her work. However, Ferlinghetti went on to pinpoint the main reason that Krauss's poetry did not acquire a wider audience at the time and is not studied today: "After your big success digging That Hole, I'm afraid you're kind of typed as a 'children's writer' and it certainly is a delightful child's fantasy and wonder at work throughout these pieces." Krauss could not escape her image as a famous and successful writer for children.[16]

In the wake of the disappointing response to his latest books, Johnson turned away from the children's book business. In December 1965, Dave started painting, inspired by mathematical formulae, which had long fascinated him, as evidenced by Atlas's speech in *Barnaby* two decades earlier. Taking the basement as his studio, he began what he called "a series of romantic tributes to the great geometric mathematicians"—Pythagoras, Euclid, Descartes, and others. Intimidated by the idea of painting on canvas, Johnson instead used inexpensive Masonite fiberboard. He started on pieces no larger than two or three square feet in size, and, after gaining some confidence, decided to enlarge one depicting Euclid's proof of the Pythagorean right triangle. He found the new version, four feet square, "a kind of imposing thing, like God or your 5B teacher confronting you."[17]

He enjoyed the work but was not sure whether it was merely a hobby or whether he was following his friends and fellow *New Masses* cartoonists Ad Reinhardt, Abe Ajay, and Adolf Dehn into a career as a serious artist. With a mixture of shyness and eagerness, he began to share his work with some of his friends, starting with Antonio and Leona Frasconi and their sons. Struck by Johnson's excitement in explaining the pictures' geometric properties, nine-year-old Miguel Frasconi thought, "This is an adult, and he's as excited as a little kid." Though the Frasconis did not understand the math, they liked Johnson's colors and thought the paintings quite beautiful. Johnson was relieved and surprised that they had not "blanch[ed] when they look[ed] at" the art and that they seemed "seriously to assume I know what I'm doing." In February 1966, he showed his paintings to Ajay, who "was kind and helpful and polite." But Johnson nonetheless thought it "possible he thinks I have gone senile, or that I have."[18]

Johnson's self-deprecating humor masked a genuine sense of doubt. For reassurance and advice, he wrote to Reinhardt, now an art professor at Brooklyn College and famous for his abstract expressionist paintings in subtly contrasting shades of black. Reinhardt immediately offered to come up to appraise the paintings and asked for more information about the work. Johnson replied that his paintings based on theorems "cannot be something that has not been done before," and "at worst" might be a "slight unifying gimmick for a show": "I wonder if I cannot con a gallery into scheduling a show say next winter after a gander at the masterpieces on hand (which I shall now call preliminary sketches). After all, there is the slight gimmick to peddle and my very famous name in other fields (I am still remembered widely as a fellow did a comic strip about a little boy with wings called Krazy Kat or something)." Johnson continued to downplay his art, describing his geometric abstractions as having "offered me ... a simple-minded chance to put something down with paint without too many cornball shapes bubbling out of my punkin head," but also found his paintings aesthetically pleasing and thought that they would "have an irresistible appeal to people that like coldly intellectual abstractions and warmly emotional realistic art." One March weekend, Reinhardt took the train up to Connecticut and looked at the paintings. Within a few months, he had put his old friend in touch with a New York gallery, and Johnson's first exhibition as a painter was in the works.[19]

Krauss's works continued to thrive on the Off-Off Broadway scene. *Practical Mother's Guide*, a short play that had recently run at the Judson Church, develops the favorite Krauss theme of spring. The doorbell rings, and Child asks, "Mama Mama, is that the bell for springtime?" When Child opens the door, a man arrives with the sun, "all tied up in ribbons and moths." The package has been sent C.O.D. Mother explains that she has "no money," but Child asks if the man can leave it anyway. He does, and Child "does a sun dance." In early March, Caffe Cino ran Krauss's *Newsletters*, a collection of news poems. In June, Charlip's version of *A Beautiful Day* opened at the Judson.[20]

In September 1964, a Delaware school district decided to name its elementary school libraries in honor of authors or illustrators of children's books. On 16 April 1966, Krauss and Johnson visited Greenville's Yorklyn Elementary School, just outside of Wilmington, for a ceremony dedicating the newly christened Ruth Krauss Library. The library housed material related to Krauss's books, including original artwork, manuscripts, and publishers' proofs. Krauss was quite pleased to be "a cornerstone," as she put it, and Johnson, too, was proud, though he joked about the library's location near the heart of the weapons industry: "A bomb shelter was dedicated to Ruth, with her name on the door and everything. They have beaten it into an elegant library, right there in the middle of Munitionsland."[21]

After visiting her cousin, Dick Hahn, and his second wife, Betty, in Baltimore, they returned home. In 1966, Johnson spent considerable time in his damp basement studio, creating two dozen paintings based on diagrams from mathematics books. Norwalk's Burndy Engineering Company had an excellent scientific library, and Johnson took advantage of the vast collection

Crockett Johnson, *Pendulum Momentum (Galileo)* (1966). Image courtesy of the Smithsonian Institution. Reprinted with the permission of the Estate of Ruth Krauss, Stewart I. Edelstein, Executor. All Rights Reserved.

of literature assembled by the corporation's founder, Bern Dibner. Johnson also bought volumes that seemed especially useful, amassing a library of nearly one hundred mathematical books. From a drawing in James R. Newman's four-volume *The World of Mathematics* (1956), Johnson's *Similar Triangles (Thales)* illustrates a theorem by the Greek mathematician Thales (c. 640–546 B.C.), who showed that corresponding sides of similar triangles are proportional. After a diagram in George Garnow's *One Two Three . . . Infinity* (1961), Johnson painted *Relativity in Time and Space (Einstein)*, depicting Albert Einstein's discovery that both time and distance are not absolute but depend on the location of the observer. Another painting inspired by *The World of Mathematics*, *Pendulum Motion (Galileo)* interprets a theorem demonstrating that as Galileo demonstrated, "motion is persistent and continues until arrested by some opposing force." According to mathematics professor J. B. Stroud, Johnson's "painting shows the path of a free-swinging pendulum along with three other paths where the string is snagged [on a nail] as it travels."[22]

In July 1966, Krauss told Nordstrom, "Dave is a full time painter at present." But Johnson was also a student of mathematics, and he did not fully understand the math behind his paintings. *Transcendental Curve (Wallis)*, another 1966 painting, illustrates a principle not of John Wallis but of René Descartes. The diagram appeared in Newman's *The World of Mathematics*, near some sentences about both Wallis and Descartes, and Johnson misla-beled the painting. As he admitted in a 1972 article, he found his math books "stimulating and helpful, though major portions of many of them are beyond me." Undeterred, Johnson kept painting and learning.[23]

Though Johnson was spending most of his creative energy on math and paintings, Krauss persuaded him to illustrate one final children's book. Perhaps recalling Nordstrom's comment a decade earlier that "the Happy Egg" (published in *Somebody Else's Nut Tree*) "could make a tiny little book by it-self," Krauss made a few small revisions and Johnson added pictures. The il-lustrations, spare even by Dave's standards, include just one color—blue, for the egg and its occupant. Published as a Scholastic paperback early in 1967, the book received no reviews until its republication by J. Philip O'Hara in 1972, when *Publishers Weekly* praised its "simplicity of text and pictures" as "a happy publication." In contrast, *School Library Journal* advised libraries to "sit on your order for this one; it's insulting to the reader for its total lack of stimulation, and Crockett Johnson's outline illustrations can't save it."[24]

In 1966, however, fans of Johnson and Krauss's children's books outnum-bered their critics. That year, as Lena Y. de Grummond founded what would become the de Grummond Children's Literature Collection at the University of Southern Mississippi, she wrote to both authors, and Johnson sent her a signed ink drawing from *Harold's Trip to the Sky*, while Krauss sent a copy of the typescript for *Open House for Butterflies*. The National Art Education Association's *Bibliography of Children's Art Literature* listed both *A Picture for Harold's Room* and *A Moon or a Button* among the books that would "stimu-late and enrich the visual imagination of the child." Norman Lear coproduced a new TV pilot for *Barnaby*, starring Sorrell Booke (who would gain fame as Boss Hogg on the *Dukes of Hazzard* in the 1980s) as Mr. O'Malley. No net-work picked it up, but Johnson was too busy painting to mind.[25]

Johnson and Krauss continued to speak out against the war. In January, Krauss was one of nearly twenty-three hundred people who signed the "Teachers Appeal for Peace in Vietnam," a full-page *New York Times* ad de-crying not only the "slaughter of innocents [and] the rapidly mounting death toll on both sides of the conflict in Vietnam" but also the suppression of civil liberties at home. In June, a statement "On Vietnam" covered three *New York Times* pages. The more than sixty-four hundred signatories included not only

This Thumbprint just jumping around to music

Ruth Krauss, illustration from *This Thumbprint* (New York: Harper and Row, 1967). Reprinted with the permission of the Estate of Ruth Krauss, Stewart I. Edelstein, Executor. All Rights Reserved.

Johnson and Krauss but many of their friends and acquaintances, among them Jean Boudin, Kay Boyle, William Gropper, Jules Feiffer, Mary Elting Folsom, Franklin Folsom, Robert Lowell, Lilian Moore, Joseph North, and Ad Reinhardt.[26]

The losses that summer of Frank O'Hara (killed at age forty in a dune buggy accident on Fire Island) and of Fred Schwed (at age sixty-four, six years after being felled by a stroke) confirmed Krauss's decision to pursue her muse where it led. That fall, as Johnson painted and studied math, Krauss continued to experiment artistically, dipping her thumbs in ink to make illustrations for *This Thumbprint*. Recalling the backyard adventures of her childhood, she had "This Thumbprint standing on his hands" and another thumbprint "in the

229

grass Alas!" Mingling ideas from her poetic mind with those from the imaginations of young people, Krauss has a thumbprint who "wants candy before supper and can't have it," and one "just jumping around to music," as well as another who "is a nut." Creating the illustrations, she discovered that black thumbprints with black doodles did not provide enough contrast, and the combination of red and black had the same problem. Following a suggestion from Johnson, she settled on purple thumbprints with black drawings, and the book was published by Harper the following year.[27]

Krauss also did a saucy update of her first self-illustrated book, *The Little King, the Little Queen, the Little Monster, and Other Stories You Can Make Up Yourself*, changing the title to *The Little Woman*. In the new version, after the Good Fairy grants the little girl's wish to be a woman, the little girl becomes pregnant, and subsequent illustrations show her as the mother of quintuplets. The tale reads like a *Mad* magazine parody of the earlier book, with a darker edge to the humor. Krauss identified with the countercultural spirit of the day.[28]

Though she never published *The Little Woman*, Krauss's creative work was finding its way into the counterculture. During the first two weeks of February 1967, some of Krauss's plays were produced during "big Peace demonstrations" in New York. In March, a musical group would perform her "Song of the Melancholy Dress," "singing and playing kazoos & combs and sitars & zithers etc." In May, Angry Arts against the War in Vietnam performed some of Krauss's work in Philadelphia. For his part, Johnson continued to lend his name to the Assembly of Men and Women in the Arts, Concerned with Vietnam. However, his main focus had become painting, and by March 1967, he had created more than forty works and was in the process of choosing thirty paintings for his first solo show. A little over a year after becoming a painter, he was about to make his debut as a serious artist.[29]

24

THEOREMS IN COLOR, POEMS ON STAGE

Modern art . . . non-representational forms. A development that puzzles
the uninitiated.
—MR. O'MALLEY, in Jack Morley and Crockett Johnson, *Barnaby*, 11
    March 1949

On the afternoon of 5 April 1967, Crockett Johnson and Ruth Krauss arrived
at the Glezer Gallery, 271 Fifth Avenue, New York. He wore a dark shirt, with a
lighter tie and jacket. She wore a simple necklace, a light-colored, loose-fitting
dress, stockings, and shoes that were formal but not entirely comfortable. At
5:00, invited guests, mathematicians, and the press began to arrive. A mere
sixteen months after deciding to pursue painting, Johnson was having his first
show, *Abstractions of Abstractions: Schematic Paintings Deriving from Axioms
and Theorems of Geometry, from Pythagoras to Apollonius of Perga, and from
Desargues and Kepler to the Twentieth Century*.[1]

If he was nervous, the photographs do not betray any anxiety. Johnson
grins broadly at the camera, lights a cigarette, talks with the guests: Jackie
Curtis (who took the photos), Jimmy and Dallas Ernst, Shelley and Jackie
Trubowitz, illustrator Bill Hogarth, Courant Institute mathematicians George
Morikawa and Howard Levi, sculptor/children's author-illustrator Harvey
Weiss, and Broadway stage designer Ralph Alswang. If Ad Reinhardt was
there, the photos do not record his presence. Having suffered a heart attack in
January, he may not have been feeling well enough to attend.[2]

Michael Benedikt was also there, representing *Art News*. He thought the
paintings had "a certain cool insouciance" but were also "intensely personal:
Johnson spaces in a lively way, converts theorem-subjects to decorative motifs,
alters colors. . . . The painting is a kind of cool Hard-Edge, but bouncy overall." The *Bridgeport Sunday Post* liked "the fanciful, often lyrical geometric abstractions which flow from Johnson's imagery."[3]

Johnson seemed uncertain about his precise professional identity. Painter?
Scholar of mathematics? Cartoonist? The exhibition program points to all

Ruth Krauss at the Glezer Gallery opening, 5 April 1967. Photo by Jackie Curtis. Used by permission of Jackie Curtis.

three. *Abstractions of Abstractions* is a witty title for a show, but its subtitle sounds like a doctoral dissertation. The back of the program features a quotation from the Museum of Modern Art's director of collections, Alfred Barr, "It's obvious today that comics are art. Just because these things are vulgar doesn't mean they are not art." In this context, the comment alludes to the fact that royalties from children's books and *Barnaby* certainly were underwriting Johnson's new artistic career.[4]

Indicative of his bemused attitude toward his new and uncertain status as painter/math student/cartoonist, when people asked what he did for a living, he would invent a job title for himself. In the late 1960s, Johnson bought a secondhand Mercedes-Benz touring car which often needed repairs. At a party, someone who did not know him would ask, "What do you do for a living?"

Crockett Johnson at Glezer Gallery opening, 5 April 1967. Photo by Jackie Curtis. Used by permission of Jackie Curtis.

Johnson's reply: "I own a Mercedes-Benz." That answer was easier than confessing his aspirations to be taken seriously as a painter.[5]

Krauss knew what she was: a poet and playwright, albeit one who continued to write for children. By the spring of 1967, she had turned in the text and artwork for *This Thumbprint* and had finished *What a Fine Day For . . .* , a collaboration with Remy Charlip (design and pictures) and Al Carmines (music) that is a hybrid of her books for children and her poem plays for adults. Charlip's loopy style and Carmines's bouncy melody sustain Krauss's sense of fun, as the book leads us through the day's many possibilities. "What a fine day for . . . ," it begins, and we turn the page to greet "a mouse and a cat / a ball and a bat." The next page offers "a ball and a throw / a stop and a go." Charlip gives a pair of feet to each letter and each noun, not only the mouse and cat but the ball, bat, glove, and arrows (for stop and go). These feet, queuing horizontally near the bottom of the page, reinforce the impression that they are performing on stage and that readers are the audience.[6]

Krauss had also created a dummy for a new book, *I Write It*, and was hoping to enlist Ezra Jack Keats as illustrator, but he declined. She wondered if Maurice Sendak could do it. He understood her work. He was then heading to England, where, during a BBC-TV interview, he suddenly felt ill and unable to speak. The interviewer ended the conversation and gave Sendak some whiskey. His editor, Judy Taylor of the Bodley Head, suspected something more serious and called an ambulance. A month before his thirty-ninth birthday, Sendak had suffered a heart attack. Thoughts of asking him to illustrate her book left Krauss's mind as she worried about his health. After he returned to the United States, she came to visit him on Fire Island, where he was recuperating. Sendak was touched by her concern, but their reunion was a bit awkward: "She was restrained or constrained when she came here, as though she had to be an old friend and no longer a collaborator—it was an uneasy feeling."[7]

Worried about Sendak's recovery and feeling herself in need of a rest, Ruth and Dave took a mid-May trip to Montauk, at the eastern end of Long Island, where the weather began to impersonate England's: cold, fog, rough seas. By mid-August, they were preparing for a return to England. To avoid another entropic homecoming, they asked Sid Landau and his new wife, Genevieve Millet, editor of *Parents* magazine, to spend weekends at 74 Rowayton Avenue, "patching the leaks, paying the taxes, running out on the dock & yelling at passing boats," as Ruth put it.[8]

Dave and Ruth spent late August and early September on a ship crossing the North Atlantic and traveling up the west coast of Britain. After a long voyage complicated by constant rain and ill health, they reached Edinburgh, Scotland, on 19 September and spent a week there sightseeing and resting. On 25 September, they decided, as Ruth said, "to continue their journeys to the Shetland Islands, home of Big Davie's Pa. Aye." They boarded "a cattle boat" for a "*rough & tough* but great" trip to the Orkneys and Shetlands. When they arrived, Ruth was amazed that the Shetlanders "all looked like Dave" and that "everyone in the Shetlands has Dave's last name (Leisk or Leask). . . . Millions of relatives, in the woolie stores, the fishing boats, the busses, taxis, weavers, *everyone*."[9]

Arriving in London on 5 October, Ruth and Dave visited Mischa Richter's son, Dan, and his wife, Jill. Richter told them about his year working with Stanley Kubrick, choreographing and casting "The Dawn of Man" opening to *2001: A Space Odyssey*, with Richter himself starring as Moonwatcher, the leader of the gorilla tribe who in the scene's final moments tosses the bone into the air. Ruth and Dave were impressed. Richter also showed them his paintings and talked with Ruth about the his underground poetry magazine, *Residu*, which had published her "There's a Little Ambiguity over There among the Bluebells" in 1964. From that day on, she called him "my publisher"—which he found both flattering and amusing. After nearly two weeks in London, Dave and Ruth left for what he called "a rush through Bruges and Brussels (if this is Tuesday this must be Belgium) to Paris." On 2 November, they boarded the *Queen Elizabeth* at Cherbourg, France, and they were home ten days later, happy to have hard beds and American plumbing.[10]

But in late August, while they were gone, their old friend Ad Reinhardt had died after suffering his second heart attack in less than year. It is not clear whether Ruth and Dave learned of his death while in Europe or when they returned three months later, but the news hit them hard. Back in the States, Ruth sent her only copy of *A Good Man and His Good Wife* (her first book, illustrated by Reinhardt) to his widow, Rita, and their thirteen-year-old daughter, Anna.[11]

The fall of 1967 and spring of 1968 brought better news, with strong reviews of *What a Fine Day For . . . . Kirkus* thought that the book of "free-swinging nonsense" was not for "routine circulation" but was nonetheless "a very original device to arouse group participation, with music (and chord indications) for an experienced pianist. Teachers from nursery school up will want to have a try." *Library Journal*, too, believed this "delightful bit of nonsense" had "great possibilities for use in both language arts and music." With this book, Krauss, Charlip, and Carmines had proved that her work for theater could be adapted for children.[12]

After the Glezer Gallery exhibit, Johnson was no longer content only to paint the theorems of others. As J. B. Stroud puts it, Johnson "fell in love with the three infamous unsolved compass and straightedge problems of the classical Greeks: squaring the circle, the 'Delian' problem of duplicating the cube (begin with a unit cube, and then construct a cube with twice its volume), and the trisection of an (arbitrary) angle." Johnson decided that he would solve these puzzles, starting with squaring the circle, a problem that also intrigued and annoyed Lewis Carroll.[13]

"Squaring the circle" means constructing a square with the same area as a circle but doing so with only a straightedge and a compass. It is impossible, but Johnson was either unaware of or undeterred by this fact. He recognized the problem as related to the squaring of a lune (a figure shaped like a crescent moon) and created a trilogy of paintings on the latter theme, each one more sophisticated than the last.[14]

Sixteen paintings related to circle squaring followed. One, *Biblical Squared Circles*, was inspired by a Bible verse, 1 Kings 7:23: "Then he made the molten sea; it was round, ten cubits from brim to brim, and five cubits high, and a line

Crockett Johnson and a version of his *Squared Circle*, ca. 1972. Photo by Jackie Curtis. Used by permission of Jackie Curtis.

of thirty cubits measured its circumference." The resulting artwork is more a reflection of Johnson's fascination in finding this biblical resonance and less a step in the actual problem solving. Johnson was using this phase of his life to read about many subjects that interested him, and one such topic was religion. Having enjoyed Robert Graves's *I, Claudius* (1934) and *The Greek Myths* (1955), he turned to Graves's *King Jesus* (1946) and *The Nazarene Gospel Restored* (1953) and to the Bible itself. Though his friends admired his wide range of knowledge and the seriousness with which he pursued it, they nonetheless were somewhat puzzled by the idea that a former communist was now studying up on Christianity. At the Rowayton post office, Johnson ran into journalist Andy Rooney, who asked, "Where you been?" Johnson answered, "Well, I've been reading the Bible." When Rooney replied, "Oh, I've never known anybody who really read the Bible. How is it?," Dave responded, "Well, there's a lot of good stuff in it." After a pause, he added, "But it's a mess overall." He joked about his reading but continued his research, concluding that Christ probably did not exist but instead was a composite of many different people. Though skeptical of the Bible as history, he found value in its spiritual and philosophical perspective.[15]

236

Krauss's poems continued to keep extremely hip company. *Intransit: The Andy Warhol Gerard Malanga Monster Issue* (1968) published four of her poems as well as work by Lou Reed, John Cale, Nico, Andy Warhol, John Ashbery, the late Frank O'Hara, Allen Ginsberg, Phil Ochs, Charles Henri Ford, John Hollander, James Merrill, May Swenson, and Charles Bukowski. That group includes two members of the Velvet Underground (plus Nico, who appears on the band's first album), the most prominent pop artist of the time (who designed that record's iconic "banana" cover), two New York School poets, the leading Beat poet, a leftist folksinger, a surrealist, and five other important poets, one of whom is Krauss. By the end of the year, Something Else Press had published Krauss's first book expressly for adults, *There's a Little Ambiguity over There among the Bluebells*, a collection of her poems and poem plays. Remy Charlip, Dick Higgins, and George Brecht contributed ideas for staging the title poem's first speech, "What a poet wants is a lake in the middle / of his sentence / (a lake appears)." The caliber of her collaborators indicates the regard in which she was held, and the book's few reviews were positive. *Library Journal* described Krauss's "delicate grammatical structuring" as "transform[ing] even our expectations of poetic reality." *The Nation* praised Krauss as "part carefree surrealist, part sober vaudevillienne, part city pantheist." Far from being "cutesy, kidsy and sudsy," "a Harpo-like insolence informs most of these pieces and sometimes turns downright diabolical."[16]

Krauss's poetic insights develop from her careful listening, experimentation, and unexpected juxtapositions. In his mathematical work, Johnson's insights were largely visual. As he admitted, he was "a desultory and very late scholar" of mathematics. He avoided algebra, he said, "because algebra, or my ineptness with it, tends to make me lose a graphic grasp of a picture." Instead, he explained, "I played with what I knew in advance to be the elements of the problem, imagining them as a construction in motion, an animated film sequence with an infinite number of frames running back and forth between plus and minus limits across the point of solution." Johnson worked out solutions by painting pictures of problems, testing different theories on his canvas.[17]

In 1968, he found a visual solution for the "squared circle" puzzle and wrote an algebraic explanation to accompany it. With the aim of publishing his discovery, he wrote to mathematicians and the scientifically minded, asking for opinions. He began corresponding with Alex Gluckman, an old friend and mathematician who worked for the Atomic Energy Commission in Washington, D.C.; Martin Gardner, author of *Scientific American*'s

"Mathematical Games" column (and of *The Annotated Alice*); and Harley Flanders, a math professor at Purdue University and editor of the *American Mathematical Monthly*. They offered advice, suggesting books and articles he might read. At Gardner's suggestion, Johnson also submitted his squared circle proof to the editor of the *Mathematical Gazette*, Dr. H. Martyn Cundy. In late May 1968, Cundy replied that Johnson had submitted what was "certainly a very close approximation to √π—one of the best I have seen. It is also delightfully simple, and I think we can spare a little space for it." Only a year after deciding that he would not only paint theorems but create them, Johnson was going to become a published scholar of mathematics. His article, "A Geometrical Look at √π," would appear in the journal's January 1970 issue.[18]

In 1968, Johnson sent a print of *Squared Circle* to the Museum of Modern Art, though officials there declined to display his work. Other institutions were more interested, however, and for the first six months of 1970, his paintings were on display at the Museum of Art, Science, and Industry in Bridgeport, Connecticut. Yet he did not call himself an artist; he said he "made diagrams." He continued to work on Masonite rather than on canvas. And instead of mixing the paint himself, Johnson would purchase wall paint in one of the colors available at Brandman's Paints, a local hardware store.[19]

Gene Searchinger asked Johnson, "Are you going to sell these paintings? You know, they must be worth a lot of money. I mean, look at that one, that must be $10,000." Johnson responded with a scornful look, saying, "$10,000— No!" He thought his paintings were worth a lot more. Johnson explained, "If I sold one, it would give the others value. And if the others had value, then on my death, I would impoverish my heirs." In one sense, he was making a joke: He had no children to pay tax on any inheritance. In another sense, he was using humor to mask his doubts about being an Artist.[20]

While he expressed indifference to selling the paintings, Johnson did consider selling color lithographs of his work. He liked a plan suggested by Los Angeles arts consultant Calvin J. Goodman: Limited-edition high-quality reproductions, sold at between $250 and $350 each, could yield Dave more than $10,000. In 1971, Goodman lined up investors and put his own money into making a few sample lithographs. The financial backers pulled out, however, and the project collapsed.[21]

Johnson and Krauss continued to earn a living through the royalties on the children's books they had published and through the foreign rights for their works. By 1970, his stories were being published in England, Germany, Holland, Italy, and Sweden, while hers were available in Czechoslovakia,

Denmark, England, Finland, Holland, and Switzerland. Their income was sub-stantial enough that 1969 saw them take two trips abroad—a February vaca-tion to South America, and another summer cruise to Europe that included stops in Galway and Cobh, Ireland; Rotterdam, Holland; Oslo, Norway; and finally Scotland.[22]

In between the two foreign jaunts, Krauss's back problems recurred, keep-ing her in bed for nearly a month. As she recovered, she was finishing the il-lustrations for *The Running Jumping Shouting ABC* and "thoroughly enjoying the drawing." Her first poetry chapbook, *If Only*, also appeared during this time, and her work was gaining a wider audience through its inclusion in Ann Waldman's *The World Anthology: Poems from the St. Mark's Poetry Project*. It featured an excerpt from her *Re-Examination of Freedom* along with poems by Ted Berrigan, Joe Brainard, Jim Carroll, Andrei Codrescu, Allen Ginsberg, Gerard Malanga, and collaborations between Frank O'Hara and Bill Berkson and between John Ashbery and James Schuyler.[23]

After Krauss and Johnson returned from Europe, Ashbery came to visit them in Rowayton. Though familiar with each other's work, they had never met. When she told Ashbery that *If Only* had drawn some inspiration from his work, he suggested "Faust" from his *The Tennis Court Oath* (1962), which begins: "If only the phantom would stop reappearing!" He offered to send her the poem if she lacked a copy.[24]

On 12 December, *If Only . . . : A Ruth Kraus Gala!* had its sole performance at the Town Hall in nearby Westport, Connecticut. Sponsored by the recently incorporated Weston-Westport Arts Council, the gala presented "theater po-ems," "stories," "ambiguities," and "scenes," according to the flyer, which was designed and illustrated by Krauss. The central image, a smiling girl wearing boots and a loose dress and carrying a star above her head, is a "self-portrait by Ruth Krauss: the artist as a young nut."[25]

Suggesting her affinity for this image, she used it as the title page illustra-tion her 1970 poetry chapbook, *Under Twenty*, which also included her self-portraits as a flower and as a young star. Making its first appearance in a Ruth Krauss book was a poem that she wrote and O'Hara arranged. One of seven pieces titled "Poem," it contains the word *lost* twenty-one times. Playing on the word's sense of absence ("lost lost / where are you") and presence ("lost / in my eyes"), this "Poem" conveys an ambivalent mixture of both lack and long-ing. The only work in the collection that had not previously appeared in print, "Tabu," offered a lyrical exploration of what we "never name" but can "write what it looks like feels like seems / like resembles."

Ruth Krauss, "Self-Portrait by Ruth Krauss: The Artist as a Young Nut," 1969. Image courtesy of the Northeast Children's Literature Collection, Dodd Research Center, University of Connecticut, Storrs. Reprinted with the permission of the Estate of Ruth Krauss, Stewart I. Edelstein, Executor. All Rights Reserved.

In early 1970, concerned that *There's a Little Ambiguity over There among the Bluebells* was not selling, Krauss wrote to Dick Higgins, Something Else Press's founder and publisher. Echoing Ferlinghetti's assessment five years earlier, Higgins explained that Krauss's fame as a children's author presented booksellers with a problem of taxonomy: "You're too well known—but for something else. Stores put the book in the juveniles section and wonder why it doesn't go from there. Or if they put it in the poetry section, the poetry buffs don't know well enough who Ruth Krauss is, so they never pull it down to give it a whirl. And they never put it in the drama section, because the plays don't look like plays and it just doesn't occur to the clerks to do so." To get the work to sell, Krauss needed to become more identified with her poetry and plays than with her children's books. While the Judson's presentation of *A Beautiful Day* had been fantastic, it was also "about four or five years ago," and "there have only been a few isolated things since." She needed "a big Off-Broadway GRAND! RETROSPECTIVE!! EVENING!!! OF!!!! RUTH!!!!! KRAUSS!!!!!! Complete with all the frills and trimmings. (Well, On-Broadway would be okay too, but harder to arrange.) Not a one night stand, but a regular production. Probably in repertoire by La Mama, but better, simply a straight commercial production. Ideally, directed by Remy. If you want my advice—and maybe you don't though I hope you do—I really think you should concentrate as much of your energies as possible toward this goal. If you do that, then I think the book will take off."[26] But Krauss was pursuing art for its own sake and was not interested in marketing her new identity as avant-garde poet.

Johnson and Krauss remained concerned about the Vietnam War and were regulars at Westport's World Affairs Center, a bookstore and organization that advocated peace and human rights. She participated regularly in the center's peace vigil, held each Saturday morning in front of Westport's Town Hall. Johnson also opposed the war but voiced his opposition through petitions and the ballot box, giving him more time to work on mathematics and painting. Having settled the matter of the squared circle, Johnson moved on to tackle duplicating the cube, the second ancient mathematical problem that had fascinated him. He created six paintings on this theme, including two based on Isaac Newton's construction and two based on his own original solution.[27]

In April 1970, Ruth and Dave took off for a brief holiday, returning to Montauk, at the eastern tip of Long Island, where they had vacationed three years earlier. Ruth thought that either Montauk or the Berkshires would be a great place to have a summer house. Dave was tiring of painting in their

241

Rowayton basement, and both he and Ruth disliked the increased noise that summer brought to their Connecticut home, where "the vicious cutout car and choked-up motorbike noise is so bad we have to flee." For the summer of 1970, they fled to Stockbridge, Massachusetts, where they rented a wing of Erik Erikson's house on Main Street. Ruth had her leg in a cast after dropping an iron on her bare foot, and the injury was driving her "nuts": "Never again! No more ironing," she vowed. But the cast was coming off soon, and she was trying to write a show that Boston University's drama department had asked her to develop for the spring of 1971. She was also sending book ideas to Harper, including a small poetry collection and a picture book based on a poem. Ursula Nordstrom was increasingly focused on her administrative duties, and Krauss was working more closely with editor Barbara Borack, who encouraged her to send in the poems. Johnson painted and corresponded with mathematicians from his Stockbridge studio but spent most of his time painting, at least until late August, when he "jumped into a lake off an unsmooth rock" and "shattered the most expensive and slowest-healing bone in the body, fifth metatarsal," landing in the hospital for a week. Ruth enjoyed the "culture-minded" community and was delighted by the many "cultural goings-on"—"theatre, symphony, dance festival, Boston University's drama school, etc." Both she and Dave wondered whether Stockbridge might be a better place for them to live.[28]

After they returned to Rowayton in mid-September, Krauss sent more poetry to Harper in hopes of interesting her editors in a new book. She had reason to be optimistic. Her latest children's book, *I Write It*, had received many notices, nearly all of them laudatory. The *Saturday Review* thought that the "poetic text bubbles along" and liked Mary Chalmers's "endearing small figures," which "romp[ed] through the pages of a book that celebrates the joy of being able to write." The *Christian Science Monitor* praised it as an "unpunctuated little enchantment . . . illustrated in truth and childhood." The reviews were a relief for Krauss. For nearly thirty years, she had wanted to address racism in her children's books. Where *I Want to Paint My Bathroom Blue* argued for integration only through metaphor, *I Write It* did so directly. She had initially worried that its illustrations of a multiracial group of children were not sufficiently sensitive to race. In light of the 1968 assassinations of Martin Luther King Jr. and Robert F. Kennedy, she had a strong "desire, at this point in our country's 'race' & ethnic problems, not to offend anyone." It would be her last book for Harper.[29]

As 1970 drew to a close, Ruth and Dave's injuries had made them painfully aware that life is short and that health can be tenuous. Three and a half months after Dave's accident, he was only just beginning to walk normally again. In July, she would turn seventy, while he would be sixty-five in October. It was time for a few changes.[30]

25

"YOU'RE ONLY AS OLD AS OTHER PEOPLE THINK YOU ARE"

"Tell me what you were like then. And all the exciting things that happened to you."

"Well," said the lion, trying to think back. "I was in better shape than I am now. My stuffing was firmer. I hadn't begun to come apart at the seams—"

—CROCKETT JOHNSON, *The Lion's Own Story* (1963)

Slim, petite, and lively, Ruth Krauss appeared to be about ten years younger than she was. Since the year of her birth contradicted her appearance, she decided to do something about it. Through 1971, reference works list her birth year as 1901, if they list it at all. From 1973 on, the books list her birth year as 1911. When she turned seventy, she became more acutely aware that people would see her as old. She felt young. So she changed her birth year. As she would later tell a female friend, "You're only as old as other people think you are, so always lie about your age—and preferably in increments of ten, because it's easier to keep track of it." Not only did Krauss's lies enter the official record, but when she died two decades later, friends were shocked to learn that she was in her nineties. They had thought her a much younger woman—at least a decade younger.[1]

In addition to changing her age, Ruth and Dave were considering changing their address. Rowayton was much busier than when they moved there a quarter century earlier. Increased traffic on Rowayton Avenue made their life noisier. As young New York executives and their families moved in, the village became more like a New York suburb. Dave observed, "It was a nice neighborhood here until the young fogies moved in and spoiled it." The river, he said, had become "so crowded now that there isn't even enough room to go sailing." Further, since the river was right across the street from their house, the basement tended to flood, requiring Johnson to wear rubber boots while he painted, often while standing in water up to his ankles. It was time to move.

As they pondered where to make their new home, Ruth and Dave decided to spend a few weeks in Montauk and made preparations for another trip—a cruise through the Arctic Circle. As she put it, "being just barely recovered from last year's broken-bone syndrome, [w]e are entitled (I think) to a crazy-type rest. (A plain rest—no.)"[2]

Johnson also enjoyed a rest from his painting and other projects, like the animated adaptation of *A Picture for Harold's Room*. Working at his Prague studio, Gene Deitch had been sending Johnson ideas. In an initial attempt, Deitch included "cinematic close-ups, camera move-ins, and cuts." Johnson called it "the worst storyboard" he'd ever seen. Communicating solely by what he called "penny postcards" (a sly comment on the fact that a postcard had risen to six cents), he helped Deitch understand that for the film to work, Harold must be "exactly the same size in relation to the film frame" and that "the entire film must appear to be one continuous scene." Ultimately, Deitch and his assistants created Harold's entire drawing and then shot the film by placing seventy-five hundred different drawings of Harold (one at a time, in reverse order) over this landscape and having him undraw the scenery, erasing the entire picture one tiny increment at a time. Only when the film was projected forward did the picture reappear. It was, Deitch said, "just about the most difficult film we ever made here, and exactly *because* it looks so simple!" With "no cuts, no zooms, and no backgrounds, . . . nothing can be hidden. It must be smooth and perfect."[3]

Eager that the book *A Picture for Harold's Room* be in print when Weston Woods released the film in 1971, Johnson began asking Harper about the status of his books, an endeavor that led to a series of skirmishes with the publisher. When the Rowayton School's fall 1970 book fair could not get any books by him or Krauss, he wrote to Ursula Nordstrom, suggesting that since Harper made most of its money through trade sales, book fairs must be "an unwieldy nuisance." He added, "I am probably romantic about books . . . , and industry and commerce cannot afford to be." Nordstrom found Johnson's letter "nasty" and resented his implication that people in publishing were "grasping and greedy"; she blamed the book fair problem on the "stupid Rowayton school people" and had Harper staff resolve the matter. Johnson apologized, but his relationship with the publisher remained difficult.[4]

Leaving the publishing world behind on 16 July, Ruth and Dave embarked on a six-week cruise that took them to twenty cities, including Reykjavik, Oslo, Stockholm, Helsinki, and Leningrad. Showing that he bore no hard feelings after their disagreements, he sent Nordstrom a postcard depicting a wintry Russian scene, writing, "No, it's 70 and sunny in Leningrad, same weather that has been following us from Iceland to the top of Norway and down into the Baltic. We will bring it home with us August 30." He had long since rejected the Soviets' totalitarian Marxism, even if a society based on international socialism still appealed to him. From Leningrad, he and Ruth sailed on to Copenhagen; Edinburgh; Scarborough, England; Rotterdam; Zeebrugge, Belgium; and Glengarriff, Ireland.[5]

Upon their return, Krauss resumed writing poetry and Johnson returned to squaring the circle, striving to craft a more elegant formula than his original. Two of the three paintings that can definitively be dated to 1972 display his thinking on the problem. He also turned his attentions to another problem posed by the ancient Greeks. Using Euclidean methods, the Greeks had been easily able to bisect angles and construct regular polygons containing multiples of those sides—the triangle led to figures of six, twelve, twenty-four, and so on sides, while the square led to figures of eight, sixteen, thirty-two, and so forth sides. But the Greeks were unable to construct regular polygons with certain numbers of sides, including seven, nine, eleven, and thirteen. Johnson wanted to use Euclidean geometry to create a regular heptagon.[6]

Johnson's mathematical correspondents had expanded to include Vince Crockett Harris, a math professor at San Diego State College, and Howard Levi, a math professor at the City College of New York. They helped Johnson express his proofs, correcting his formulae or working out their own proofs. Levi came to visit Johnson in Rowayton several times and thought that his "geometrical discoveries" were "all unconventional, and in many cases seem to have considerable substance."[7]

In the summer of 1972, Dave and Ruth left Rowayton behind, buying a house at 24 Owenoke Park in Westport, seven miles up the coast. Though it also overlooked Long Island Sound, the new house had space for an above-ground studio, where Dave could paint undisturbed by noise or water. After twenty-seven years, they were, in Ruth's words, "upheaving from the Old Rowayton Poetry Sweatshop & Geometry Grounds to the New Owenoke Peninsula Poetry, Geometry and Coffee Grounds—in among the swamp birds, politely called 'marsh birds.'" By August, Dave and Ruth had moved into their new home.[8]

They unpacked boxes, trying to locate books and manuscripts and recovering from their moving injuries. As Ruth said, "I've strained my something or other and Dave strained his something also." Strained or not, she was working on illustrations and, with the help of her friend Valerie Harms, selecting poems for *This Breast Gothic*, a collection to be published the following year by the Bookstore Press, a small outfit based in Lenox, Massachusetts, and run by poet Gerald Hausman; his wife, Lorry; and David Silverstein, all of whom Krauss had befriended during her summer in Stockbridge.[9]

Thinking that their conversation would make an interesting interview, Harms brought a tape recorder. Krauss explained that she wanted poems that have "the same feeling" as "This Breast" and discussed the order in which the selections should appear. Krauss also offered interpretations of some of her work, such as "Silence," a poem consisting of fourteen lines of four underscored blank spaces. Citing John Cage's *Silence* as an inspiration, Krauss described her poem as a "sonnet" that "you can fill . . . in yourself": "You can read anything into it you want." Given the themes of some poems in the collection, Krauss suggested that the blank four-letter words might be "sex in situations.

I mean, f-u-c-k, f-u-c-k, f-u-c-k. Or it can mean l-o-v-e, l-o-v-e, l-o-v-e. Or it can mean s-h-i-t, s-h-i-t, whatever."[10]

Krauss had mostly stopped writing poetry. Without classroom assignments to prompt her, she listened to her doubts and was afraid to write something inferior. In an undated statement on poetics, she revealed that Kenneth Koch's emphasis on freshness had stuck with her yet seemed to be an impediment: "At the height of my enthusiasm and freshness in poetry, I had no techniques or judgment—now I have a little techniques whatever that means and a little judgment, and I've lost my freshness—for the moment anyway." She simultaneously questioned the idea that "good poetry should necessarily be astonishing and surprising all the time. The astonishment of one year is not that of another." If that statement predicts her verse's fall from critical favor, it also invites a reappraisal of Krauss's poetry—its disregard for generic boundaries, its exuberant experimentation, and its curious blend of progressive education, children's literature, and the twentieth-century avant-garde.[11]

In the early 1970s, however, Krauss remained a critical favorite. Albert Poland and Bruce Mailman's *The Off Off Broadway Book: The Plays, People, Theatre* (1972) featured her work along with that of Amiri Baraka, John Guare, A. R. Gurney Jr., Terrence McNally, David Rabe, Sam Shepard, and Lanford Wilson. In late March 1973, Joseph Gifford offered *There's a Little Ambiguity over There among the Bluebells*, an ambitious staging of her poetry at Boston University Theatre. The show was a multimedia experience. Accompanying the actors' performance of Krauss's poems, six large screens displayed projections of "a myriad of eclectic images from Picasso to Playboy," as the *Boston Phoenix*'s Carolyn Clay noted. Clay declared that the show had "definite commercial possibilities" and constituted "a fascinating if frightening realm— one in which an effusive, slightly idiotic Bill Shakespeare can take a friendly tumble with a sluggish Winnie the Pooh, where Molly Bloom can reject Apollinaire for an NYU poetry student, where grotesquerie and naturalism are so adroitly fused that the boundaries cease to be evident." The *Boston Globe*'s William A. Henry 3rd also praised the performance's blurring of boundaries: "The collage of poetry, movement, hard-edged but lyrical music, bright, coordinated costumes . . . is a giddy delight. . . . Whimsy predominates on the surface of *Bluebells*. But . . . the playing of the poems suggests that the distortion of reality is frightening as well as funny."[12]

In her illustrations for *This Breast Gothic*, Krauss strove more for funny than for scary. For the poetry chapbook's cover image, she drew a portrait of a woman whose torso was made up entirely of breasts, with two stick legs sticking out below and with a head and waving arms on the top. Wild, explicit, and vibrant against its pink background, the image certainly shifts the possible meanings for the title poem, encouraging a reappraisal of lines like "This breast boom-boom yippee slurp strawberries cabañas / This breast as we go whizzing along," and "This breast we have a fine view of everything that happens." The poem suddenly seems an exuberant celebration of a woman's power: from her breast comes life, food, art, literature, cities, history, news—everything.

While Krauss pursued art for its own sake, *This Breast Gothic*'s cover and title poem display her feminism. Krauss was a regular at events sponsored by Connecticut Feminists in the Arts, a group that sought to empower women to see "that we could create our own lives, that our lives could be more than our mothers' lives." That idea very much appealed to Krauss.[13]

Bookstore Press editor Gerald Hausman wanted to write a book called *Hooray for Everyday: Conversations with Ruth Krauss* and so spent a few hot, humid days, probably early in the summer of 1973, visiting her and Johnson in Westport. Outside, Krauss, dressed in a blue-and-white Japanese robe, lay on the sun deck, flat on her back, "her silvery shoulder-length hair let down," her head propped up on two thick hardcover books, with handwritten pages "full of poems and scribbles" nearby. Inside the window-filled studio over the garage, Johnson spent the entire day painting, moving "gracefully, slowly, effortlessly . . . perfecting a geometric angle in blue or gray, demonstrating a theory that has been left untouched since the time of Archimedes." In the evening, Johnson emerged wearing khaki shorts and no shirt and bearing "a small tankard of vodka and tomato juice" for his Bloody Mary. Out at dinner (Johnson now wearing a shirt), and Krauss's "joyous" laughter attracted looks and smiles from tables away. The next morning, she and Hausman went out for breakfast at Franny's, where she ate "spoonfuls of grape jelly, no toast, just good old gooey globs of grape." Not having seen anyone do that since he was a summer camp counselor, Hausman thought, "Her white hair is the white hair of a child," he writes.[14]

Krauss's interest in the poetic imagination led her to a poetry discussion group founded in the early 1970s by Cynthia Luden. Every other Monday afternoon, participants read poetry ranging from Homer and *Beowulf* to contemporary poets such as Lucille Clifton. Krauss was the oldest member of a group that included photographer Barbara Lans; children's author Freya Littledale; poets Janet Krauss and Ruth Good; and aspiring poets Peggy Heinrich and Peter Felsenstal. Enjoying the company of fellow lovers of

Ruth Krauss, cover for *This Breast Gothic* (Lenox, Mass.: Bookstore, 1973). Reprinted with the permission of the Estate of Ruth Krauss, Stewart I. Edelstein, Executor. All Rights Reserved.

poetry, Krauss would arrive, take off her shoes and socks, and join in the conversation until she fell asleep. The group nicknamed her the dormouse after the sleepy Mad Tea Party guest in *Alice's Adventures in Wonderland*.[15]

Inspired by her conversations with Gerry Hausman, Krauss conducted some 1972 and 1973 poetry-writing workshops modeled loosely on Kenneth Koch's classes. She did one in the Westport area and another in Lenox, Massachusetts, but turned down requests to do more in "too hard to get to places—Northern Pa—etc." Participants would write a standard poetic form (such as a sestina) but "take end-words from some science (book or article)." Or they would "do a dialogue-poem using 2 incongruous characters," possibly from literary sources. Writers could "'team-up' a human-made thing with a 'natural' one," as in Krauss's line, "sad as a shoe and no foot." She wrote more than two dozen such prompts, all designed to ignite her students' creativity.[16]

Early in the summer of 1973, Johnson met one of his creative partners when Gene and Zdenka Deitch visited Westport, admiring the new Johnson-Krauss home and Johnson's paintings. Gene Deitch was then working on an animated adaptation of *Harold's Fairy Tale*, also for Weston Woods. Johnson had been pleased with Deitch's film of *A Picture for Harold's Room* and responded warmly to the idea of more animated Harold films and even an animated *Barnaby*. An earlier *Barnaby* cartoon had won first prize at the 1967 Venice Film Festival, but Johnson thought it "much inferior" to Deitch's work and was excited at the prospect of an adaptation that might live up to his exacting standards.[17]

For her part, Krauss was toying with the idea of a poetry collection that explored sexuality. In early August 1973, she sent her friends at the Bookstore Press a "rough of what the end-papers for [a] proposed sex-maniac book might look like." At different angles, she juxtaposes lines of verse, including "This breast plumbers here ask five-hour day / This breast expelled from the universities for crazy" and "I / I take / I take off / I take off my clothes" and "summer is gone / the leaves are gone / and I am gone (torrents of gone) / on you." She called the proposed book "my famous porm? collection," combining the words *porn* and *poem*. The book was never published.[18]

At the end of the month, Ruth and Dave embarked from New York on another cruise—this one to the western Mediterranean, with stops in the Azores, Lisbon, Cadiz, Tangier, Ibiza, and Syracuse, on the island of Sicily, the home of Archimedes. One afternoon there, as Dave and Ruth sat in an outdoor cafe waiting for their lunch, he began thinking about the regular heptagon problem. On the table in front of him were a menu, a wine list, and a container of toothpicks. Turning his menu and wine list so that they formed the two equal sides of an isosceles triangle, he placed the toothpicks in a criss-cross pattern across the space in between these two sides. He then hypothesized that the angle where the menu and wine list intersected would be $\pi/7$ degrees. His supposition was correct. As J. B. Stroud has shown, this discovery permitted Johnson to "construct a regular seven-sided figure using a compass and straightedge with only one mark on it." According to Stroud, "The details of how he did it are high school mathematics, but it's not trivial. It's darn clever."[19]

Ruth and Dave continued on to Naples, Cannes, Monte Carlo, Barcelona, and Majorca, where Ruth grew overwhelmed by the pace of their travels. Still they sailed on, stopping in Alicante, Gibraltar, and Casablanca before finally returning to New York on 5 October. They arrived home exhausted and sick with colds, and Ruth soon developed laryngitis.[20]

As they recovered, Johnson began to write up the equation he had devised in Sicily, while Krauss resumed work on both *Little Boat Lighter Than a Cork* and the poetry collection that would become *Under Thirteen*. For both projects, she would work with smaller presses. In August 1973, Nordstrom stepped down as director of Harper's Department of Books for Boys and Girls, and although Krauss had a Harper contract for *Running Jumping ABC*, delays in finding the right illustrator postponed the project. In late 1973, Scholastic published her first children's book in three years, *Everything under a Mushroom*, which garnered mostly praise. In the *New York Times Book Review*, poet Karla Kuskin did not think that Krauss "succeeds here very well" but nonetheless considered her "a step ahead of many who write for children." *Publishers Weekly*, however, praised the "inspired nonsense" in the book's "series of glimpses of little ones at play. . . . It all adds up to enchantment." Similarly, the *Christian Science Monitor* said the "glorious" book "sends us down below to a world of whimsy."[21]

Johnson spent March and April 1974 mired in, as he put it, "an endless round of flu and colds and sinus treatments with anti-biotics worse than the ailment." But he and Ruth were cheered by both the beginning of the House Judiciary Committee's impeachment hearings against President Richard Nixon and the news that Deitch's studios had finished what Johnson thought was a "beautiful" animated version of *Harold's Fairy Tale*. Johnson was irritated, however, when he learned that the book had gone out of print, squandering the opportunity to sell copies in conjunction with the film's release. Further inquiries revealed that although the book had gone out of print the previous year, Harpers had sold reprint rights to *Reader's Digest*, and

Crockett Johnson with *Heptagon from Its Seven Sides*, ca. 1972. Photo by Jackie Curtis. Used by permission of Jackie Curtis.

paperbacks would be out soon. Grumbling that publishers should keep authors informed about the status of their books, Johnson returned to painting and mathematics.[22]

As he worked on his construction for a regular heptagon, Johnson had been corresponding with the *Mathematical Gazette* and with scholars such as Harley Flanders, Howard Levi, and Stanley Smith, who were checking Johnson's work and helping him refine his formula. In June 1974, the editor of the *Mathematical Gazette*, Douglas A. Quadling, wrote to Johnson, "This construction is certainly new to me, and would I am sure be of interest to Gazette readers. I'm glad that your perseverance has borne fruit." Another mathematical triumph: His second original formula would be published.[23]

In the fall of 1974, Dave and Ruth returned to England, where the highlight of their trip was a visit with Smith and his wife, Gladys, in East Sussex. Too much of the rest of their time was spent in or near their hotel: Dave "couldn't walk far because of a pulled calf muscle and . . . the worst weather in history swept the Channel coast."[24]

In early February 1975, Dave went to the doctor. Perhaps his ailing leg prompted the visit. Or maybe that persistent cough had returned, and he was feeling short of breath. Five decades of smoking had caught up with him. He had lung cancer.

26

WHAT WOULD HAROLD DO?

Up and up, he went, into the dark.
—CROCKETT JOHNSON, *Harold's Trip to the Sky* (1957)

The news of Dave's cancer threw Ruth into a state of collapse. For thirty-five years, he had been the one person on whom she had allowed herself to depend. Life without him was inconceivable.[1]

At the end of the first week of February, Dave checked in to Norwalk Hospital. He learned that although the doctors there could not do much for him, there was some chance that more skilled surgeons elsewhere might be able to remove the cancerous parts of his lungs. Buoyed by this possibility, he managed to keep a sense of humor. When neighbor Doris Lund saw him just after the diagnosis, she asked, "How are you doing, Dave?" He replied, "They're all rushing around, looking for the fastest switchblade in the West."[2]

Gene Searchinger arranged for Dave to be seen at New York's Sloan-Kettering Cancer Center, and Dave and Ruth traveled there at the beginning of the second week of February. So that she would not have to commute from Westport, she stayed with their old friends, Nina and Herman Schneider. In early March, Dave had an operation to remove part of his lungs, and by 17 March, Ruth reported that he was "rapidly improving," "pacing around (when not asleep)," and doing "whatever one does in hospitals while waiting (to get out)." Encouraged by his progress, Ruth wrote, "we hope to be home soon."[3]

The operation's ameliorative effects were temporary, however. After Dave recovered sufficiently from the surgery, the doctors ran some more tests, which showed that the cancer had already spread. Further operations would be both dangerously invasive and unlikely to succeed. Out of options, Sloan-Kettering sent Dave back to Westport. At home, Dave received many visitors. Ruth's cousin, Dick Hahn, and his wife, Betty, drove up from Baltimore every weekend. Frank O'Hara's sister, Maureen; Jackie Curtis; Shelley Trubowitz; Doris and Shelley Orgel; Stefan and Marion Schnabel; and other friends visited him regularly. As the cancer made him cough and shortened his breath,

...before it TALKS

... is the way our doctors put it—"Our chances of curing cancer are so much better when we have an opportunity to detect it *before it talks.*"

That's why we keep urging you to make a habit of having periodic health check-ups, no matter how well you may *feel* ... check-ups that *always* include a thorough examination of the skin, mouth, lungs and rectum and, if you are a woman, the breasts and generative tract. Very often doctors can detect cancer in these areas long before the patient has noticed any symptoms in himself.

The point to remember is that most cancers are curable if properly treated before they begin to spread, or "colonize" in other parts of the body... For other life-saving facts about cancer, phone the American Cancer Society office nearest you or write to "Cancer"—in care of your local Post Office.

American Cancer Society

Crockett Johnson, advertisement for the American Cancer Society, 1958. Reprinted with the permission of the Estate of Ruth Krauss, Stewart I. Edelstein, Executor. All Rights Reserved.

Dave had to slow down. He knew what was happening, and when he felt frustrated, he would say, "Oh, balls!"[4]

By June, Dave was no longer able to live at home and was back at Norwalk Hospital. He remained hopeful, trying to eat to keep up his strength. He showed Jackie Curtis and her daughter, Karen, his new theorem, "A Construction for a Regular Heptagon," just published in the *Mathematical Gazette*, and received the news that his painting *Heptagon from Its Seven Sides*—the artistic realization of that theorem—would be exhibited in the Smithsonian Institution's Hall of Mathematics. He wanted to pursue other theorems and had plans to build more furniture. His once large body was wasting away, but his mind remained alert and active. Nevertheless, it was a daily struggle. "Oh, balls!" Talking to Searchinger on the phone from his hospital bed, Dave said, "I want to get out of here, one way or another."[5]

By early July, the end was near. One evening, Gil Rose and Andy Rooney came to visit. They found Dave scared, in pain, and slipping in and out of consciousness. To help Dave deal with his anxiety and fear, Rose asked, "Well, what would Harold do?" Dave grew interested in looking at his illness from Harold's perspective, and as he thought about what Harold would do, he calmed down.[6]

On Thursday, 10 July, Dick and Betty Hahn arrived for the weekend a little earlier than usual. As they were leaving the hospital, Dave said, "Oh, balls!" Later that day, he fell into a coma. For most of the next day, the Hahns and Ruth stayed at Dave's bedside. He was alive but unconscious. As evening approached, they left to get dinner and then returned to 24 Owenoke for the night. Exhausted, the three of them were lying on a bed and talking when the phone rang. Ruth was in no state to answer. Dick Hahn picked up the receiver. After a moment, he turned to Ruth and said, "Ruth, it's over. And Dave is gone." She began to sob softly. Dick and Betty tried to console her, talking with her until she fell asleep around midnight.[7]

In its obituary, the *New York Times* described him as a cartoonist and creator of *Barnaby*, mentioning his authorship of "more than a dozen children's books, including *Harold and the Purple Crayon* and *Harold's Fairy Tale*," only in the penultimate paragraph. In addition to a photo of Johnson, the *Times* ran a drawing of Barnaby and Mr. O'Malley. The little boy and his fairy godfather would be Crockett Johnson's artistic and intellectual legacy.[8]

Johnson's ashes were scattered in Long Island Sound, laying him to rest in the waters through which he had so often sailed.[9]

27

LIFE AFTER DAVE

"I wonder if there was time," said Ann.
"Time for what?" said Ben.
"For a happy ending," said Ann.
"The tide came in too soon," said Ben.
—CROCKETT JOHNSON, *Magic Beach* (1959)

Ruth never got over the loss of Dave. After the mute shock of bereavement, she struggled to cope, seeking a way forward. Immediately after his death, she knew she could not bear to stay in the house alone. So, Dick and Betty Hahn took her back to Baltimore to stay with them. A few weeks later, they brought her along on a planned holiday to Maine. Feeling a little better, Ruth decided to apply for a fellowship at the MacDowell Colony in Peterborough, New Hampshire. There, she would be able to work among fellow artists, away from the memories evoked by Westport.[1]

In October 1975, when the MacDowell Colony contacted Ursula Nordstrom for a reference, she must have paused for a moment before responding. Over the years, she and Krauss had had a full measure of dramatic conflicts. Three months earlier, Nordstrom had struggled with her note of condolence about Johnson's death: Though it "came from the heart," she thought it likely "the worst 'sympathy' note ever written" because she "adored Dave, . . . and didn't see how he ever stayed married to dear Ruth who used to be able to drive me up the wall." Yet when MacDowell inquired whether Krauss had "any personality problems of which you may know," Nordstrom said, "I have always found her a delightful person." Asked for a "frank assessment" of Krauss's abilities, Nordstrom said that Ruth "brings to all her work the most important qualities—regard for the child's individuality, imagination, depth of feeling, sensitivity. She is an artist in the true sense of the word." Despite their differences, Nordstrom and Krauss respected each other.[2]

Krauss also sought the company of poets closer to home. In late 1975 or early 1976, she joined Dale Shaw's Westport Poetry Workshop, which included

Peggy Heinrich, Janet Krauss, and children's authors Freya Littledale and Doris Lund. Once a week, they met at the Unitarian Church and later at the Westport Arts Center. Krauss's energy and work ethic inspired the other participants. Introducing her poem "If Only" as a new work (even though she wrote the first version in 1959), she explained its composition. She had filled many, many sheets of paper, she said, because doing so stimulated her memory, giving her access to the possibilities of accident and of unconscious associations. Then she threw out most of her drafts. When she was stuck for a word, she would stick a pin through the *New York Times*, see where it landed, and make fresh combinations of words that suited her. Once a month, Julius Gold kept his delicatessen open late so that Shaw's group could meet for "Poem and Pickle" readings and discussions. Though Krauss was often reluctant to read her work in public, on one of those evenings she did. As the best-known poet in the group, she entered the deli to a standing ovation; more applause followed her reading of "If Only." For the next seven years, Krauss remained an active participant in their readings—at Gold's Deli, at the Westport Arts Center, at libraries, and even in New York on a few occasions.[3]

In the fall of 1977, Ruth had her first residency at the MacDowell Colony. She enjoyed the experience enough to spend the summer of 1978 at another artists' colony, Yaddo, in Saratoga Springs, New York. She returned to MacDowell that fall and again in August and September 1979, 1980, 1981, and 1982. During her weeks at MacDowell, Krauss was able to write unimpeded. The colony provided her with a studio, a bedroom, a bathroom, and meals. She ate breakfast and dinner in the main dining room, with the other artists. To avoid midday interruptions, MacDowell's staff quietly left lunch in a picnic basket on Krauss's doorstep.[4]

Back home, Ruth had to learn how to take care of the details of daily life—all of the things that Dave had done for her. As she told a friend who asked how she was coping, "I lose and break things and cut and burn myself." Dave had also paid the bills, looked after the property, and done all the driving. Shelley Trubowitz took her to buy a small, easily manageable car, which she refused to drive on highways, where the speed and traffic frightened her. She preferred the slower, more comfortable pace of back roads.[5]

She missed Dave terribly. If a friend brought up his name, she would become agitated and change the subject. By July 1976, Harper stopped forwarding Crockett Johnson fan mail because it upset Ruth. However, as Dave's heir and executor, she could not avoid him. That year, the IBM Research Division in Yorktown Heights, New York, held an exhibition of twenty-one of his paintings. The paintings had to be picked up from Ruth's house. She needed to sign the contract granting permission for the exhibit. She had to be involved. Ruth wanted Dave's work to be seen, even if remembering him grieved her.[6]

As she was then still so upset, it is hard to know whether Krauss even saw the mixed reviews of *Little Boat Lighter Than a Cork*. *Publishers Weekly* praised the "tiny book" as "gentle as a lullaby, just right for introducing the joys of books to toddlers." In contrast, *School Library Journal*'s Helen Gregory called it "a gentle if pointless tone poem" and noted that Maurice Sendak's "entire Nutshell Library can be purchased for less than this unmemorable extravagance." The book was published by Magic Circle Press, run by Ruth's friend, Valerie Harms, which had limited distribution, and *Little Boat Lighter Than a Cork* was not a big seller.[7]

Ruth did not want to live alone. She had been renting a room to a young woman, but they were not getting along. In 1977, Ruth responded to an ad in the *Westport News*: "20-something-year old woman poet seeks place to live and write." The woman was Binnie Klein, whom Ruth had heard at a Westport poetry reading a few years earlier. She had enjoyed Klein's work and had invited her back to the house, where the two women and Dave drank chocolate milk before Ruth sent Klein home with some volumes of poetry. Ruth was delighted to rent Dave's studio to Klein.[8]

The studio was exactly as Dave had left it: his paintings on the walls, his things in the desk, his mathematical equations on a bulletin board, and his bed. When Klein moved the equations from the board into a desk drawer, Ruth responded angrily: "How dare you touch these things! I told you not to move anything!" Klein apologized, and Ruth consented to let her bring in a free-standing rack to hold her clothes and to have a better door put up for more privacy.[9]

Just as Ruth had depended on Dave, so she came to depend on Klein. As Ruth said at the time, "I can't even change a lightbulb." Home alone, she felt vulnerable, and she did not sleep well unless Klein was home: On nights when her tenant did a radio show that lasted until 3:00 in the morning, Ruth would get up and slam doors to vent her frustration.[10]

Ruth was also struggling with her body, angry that it would no longer work just as she wanted it to. For a few years, her hip had been causing her pain. Though she disliked hospitals, she at last scheduled a hip replacement operation but arranged to have the procedure in Baltimore so she could recuperate at the home of Dick and Betty Hahn. On the way to the hospital, Ruth proposed that they go to lunch, and Betty suggested Bertha's, a restaurant famous for its mussels. Ruth said, "I'm going to go there and have mussels. I think I'm allergic to them. But if I'm allergic, I'm going to the right place to be treated!"[11]

The surgery was a success and restored Ruth's mobility, but the need for the operation contributed to her feeling that her body was betraying her. As she wrote at the time, "I loved physical activity, and love it now but cannot i.e. 'run.' ... Now my body is a pain in the neck."[12]

Back in Westport, Klein took care of practical matters, while Ruth served as mentor and friend. Despite the fifty-year difference in their ages, both women were free spirits who loved poetry. Ruth was very generous with both her books and her encouragement. After Ruth showed her André Breton's poem, "My Wife with the Woodfire Hair," Klein went up to Dave's studio and wrote "My Nightmare with Its Mother Just Off to the Left." When Ruth saw it, she told Klein, "It's the best thing you've ever written." Ruth urged her friend to keep writing, telling her that some of her poems might make good children's books. She would be happy to help if Klein wanted to publish them for younger readers. Ruth also welcomed Klein into her social circle, which then included Jean and Leonard Boudin; Freya Littledale; and conservative art critic Hilton Kramer and his wife, Esta.[13]

After Klein moved out in 1979, Pablo Frasconi was back from York University and looking for a place to live. Ruth had known Frasconi since his childhood and offered to rent him Dave's studio, still nearly just as Dave had left it. Frasconi did not mind: Living with Ruth was like living with family. They saw each other every day. They shared friends, and he occasionally did chores for her. Every once in a while, he would stay away for a night, and Ruth would say, "Well, you know, if you're going to rent, you have to stay here. I want someone who will check up on me."[14]

Near the end of 1979, Dick Hahn's daughter, Linda Graetz, wrote to Ruth for help. Living in Italy with her eleven-year-old son, Graetz had left a bad marriage but had no job prospects and no way to get home. Ruth sent them plane tickets, met them at the airport, and invited them to live with her. After a couple of weeks, Graetz realized that she and her son needed a place of their own. Though Ruth felt "abandoned" by this decision, she helped them find an apartment and got Graetz a job. Ruth also introduced Graetz to her friends, paid for the boy to go to summer camp, and paid the bill when Graetz decided to go to nursing school.[15]

As curator of Dave's legacy, Ruth was pleased when the Smithsonian Institution's Mathematics Division came to collect Dave's mathematical paintings and related materials. Dave would be recognized for his mathematical

Eleanor Hazard, cover for Ruth Krauss, *Somebody Spilled the Sky* (New York: Greenwillow, 1979). Used by permission of Eleanor (Hazard) Lanahan.

ideas, which had been very important to him during the final years of his life. However, Ruth let them take only eighty of the more than one hundred paintings, keeping the remainder hanging up in the house; the Smithsonian could have them after she was gone.

Some people thought she was already gone. As her most popular books were decades old and her newer books were appearing only every three or

four years, the name Ruth Krauss was gradually slipping out of public consciousness. One day, when she and her friend, Ina Chadwick, were browsing
the aisles of a Westport bookstore, they overheard a customer in a neighboring aisle: "Oh, look at this book by Ruth Krauss! Do you think she's still alive?"
Krauss and Chadwick started laughing, and Krauss asked, "Do you want me
to go back there and look like a ghost?" *Somebody Spilled the Sky* (1979) was
easily Krauss's best children's book since her creative heyday with Maurice
Sendak, but it received only mixed reviews. In the *New York Times Book
Review*, poet Donald Hall wrote that perhaps Krauss's "special well is running
dry; at any rate it seems a trifle shallow." *Kirkus* was skeptical of the fact that
several of the items in *Somebody Spilled the Sky* had appeared in other books
but assigned blame to Eleanor Hazard's comic illustrations, which were "too
linear" and not "wiggly enough." In contrast, *Publishers Weekly* loved Hazard's
"crazy drawings," praised Krauss's "genius for echoing the daft but unassailable
logic of children," and predicted that children would "read and reread" the
book.[16]

Though most of her published and performed work in the late 1970s and
the 1980s had been written earlier, Krauss remained receptive to creative discovery. Beneath her living room's vaulted ceiling, she created what Chadwick
calls "a kitchen of the mind." As a concession to living room furniture, she set
up two chairs in front of the fireplace, but the rest of the room was devoted to
work tables covered with paper, pens, and crayons. When inspiration struck,
Krauss would be ready.[17]

A few years after Johnson's death and much to Krauss's surprise, she received a telephone call from her first husband, Lionel White, who was now
on his fourth marriage and had decided that it was time to reach out. Still an
alcoholic, he also remained an entertaining storyteller, and he wished Krauss
well. They spoke once or twice a year until his death in late 1985.[18]

Though she was pleased to hear from White, their divorce still ranked
among her most painful experiences, and that early marriage left wounds that
had never fully healed. In October 1979, Ruth confronted those memories as
she tried to sort through the loneliness of her life without Dave. Encouraged
by her psychiatrist, she recorded her thoughts. She felt "anguish" and was
"almost ready to give up," but she thought that this outlook "is something I
should work on. . . . I've got to change the behavior of my *feelings*." Dave's illness and death, she reflected, "chang[ed] the entire way of my living & I am
sure that each goodbye or rejection is an echo of that death." Further, she didn't
want to be single. "I need a man. What man? Any? Well—not quite—although

if I think hard enough one guy is the same unconscious as the other." But no, she reminded herself, "after all men are not just sex objects & I guess that's part of my problem. . . . I *must* become independent." More than a quarter of the narrative concerned her life with White, and she concluded, "I guess it was like a living fantasy & I loved it all when we were together—before he began drinking."[19]

In the unpublished anti-ageist children's book she wrote as a young woman, Krauss had noted that among the Northwest Coast Indians of the United States and Canada, "the high point of romantic sex is old-age, about seventy to ninety. You're supposed to be romantic then; so, consequently, you are romantic then." She attempted to follow this advice. Describing Krauss as "coquettish," Klein found her flirtatiousness "very liberating," showing that older women need not abide by cultural conventions. Dale Shaw remembered her falling in love with a man at a writer's retreat and then being quite distraught when he called it off. At one point in the 1980s, she had a male boarder much younger than she whom she hoped would become her lover. On another occasion, she told Peggy Heinrich that a priest was interested in her but quickly changed the subject.[20]

In 1979 or 1980, Susan Carr Hirschman approached Krauss about having Greenwillow, the children's imprint Hirschman had founded at William Morrow, publish an anthology of Krauss's work. She agreed but then panicked, phoning Heinrich and saying, "Oh, I just can't handle it any more. I can't do these things any more. What am I going to do? This is so much." When Heinrich arrived to help, she discovered that Krauss was more than able to handle the project, though she seemed to need Heinrich's presence for reassurance. Reviewers either loved or hated *Minestrone: A Ruth Krauss Selection*, published in the fall of 1981. *Publishers Weekly* saluted Krauss's "unchained imagination" and her "unique contributions to children's books, creations that delight grownups and boys and girls of all ages," predicting that the "book will surely be among the new bestsellers." *Language Arts*, a magazine for English teachers, pronounced the book "definitely for sharing. Calmer than Silverstein, and for a younger audience. I love them both." In contrast, *School Library Journal* saw Krauss as "unsure of which age group she wishes to address" and "striv[ing] to be childlike," with results that were "childish and condescending." *Kirkus* dismissed this "recycled collection" of "disparate material," mocking it as dated: "There's a shade of '60s twee (admittedly staked out by Krauss in the '50s) to the best of her stuff; and at worst it verges on airy nothings."[21]

Just as Krauss resisted being classified as a children's writer or a writer for grown-ups, so she resisted any fashion trend that made her uncomfortable. Starting in the early 1970s, she began wearing loose, comfortable clothing—cotton drawstring pants, a cotton pullover top, and soft leather shoes. Klein "never saw Ruth in a skirt or a dress. She dressed for comfort. She was just the essence of 'This is me.'"[22]

Krauss took a stand in her poetry, too. Though her proposed collection, *Small Black Lambs Wandering in the Red Poppies,* was not as overtly political as *This Breast Gothic,* she nonetheless saw it as having the potential to raise consciousness. In June 1982, an antinuclear demonstration featured a performance of selections from this unpublished book, intended, Krauss said, "for adults-and-children-together." The combination of old and new verses does include a few with pacifist implications. One iteration of the title poem reads, "when I saw the small black lambs wandering in the red poppies / I threw my arms around the world and / loved it."[23]

Although Krauss wrote on her own, usually in the morning at her kitchen table, she relied on feedback from others. In 1985, as she drifted away from the Westport Poetry Workshop, she found artistic fellowship in a collaborative writing workshop run by sculptor Harvey Weiss. Though he had known Krauss for decades, Weiss was initially "surprised . . . that she wanted to enter into the give-and-take of a workshop." She also enjoyed the attention: "Ruth's position in the workshop was always a paramount one. People did not approach her work in the same way that any of the others in the workshop were approached. We had to learn how to work with Ruth, with her sentences, with her imagination, with her tremendous energy—rather than imposing anything from traditions or expectations that we had as writers or as poets or as academics or whatever. And she came to us with a number of poems that were sometimes astonishing." Though it was Weiss's workshop, Krauss's experience and creative verve often gave her a starring role. She stayed with the group for a few years, attending semiregularly until at least 1987.[24]

Beyond the attention a writing group provided, Krauss simply enjoyed the company. In 1985, when Chadwick spoke of construction problems with her new house, Krauss was sympathetic, inviting her friend to move in temporarily. For the month that Chadwick stayed in the guest room, she would come home from work, open the front door, and hear Krauss call out jokingly from the kitchen, "My husband is home! My husband is home!" Krauss no longer ate unless someone else cooked. So, Chadwick prepared dinner each night as well as loaded and ran the dishwasher and saw to other domestic tasks that seemed beyond Krauss's grasp.[25]

Though Dave had always taken care of anything practical, Ruth at times seemed to be craving not just her late spouse but a parent figure. When Chadwick asked why Krauss had never learned to do so many basic things, she claimed that she had been an indulged child-prodigy violinist and that no one had ever forced her to do anything. She remained determined that she would not be forced to do things now. She told friends that she had a "wonderful system" for taking care of her finances: "I put everything in this box, and Sidney [Kramer] takes care of it." She also called Kramer if she needed to change a lightbulb or if her plumbing were acting up. When she needed a new car, Morton Schindel took her to a dealer, but Krauss was unable to decide. Schindel finally picked one out and said, "Look, this would be a good car for you," and Krauss "never questioned it. She just got delivery of the car and paid the bill and drove that car for the rest of her life." As Kramer said, "She was a *luftmensch*. She operated way up in the sky."[26]

Though Krauss depended on others to help with life's daily challenges, in other respects she remained a parent figure and mentor to younger people. In the fall of 1986, she returned to an idea she had had fifteen years earlier: having Nina Stagakis, the daughter of her old friends Phyllis Rowand and Gene Wallace, illustrate *Running Jumping ABC*. Influenced by Krauss's poetry career, the ABC book is both whimsical and gently lyrical. For *D*, Krauss has "Dance with a leaf / Duckwalk all around the world / Draw your dreams on an old bathrobe / Dress up like the sun and stand on a mountain." *Y* is "Yell 'Good Morning Big Fat World!'" Scholastic senior editor Phyllis Hoffman loved the text and invited Krauss to send Stagakis's drawings. Hoffman found the artwork "dear and kind of 'Sendakian' but . . . , at times, very awkward." Stagakis submitted some new sketches, but Scholastic passed, and *Running Jumping ABC* remains unpublished.[27]

But for the first time in eight years, Krauss was working on a new picture book, *Big and Little*, and Scholastic liked it enough to send a contract. In consultation with editor-in-chief Jean Feiwel, Hoffman sought an illustrator for the book. Accustomed to working with Nordstrom at Harper and Hirschman at both Harper and Greenwillow, Krauss expected to be consulted. But the children's book business had changed: It was less common for authors to have a say in choosing their illustrators. When the finished art arrived in late March 1987, Krauss was surprised and upset: Who was Mary Szilagyi, and why had she drawn only white children for *Big and Little*? Probably because of time constraints, Szilagyi refused to redo the illustrations to add a black child as a friend of the central character, and an angry Krauss vowed never to write for children again. Published in the fall of 1987, *Big and Little* would be Ruth's final children's book.[28]

At around that time, Krauss traveled to Baltimore to see a doctor about her hip because she was growing more frail. Ralph Nazareth, a poet she had met through Dale Shaw's workshops, drove her down. A young man from India interested in American mores, Nazareth asked many questions. Krauss answered each with a whimsical comment. Just after they crossed into Maryland, they saw a sign for the town of Havre de Grace, and Krauss began chanting, "Havre de Grace." Nazareth joined in. The town's name made Krauss think of France, and she told Nazareth how exquisite and extraordinary the French were as lovers and how Americans did not know how to make love. Then she changed the subject again. It was, Nazareth recalled, a "very memorable trip."[29]

In Baltimore, she stayed with Richard and Betty Hahn. Dave's studio was empty again, and Ruth considered moving down to Baltimore, where she would be close to family. After spending about four weeks with the Hahns and pondering her options, she realized that she would not be able to drive in Baltimore, though she could still drive in Westport. She concluded that the best decision was to remain in her house but have people come in to help her, and she returned to Westport.[30]

Living alone (when she could not find a boarder) or with company (when she could), Krauss continued to write when inspiration struck and to curate her husband's literary legacy. During the summer of 1989, Theatreworks USA's Barbara Pasternack, composer-lyricist Jon Ehrlich, and adapter Jane Shepard came up to Westport to perform for her a musical adaptation of *Harold and the Purple Crayon*. Theatreworks USA had asked Ehrlich to adapt the book, and he believed that the company already had the rights, so he was surprised to discover that Krauss's final approval was required. Confident that he had done a good job but a little anxious about her reaction, Ehrlich and Shepard talked and sang their way through the show in Krauss's living room with her and a friend as the audience. To convey the idea that the drawings truly come alive, the play has four Purple People emerge as the result of Harold's first scribbles: They embody what Harold draws (a dragon, an apple tree, the moon) or help display the action (turning Harold around in the air when he falls from the mountain). For an hour, Krauss listened and watched. When it was over, she gladly gave Ehrlich and Shepard permission to stage their play. The show made its debut at Broadway's Promenade Theatre in November 1990 and then toured the country for a few seasons.[31]

At the end of the show, Harold draws himself into bed, drops his crayon, and falls asleep. Harold's imagination guides him toward home and rest, but Ruth Krauss's imagination guided her toward anxiety. In her big empty house, she could not feel fully at home, nor could she sleep soundly. Fourteen years after Dave's death, Ruth still could not adapt to living alone.

28

CHILDREN ARE TO LOVE

—and when we pass a cemetery, we both
hold our breath alike, like twins,
even when we're not together.
—RUTH KRAUSS, *I'll Be You and You Be Me* (1954)

In the fall of 1989, Dave's studio was empty again. When Nina Stagakis visited, Ruth asked whether she and her family could move in, living there rent-free in exchange for serving as her caretakers. Stagakis realized that having the five members of her family living in a single room would be impractical. So Ruth placed another ad in the paper.[1]

The ad was answered by Joanna Czaderna, a Polish immigrant who was seven months pregnant at the time. Although she was employed, she was having difficulty finding a place to live because landlords refused to rent to a pregnant woman. But when she knocked on the door of 24 Owenoke, Ruth opened it and said, "Oh, welcome! So, where is your stuff?" Czaderna and her husband, Janusz, became a part of the household, followed by their daughter, Bianca, who arrived in December 1989. Needing to care for her newborn as well as her mentally unstable husband, Czaderna was unable to work, and she began to worry about how she would afford the rent. Though she did not raise the matter, Ruth understood and offered to let the Czadernas stay for free if Joanna would help around the house. The younger woman gratefully agreed.[2]

Ruth's other friends wondered how she would adapt to having an infant in the household, but much to their surprise, she enjoyed Bianca's company. A very easygoing baby, Bianca would play quietly next to her mother and Ruth, and when the girl got older, she would crawl over and sit in the eighty-nine-year-old author's lap, where Ruth would hug her "little angel." Ruth would also read her books to Bianca, the grandchild she never had.[3]

Joanna Czaderna became Ruth's confidant and chauffeur. Traveling in Ruth's little Honda, they began to visit the places Ruth had lived and worked— the Rowayton house, the schools where had interviewed children. She finally became able to talk about Dave without being overcome by grief. Her face lighting up, Ruth described Dave as a gentleman who treated her like a princess. Czaderna was surprised: "I just never heard anyone speaking with such a love about another person, and especially coming from her, it was even more powerful to me."[4]

Returning to one of her favorite childhood activities, Ruth began making books for her own amusement—writing the story, drawing the pictures, and sewing the pages together with yarn. In one of these stories, a variation on "Love Song for Elephants" from *I'll Be You and You Be Me*, she wrote of a stuffed elephant who grows old, gets worn out, and is thrown in the garbage. A little girl finds the sad elephant, takes him home, and repairs him.[5]

In July 1992, Ruth's good health suddenly deserted her, and she took to her bed, requiring round-the-clock care. Nurses came in for a few hours each day, but Czaderna became her primary caregiver. Helplessness devastated Ruth, and she fought to lift herself out of bed, though she lacked the strength. Her body was failing, but her will remained strong.[6]

Friends and fans came to visit. Barbara Lans, Lillian Hoban, Morton Schindel, and Maureen O'Hara came regularly. Maurice Sendak visited several times, and Shel Silverstein visited once. Ruth began giving things away. When Dan Richter stopped by, she gave him some of Dave's books—Boswell's *Life of Johnson* and a book on seventeenth-century thought.[7]

Another regular visitor, Janet Krauss, was struck by Ruth's humor and defiance. When Janet mentioned that she was going to attend a poetry festival, Ruth asked, "A poverty festival?" "No, a poetry festival," Janet replied. "Oh, those things," Ruth laughed, enjoying the misheard phrase. After sitting at Ruth's bedside and noticing her fist, Janet composed a poem comparing Ruth to "an aged Barbie doll / with flowing white hair," and asks, "Why do you never let go / let your hand fly open? / A fist of anger / or defiance / against your still life." Bianca and Joanna Czaderna also sat with Ruth, but she was hard to comfort. She was frustrated, imprisoned by a body she could no longer control. She ultimately stopped fighting and simply lay in bed, waiting for the end.[8]

Aware that Ruth might not last much longer, Maureen O'Hara phoned Sendak to suggest that he come back for a final visit. Ruth was annoyed that O'Hara had made the call, and when Sendak arrived, she ignored him. He tried making conversation but got no response, and he was not sure if Ruth even recognized him. As he prepared to go, he leaned over and asked, "Could I kiss you goodbye?"

Ruth Krauss, late 1980s.
Courtesy of Betty Hahn.

She did not object. He gently took her chin in his hand and kissed her on the lips. She giggled, and said, "Oh, Maury." Sendak recalled, "I can't tell you how much that meant. That she knew it was me all the time and that I had done just what she would have liked me to have done—to not have treated her like a dying person, but to have treated her like the beautiful woman that she was."[9]

On 9 July 1993, Czaderna could see that Ruth was fading. Czaderna sat up with her friend all night and into the next day, stepping outside into the sunshine for a walk with her daughter only after one of the nurses arrived to tend to Ruth. When Joanna and Bianca returned, the nurse told them that Ruth had died. Three-and-a-half-year-old Bianca refused to leave Ruth's side until the coroner came to take away her body.[10]

Ruth died on 10 July, one day before the eighteenth anniversary of Dave's death and two weeks shy of what would have been her ninety-second birthday. The *New York Times* ran a short, error-laden obituary, suggesting that her life, though noteworthy, did not merit some basic fact-checking. The paper did, however, get her age correct.[11]

When Valerie Harms had asked fifteen years earlier whether Ruth ever thought of her creations as having an immortality of their own, Ruth responded, "How long can anything last? Especially in this time of space travel and exploration of other parts of the universe, posterity means nothing." Amending her statement slightly, Ruth added, "Everything of course has repercussions or, rather, intersects with everything."[12]

Conscious of those repercussions, Ruth did not forget the people and ideals that were important to her. She had finally made a will in early 1991, after decades of avoiding the subject. She consulted her cousin, Dick Hahn, and his wife, Betty, and initially planned to leave her entire estate to him. When he said he did not want her money, she made other arrangements. Bianca Czaderna received fifty thousand dollars to help with her education. Crockett Johnson's paintings went to the Mathematical Division of the Smithsonian Institution. Ruth Krauss left the remainder of her estate (which also included Johnson's estate) to charitable "organizations which are dedicated to meeting the needs of homeless children in the United States," stipulating only that the organizations "have no particular religious affiliation." As she had written forty years earlier in *A Hole Is to Dig*, "Children are to love."[13]

At the time of Ruth's death, Sendak's new book about homeless children, *We're All in the Dumps with Jack and Guy*, was in production. When working on the book, Sendak found himself "going back to the *A Hole Is to Dig* kids." He had been "unnerved" by reports of homeless children in "Venezuela, South America, children being killed on the street by police like rats and vermin." Thoughts of these kids "brought [him] back to the happy little ragamuffins in the Krauss books." *We're All in the Dumps* was released in the fall, and the cover of the 27 September issue of the *New Yorker* featured a Sendak illustration of the book's homeless children. Sleeping on the ground, a boy uses *A Hole Is to Dig* as a pillow. Standing beneath a makeshift shelter is a girl who has Ruth Krauss's dark curly hair and who is holding a copy of *I Can Fly*. The girl's eyes are closed, as if dreaming of flying.[14]

Sendak was unable to attend her memorial service but sent a loving reminiscence that Hoban read at the gathering and that formed the basis of his appreciation of Krauss published in the *Horn Book* the following year. Sendak said, "Ruth broke rules and invented new ones, and her respect for the natural ferocity of children bloomed into poetry that was utterly faithful to what was true in their lives." Remy Charlip, who also could not attend the service, sent a piece in which he spoke of how Krauss inspired him. When he asked where she had come up with the wonderful title "The Song of the Melancholy Dress," Krauss replied, "I misunderstood a woman at a party, who told me she just bought a melon-colored dress." So, Charlip concluded, "Ruth taught me how to use my misunderstandings and my so-called failures and mistakes. And in the process I learned how to respect other people's creative interpretations of what I say or do. For this path to artful enlightenment, I will be forever grateful to Ruth."[15]

In accordance with Ruth's wishes, she was cremated and her ashes scattered in Long Island Sound. At 5:00 A.M., on 21 June 1994, the day of the summer solstice, Ruth's executor, attorney Stewart Edelstein, got into a canoe in Fairfield, Connecticut, and paddled out onto the sound. Dave had loved to sail there. For more than three decades, Ruth and Dave had lived together on the shore. And nineteen years earlier, his ashes had been scattered there. If Dave's spirit were anywhere, it would be there.[16]

Out on the water, Edelstein recalled one of several visits to Ruth's house, during which they ate cookies and worked on her will. Either he or Ruth had said something funny, and Ruth laughed—not a polite laugh, but a deep belly laugh. He thought of that moment, and "it was like she was there with me." As he scattered Ruth's ashes into the water, the sun rose.[17]

EPILOGUE

The handclapping and cheering went on even after the lion fell off the table and lay on the floor again and it continued until everyone forgot who the applause was for or what it was he was famous for having done.
—CROCKETT JOHNSON, *Ellen's Lion* (1959)

In the decades since their deaths, Ruth Krauss and Crockett Johnson have receded in the public memory, she more quickly than he. Where once her poetic and dramatic achievements ranked among the best of the contemporary avant-garde, they are today a footnote to her better-known career as children's author. That career, too, does not shine as brightly as it once did. All of her poetry is out of print, and less than a dozen of her thirty-six children's books remain available.

However, new editions of some of her books have been published. *The Bundle Book* (1951) gained new life as *You're Just What I Need* (illustrated by Julia Noonan, 1999); *Eyes Nose Fingers Toes* (1964) returned as *Goodnight Goodnight Sleepyhead* (illustrated by Jane Dyer, 2004); and *Big and Little* reappeared as *And I Love You* (illustrated by Steven Kellogg, 2010). In 2005, Maurice Sendak reworked *Bears* (1948), using new pictures featuring Max from *Where the Wild Things Are* to create a story that runs parallel to and intersects with Krauss's original verse. He dedicated the new volume to Krauss and Johnson. In 2007, Helen Oxenbury's art gave a fresh look to *The Growing Story* (1947), and the New York Review of Books' Children's Books imprint brought *The Backward Day* (1950) back into print.

While these republications augur well for Krauss's literary legacy, Johnson has far better name recognition for two reasons. First, his comic garners much more respect than her poetry. *Barnaby* ranks among the twentieth century's classic comic strips, alongside Winsor McCay's *Little Nemo in Slumberland*, George Herriman's *Krazy Kat*, Walt Kelly's *Pogo*, Charles Schulz's *Peanuts*, and Bill Watterson's *Calvin and Hobbes*. Moreover, *Barnaby* has prominent fans ready to speak on its behalf. Pulitzer Prize–winner Art Spiegelman and *New*

Yorker art editor Françoise Mouly included *Barnaby* in the second of their three-volume Little Lit series (2000–2003). Daniel Clowes, best known for his *Ghost World* graphic novel (1997) and film (2001), frequently cites the strip as a favorite, even alluding to *Barnaby* in his graphic novel, *Ice Haven* (2005). Though the *Comics Journal* ranked *Barnaby* only at number 68 in its Top 100 Comics of the twentieth century, the issue's cover featured two *Barnaby* characters, O'Malley and Gus the Ghost.[1]

The second reason for Johnson's endurance is *Harold and the Purple Crayon*, which has sold more than two million copies and been translated into fourteen languages. It and its sequels have inspired an Emmy-winning animated HBO series (2001–2), a board game (2001), and a new stage play (2009). Many creative people, including cartoonist Peter Kuper and children's author-illustrators William Joyce and Thacher Hurd, also cite Harold as an inspiration. Harold is the ancestor of the crayon-wielding protagonists in Chris Van Allsburg's *Bad Day at Riverbend* (1995) and Patrick McDonnell's *Art* (2006) and the pencil-powered characters in Anthony Browne's *Bear Hunt* (1979) and Allan Ahlberg and Bruce Ingman's *The Pencil* (2008). In a February 2009 Sunday *Zits* comic, Jerry Scott and Jim Borgman show Connie Duncan finding a box of her son Jeremy's old picture books, with five of the strip's seven panels devoted to *Harold and the Purple Crayon*. Though Jeremy usually displays a teenager's reluctance to hang out with his parents, he happily recalls the book's plot with his mother. In the final panel, he has become a child waiting for story time: His gangly adolescent body rests in his mother's lap, she holds the book in her hands, and he says, "Start from the beginning."[2]

Crockett Johnson shows us that a crayon can create a world, while Ruth Krauss demonstrates that dreams can be as large as a giant orange carrot. Whenever children and grown-ups seek books that invite them to think and to imagine, they need look no further than Johnson and Krauss. There, they will find a very special house, where holes are to dig, walls are a canvas, and people are artists, drawing paths that take them anywhere they want to go.

NOTES

INTRODUCTION

1. New Haven Office of the FBI, "David Johnson Leisk, wa. Crockett Johnson," 10 Nov. 1950, 5, FBI-CJ.

2. Mickenberg, *Learning*, 15, 141–42; Mickenberg and Nel, *Tales*, 101, 205.

3. Marcus, *Minders*, 216.

4. *The Simpsons*, season 21, episode 22, 16 May 2010; Dove, "Maple Valley Branch Library," 32.

5. Solomon, "Beyond Finger Paint," 25.

6. Bader, "Ruth Krauss," 416; Sendak, "Ruth Krauss and Me," 287.

7. Parker, "Mash Note," 16; Wepman, "Barnaby," 47.

8. Waugh, *Comics*, 306.

CHAPTER 1

1. IJW, 17–20 Oct. 1979; RK birth certificate, Maryland State Archives; Baltimore City Directories for 1901, 1933, MD; Sanborn Maps of Baltimore, 1901–2, MD; Wertz and Wertz, *Lying-In*, 133.

2. Baltimore City Directories for 1892, 1901, MD; 1880 U.S. Census; Swyrich, "Ancient History"; IJW, 19 Oct. 1979.

3. Fein, *Making*, 134; IJW, 19 Oct. 1979; Baltimore City Directories, 1891–1921, MD.

4. "Mrs. Albert A. Brager," *Baltimore Sun*, biography files, MD; 1910 U.S. Census, Maryland, Baltimore 13, Enumeration District 201; 1920 U.S. Census, Maryland, Baltimore 13, Enumeration District 204; 1880 U.S. Census, St. Louis, Missouri; IJW, 17–20 Oct. 1979. Carrie Mayer was the sister of Hollywood producer Samuel Mayer.

5. Marriage record, Baltimore City Court of Common Pleas, Maryland State Archives; Pruce, *Synagogues*, 126–29; William Rosenau, "Oheb Shalom Congregation," in Blum, *Jews*, 65; Fein, *Making*, 178; IJW, 20 Oct. 1979; Baltimore City Directories, 1890–1900, MD; Bowditch, *Images*, 12–43; Sandler, *Jewish Baltimore*, 55.

6. Brian Alverson to author, 20 September 2004; IJW, 19 Oct. 1979.

7. IJW, 19 Oct. 1979; Hahn, interview.

8. RKA, 2.

9. Baltimore City Directories, 1903–15, MD; 1910 U.S. Census; Sandler, *Jewish Baltimore*, 44; Sanford Maps of Baltimore, 1901–2, 1915, MD.

10. "Where," 39–40.

11. Ibid., 40.

12. IJW, 20 Oct. 1979; "Krauss, Ruth (Ida) 1911–," in *Something about the Author*, 135; *Baltimore Sun*, index for 1913, PR.

13. "Ruth Krauss: Let Me Tell You a Story," 3–4; Graetz, interview; "Krauss, Ruth (Ida) 1911–," in *Something about the Author*, 134; Harms, "Interview," 9.

14. Sandler, *Jewish Baltimore*, 43; Baltimore City Directories, 1916–18, MD; Chico, "Cone Sisters," 82–83; "The Marlborough Apartment House" (promotional brochure), ca. 1905, MD; RKA, 2–3.

15. Klapper, *Jewish Girls*, 78, 90, 202.

16. RK, "Ruth Krauss," in *More Junior Authors*, 126; information provided by Joan Schwartz, Alumni Office, Maryland Institute of Art, 2 June 2005; "N.Y. Artists Out

for Cash," *Baltimore Sun*, 30 Jan. 1917, J.O.L., "The Three Arts: Music Drama Painting," *Baltimore Sun*, 4 June 1918, "Consulting Engineers in the Art of Dress," [*Baltimore Sun*?], 1921, all in Decker Library, Maryland Institute College of Art; Maryland Institute for the Promotion of the Mechanic Arts, *Announcement: Schools of Art and Design, Baltimore, Md., 1917–1918*, 13, Maryland Institute College of Art.

17. Baltimore City Directories, 1918, 1919, 1920, MD; 1920 U.S. Census; information provided by Joan Schwartz, Alumni Office, Maryland Institute of Art, 2 June 2005; "Consulting Engineers in the Art of Dress," [*Baltimore Sun*?], 1921, Decker Library, Maryland Institute College of Art; Maryland Institute for the Promotion of the Mechanic Arts, *Announcement*, 30.

18. Cohen, interview.

CHAPTER 2

1. Nicholson, *Shetland*, 11, 16, 44–45, 135; Gott, *Shetland Family History*; Linklater, *Orkney and Shetland*, 189; Scotland Online, *Scotland's People*; Thomson, "Population and Depopulation," 151; Else Frank, interview.

2. 1900 U.S. Census, Buffalo, Ward 11, Erie, New York; Else Frank, interview.

3. *Newtown Register*, 13 May 1915, qtd. in Seyfried, *Corona*, 53, 50–51, 70–71; Else Frank, interview.

4. Else Frank, interview; "May Go to the Grand Jury"; Seyfried, *Corona*, 55.

5. Seyfried, *Corona*, 67–68; Fitzgerald, *Great Gatsby*, 27.

6. Hopkins, "Ruth Krauss [and] Crockett Johnson," 124; Else Frank, interview. At varying times, Crockett Johnson gave different reasons for having changed his name. On one occasion, he said that "Leisk was too hard to pronounce" (Hopkins, "Ruth Krauss [and] Crockett Johnson," 124), and according to "O'Malley for Dewey," "Crockett Johnson dropped his real name, David Johnson Leisk (pronounced Lisk) because he got tired of spelling it out."

7. Else Frank, interview.

8. Ibid.; Fisher, "Barnaby and Mr. O'Malley."

9. Else Frank, interview.

10. John Hyslop to author, 19 Nov. 2006; Seyfried, *Corona*, 65–66.

11. Theodore Roosevelt, *America*, 392–93; New York State Census, 1915, 1925; Seyfried, *Corona*, 52.

12. Else Frank, interview; "Cushlamochree!," 102, 104; Leslie Howard, "What's in a Song?"

13. *Newtown High School Handbook*, 9, 12, 18, 108, 82–83, 42–62.

14. Else Frank interview; *Newtown High School Lantern*, May 1922, cover, May 1923, cover; H[annah] B[aker], "Crockett Johnson," 1.

15. Else Frank interview; "Newtown High Decides to Play," 10; "Newtown Swamps Schools," 8; "27 Newtown High Students," 12; "Corona & Elmhurst," 12; Doggett, *Newtown High School*, 29.

16. "Newtown H.S. Graduates," 12; "Newtown Loses Baseball Stars," 14; Norris, "Meet the Man," 24; "Newtown High School, Elmhurst," 5.

CHAPTER 3

1. "Walden Past"; *Camp Walden, Denmark Maine, 1917*, 4, Camp Walden Papers, Schlesinger Library, Radcliffe Institute for Advanced Studies; Cohen, interview.

2. *Splash*, 1920, Camp Walden Archives, Denmark, Maine; Cohen, interview.

3. Cohen, interview; "Brief History"; *Camp Walden, Denmark Maine, 1917*, 11; RK to UN, [Mar.–Apr. 1963], RK Papers-HC.

4. Cohen, interview; *Splash*, 1919, Camp Walden Archives.

5. Ibid., 1920.

6. RK student records, Peabody Archives, Friedheim Music Library, Peabody Institute.

7. Ibid.

8. Hahn, interview; Graetz, interview; Baltimore City Directories, 1923, 1924–25, 1926, 1927, MD.

9. RKA, 3.

10. "Necessary Information for Inquiring Students," in *New York School of Fine and Applied Art: General Prospectus, 1927–1928*, 44–45, 47–48, Parsons School Archives, Anna-Maria and Stephen Kellen Archives Center, Parsons School of Design, New School University; Marjorie F. Jones, "History," 117; "Necessary Information for All Who Are Inquiring," in *New York School of Fine and Applied Art (Parsons): General Prospectus, 1928–1929*, 40, Parsons School Archives.

10. Ibid.

11. Marjorie F. Jones, "History," 91–92; Gropius, qtd. in Read, *Art and Industry*, 40; Parsons, qtd. in Marjorie F. Jones, "History," 297, 361.

12. Marjorie F. Jones, "History," 141; Hambidge, *Practical Applications*, intro., 3, 20.

13. RKA, 4.

14. IJW, 17–20 Oct. 1979; RKA, 3–4.

15. Kimmel, interview; "Costume Design, Construction and Illustration," in *New York School of Fine and Applied Art (Parsons)*, 16; "Georges Lepape"; Jewell, "Students," 10; Yohannan and Nolf, *Claire McCardell*, 19–21; Valerie Steele, "McCardell's American Look," in Yohannan and Nolf, *Claire McCardell*, 13.

16. IJW, 17–20 Oct. 1979; Kimmel, interview; Jackie Curtis and Maureen O'Hara, interview; Valerie Harms to author, 5 Aug. 2002; Chadwick, interview; Noguchi, *Sculptor's World*, 19; Torres, *Isamu Noguchi*, 311.

17. RKA, 4; Harms, "Interview," 8.

18. "Albert A. Brager to Wed," 7; "Albert A. Brager Married," 3; "Albert A. Brager's Funeral," 18.

19. "Lionel White 1905–"; Hedy White, interview; Helaine White, interview; IJW, 19 Oct. 1979.

CHAPTER 4

1. Else Frank, interview; Miller, interview.

2. Leach, *Land of Desire*, 22; Fisher, "Barnaby and Mr. O'Malley"; Hungerford, *Romance*, 90–91, 93, 176.

3. Lears, *Fables*, 226; Norris, "Meet the Man."

4. Norris, "Meet the Man," 24; Else Frank, interview; "Ice Business," *Donnelley's Red Book Classified Telephone Directory: Queens, Winter Issue 1927–1928, Dec. to June,* Long Island Division, Queens Borough Public Library; Folsom, interview; Searchinger, interview; Trubowitz, interview.

5. "Looking Back at 1927," 22–25, 50–54; Burlingame, *Endless Frontiers,* 265.

6. "Leisk, David Johnson," in *Something about the Author* (1971), 141; "Leisk, David Johnson 1906–," 505; "Leisk, David Johnson," in *Something about the Author* (1983), 141–44; "Crockett Johnson," 152–53; MacLeod, "Johnson, Crockett," 499; "Johnson, Crockett," 346; Film Designers, promotional brochure, box 28, folder 857, RK Papers-NCLC; *New York University Department of Fine Arts: Announcements for the Summer Term, 1926—Fall Term, 1926–1927—Spring Term, 1927,* 9, New York University Archives; Goudy, introduction, 20; Boone, "Type," 114; Orton, *Goudy,* 27; "Johnson, Crockett, pseud.," 126.

7. "Pioneer Manufacturer," 1049; McGraw, "Why McGraw-Hill Desires to Serve," 629; H[annah] B[aker], "Crockett Johnson," 2; Fisher, "Barnaby and Mr. O'Malley"; "Cushlamochree!," 104; "Editorial: Styled for Today," 769; Burlingame, *Endless Frontiers,* 291, 267–68, 271, 273.

8. 1930 U.S. Census; Else Frank, interview; Folsom, interview; 1930 U.S. Census; *New York City 1933 Directory H–R,* 287, New York Public Library.

9. Folsom, interview.

10. Chandler, *America's Greatest Depression,* 5–6; "Treasury's Position," 22; "Milk Strike," F21; Denning, *Cultural Front,* xiii, 200.

CHAPTER 5

1. "Writer Is Rescued," 32; "Recovering from Submersion," 17; Hahn, interview.

2. Helaine White, interview; "Lionel White 1905–"; Hedy White, interview; "Books and Authors," 18; RK to Miss Coker, 27 Mar. 1944, RK Papers-HC; Goulart, *Cheap Thrills,* 13; Georgia M. Higley to author, 11 July 2005. Decades later, White's detective novels would become classic films: Stanley Kubrick adapted *Clean Break* (1955) as *The Killing* (1956), and Jean-Luc Godard filmed *Obsession* (1962) as *Pierrot le fou* (1965).

3. RK to Miss Coker, 27 Mar. 1944, RK Papers-HC; RK to Dorothy Warner, 10 Dec. 1986, folder 42, box 2, series I, RK Papers-NCLC; IJW, 19 Oct. 1979; Lionel White and RK, marriage certificate, Orphans' Court Division, Court of Common Pleas of Bucks County, Pennsylvania; Hahn, interview.

4. IJW, 19 Oct. 1979; Hahn, interview; "Where," 122; RK to Miss Coker, 27 Mar. 1944, RK Papers-HC.

5. Hahn, interview; "Wife and Children," 36; RK, "Poem for the Depression," 1960, folder 33, box 2, series I, RK Papers-NCLC.

6. IJW, 19 Oct. 1979; Graetz, interview.

7. RK, "The House," 1, 16, 17–18, 14, 20, 21, box 19, folder 690, RK Papers-NCLC.

8. "Where," 72.

9. Ibid., 72–73; RK to Miss Coker, 27 Mar. 1944, RK Papers-HC.

10. "Where," 69–71.

11. Hahn, interview.

CHAPTER 6

1. Mischa Richter, interview.

2. Bergman, *We're in the Money*, 115–20.

3. Denning, *Cultural Front*, 9.

4. "To Our Readers"; Lerner, "American League," 31; Klehr, *Heyday*, 116; "With the Readers," 5.

5. Magil, interview; "Johnson, Crockett," 346; *News Letter of the American Institute of Graphic Arts* 40 (July 1936), American Institute of Graphic Arts, New York; Joe Freeman to Granville Hicks, 6 June 1936, box 44, folder: New Masses, 1936–1939, Granville Hicks Papers, Syracuse University Library, Special Collections Research Center; Joe Freeman to Rockwell Kent, 24 July 1936, Rockwell Kent to Joseph Freeman, 29 July 1936, reel 5217, frames 0934–35, Kent Papers; "Rockwell Kent Biography."

6. CJ, qtd. in Hemingway, *Artists*, 105.

7. Dutt, "Britain and Spain," 3; "Challenge and the Answer," 20; "Cement," 10.

8. Joe Freeman to Granville Hicks, 6 June 1936, box 44, folder: New Masses, 1936–1939, Hicks Papers; Mischa Richter, cartoon, *New Masses*, 19 Oct. 1937; AR, cartoon, *New Masses*, 14 July 1936; Abe Ajay, cartoon, *New Masses*, 8 Sept. 1936; Lee Hall, *Abe Ajay*, 31; "With the Readers," 5; AR, artist's chronology, reel N69-99, frame 115, AR Papers; Anna Reinhardt, interview; NS, interview; McMahon, interview; Landau, interview; Alice McMahon, biographical sketch of George Annand (1980), George Annand Papers, in possession of Alice McMahon.

9. AR, artist's chronology; Anna Reinhardt, interview.

10. CJ to Rockwell Kent, 11 May 1937, reel 5217, frame 0971, Kent Papers; Syd Hoff to author, 8 July 2000.

11. Mickenberg, "Pedagogy."

12. Magil, interview; Browder, "Isolationist Front," 3–4; Browder, "Historic Report," 3–4.

13. Magil, interview; Communist Party U.S.A. Records, Library of Congress; Linder, "Samuel Liebowitz"; Klehr and Haynes, *American Communist Movement*, 79, 86; Harold Strauss to William Gropper, 20 Oct. 1936, roll 3501, frame 556, William Gropper Papers, Syracuse University Library, Special Collections Research Center.

14. McCloud, *Understanding Comics*, 30, 37.

15. "Public Speaking Zooms"; Cobb, *Radical Education*, 36, 148, 204, 116, 63; Randolph, "Utopia in Arkansas," 147; Oser, interview.

16. Syd Hoff to author, 15 July 2001; Redfield, "'When the Locomotive'"; Magil, interview.

CHAPTER 7

1. RKA, 5.

2. Lapsley, *Margaret Mead*, 275; NS to author, [Mar. 2001?].

3. RKA, 6.

4. Ibid., 7; "Where," 98, 99.

5. RKA, 7–8.

6. Benedict, "Primitive Freedom," 760, 762; Caffrey, *Ruth Benedict*, 291.

7. *Columbia University in the City of New York: Directory Number for the Sessions 1939–1940*, 162, 76, Columbiana Library, Columbia University Archives; *Columbia University*

in the City of New York: Catalogue Number for the Sessions of 1940–1941, 207, Columbiana
Library, Columbia University Archives; "Between Ourselves," 28 Mar. 1939, 2; Rovere,
"What Every Appeaser Should Know," 5–6; "Why the Pact Was Signed," 10–12.

8. RKA, 5–6.

9. Beckwith, "Barnaby," 33; "Wife of Barnaby's Creator Is Baltimore Authoress,"
Baltimore Sun, ca. 1 Oct. 1944, RK Papers-HC; Hahn, interview.

10. Mischa Richter, interviews; Sparber, interview.

11. "This Little Gag"; Mischa Richter, interview. Richter remained at *New Masses* until
late 1941, when he became a *New Yorker* cartoonist.

12. Though officially untitled, the comic strip is known by the name *Little Man with the
Eyes*.

13. Norris, "Meet the Man," 24; original drawing dedicated "To Ben Gray Moore with
Thanks," and CJ to Ben Gray Moore, 20 Mar. 1942, in possession of Ben Gray Moore Jr.; CJ,
"Watch Ford in '48." I thank Mark Newgarden for his help in figuring out CJ's method of
composition.

14. "Between Ourselves," 2 Apr. 1940.

15. Gurney Williams, *Collier's Collects Its Wits*, 80; FBI-CJ, 11 May 1951.

16. *Columbia University in the City of New York: Supplement to the Directory Number
1941*, 22, Columbiana Library, Columbia University Archives; 1941 New York phone book;
"Crockett Johnson," in *Major Authors*, ed. Collier and Nakamura, 1436; "Leisk, David
Johnson," in *Something about the Author* (1971), 141; "Leisk, David Johnson," in *Something
about the Author* (1983), 141; "A Hole Is to Dig? Harold Should Know," 2; "Johnson,
Crockett," 347; "Wife of Barnaby's Creator"; New York Office of the FBI, 11 May 1951, FBI-
CJ; Heinrich, interview; RKA, 6.

17. New York Office of the FBI, 11 May 1951, FBI-CJ; World War Two Bonds Cartoons,
Terry-D'Alessio Collection. Ruth was enrolled at Columbia University in the fall of 1941,
although she was not a degree student, and there is no record of what classes she took.

18. World War Two Bonds Cartoons, Terry-D'Alessio Collection. Johnson's cartoon
featuring Hitler and the clock and the globe was reprinted in the 24 February 1942 issue of
New Masses, his first drawing to appear in that publication since May 1940.

19. "Where," 44–46.

20. Colored Comic Continuities stock certificate, 10 May 1941, signed George Annand,
George Annand Papers, in possession of Alice McMahon; Alice McMahon to author, 3 July
2001; McMahon, interview; Norris, "Meet the Man"; Tom Hopps to author, 9 Apr. 2000;
Raymond, *Rowayton*, 86, 88.

21. Norris, "Meet the Man"; Fisher, "Barnaby"; Mischa Richter, interview.

22. "The Saga of Barnaby," *Barnaby Quarterly* 1.1 (July 1945): 25; Norris, "Meet the Man."

CHAPTER 8

1. "The Saga of Barnaby," *Barnaby Quarterly* 1.1 (July 1945): 25; "Cushlamochree!";
Fisher, "Barnaby and Mr. O'Malley."

2. Milkman, *PM*, 49, 43, 1, 41; Nevins, "Pulp and Adventure Heroes: J"; Nevins, "Pulp
and Adventure Heroes: P."

3. Geisel, qtd. in Ralph Ingersoll, "Memo to the Staff," 24 Mar. 1942, 2–3, MSS 0230, box
18, folder 27, Dr. Seuss Collection, Mandeville Special Collections, University of California

at San Diego. For nine months, *PM* ran cartoons by both Johnson and Geisel. Although they knew each other's work and may have met socially, they were not friends, and Johnson disliked Geisel's style of illustration (NS, interview).

4. Norris, "Meet the Man."

5. Fisher, "Barnaby and Mr. O'Malley."

6. Norris, "Meet the Man," 24.

7. *Columbia University Bulletin of Information: Announcement for the Division of Philosophy, Psychology, and Anthropology for the Winter and Spring Sessions 1942–1943*, 38–39, Columbiana Library, Columbia University Archives; RK to Miss Coker, 27 Mar. 1944, RK Papers-HC; "Where," 24.

8. Benedict and Weltfish, *Races*, 3, 16, 18; Caffrey, *Ruth Benedict*, 298.

9. Ellington, "He Trusts"; Parker, "Mash Note."

10. Norris, "Meet the Man," 24; FBI-CJ, 11 May 1951.

11. Foster, *This Rich World*, rear dust jacket, 143, 125.

12. Hahn, interview.

13. Charlotte Zolotow, interview; Charlotte Zolotow, speech at RK memorial service, July 1993, cassette tape provided by Maureen O'Hara; Bader, "Ruth Krauss," 416.

14. Mickenberg and Nel, *Tales*, intro. to sec. 7. See also Mickenberg, *Learning*, chaps. 3, 5, 7.

15. Norris, "Meet the Man," 24; McNell and McNell, interview.

CHAPTER 9

1. "Wife of Barnaby's Creator Is Baltimore Authoress," *Baltimore Sun*, ca. 1 Oct. 1944, RK Papers-HC; Norris, "Meet the Man," 24; Mischa Richter, interview; David Johnson Leisk and RK marriage certificate, Estate of RK, Cohen & Wolf, Bridgeport, Conn.

2. "Where," 114.

3. UN to RK, 16 Nov. 1943, RK to UN, 1 Jan. 1944, both in RK Papers-HC.

4. Kent, Benét, Untermeyer, McKenney, qtd. in CJ, *Barnaby*, back dust jacket; Parker, "Mash Note"; S[eaver], "Books," 14, Barnaby Fan Mail II, CJ Papers-SI.

5. *Philadelphia Record*, 18 Oct. 1943, Henry Holt and Company advertisement, *New York Times Book Review*, 12 Nov. 1943, both in Barnaby Fan Mail II, CJ Papers-SI; *Publisher's Weekly* clipping, 22 Nov. 1943, photograph and handwritten note by Elenore Lust, both in Elenore Lust Papers, Archives of American Art, Smithsonian Institution; "Speaking of Pictures"; "Cushlamochree!," 102; "Tonight," *New York Times*, 9 Nov. 1943.

6. Charles Frederick Lehmann to managing editor of *PM*, 27 May 1944, Pvt. Daniel H. Distler to CJ, 22 Nov. 1944, George A. Elliott III to CJ, 30 Sept. 1944, "The Things to Do," *Wilmington (Del.) Experiment Station Beacon*, 4 Feb. 1944, Joseph H. Firman to CJ, 19 May 1944, "O'Malley Foiled by Crown Zippers," *Life*, 10 Apr. 1944, 82, Hannah Baker to Lillian Schwartz, 28 June 1944, 21 Jan. 1946, all in Barnaby Fan Mail II, CJ Papers-SI; Bob Miller, "Mr. O'Malley's March" (sheet music) (1944), CJ Papers-SI.

7. RK to UN, 12 Jan., 27 Feb. 1944, both in RK Papers-HC.

8. "Ruth Krauss: Let Me Tell You a Story," 3; "Krauss, Ruth (Ida) 1911–," in *Something about the Author*, 135; unsigned letter to RK, RK to UN, [Oct. 1944?], both in RK Papers-HC.

9. RK to UN, n.d., RK Papers-HC.

10. Korff, "Children's Books"; RK to UN, 25 Aug. 1960, RK Papers-HC; Bader, "Ruth Krauss," 418.

11. "Wife of Barnaby's Creator"; Sparber, interview.

12. Sparber, interview. The first strip to use type was George Herriman's *The Dingbat Family* of 26 July 1910 (notable for the debut of Krazy Kat and Ignatz Mouse), but Herriman abandoned the experiment, preferring hand-lettering (McDonnell, O'Connell, and de Havenon, *Krazy Kat*, 55). I thank Chris Ware for pointing me to this Herriman strip. My description of Futura owes a debt to Burke, *Paul Renner*, 96–98, 113.

13. Sparber, interview.

14. Skelly, interview; Christopher Skelly to author, 13 July 2007; Stroud, "Crockett Johnson's Geometric Paintings," 78–79; E. H. C. Hildebrandt to CJ, 3 Mar. 1944, Barnaby Fan Mail II, CJ Papers-SI; Gray, "Engineering Research Associates."

15. Miles H. Wolff to Harry Elmlark, 10 July 1944, Mary E. O'Malley to editor, *Baltimore Evening Sun*, ca. 23 June 1944, Stephen G. May et al. to editor, *Baltimore Evening Sun*, ca. 24 June 1944, all in Barnaby Fan Mail II, CJ Papers-SI.

16. Beckwith, "Barnaby."

17. Jo Davidson to CJ, 17 Jan. 1944, Barnaby Fan Mail I, CJ Papers-SI; *President's Speech*, Hugo Gellert Papers, Archives of American Art, Smithsonian Institution.

18. Hannah Baker to Norman Dine, 26 Sept. 1944, "Ex-Rep. O'Malley's Program: Woolgathering," *PM*, 25 Oct. 1944, both in Barnaby Fan Mail II, CJ Papers-SI.

19. Mallet, "Godfather," 9; Mallet, "Cartoonists," 7; Conroy, "Leisk," 73; Binsse, "Children's Books," 127.

20. UN to CJ, 2 Nov. 1944, CJ to UN, 27 Nov. 1944, both in CJ Papers-HC.

21. "Events Today," 21; "Dinner Will Honor Gropper," 8; "Edward Chodorov Invites You to a Dinner Honoring William Gropper on Monday Evening, December Fourth at Six-Forty-Five" (program), Box 11, William Gropper Papers, Syracuse University Library, Special Collections Research Center.

22. FBI-CJ; Henrietta Buckmaster to Rockwell Kent, 6 Feb. 1945, reel 5169, frame 269, Kent Papers; Loewen, *Lies across America*, 246–50; Katherine Shryver to CJ, 18 Mar. 1944, Barnaby Fan Mail I, CJ Papers-SI; Hannah Baker to Katherine Shryver, 22 Mar. 1944, Barnaby Fan Mail II, CJ Papers-SI.

23. Schallert, "Dorothy McGuire," A10; "Musical Revivals," 10; Denning, *Cultural Front*, 295–300.

24. "Nugent's Comedy," 16; Margolick, *Strange Fruit*, 40–41; Lyons, "Lyons Den," 18; Sam Zolotow, "New Variety Show," 17; Denning, *Cultural Front*, 115; "Jimmy Savo Celebrates First Anniversary, and a Comeback, at Café Society Uptown, Monday, May 22" (press release), 17 May 1944, Barnaby Fan Mail II, CJ Papers-SI.

25. Deed of sale, 13 Feb. 1945, Probate Court, Norwalk, Conn., 307:198–99.

26. RK to UN, [Oct. 1944?], 27 Mar. 1945, both in RK Papers-HC; review of *The Carrot Seed*, *Virginia Kirkus' Bookshop Service*, 180; Buell, review of *The Carrot Seed*, 18.

27. Hopkins, "Ruth Krauss [and] Crockett Johnson," 122; Raymond Eisenhardt to CJ, 27 Aug. 1945, RK Papers-HC; RK, untitled short story (about the writing of *The Great Duffy*), 29, box 7, folder 242, RK Papers-NCLC; "Krauss, Ruth (Ida) 1911–," in *Something about the Author*, 135.

CHAPTER 10

1. CJ, *Barnaby*, 8 June, 6 Dec. 1944, both in *Barnaby #4*, 28, 183; *American Statistical Association Bulletin* 3.4 (Aug. 1944); "Small Cigaret Firms," 8; CJ, *Barnaby*, 30 Jan. 1945, in *Barnaby #5*, 15; "Soap Opera"; Agnes Allen to CJ, 12 Apr. 1945, Barnaby Fan Mail II, CJ Papers-SI.

2. Fisher, "Barnaby and Mr. O'Malley"; Norris, "Meet the Man," 24.

3. RK, untitled short story (about the writing of *The Great Duffy*), box 7, folder 242, RK Papers-NCLC 1–2.

4. Ibid., 2, 3.

5. Antler, *Lucy Sprague Mitchell*, 322–23; Marcus, *Margaret Wise Brown*, 52.

6. Dan Richter, interview.

7. RK, untitled short story (about the writing of *The Great Duffy*), 22, 14, 13, 16–17.

8. Ibid., 26–27.

9. *Baby Talk*, in possession of NS.

10. NS, interview; RK to UN, [Feb. 1945], "Ruth Krauss, 1943–1950," RK Papers-HC.

11. Ray and Stewart, *Norwalk*, 159, 212n; Elizabeth Ring Hennefrund to author, 11 Sept. 2004; Edwards, "Journalist and the G-Man," 119, 152–54; Schnabel, interview; Marinsky, interview. Schwed, *Pleasure Was Mine*, 201, also uses the phrase "the Athens of South Norwalk."

12. Fay, interview; Schwed, *Where Are the Customers' Yachts?*, xii, 19, 20.

13. CJ, *Barnaby*, 21, 25 Feb., 24, 25, 9 Apr. 1945, all in *Barnaby #5*, 34, 38, 87, 88, 74.

14. New Haven Office of the FBI, "David Johnson Leisk, wa. Crockett Johnson," 27 Feb. 1952, 8. FBI-CJ; *The Independent*, 13 Feb. 1946, 2, Reel 4625, Carl Zigrosser Papers (microfilm), Archives of American Art, Smithsonian Institution; *For the People's Health*.

15. U.S. House of Representatives, Committee on Un-American Activities, *Review*, 41; Ben Goldstein to sponsor, 18 Aug. 1945, reel 5167, frames 669, 670, Kent Papers; letterhead and list of sponsors, Milton Wolff to Shirley Johnson, 6 Dec. 1945, reel 5155, frame 181–182, Kent Papers; *Stamford Shopper*, 9 Aug. 1945; New Haven Office of the FBI, "David Johnson Leisk, wa. Crockett Johnson," 27 Feb. 1952, 8, FBI-CJ.

16. RK to UN, [early July 1945], RK Papers-HC.

17. RK, "Suggestion for a Movie for Adults from a Book for Children, The Great Duffy," 1, 2, 3, 6, RK Papers-NCLC.

18. UN, "File Ruth Krauss," 2 Nov. 1945, "Ruth Krauss 1943–1950," RK Papers-HC.

19. Hannah Baker to CJ, 2 Nov. 1945, Barnaby Fan Mail II, CJ Papers-SI; "Escape Artist," 49–50; CJ to Theodore E. Ferro, 16 Dec. 1946, CJ to Jack Morley, 16 Dec. 1946, both in CJ Papers-ERK.

CHAPTER 11

1. CJ, "Assorted Facts about Crockett Johnson," *Barnaby* (Pocket Books, 1946), 362.

2. "Ickes for Free Speech," 14; "Noted Professionals Back May Day," 4.

3. Lieberman, *Strangest Dream*, 10; New Haven Office of the FBI, "David Johnson Leisk, wa. Crockett Johnson," 28 July 1950, 5–6, New York Office of the FBI, "David Johnson Leisk, wa. Crockett Johnson," 31 July 1950, 2, both in FBI-CJ; "New Yorkers Are Moving"; "Win the Peace for Whom?"; Shiefs, "600 at Win-Peace Parley," 7.

4. CJ, *Barnaby*, *PM*, 26 Aug. 1946, 19.

5. Barney Josephson to CJ, 4 May 1946, CJ Papers-ERK; "RKO·Will Produce 'Barnaby,'" 9; "Two Plays Tonight," 34.

6. Barney Josephson to CJ, 4 May 1946, CJ Papers-ERK; Hamilton, interview; "Two Plays Tonight," 34; Seeley, "Barnaby's Coming to Town," 14; Jerome Chodorov, *Crockett Johnson's Barnaby and Mr. O'Malley* (script, 1946), I-39, 2–58, in possession of Thomas Hamilton.

7. "Plan of the Book (The Following Aren't Titles; Just Contents)," n.d., RK Papers-HC.

8. Little, "For Small Children," 4; Fischer, review of *The Great Duffy*, 3; review of *The Great Duffy*, *Virginia Kirkus' Bookshop Service*, 490; RK, untitled short story (about the writing of *The Great Duffy*), 29, box 7, folder 242, RK Papers-NCLC.

9. Hamilton, interview; Sam Zolotow, "Canada Lee," 10; Jerome Chodorov to Terry Josephson, 15 Apr. 1992, in possession of Terry Josephson; Hamilton, interview; unidentified clipping, 7 Oct. 1946, in possession of Thomas Hamilton; CJ to Barney Josephson, ca. Sept. 1947, CJ Papers-ERK.

10. RK to UN, [first half of 1947?], RK Papers-HC; "Where," 91, 6, 103, 111; *Greenwich Time*, 27 Dec. 1946, qtd. in New Haven Office of the FBI, "David Johnson Leisk, wa. Crockett Johnson," 28 July 1950, 4, New Haven Office of the FBI, "David Johnson Leisk, wa. Crockett Johnson," 28 July 1950, 5, both in FBI-CJ; "Plans Reception," 12; "Increase Seats," 1, 12; "Debate on Peace Formula, 1, 12; "Wallace Raps," 1, 6.

11. UN to RK, 11 July 1947, RK to UN, [early July 1947], both in RK Papers-HC; Dorothy A. Bennett to RK, 26 June 1947, box 2, folder 46, RK Papers-NCLC.

12. CJ to Barney Josephson, ca. Sept. 1947, CJ, draft of telegram to Barney Josephson and James Proctor, [Feb. or July?] 1947, CJ to Kay Van Riper, 4 Sept. 1947, all in CJ Papers-ERK.

13. "Where," 117–18; "This Is the Kind of Book I Like"; Waugh, *Comics*, 306, 309, 310.

14. NS to author, [Mar. or Apr. 2001]; "Where," 119; *Baby Talk*, in possession of NS.

15. "Where," 47; McMahon, interview. For some of the 1947–52 period, Johnson appears to have left all or most of the work to Morley. In February 1949, for example, the strip is credited only to Morley.

16. Becker, review of *The Growing Story*, 14; Darling, review of *The Growing Story*, 16A; Gerard, review of *The Growing Story*, 42; review of *The Growing Story*, *Virginia Kirkus' Bookshop Service*, 335.

CHAPTER 12

1. Nona Brown, "It's Been a Tough Winter," E9; "City's Snow Costs," 28; Tracy, "Climatological Data," Dec. 1947, 94, Jan. 1948, 23, Feb. 1948, 23; "Where," 2; James, qtd. in Perry, *Thought and Character*, 355.

2. "Where," 1, 11, 37.

3. Ibid., 9, 10, 12.

4. Ibid., 4–6, 7, 7a–c, 25, 93.

5. Ibid., 94, 41, 42, 44, 45.

6. McNell and McNell, interview; "Where," 29, 27.

7. "Where," 64–65.

8. Ibid., 20, 21.

9. Jackie Curtis and O'Hara, interview; "Where," 18.

10. "Where," 18, 16, 17, 77–81, 109, 110.

11. "Where," 22, 42, 55; Hopps, interview.

12. "Where," 37.

13. Ibid., 49; Twain, *Pudd'nhead Wilson*, 211; CJ, *Barnaby*, 8 Dec. 1948.

14. "Where," 31, 35–36; "Wallace Returns," 2; "Group from Connecticut," 1; New Haven Office of the FBI, "David Johnson Leisk, wa. Crockett Johnson," 28 July 1950, 5, FBI-CJ; "We Are for Wallace," 32; Wallace, qtd. in Culver and Hyde, *American Dreamer*, 457.

15. "Where," 87; Furman, "Johnston Stresses," 32; "Aid to Family Life," 22; Marcus, *Golden Legacy*, 79.

16. "Where," 36–37, 83–86, 88, 89.

17. Furman, "Johnston Stresses," 32; Truman, "President's Speech," 10; Truman, "Statement"; Masters and Masters, *Barnaby: A Play for Children in Two Acts*; Mabel McKee, "'Barnaby' Pleases in Its First Run," *Terre Haute Tribune*, 3 May 1948, CJ Papers-ERK; "Agreement between Samuel French Incorporated 1899 and Robert and Lillian Masters," CJ Papers-ERK.

18. *Barnaby and Mr. O'Malley*, presented by Ben Pearson (Radio Recorders, Hollywood, Calif.), acetate disc, CJ Papers-SI; Brown, interview.

19. Milkman, *PM*, 201, 198, 208; Harvey, "Introducing Walt Kelly," v.

20. CJ, *Barnaby*, 29 May–2 June, 26 May 1948.

21. "Text of Wallace Letter," 14; U.S. House of Representatives, Committee on Un-American Activities, *Review*, 51.

CHAPTER 13

1. U.S. Code 2385 (Advocating Overthrow of Government); Michael Steven Smith, "Smith Act Trials, 1949," 755–56.

2. "Text of the Platform," 32; CJ, *Barnaby*, 21, 22 Sept., 27 Sept.–1 Oct., 11 Oct., 10 Nov. 1948.

3. New Haven Office of the FBI, "David Johnson Leisk, wa. Crockett Johnson," 28 July 1950, 6, FBI-CJ.

4. CJ, *Barnaby*, 15, 16, 17, 31 Dec. 1948.

5. Dedman, "Celebrating," 21; Bechtel, review of *Bears*, 6; Eaton, review of *Bears*, 11; Jordan, "Mid-Winter Booklist," 33–34.

6. RK to UN, [prior to May 1949], RK Papers-HC; Marcus, *Golden Legacy*, 79–80, 139; Canemaker, *Art and Flair*, ix.

7. RK to UN, [prior to May 1949], RK Papers-HC; Leonard S. Marcus to author, 25 July 2008; Marcus, *Margaret Wise Brown*, 58, 84, 85, 168.

8. Marcus, *Golden Legacy*, 141; Canemaker, *Art and Flair*, 72–73.

9. RK to UN, 31 Dec. 1948, RK Papers-HC.

10. "Marc Simont"; Pittman, "Finding Aid"; Marcus, "Marc Simont's Sketchbooks"; Simont, interview.

11. Elizabeth Ring Hennefrund to Adolf Dehn, 20 July 1961, reel 287, frame 133, Adolf and Virginia Dehn Papers, Archives of American Art, Smithsonian Institution; Adolf Dehn, handwritten note on H. Harvard Arnason's telegram to Dehn, 13 Jan. 1949, Dehn Papers; Parke, "Culture Sessions," 1, 44, 45, 46, 47; O'Connor, "News," 438–40; Price,

Threatening Anthropology, 118; "Pickets Denounce Soviet, Communism," 1, 3; "2 'Peace' Meetings," 1, 47; Parke, "Global Unity Call," 1–4; Lieberman, *Strangest Dream*, 33. On 16 Mar. 1949, Harper sent Ruth's contract for *Flower in the Snow* (*The Happy Day*) to her at Dehn's address (RK Papers-HC).

12. "1000 Notables," 2, 11; U.S. House of Representatives, Committee on Un-American Activities, *Review*, 2, 9, 20, 47, 54, 57.

13. CJ, *Barnaby*, 7–12 Mar. 1949.

14. "Secretary, Department of Books for Boys and Girls" to RK, 16 Mar. 1949, RK Papers-HC; "Where," 93, 108, 113; RK, manuscript page of *The Happy Day* sent to Marc Simont, in possession of Marc Simont; Hirschman, "1998 May Hill Arbuthnot Lecture," 362–77. Susan Carr married in September 1959 and after 1964 was known professionally as Susan Carr Hirschman.

15. RK, manuscript page of *The Happy Day* sent to Simont, in possession of Marc Simont; Simont, interview.

16. Hirschman, interview; review of *The Happy Day*, *Atlantic Monthly*, 103; Bechtel, review of *The Happy Day*, 6; Moore, review of *The Happy Day*, 520–23.

17. Winn, "How a Family," 12; review of *Big World*, *Bulletin of the Children's Book Center*, 16–17; Palmer, review of *Big World*, 14; Blasco, review of *Big World*, 1917; review of *Big World*, *San Francisco Chronicle*, 6.

18. RK to UN, Mar. 1949, RK Papers-HC.

19. Ibid., [early 1949].

20. CJ to William Morris Jr., 1 Dec. 1949, Sidney Buchman to CJ, 14 Nov. 1949, "A Formula for Some Required Revision," all in CJ Papers-ERK.

CHAPTER 14

1. FBI-CJ.

2. Hoover, *Masters of Deceit*, 83, 86.

3. FBI-CJ; New Haven Office of the FBI, "David Johnson Leisk, wa. Crockett Johnson," 10 Nov. 1950, 5, FBI-CJ.

4. Trubowitz, interview.

5. CJ, *Barnaby*, 15 May 1950.

6. UN to RK, 8 May 1950, RK Papers-HC; New Haven Office of the FBI, "David Johnson Leisk, wa Crockett Johnson," 28 July 1950, 5, 1, Baltimore Office of the FBI, "David Johnson Leisk, wa.," 18 Nov. 1950, 1–2, both in FBI-CJ.

7. Graetz, interview.

8. Bechtel, review of *The Backward Day*, 9; Buell, review of *The Backward Day*, 36.

9. Gesell, *First Five Years*, 55; RK to UN, [June or July 1951?], RK Papers-HC.

10. RK to UN, 5 Jan. 1951, RK Papers-HC; Hopkins, "Ruth Krauss [and] Crockett Johnson," 122.

11. Lanes, *Art*, 42, 40; Braun, "Sendak Raises," 47, 49; Sendak, interview; Harms, "Interview," 8.

12. Sendak, interview; Sendak, "Ruth Krauss and Me," 287; *A Hole Is to Dig* draft, RK Papers-NCLC; Lanes, *Art*, 42.

13. CJ, "The Five-Inch Shelf: Tiny Golden Books as Miniature 'Sets of Classics' for Younger Children," 2–4, RK Papers-NCLC.

14. U.S. House of Representatives, Committee on Un-American Activities, *Report*; Cronan, "Washington Close-Up," A12; New Haven Office of the FBI, "David Johnson Leisk, wa," 9 May 1952, 2–3, FBI-CJ; Mellen, *Kay Boyle*, 336–37; Elizabeth Ring Hennefrund to author, 11 Sept. 2004; Price, *Threatening Anthropology*, 120.

15. Simon, interview; RK to UN, 3 Oct. 1951, UN to RK, 8 Oct. 1951, both in RK Papers-HC; Sendak, "Ruth Krauss and Me," 289.

16. RK to UN, 8 Jan. 1952, RK Papers-HC; UN, *Dear Genius*, 44; Sendak, "Ruth Krauss and Me," 288.

17. Sendak, interview; Sendak, "Ruth Krauss and Me," 289.

18. Review of *Bundle Book*, *Virginia Kirkus' Bookshop Service*, 575; Lindquist and Andrews, review of *Bundle Book*, 403; Palmer, review of *Bundle Book*, 42; UN to RK, 29 Nov. 1951, RK Papers-HC.

19. Marcus, *Margaret Wise Brown*, 261; UN to RK, 15 Nov. 1951, RK Papers-HC.

20. CJ, *Barnaby*, 5, 7, 31 Jan., 2 Feb. 1952.

21. CJ to Charles Fisher, 11 Feb. 1952, in possession of Chris Wheeler; Dwight Marvin to CJ, 12 Dec. 1951, Barnaby Fan Mail II, CJ Papers-SI; Ray Armstrong to CJ, 11 Feb. 1952, CJ Papers-SI.

22. Brown University, Pembroke College, *Brun Mael*, 1953, RK Papers-NCLC.

23. NS, interview; Tayler, "Barnaby's Creator," B5.

24. Palmer, "Bewildered Kangaroo," 52.

25. Buell, review of *A Hole Is to Dig*, 31; Lindquist, review of *A Hole Is to Dig*, 315; *A Hole Is to Dig*, dust jacket.

26. Sendak, interview.

27. Hahn, interview; RK to UN, [26 Aug. 1952?], RK Papers-HC; Graetz, interview; "Deaths [Leisk, Mary]," 23.

28. Mickenberg, *Learning*, 33; Fay, "Ruth Ida Krauss," 31.

29. Mickenberg, *Learning*, 142, 15; SAC, New Haven to Director, FBI, 20 Dec. 1954, FBI-CJ.

CHAPTER 15

1. Lund and Lund, interview; Lichtenstein, interview; Marion Schnabel to author, 20 Jan. 2003; Schnabel, interview; "ILWU's Kent Tangles With McCarthy," *The Dispatcher*, 10 July 1953, reel 5211, frame 0658, Kent Papers.

2. Willcox, interview; Roger Willcox, "President's Report: Welcome to our 50th Anniversary Celebration," in *Village Creek*, 1.

3. Openheimer, reminiscence, in *Village Creek*, 13; Seidman, reminiscence, in *Village Creek*, 30; Willcox, interview.

4. Simon, interview; Garment, interview.

5. Dan Richter, interview; Levine, interview.

6. Mellen, *Kay Boyle*, 359, 361, 365, 378, 373, 400; Elizabeth Ring Hennefrund to author, 11 Sept. 2004. Hennefrund recalls meeting Krauss and Johnson in 1956 or 1957.

7. "Jack A. Goodman," 27; Trubowitz, interview; Charles Lederer, in *Jack A. Goodman*, 11; Peter Schwed, in *Jack A. Goodman* 5; Elizabeth Ring Hennefrund to author, 11 Sept. 2004; Searchinger, interview.

8. Feiffer, interview; Feiffer, *Backing into Forward*, 241.

9. Kieran, review of *A Very Special House*, 97; Haviland, review of *A Very Special House*, 452–53.

10. Tyler, "As an Author Sees," B4; Sendak, interview; Marcus, interview.

11. Marcus, *Margaret Wise Brown*, 279; NS, interview.

12. *Is This You?*, sketches by RK and CJ, Series II, Box 10, RK Papers-NCLC.

13. *Is This You?*, sketches by CJ, Series II, Box 10, RK Papers-NCLC

14. Buell, review of *Is This You?*, 28; review of *Is This You?*, *Bulletin of the Children's Book Center*, 9; Bechtel, review of *I'll Be You*, 32; Buell, review of *I'll Be You*.

15. Tyler, "As an Author Sees," B4.

16. Donlon, review of *How to Make an Earthquake*, 15; Palmer, review of *How to Make an Earthquake*, 24; review of *How to Make an Earthquake*, *Bulletin of the Children's Book Center* 4; Mrs. Donn Grinn to Harper and Brothers, 18 Jan. 1955, RK Papers-HC; Hopkins, "Ruth Krauss [and] Crockett Johnson," 123.

17. UN to RK, 15, 21 Sept. 1954, Mary Russell to RK, 21 Sept. 1954, RK to UN, [Sept. 1954], all in RK Papers-HC.

18. Gene Wallace death certificate, in possession of NS; "Gene Wallace," 24; NS, interview; McMahon, interview; NS to author, July 2004.   19. NS to author, July 2004, [Mar. or Apr. 2001], 13 Aug. 2008.

20. RK to UN, [Sept. 1954] (two letters), UN to RK, 21 Sept. 1954, all in RK Papers-HC; RK to Claudia Lewis, 20 Sept. 1954, archives, Bank Street College of Education, New York.

CHAPTER 16

1. Else Frank interview; Harold Frank, interview.

2. Mickenberg, *Learning*, 142.

3. UN, *Dear Genius*, 83; A[nn] P[owers], reader's report for *Harold and the Purple Crayon*, 23 Nov. 1954, CJ Papers-HC.

4. UN, *Dear Genius*, 83, 84.

5. New Haven Office of the FBI, "David Johnson Leisk, wa. Crockett Johnson Security Matter—C," 20 Dec. 1954, 1, 2, FBI-CJ; Philbrick, *I Led 3 Lives*; "Request for Payment," Harper and Brothers, 20 Dec. 1954, CJ Papers-HC.

6. Director, FBI, "David Johnson Leisk, wa Security Matter—C," 4 Jan. 1955, New Haven Office of the FBI, "David Johnson Leisk, wa. Crockett Johnson Security Matter—C," 24 Feb. 1955, Director, FBI, "David Johnson Leisk, wa Security Matter—C," 8 Mar. 1955, all in FBI-CJ.

7. Mellen, *Kay Boyle*, 382–83; New Haven Office of the FBI, "David Johnson Leisk, wa. Crockett Johnson Security Matter—C," 22 Apr. 1955, FBI-CJ.

8. Director, FBI, "David Johnson Leisk, wa Security Matter--C," 5 May 1955, New Haven Office of the FBI, "David Johnson Leisk, wa. Crockett Johnson Security Matter—C," 16 May 1955, both in FBI-CJ.

9. Tyler, "As an Author Sees," B4.

10. Ibid.

11. "Personal & Otherwise," 23; CJ to UN, 2 Feb. 1955, CJ Papers-HC; CJ, "Fantastic Companions," 32–34; Stacy V. Jones, "Inventor," 22; Tayler, "Barnaby's Creator," B5.

12. UN to CJ, 13, 28 Oct. 1955, both in CJ Papers-HC.

13. Hopkins, "Ruth Krauss [and] Crockett Johnson," 121; Tayler, "Barnaby's Creator," B5; New Haven Office of the FBI, "David Johnson Leisk, wa. Crockett Johnson," 28 July 1950, 18, FBI-CJ; Searchinger, interview; Simon, interview; Trubowitz, interview; Marinsky, interview.

14. UN to CJ, 13 Oct. 1955, CJ Papers-HC.

15. Mickenberg, *Learning*, 33.

16. Haviland, "Crockett Johnson," 362–63; Buell, "Traveler," 34.

17. Dove, "Rita Dove," 70; Van Allsburg, "Books I Remember."

18. Doty, interview; Tayler, "Barnaby's Creator," B5.

CHAPTER 17

1. "Draws Anything"; CJ to UN, [13 Nov. 1955], CJ Papers-HC.

2. Martin, "Ruth Krauss," 427, 428, 432, 434.

3. Sendak, interview.

4. Review of *Charlotte and the White Horse*, *Horn Book*, 363; Palmer, "Milky Way," 47; Kinkead, review of *Charlotte and the White Horse*, 205; review of *Charlotte and the White Horse*, *New York Herald Tribune*, 5; "Collector's Item," 7.

5. UN to CJ, 14 Dec. 1955, CJ to UN, 24 Dec. 1955, both in CJ Papers-HC.

6. Tayler, "Barnaby's Creator," B5; Beckwith, "Monkey Business," 4; Tyler, "As an Author Sees," B4.

7. Henry Miller to Harper, 22 Nov. 1956, RK Papers-HC; UN to Henry Miller, 5 Dec. 1956, in UN, *Dear Genius*, 88.

8. CJ to SC, 28 Jan. 1956, SC to CJ, 30 Jan. 1956, both in CJ Papers-HC.

9. CJ to UN, 4 Apr. 1956, CJ to Miss Hahn, 14 Sept. 1957, Dorothy B. Fiske to Juliet Piggott, 25 Oct. 1956, Dorothy B. Fiske to Kurt E. Michaels, 26 June 1956, all in CJ Papers-HC.

10. UN, handwritten note on CJ to UN, 4 Apr. 1956, Bunny Aleshire, reader's report on *Terrible Terrifying Toby* and *Time for Spring*, 5 Apr. 1956, both in CJ Papers-HC.

11. CJ to UN, 11 June 1956, UN to CJ, 23 July 1956, both in CJ Papers-HC.

12. Sendak, interview; NS, interview; Jackie Curtis and O'Hara, interview; IJW, 20 Oct. 1979.

13. UN to CJ, 31 May 1956, CJ to UN, 11 June 1956, both in CJ Papers-HC; Irving L. Fisher to Norman W. Schur, 24 July 1956, RK Papers-NCLC; Mickenberg, *Learning*, 176.

14. Sendak, interview.

15. Ibid.

16. NS to author, 3 Mar. 2001; ["Little Girl and Little Stream"] typescript and manuscripts, series II, box 11, folder 395, RK Papers-NCLC; Michaels and Michaels, interview; Schneider, *Psychoanalyst and the Artist*, 18–19, 55, 230.

17. UN to CJ, 14, 29 Nov. 1956, both in CJ Papers-HC.

18. CJ to UN, 15 Dec. 1956, UN to CJ, 15 Jan. 1957, both in CJ Papers-HC.

19. Lieberman, *Strangest Dream*, 136.

20. Ambrose, *Eisenhower*, 348, 313, 349.

21. Palmer, review of *I Want to Paint*, 38; Libby, review of *I Want to Paint*, 6; Hormel, review of *I Want to Paint*, 7; IJW, 19 Oct. 1979; RK to UN, 12 Nov. 1970, RK Papers-HC.

22. Beckwith, "Monkey Business," 4; Sendak, interview.

CHAPTER 18

1. Simon, interview.

2. UN to RK, 30 Apr. 1957, JR, "Tales from Children," handwritten notes, n.d., SC, memo, 30 July 1957, all in RK Papers-HC.

3. "Jack A. Goodman"; Landau, interview; Amateau, "Sidney Landau"; NS to author, 24 June 2009.

4. Berry, review of *Monkey Day*, 3242–43; Woods, review of *Monkey Day*, 59; Libby, review of *Monkey Day*, 11; review of *Monkey Day*, *Virginia Kirkus' Service*, 410.

5. Bader, "Crockett Johnson," 437; Buell, review of *Harold's Trip to the Sky*, 51; Goodwin, review of *Harold's Trip to the Sky*; review of *Harold's Trip to the Sky*, *Booklist*.

6. CJ to UN, 12 Oct. 1957, CJ to Mary [Russell], 28 Sept. 1956, both in CJ Papers-HC.

7. Jim Blake to Fitz, [2 July 1957], UN to Jim Bradley, 2 July 1957, UN to Jim Blake, 2 July 1957, all in CJ Papers-HC.

8. Rose Moudis to David Piel 31, Oct. 1957, Rose Moudis to CJ, 31 Oct. 1957, CJ to UN, 15 Dec. 1957, all in CJ Papers-HC; Schindel, interview.

9. CJ to UN, 29 June, 15 Dec. 1957, both in CJ Papers-HC.

10. "Arms Are to Hug," *Tide*, 25 Jan. 1957, 11, "A Faucet Is to Splash," *Tide*, 9 Nov. 1956, 39, "A Shovel Is to Dig," *Tide*, 28 Sept. 1956, 43, Frank S. MacGregor to the Joint Ethics Committee, 28 May 1957, Tran Mawicke to Frank S. MacGregor, 6 June 1957; Frank S. MacGregor to Tran Mawicke, 14 June 1957, all in RK Papers-HC.

11. Belkin and Belkin, "Going through a Phrase Dept."

12. Sendak, "Ruth Krauss and Me," 286; Dorothy B. Fiske to Gerald Pollinger, 4 Dec. 1956, RK to UN, [Dec. 1957?], UN to RK, 6 Dec. 1957, all in RK Papers-HC; RK to Barthold Fles, 18 May 1958, 2, box 2, folder 58, RK Papers-NCLC.

13. CJ to UN, 14 June 1957, 14 May 1958, CJ to Bob Cheney, 30 Jan. 1958, Louise F. Haynie to Mr. Bradley, 6 May 1958, all in CJ Papers-HC.

14. RK to UN, n.d., box 2, folder 65, RK Papers-NCLC; RK, "A Little Boy Said to His Mother," box 11, folder 393, RK Papers-NCLC.

15. Elizabeth Ring Hennefrund to author, 11 Sept. 2004; Brooks, interview.

16. *Is This You?*: Notes and sketches by RK, series II, box 10, folder 349, RK Papers-NCLC; Children's Record Guild, copy of unsigned contract with Raymond Abrashkin, 8 Mar. 1950, courtesy of David Bonner; Snodgrass, "Tact," 419.

17. UN to CJ, 11, 12 Dec. 1957, both in CJ Papers-HC; UN to RK, 9 Dec. 1957, RK Papers-HC.

CHAPTER 19

1. RK, "Child's Eye Visual," series 6, folder 193, RK Papers-NCLC.

2. UN to CJ, 14 Mar. 1958, CJ Papers-HC.

3. CJ to UN, 26 Feb. 1958, SC, memo, [13 or 14 Mar. 1958], both in CJ Papers-HC.

4. CJ to UN, 7 Apr. 1958, UN to CJ, 12 May 1958, both in CJ Papers-HC.

5. RK to Barthold Fles, 18 May 1958, 2, box 2, folder 58, RK Papers-NCLC.

6. "50 Years Ago"; Chusid, *Mischievous Art*, 21, 22, 55, 95, 97.

7. Helen M. Lothian to CJ, 13 Mar. 1958, CJ to UN, 13 Apr. 1958, CJ to Helen M. Lothian, 13 Apr. 1958, UN handwritten note, n.d., all in CJ Papers-HC.

8. Sendak, "Magic Beach: An Appreciation," in CJ, *Magic Beach*; Blechman, *Dear James*, 3–4; CJ, quoted in "Animating Harold."

9. Sendak, interview.

10. Ibid.

11. Ibid.

12. Charlip, interview; Remy Charlip, "Ruth Krauss" (reminiscence read at her memorial service), 1993, in possession of Remy Charlip.

13. Charlip, interview; Charlip, "Ruth Krauss"; UN to RK, 8 Sept. 1958, RK Papers-HC.

14. Review of *Harold at the North Pole*, *Kirkus*; review of *Harold at the North Pole*, *Oakland Tribune*; review of *Harold at the North Pole*, *New York Times Book Review*.

15. CJ to UN, 26 Feb. 1958, CJ to SC, 15 July, [before 14 Aug.] 1958, SC to CJ, 17 July 1958, all in CJ Papers-HC.

16. RK to SC, n.d., RK Papers-HC; Soby, *Arp*, 7.

17. "Where," 106.

18. Mickenberg, *Learning*, 12, 287 n. 35; Adelson, interview.

19. Mickenberg, *Learning*, 12.

20. Schneider, interview.

21. RK to UN, 12 Jan. 1959, RK Papers-HC.

CHAPTER 20

1. RK to UN, 12 Jan. 1959.

2. Lehman, *Last Avant-Garde*, 206; Koch, *Collected Poems*, 260, 263, 262; "'A Hole Is to Dig?' Harold Should Know," 2.

3. Gerard Malanga, interview by Gerald Hausman, n.d., Bookstore Press, tape 5, BP Records.

4. CJ to SC, 27 Mar. 1959, CJ Papers-HC.

5. UN, *Dear Genius*, xxvi.

6. CJ to UN, 7 Apr. 1959, CJ Papers-HC.

7. SC, reader's report on *Magic Beach*, 8 Apr. 1959, CJ to UN, 28 Apr. 1959, both in CJ Papers-HC.

8. CJ to UN, 31 July 1959, Ann Jorgensen, memo, 3 Aug. 1959, both in CJ Papers-HC. Ann Jorgensen married in September 1959 and subsequently was known as Ann Jorgensen Tobias.

9. Searchinger, interview.

10. CJ to UN, 7 Aug. 1959, RK Papers-HC; "'A Hole Is to Dig? Harold Should Know," 2; RK to UN, 31 Aug. 1959, RK Papers-HC.

11. RK to UN, 15 Sept. 1959, RK to SC, 3 Apr. 1960, both in RK Papers-HC; Sendak, interview.

12. Sendak, interview.

13. RK to UN, [31 Aug. 1959], 30 July 1960, 1960, all in RK Papers-HC.

14. Lehman, *Last Avant-Garde*, 184; RK, "From Poet in the News," *Bards' Bugle* 1.1, RK Papers-NCLC, repr. in *There's a Little Ambiguity*, n.p.

15. Lehman, *Last Avant-Garde*, 83, 240; RK, *There's a Little Ambiguity*, n.p.

16. Lehman, *Last Avant-Garde*, 233–34; RK, "If Only," box 1, Gerard Malanga Papers, Syracuse University Library, Special Collections Research Center; Breton, *Selected Poems*, 23; Koch, *Rose*, lxi.

17. RK, "Four Prose Poems," x, RK Papers-NCLC; RK to UN, [Dec. 1959–Jan. 1960], RK Papers-HC.

18. Antonio Frasconi, interview; Mischa Richter, interview; Murray, *Musician*, 209–10.

19. Gould, "Vet., Youngster Join Forces"; "Tele Review."

20. RK to UN, [March?] 1960, RK Papers-HC; CJ to UN, 14 Mar. 1960, CJ Papers-HC.

21. RK to UN, [early Jan. 1960?], RK Papers-HC.

22. CJ to UN, 25 Jan. 1958, 2, CJ Papers-HC; Hilberman, interview; Barrier, *Hollywood Cartoons*, 513–15; Canemaker, "David Hilberman," 17–21.

23. CJ to UN, 14 May 1958, CJ to SC, 24 Mar. 1959, both in CJ Papers-HC; CJ to Lou Bunin, 24 Apr. 1959, n.d., both in possession of Amy Kaiman.

24. Unsigned to UN, 1 Apr. 1960, notes headed "toes are to wiggle / arms are to hug with" at top, RK to SC, 3 Apr. 1960, all in RK Papers-HC; "Next Sunday," X7.

25. RK to UN, 23 Apr. 1960, RK Papers-HC; "Rowayton Arts Center."

26. Review of *Open House for Butterflies*, *Virginia Kirkus' Service*, 288; Woods, review of *Open House for Butterflies*, 30; Miles, review of *Open House for Butterflies*, 37–38.

27. Ambrose, *Eisenhower*, 573; Jackie Curtis, interview.

28. RK to UN, 21 June, 30 July 1960, both in RK Papers-HC; RK to Paul Carroll, 4, 21 June 1960, both in box 2, folder 58, RK Papers-NCLC.

29. AR, calendar for July 1960, AR Papers; RK to UN, 30 July 1960, RK Papers-HC; Lee Hall, *Abe Ajay*, 20, 46–47.

CHAPTER 21

1. RK to UN, Thursday [early August?] 1960, RK Papers-HC; NS to author, [3 Mar. 2001].

2. E. Y. Harburg to CJ, 26 Sept. 1960, RK Papers-NCLC.

3. Erwin, "'Barnaby' Returns," 52; CJ to UN, 1 June 1960, CJ Papers-HC.

4. Annotated list of CJ's works, Hall Syndicate, Estate of RK, Cohen & Wolf, Bridgeport, Conn.; "American Cyanamid."

5. Antonio Frasconi, interview; Brooks, interview.

6. Trubowitz, interview; Antonio Frasconi, interview.

7. RK to UN, 5 Feb. 1961, UN to RK, 28 Mar. 1961, both in RK Papers-HC.

8. Marcus, *Minders*, 220; RK to UN, Easter 1961, Dec. 1962, both in RK Papers-HC; Marcus, *Golden Legacy*, 178.

9. RK to UN, Apr. 1961, RK Papers-HC.

10. CJ to UN, 11 Dec. 1960, CJ Papers-HC.

11. SC, jacket copy for *Harold's Republic*, 19 Apr. 1961, CJ Papers-HC.

12. CJ to UN, 1 July, 12 Oct. 1961, 9 June 1962, UN to CJ, 6 July 1961, 11 July 1962, SC, reader's report on *The Lion's Own Story*, 20 June 1962, Ann Jorgensen Tobias, reader's report on *The Lion's Own Story*, 22 June 1962, all in CJ Papers-HC; "End of the Conversation"; "Prognosis"; "Post Time."

13. RK to UN, 5 June 1961, UN to RK, 8, 28 June 1961, all in RK Papers-HC.

14. RK to UN, 3 July 1961, UN to RK, 6 July 1961, both in RK Papers-HC; RK, *Cantilever Rainbow*.

15. CJ to UN and SC, 17 July 1961, CJ Papers-HC; Willard Maas to Kay Boyle, 21 Aug. 1961, RK Papers-NCLC; "Schedule cont.," 2, box 9, "Writer's Conference" folder, RK Papers-NCLC; Gussow, *Edward Albee*, 185–86.

16. Orgel, interview.

17. Orgel, interview; Searchinger, interview; Gene Searchinger to author, 28 Feb. 2004.

18. RK to UN, [Mar.–Apr. 1963], RK Papers-HC.

19. CJ to Robert M. Hall, 2 Jan. 1962, CJ Papers-ERK.

20. CJ to UN, [7 May 1962], Ann Jorgensen Tobias, reader's report on *Magic Beach*, 8 May 1962, UN to CJ, 9 May 1962, all in CJ Papers-HC.

21. Review of *Mama, I Wish I Was Snow*, *Kirkus*, 15 Jan. 1962, 53; Woods, review of *Mama, I Wish I Was Snow*, 5; review of *Mama, I Wish I Was Snow*, *Christian Science Monitor*, 2B.

22. RK to UN, [received 26 Mar. 1962], [late Apr. 1962?], UN to RK, 2 May 1962, all in RK Papers-HC.

23. RK to UN, [May 1962?], [May–June 1962], both in RK Papers-HC; Schneider, interview.

24. RK to UN, [May–June 1962], RK Papers-HC; Schneider, interview.

25. Gerard Malanga, interview by Gerald Hausman, n.d., tape 5, BP Records; Gussow, *Edward Albee*, 185; RK to Ted Berrigan, 22 July 1963, box 1, Ted Berrigan Papers, Syracuse University Library, Special Collections Research Center; RK to UN, [summer 1962], RK Papers-HC; "What They Say about Wagner Literary Magazine," box 31, RK Papers-NCLC.

26. CJ to UN, 29 Aug. 1962, 12 Jan. 1963, Ann Jorgensen Tobias, reader's report for *Harold's ABC*, [Sept. 1962], SC, reader's report for *Harold's ABC*, 5 Oct. 1962, typeset text for *Harold's ABC*, UN to CJ, 23 Jan. 1963, all in CJ Papers-HC.

27. RK to UN, 4 Dec. 1962, RK Papers-HC.

28. Jackie Curtis and O'Hara, interview; *New School Poets* (Fall 1962), RK Papers-NCLC; Social Security Death Index search for Meyer Zinman.

29. "The Living Theatre Presents a Reading of Poetry of Wagner Poets" (flier), Box 31, RK Papers-NCLC.

30. CJ to UN, 12 Dec. 1962, CJ Papers-HC.

31. RK to UN, 4 Dec. 1962, UN to RK, 5 Dec. 1962, both in RK Papers-HC; Schneider, interview.

32. UN to CJ, 9 May 1962, CJ Papers-HC; Marcus, *Minders*, 220, 222.

CHAPTER 22

1. CJ to AR, 27 Apr. 1963, N/69-100, frame 697, AR Papers.

2. Ibid.; Gussow, *Edward Albee*, 185; "Visions of Warhol."

3. RK, draft of "This Breast," with comments from Frank O'Hara, RK Papers-NCLC; Koch, "Thank You," in *Collected Poems*, 137; Gerard Malanga interview by Gerald Hausman, n.d., tape 5, BP Records. "This Breast" also appeared in *There's a Little Ambiguity over There among the Bluebells* (1968) and as the title poem in *This Breast Gothic* (1973).

4. Jean Karl to RK, 28 Mar., 9 Apr. 1963, both in box 1, folder 3, RK Papers-NCLC.

5. UN to Maurice Sendak, 31 Jan., 19 Feb. 1963, in UN, *Dear Genius*, 153–58; Lanes, *Art*, 92; Sendak, interview; Jennifer M. Brown, "Rumpus"; Marcus, *Caldecott Celebration*, 20–21; Ludden, "Conversation."

6. Untitled document beginning "*A Beautiful Day* was the first poem-play," RK Papers-NCLC; Remy Charlip, "Ruth Krauss" (reminiscence read at her memorial service), 1993, in possession of Remy Charlip.

7. "Phyllis Rowand," 25; NS, interview; David Johnson Leisk, Last Will and Testament, Probate Court, Westport, Conn., 2.

8. Pablo Frasconi, interview; Miguel Frasconi, interview; Antonio Frasconi, interview.

9. Sutherland, review of *Bouquet of Littles*, 96; Taylor, "Reviewer Picks," B16; R.M.B., "Dolls and Dogs," K22-A; Buell, review of *The Lion's Own Story*, 20; Heins, review of *Harold's ABC*, 495; review of *Harold's ABC*, *New York Times Book Review*; review of *Harold's ABC*, *Kirkus*; review of *Harold's ABC*, *Bulletin of the Center for Children's Books*; CJ to UN, 2 Feb. 1963, CJ Papers-HC.

10. BD to RK, 11 Dec. 1963, CJ to UN, 13, 26 Dec. (two letters) 1963, UN to CJ, 20 Dec. 1963, all in CJ Papers-HC.

11. RK, "Poem-Plays," 45; RK to UN, [Jan. 1964], RK Papers-HC.

12. Loretta Fasolina to RK, 3 Feb. 1964, RK to Loretta Fasolina, 8 Feb. 1964, RK Papers-NCLC.

13. CJ to UN, [Jan or Feb.] 1964, CJ Papers-HC.

14. SC, handwritten comment on note by UN, n.d., UN to CJ, 6 Mar. 1964, both in CJ Papers-HC.

15. UN to CJ, 6 Mar. 1964, CJ to UN, 6 Oct. 1964, both in CJ Papers-HC; Marcus, *Minders*, 230–31; Sendak, *Caldecott and Co.*, 146; UN to RK, 6, 11 Feb. 1964, RK to UN, 9 Feb. 1964, all in RK Papers-HC.

16. CJ to BD, 27 Mar. 1964, CJ to UN, 8 Apr. 1964, UN, handwritten marginalia on letter from CJ, 8 Apr. 1964, all in CJ Papers-HC; RK to BD, [late Apr.–early May 1964], RK to UN, [early May 1964], both in RK Papers-HC; Frank O'Hara to RK, 20 Apr. 1964, box 1, folder 35, RK Papers-NCLC; Simon, interview.

17. Walter, "Theatre," 10.

18. RK to Ted Berrigan, 2, 12 July 1964, Ted Berrigan Papers, Syracuse University Library, Special Collections Research Center; Michael Benedikt to RK, 7 July 1964, Box 9, RK Papers-NCLC; Poland and Mailman, *Off Off Broadway Book*, xix–xxi.

19. Gibson, review of *Little King*, 2090.

20. Rose, interview.

21. Landau, interview; Sidney Landau to author, 14 Jul, 2 Aug. 2005; CJ to Frank Boyle, 16 July 1964, in possession of Sidney Landau.

22. Antonio Frasconi, interview; "Chronologies of the Conflict."

23. *Wild Dog* 2.10 (Sept. 1964); *Wild Dog* 2.11 (28 Oct. 1964); *Nadada* 1 (Aug. 1964).

24. CJ to UN, 19 Sept. 1964, CJ Papers-HC; SC, "Straight Home from School" (reader's report), 25 Sept. 1964, UN to CJ, 8 Oct. 1964, both in CJ Papers-HC.

25. Gerald Harrison to RK, 14 May 1979, RK Papers-NCLC.

CHAPTER 23

1. Small, *Antiwarriors*, 14; "Assembly of Men and Women in the Arts, Concerned with Vietnam," N/69-101, Frame 82, AR Papers.

2. Small, *Antiwarriors*, 20; "End Your Silence," E5; Jackie Curtis, interview.

3. RK to UN, 8 June 1965, RK to UN, [before 17 May 1965], both in RK Papers-HC.

4. RK to UN, 8 June, [20 or 21 June] 1965, RK to BD, [received 6 July 1965], all in RK Papers-HC; CJ to BD, 26 July 1965, CJ Papers-HC.

5. CJ to BD, 26 July, [late June–early July], [mid-June] 1965, BD to RK and CJ, 4 June 1965; all in CJ Papers-HC.

6. RK to UN, [13 July 1965], RK Papers-HC; UN to CJ, 13 Oct. 1955, 30 Dec. 1964, both in CJ Papers-HC.

7. CJ to UN, 31 May 1965, CJ Papers-HC; RK to UN, 8 June 1965, RK Papers-HC.

8. RK to Ted Berrigan, [1964 or 1965], Box 1, Ted Berrigan Papers, Syracuse University Library, Special Collections Research Center; RK to UN, 8 June 1965, UN to RK, 10 June, 28 July 1965, all in RK Papers-HC.

9. RK to UN, 8 June 1965, UN to RK, 10 June 1965, both in RK Papers-HC; Morrison, review of *Cantilever Rainbow*, 5527; review of *Cantilever Rainbow, Kirkus*, 986; Richard Howard, "What Comes Naturally."

10. Fraser, interview.

11. O'Doherty, "World," 4; review of *Castles in the Sand, Kirkus Reviews*, 171; Izard, review of *Castles in the Sand*, 2396.

12. Kluger, "Hi-Jinks and Low," 16; Hurwitz, review of *Emperor's Gifts*, 4606; Finne, "Emperor's Gifts," 18; McCauley, "Heroes," B3; review of *Gordy and the Pirate, Kirkus Reviews*, 1116; review of *Gordy and the Pirate, Bulletin of the Center for Children's Books*, 13.

13. NS, interview.

14. Document beginning "*A Beautiful Day* was the first poem-play," RK Papers-NCLC; Hopkins, "Ruth Krauss and Crockett Johnson," 124.

15. Michael Smith, "Theatre Journal," 25; Lawrence Ferlinghetti to RK, 9 Nov. 1965, RK Papers-NCLC.

16. Document beginning "Lawrence Kornfeld has directed at Judson since 1961," Ferlinghetti to RK, 9 Nov. 1965, both in RK Papers-NCLC.

17. CJ to AR, 27 Feb. 1966, N/69-101, frame 241, AR Papers.

18. Ibid., frames 241–42; Miguel Frasconi, interview.

19. CJ to AR, 27 Feb. 1966, N/69-101, frame 241, AR Papers; AR, interview.

20. Poland and Mailman, *Off Off Broadway Book*, xxii; "Judson Poets' Theater Productions."

21. "The Ruth Krauss Library" (news release), n.d., RK to UN, [received 18 Apr. 1966], both in RK Papers-HC; CJ to BD, 19 Apr. 1966, CJ Papers-HC.

22. RK to UN, [received 18 Apr. 1966], RK Papers-HC; "Painting No. 3: Similar Triangles (Thales)," Stroud Notes; "Painting No. 30: Relativity in Time and Space (Einstein)," Stroud Notes; author's notes from discussion with and slides shown by J. B. Stroud, Charleston, S.C., 6 Jan. 2000; Stroud, "Crockett Johnson's Geometric Paintings," 88; Burndy Library flyer, Bern Dibner to CJ, 18 Apr. 1968, both in RK Papers-NCLC; NS, interview.

23. RK to UN, [July 1966], RK Papers-HC; "Transcendental Curve (Wallis)," Stroud Notes; CJ, "On the Mathematics," 97.

24. Review of *Happy Egg, Publishers Weekly*, 263; review of *Happy Egg, School Library Journal*, 71.

25. CJ to Lena Young de Grummond, 27 Feb. 1966, Finding Aid for RK Papers, both in RK Papers, de Grummond Collection, University of Southern Mississippi; UN to CJ, 18 Aug. 1966, CJ Papers-HC.

26. "To the President," 12; "On Vietnam," E5–E7.

27. RK to UN, 8 Sept. 1966, RK Papers-HC.

28. RK, Dummy A, "Little Woman," box 11, folder 409, RK Papers-NCLC.

29. RK to UN, 23 Jan., [late Feb.–early Mar. 1967], RK to UN, 15 May 1967, all in RK Papers-HC; list accompanying form letter from Debbie Louis to Lynd Ward, 14 Mar. 1967, Lynd Ward Papers, reel 3519, frame 394, Archives of American Art, Smithsonian Institution.

CHAPTER 24

1. Invitation to opening of *Abstractions of Abstractions*, exhibit at Nechemia Glezer Gallery, Box 35, RK Papers-NCLC; photos taken at Glezer Gallery, 5 Apr. 1967, in possession of Jackie Curtis.

2. Jackie Curtis to author, 12 Jan. 2003; Jackie Curtis and O'Hara, interview; Howard Levi to CJ, 29 Mar. 1971, Mathematical Correspondence, folder 3, CJ Papers-SI; Sparber, interview.

3. Michael Benedikt, blurb, *Abstractions of Abstractions*, CJ Papers-SI; B[enedikt], "Reviews and Previews"; "Creator of 'Barnaby' in First Serious Show."

4. *Abstractions of Abstractions*; "Creator of 'Barnaby' in First Serious Show."

5. Landau, interview.

6. RK to UN, 23 Jan., 10 Feb. 1967, UN to RK, 27 Feb. 1967, all in RK Papers-HC.

7. RK to UN, 14 Mar., 2 Apr., 15 May 1967, RK to BD, [8 or 9] Oct. 1967, all in RK Papers-HC; Lanes, *Art*, 151; Sendak, interview.

8. RK to BD, [8 or 9] Oct. 1967, RK Papers-HC.

9. CJ to Jackie Curtis, 4 Oct. 1967, in possession of Jackie Curtis; RK to UN, 19, 24 Sept. 1967, RK to BD, [8 or 9] Oct. 1967, all in RK Papers-HC; Landau, interview.

10. RK to BD, [8 or 9] Oct., 13 Nov. 1967, RK Papers-HC; Dan Richter, *Moonwatcher's Memoir*; CJ to Mischa Richter, 8 Oct. 1967, Mischa Richter Papers, Archives of American Art, Smithsonian Institution; Dan Richter, interview; CJ to BD, 15 Oct. 1967, CJ Papers-HC.

11. Jackie Curtis and O'Hara, interview; RK to Barbara Borack, [Jan. or Feb.] 1970, RK Papers-HC.

12. Review of *What a Fine Day For . . .*, *Kirkus*, 1317; Gibson, review of *What a Fine Day For . . .*, 680.

13. Stroud, "Crockett Johnson's Geometric Paintings," 83.

14. "Painting No. 35: Squared Lune (Hippocrates)," "Painting No. 67: Squared Lunes (Hippocrates)," "Painting No. 68: Squared Lunes (Hippocrates)," all in Stroud Notes.

15. "Painting No. 92: Biblical Squared Circles," Stroud Notes; CJ to NS, 30 May 1970, in possession of NS; Andy Rooney, interview; Mischa Richter, interview; Simon, interview.

16. RK, "Lost," "Poem," and "This Breast," 162–63; Robert Baker, review of *There's a Little Ambiguity*, 565; Bermel, "Closet Openings," 156–57.

17. CJ, "On the Mathematics," 97, 99.

18. H. Martyn Cundy to CJ, 23 May 1968, Mathematical Correspondence, CJ Papers-SI.

19. Sarah Weiner to CJ, 22 Nov. 1968, Mathematical Correspondence, CJ Papers-SI; "Crockett Johnson's Art," 16; Antonio Frasconi, interview; Searchinger, interview.

20. Searchinger, interview.

21. Cal Goodman to CJ, 9 July, 24 Sept., 8, 13 Dec. 1971, 14 Jan., 26 Sept. 1972, 10 Jan. 1973, all in RK Papers-NCLC; Searchinger, interview.

22. RK to Barbara Borack, 6 May 1969, RK to Ellen Rudin, 1969, both in RK Papers-HC; RK to UN, [summer] 1969, HarperCollins Archives.

23. RK to UN, [summer] 1969, HarperCollins Archives.

24. John Ashbery to RK, 29 Oct. 1969, series I, box 2, folder 31, RK Papers-NCLC.

25. Alyssa Crouse to author, 10 Sept. 2009; "Westport Arts Center"; "If Only . . . : A Ruth Krauss Gala!" (flyer), RK Papers-NCLC.

26. Dick Higgins to RK, 15 Mar. 1970, RK Papers-NCLC.

27. Wendy Newton to author, 21 Nov. 2007; Dmitri Belser to author, 1 Dec. 2008; Stroud, "Crockett Johnson's Geometric Paintings," 85.

28. RK to UN and Barbara Borack, [late] Apr. 1970, RK Papers-HC; CJ to NS, 30 May 1970, in possession of NS; RK to Barbara Borack, [late May–early June], [31 Aug.], 5, 8, 20 Sept. 1970, all in RK Papers-HC; CJ to NS, 30 May 1970, RK to NS, 16 June 1970, both in possession of NS; Alex and Else Gluckman to CJ and RK, Aug. 1970, Mathematical Correspondence, CJ Papers-SI; RK to David Silverstein, 13 Oct. 1970, Box 1, Folder 26, BP Records; CJ to Florence and Lou Bunin, 23 Dec. 1970, in possession of Amy Kaiman.

29. Sutherland, review of I Write It, 52; N.M., "Things That Rhyme," B4; RK to Barbara Borack, Dec. 1969, RK Papers-HC.

30. RK to UN, 12 Nov. 1970, RK Papers-HC.

CHAPTER 25

1. Sainer, "Krauss, Ruth (Ida)," 449–51; "Krauss, Ruth (Mrs. Crockett Johnson)," in American Authors, 357; "Krauss, Ruth Ida," in Author's and Writer's Who's Who, 468; "Krauss, Ruth," in Foremost Women, 356; "Krauss, Ruth," in Contemporary Authors, 553; Blake, interview.

2. Harry Marinsky, interview; Hopkins, "Ruth Krauss [and] Crockett Johnson," 121; RK to BD, 6 July 1971, RK Papers-HC; CJ to Florence and Lou Bunin, 20 July 1971, in possession of Amy Kaiman.

3. Gene Deitch to author, 28 Oct. 2000; Dart, "History"; Deitch, "Picture Book Animated," 147; Gene Deitch to Morton Schindel, 28 Feb. 1971, RK Papers-NCLC.

4. CJ to UN, 18, 30 Nov. 1970, UN to CJ, 23, 24 Nov. 1970, all in CJ Papers-HC.

5. "Holland America Mail and Cable Information: 1971 North Cape Cruises, S.S. Statendam" (brochure), RK Papers-HC; RK and CJ [postcard signed by both but written by CJ] to UN, [7–8 Aug. 1971], RK Papers-HC; RK to David Silverstein, 21 Aug. 1971, BP Records.

6. Stroud, "Crockett Johnson's Geometric Paintings," 86, 91–92; "Painting No. 91: Circle Squared to 0.0001," "Painting No. 94: Rectangle Squared on an Euler Line," both in Stroud Notes.

7. Mathematical Correspondence, CJ Papers-SI.

8. Deed of sale, June 1972, Probate Court, Westport, Conn.; Howard Levi to CJ, 4 July 1972, CJ Papers-SI; Beatrice de Regniers to RK, 15 Aug. 1972, RK to UN, 11 June 1972, both in RK Papers-HC.

9. RK to Elizabeth Ring Hennefrund, in possession of Elizabeth Ring Hennefrund; RK to Gerald Hausman, [10 Sept. 1972], BP Records.

10. RK, interview by Valerie Harms, ca. 1972, Tape 4, BP Records.

11. RK, "Preliminary Statement to a Statement on Poetics," 1, 5, box 20, folder 696, RK Papers-NCLC.

12. Clay, "Theatre," 14; Henry, "Levels of Reality."

13. Colby, interview; Valerie Harms to author, 23, 24 Oct. 2002.

14. Gerald Hausman, "One," 1–2, 3, 6–7, BP Records.

15. Holmes, interview; Janet Krauss, interview; Janet Krauss to author. 18 Apr. 2010.

16. RK to Gerald Hausman, 2 Dec. 1972, [Dec. 1972], 25 Jan. 1973, all in BP Records.

17. Gene Deitch to CJ, 22 June 1973, RK Papers-NCLC; CJ to UN, 27 May 1971, CJ Papers-HC.

18. RK to Gerald Hausman, Aug. 1973, [Nov. 1972], both in BP Records.

19. RK to Gerry [Hausman], Lorry [Hausman], David [Silverstein], and Mariah [Hausman], [early Sept. 1973], BP Records; "Stroud Studies," 7; Stroud, "Crockett Johnson's Geometric Paintings," 94–95.

20. RK to Gerry [Hausman], Lorry [Hausman], David [Silverstein], and Mariah [Hausman], [early Sept. 1973], RK to Gerald and Lorry Hausman, [23 Sept. 1973], both in BP Records; RK to BD, 13 Oct. 1973, RK to Ellen Rudin, Oct. 1973, both in RK Papers-HC.

21. UN, *Dear Genius*, xxxvii–xxxviii; Kuskin, review of *Everything under a Mushroom*, 46; review of *Everything under a Mushroom*, *Publishers Weekly*, 72; Komaiko, "3–6's," F2.

22. CJ to BD, 14 Apr., 9 May 1974, CJ to Ellen Rudin, 30 May 1974, all in CJ Papers-HC.

23. Douglas A. Quadling to CJ, 9 June 1974, Mathematical Correspondence, CJ Papers-SI.

24. CJ to BD, 8 Jan. 1974 [1975], CJ Papers-HC; Stanley Smith to CJ, 25 Dec. 1974, Mathematical Correspondence, CJ Papers-SI.

CHAPTER 26

1. UN to BD, 10 Feb. 1975, HarperCollins Archives.

2. RK to Gerald and Lorry Hausman, 8 Feb. 1975, BP Records; Lund and Lund, interview.

3. Searchinger, interview; UN to BD, 10 Feb. 1975, HarperCollins Archives; RK to UN, 17 Mar. 1975, RK Papers-HC.

4. Searchinger, interview; Hahn interview.

5. Jackie Curtis, interview; Jackie Curtis and O'Hara, interview; "Westporter's Painting," 7; "Geometric Abstraction," 22.

6. Rose, interview.

7. Hahn, interview.

8. "Crockett Johnson, Cartoonist," 38.

9. Hahn, interview.

CHAPTER 27

1. Hahn, interview; RK to Gerald Hausman, Lorry Hausman, and David Silverstein, 5 Aug. 1975, BP Records.

2. UN to BD, 21 July 1975, UN to Shirley Blanchard, 16 Oct. 1975, both in RK Papers-HC.

3. Fran Pollak to author, Jan. 2006; Fran Pollak, "Poems and Pickles in Westport," *Sunday Connecticut Post*, c. 1976, in possession of the author; Ina Chadwick to author, 19 Oct. 2009; Shaw, interview.

4. Information provided by Robin Lynn Rausch, 2005; "MacDowell Colony."

5. Sally Fisher to author, 2 Apr. 2011; Ernst, interview; Trubowitz, interview.

6. BD to Robert I. Fitzhenry, 7 July 1976, RK Papers-HC; Stewart I. Edelstein to RK, 9 Mar. 1976, Stewart I. Edelstein to Joseph Rosenbloom, 9 Mar. 1976, F. McAllister to and contract with RK, all in RK Papers-NCLC.

7. Review of *Little Boat*, *Publishers Weekly*, 99; Gregory, review of *Little Boat*, 84.

8. Binnie Klein, interview.

9. Ibid.

10. Ibid.

11. Chadwick, interview; Binnie Klein, interview; Hahn, interview.

12. IJW, 20 Oct. 1979.

13. Binnie Klein, interview.

14. Pablo Frasconi, interview.

15 Graetz, interview; Linda Graetz to author. 4 Nov. 2009.

16. Chadwick, interview; Donald Hall, "Third Hand," 25; review of *Somebody Spilled*, *Kirkus*, 324; review of *Somebody Spilled*, *Publishers Weekly*, 370.

17. Chadwick, interview.

18. Hedy White, interview.

19. IJW, 19, 20 Oct. 1979.

20. RK to UN, 1 Jan. 1944, RK Papers-HC; Binnie Klein, interview; Shaw, interview; Janet Krauss, interview; Sally Dimon to author, 28 June 2010; Heinrich, interview.

21. Peggy Heinrich, recollection of RK, RK memorial service, July 1993, cassette tape provided by Maureen O'Hara. Review of *Minestrone*, *Publishers Weekly*, 55; Stein, review of *Minestrone*, 606; Sanhuber, review of *Minestrone*, 94; review of *Minestrone*, *Kirkus*, 1346–47.

22. Binnie Klein, interview.

23. RK, "The Enclosed Collection of Poems," [1983], box 2, folder 65, RK Papers-NCLC; RK, "Small Black Lambs Wandering in the Red Poppies," box 13, folder 519, RK Papers-NCLC.

24. Harvey Weiss, recollection of RK, RK memorial service, July 1993, cassette tape provided by Maureen O'Hara.

25. Chadwick, interview.

26. Ibid.; Heinrich, interview; Kramer, interview; Schindel, interview.

27. Phyllis Hoffman to RK, 14 Jan., 20 Feb., 21 Aug. 1987, RK to Phyllis Hoffman, 2, 11 Jan., 1 Feb. 1987, all RK Papers-NCLC; RK, ABC Notes, [1960], box 9, RK Papers-NCLC.

28. Phyllis Hoffman to RK, 31 Mar. 1987, RK Papers-NCLC

29. Nazareth, interview.

30. Graetz, interview; Hahn, interview.

31. Jon Ehrlich to RK, 6 Nov. 1990, RK Papers-NCLC; John Ehrlich, Robin Pogrebin, and Jane Shepard, *Harold and the Purple Crayon* script, final draft, Jan. 1992, courtesy of Theatreworks USA; Ehrlich, interview.

CHAPTER 28

1. NS to author, July 2004.

2. Wood, interview.

3. Ibid. Janusz Czaderna continued to live with his wife and daughter at Ruth's house, but he was rarely around, disappearing in the mornings, wandering the beaches, and coming back when it suited him.

4. Ibid.

5. Graetz, interview.

6. Wood, interview.

7. Ibid.; BD, interview; Dan Richter, interview.

8. Janet Krauss, "A Good Visit" (poem), courtesy of Janet Krauss; Janet Krauss, "The Clenched Hand" (poem), courtesy of Janet Krauss.

9. Jackie Curtis and O'Hara, interview; Sendak, interview.

10. Wood, interview.

11. "Ruth Krauss, 91," D22.

12. Harms, "Interview," 9.

13. Hahn, interview; RK, Last Will and Testament, 28 Feb. 1991, Probate Court, Westport, Conn.

14. Sendak, interview.

15. RK, memorial service, July 1993, cassette tape provided by Maureen O'Hara; Sendak, "Ruth Krauss and Me," 287.

16. Hahn, interview.

17. Edelstein, interview.

EPILOGUE

1. CJ, "Barnaby," in *Strange Stories*, ed. Spiegelman and Mouly, 43–51; Hignite, "Daniel Clowes," 31; Clowes, *Ice Haven*, 33; *Comics Journal* 210 (Feb. 1999).

2. "Harold and the Purple Crayon," in *Everything I Need to Know*, 113; "Auteur-Illustrateur," 2; Meyers, "Cold War Illustrated," 24; "Features"; Thacher Hurd to author, 19 June 2005; Jerry Scott and Jim Borgman, *Zits*, 1 Feb. 2009.

BIBLIOGRAPHY

ARCHIVES AND SPECIAL COLLECTIONS

Archives of American Art, Smithsonian Institution, Washington, D.C.
    Adolf and Virginia Dehn Papers
    Hugo Gellert Papers
    Rockwell Kent Papers
    Elenore Lust Papers
    Ad Reinhardt Papers
    Mischa Richter Papers
    Stuyvesant Van Veen Papers
    Lynd Ward Papers
    Carl Zigrosser Papers (microfilm; originals in Van Pelt Library, University of
Pennsylvania, Philadelphia)
Aviation Weekly Archives, McGraw-Hill, New York
Camp Walden Archives, Denmark, Maine
Columbia University Archives, Columbiana Library, New York
de Grummond Children's Literature Collection, University of Southern Mississippi,
Hattiesburg
    Crockett Johnson Papers
    Ruth Krauss Papers
Enoch Pratt Free Library, Baltimore
    Maryland Department
    Periodicals Department
Estate of Ruth Krauss, Cohen & Wolf, Bridgeport, Conn.
    Crockett Johnson Papers
    Ruth Krauss Papers
HarperCollins Publishers' Archives, New York
    Crockett Johnson Papers
    Ruth Krauss Papers
Harry Ransom Center, University of Texas at Austin
    Pascal Covici Papers
Harvard University Archives, Cambridge, Mass.
    PM Papers
Library of Congress, Washington, D.C.
    Communist Party U.S.A. Records
    Prints and Photographs Division
    Serial and Government Publications Division

BIBLIOGRAPHY

Long Island Division, Queens Borough Public Library, Jamaica, New York
Mandeville Special Collections, University of California at San Diego
    Dr. Seuss Collection
Maryland Institute College of Art Historical Archives, Baltimore
Maryland State Archives, Annapolis
Mathematics Division, National Museum of American History, Smithsonian Institution
    Crockett Johnson Papers
McGraw-Hill Archives, New York
National Archives II, College Park, Maryland
New York Public Library, New York
New York University Archives, New York
Northeast Children's Literature Collection, Dodd Research Center, University of
Connecticut, Storrs
    Bookstore Press Records
    Ruth Krauss Papers
Parsons School Archives, Anna-Maria and Stephen Kellen Archives Center, Parsons
School of Design, New School University, New York
Peabody Archives, Friedheim Music Library, Peabody Institute, Baltimore
Reference Center for Marxist Studies, New York
Schlesinger Library, Radcliffe Institute for Advanced Study, Cambridge, Mass.
    Camp Walden Papers
Syracuse University Library, Special Collections Research Center, Syracuse, N.Y.
    Ted Berrigan Papers
    William Gropper Papers
    Granville Hicks Papers
    Gerard Malanga Papers
Terry-D'Alessio Private Collection
    World War Two Bonds Cartoons (some of which were exhibited as part of *Cartoons
    against the Axis: World War Two War Bonds Cartoons from the Terry-D'Alessio Collection*,
    curated by Sandy Schechter, Museum of Comic and Cartoon Art, New York, 8 Oct. 2005–6
    Feb. 2006)
University of Delaware Library, Special Collections, Newark

PRIVATE COLLECTIONS

Remy Charlip
Jackie Curtis
Betty Hahn
Thomas Hamilton
Elizabeth Ring Hennefrund
Amy Kaiman
Sidney Landau
Alice McMahon
Marc Simont
Nina Stagakis
J. B. Stroud

INTERVIEWS (BY AUTHOR)

Leone Adelson. 21 Nov. 2001 (telephone), 20 Dec. 2001 (in person).
Isabella Blake. 4 June 2001 (telephone).
Pat Brooks. 17 Sept. 2004 (telephone).
Jared Brown. 16 May 2004 (telephone).
Ina Chadwick. 19 Oct. 2009 (telephone).
Remy Charlip. 23 Mar. 2003 (telephone).
Helen Herz Cohen. 21 July 2005 (in person).
Sas Colby. 15 Oct. 2002 (telephone).
Norman Corwin. 18 Nov. 2008 (telephone).
Jackie Curtis. 18 June 2001 (telephone), 15 Dec. 2004 (in person).
Jackie Curtis and Maureen O'Hara. 18 June 2002 (in person).
Karen Curtis. 1 May 2002 (telephone).
Bianca Czaderna. 3 Feb. 2008 (telephone).
Barbara Dicks. 16 Mar. 2004 (in person).
Roy Doty. 4 Feb. 2006 (telephone).
Stewart Edelstein, 17 June 2002 (in person).
Jon Ehrlich. 24 Oct. 2009 (telephone).
Dallas Ernst, 5 Aug. 2000 (telephone).
Frank Fay. 20 Jun. 2000 (in person).
Jules Feiffer. 16 Sept. 2000 (telephone).
Mary Elting Folsom. 12 Dec. 2001 (telephone).
David Frank. 26 Dec. 2000 (in person).
Else Frank. 26 Dec. 2000, 18, 20 Mar. 2001 (in person).
Harold Frank. 2 November 2000 (telephone).
Antonio Frasconi. 12 Oct. 2000 (telephone).
Miguel Frasconi. 2 Dec. 2007 (telephone).
Pablo Frasconi. 28 Nov. 2007 (telephone).
Betty Fraser. 12 June 2000 (telephone).
Martin Garment. 24 Sept. 2002 (telephone).
Linda Graetz. 1 Nov. 2009 (telephone).
Betty Hahn. 27 June, 6 Aug. 2001, 15 Feb. 2010 (telephone).
Thomas Hamilton. 12 Aug. 2006 (telephone).
Valerie Harms. 12 July 2002 (telephone).
Peggy Heinrich. 30 Mar. 2001, 18 Apr. 2010 (telephone).
David Hilberman. 19 Mar. 2003 (telephone).
Susan Carr Hirschman. 18 Mar. 2004 (telephone).
Syd Hoff. 1 July 2001 (telephone).
Ann Holmes. 13 Apr. 2010 (telephone).
Lee Hopkins. 14 Jan. 2001 (telephone).
Tom Hopps. 4 Apr. 2000, 1 Aug. 2008 (telephone).
Leonard Kessler. 14 Oct. 2002 (telephone).
Bill Kimmel. 1 June 2004 (in person).
Binnie Klein. 10 Jan. 2001 (telephone).
Henry F. Klein. 20 Mar. 2003 (telephone).

Sidney Kramer. 26 Jan. 2006 (telephone).
Janet Krauss. 18 Apr. 2010 (telephone).
Sidney Landau. 16 Feb. 2001 (telephone).
Emily Levine. 25, 31 Jan. 2003 (telephone).
Grace Lichtenstein. 8 July 2002 (telephone).
Sid and Doris Lund. 20 June 2000 (in person).
Leonard Marcus, 12 Jun. 2010 (in person).
A. B. Magil. 19 Aug. 2001 (telephone).
Harry Marinsky. 10 Dec. 2000 (telephone).
Ann McGovern. 18 Jun. 2001 (telephone).
Alice McMahon. 4 Mar. 2001 (telephone).
Bob and Helen McNell. 15 Apr. 2000 (telephone).
Mike and Steffie Michaels. 27 June 2005 (telephone).
George Miller, 28 Jun. 2007 (in person).
Ralph Nazareth. 18 Apr. 2010 (telephone).
Wendy Newton. 23 Nov. 2007 (telephone).
Maureen O'Hara. 10 June 2001 (telephone).
Doris Orgel. 21 Jun. 2006 (telephone).
Nathan Oser. 1 June 2004 (telephone).
Fran Pollak. 24 Jan. 2006 (telephone).
Ad Reinhardt. 22 June 2002 (telephone).
Anna Reinhardt. 2 Dec. 2007 (telephone).
Dan Richter. 28 June 2005 (telephone).
Mischa Richter. 5, 7 Feb., 5, 7, Mar. 2001 (telephone).
Andy Rooney. 16 Oct. 2000 (telephone).
Marge Rooney. 18 Oct. 2000 (telephone).
Gilbert Rose. 19 June 2000 (in person).
Stanley Rubin. 27 Apr. 2006 (telephone).
Warren Sattler. 17 Dec. 2001 (telephone).
Morton Schindel. 26 June 2001 (in person).
Marion Schnabel. 18 Jan. 2003 (telephone).
Elizabeth Schneïder. 18 Feb. 2009 (telephone).
Gene Searchinger. 22 June 2002 (telephone).
Maurice Sendak. 21 June 2001, 10 Sept. 2008 (telephone).
Dale Shaw. 11 Apr. 2010 (telephone).
Norma Simon. 20 June 2002 (telephone).
Marc Simont. 12 July 2000 (telephone).
Christopher Skelly. 7 July 2007 (telephone).
Howard Sparber. 27 Nov. 2000 (telephone).
Nina Stagakis. 31 Jan. 2001 (telephone), 30 June 2001 (in person).
Shelley Trubowitz. 7, 14 Aug. 2000 (telephone).
Hedy White. 10 May 2004 (telephone).
Helaine White. 18 May 2004 (telephone).
Roger Willcox. 26 Sept. 2004 (telephone).
Joanna Czaderna Wood. 10 Feb. 2008 (telephone).
Charlotte Zolotow. 26 Mar. 2004 (telephone).

WORKS BY CROCKETT JOHNSON

BOOKS

Barnaby. New York: Holt, 1943.

Harold and the Purple Crayon. New York: Harper, 1955.

Barkis: Some Precise and Some Speculative Interpretations of the Meaning of a Dog's Bark at Certain Times and in Certain (Illustrated) Circumstances. New York: Simon and Schuster, 1956.

Harold's Fairy Tale: Further Adventures with the Purple Crayon. New York: Harper, 1956.

Harold's Trip to the Sky: More Adventures with the Purple Crayon. New York: Harper, 1957.

Terrible, Terrifying Toby. New York: Harper, 1957.

Time for Spring. New York: Harper, 1957.

Harold at the North Pole: A Christmas Journey with the Purple Crayon. New York: Harper, 1958. First published in an abbreviated form as "Harold and the Big Day," *Good Housekeeping*, December 1957.

The Blue Ribbon Puppies. New York: Harper, 1958.

Merry Go Round. New York: Harper, 1958.

Ellen's Lion: Twelve Stories. New York: Harper, 1959.

The Frowning Prince. New York: Harper, 1959.

Harold's Circus: An Astounding, Colossal Purple Crayon Event. New York: Harper, 1959.

Will Spring Be Early? Or Will Spring Be Late? New York: Crowell, 1959.

A Picture for Harold's Room: A Purple Crayon Adventure. New York: Harper, 1960.

Harold's ABC: Another Purple Crayon Adventure. New York: Harper, 1963.

The Lion's Own Story: Eight New Stories about Ellen's Lion. New York: Harper, 1963.

We Wonder What Will Walter Be? When He Grows Up. New York: Holt, Rinehart, and Winston, 1964.

Gordy and the Pirate and the Circus Ringmaster and the Knight and the Major League Manager and the Western Marshal and the Astronaut and a Remarkable Achievement. New York: Putnam's, 1965.

The Emperor's Gifts. New York: Holt, Rinehart, and Winston, 1965.

Castles in the Sand. Illustrated by Betty Fraser. New York: Holt, Rinehart, and Winston, 1965.

Who's Upside Down? New York: Scott, 1952. Also published as *Upside Down*. Park Ridge, Ill.: Whitman, 1969.

Barnaby and Mr. O'Malley. New York: Holt, 1944; New York: Dover, 1975.

Barnaby #1: Wanted, a Fairy Godfather. New York: Ballantine, 1985.

Barnaby #2: Mr. O'Malley and the Haunted House. New York: Ballantine, 1985.

Barnaby #3: Jackeen J. O'Malley for Congress. New York: Ballantine, 1986.

Barnaby #4: Mr. O'Malley Goes for the Gold. New York: Ballantine, 1986.

Barnaby #5: Mr. O'Malley, Wizard of Wall Street. New York: Ballantine, 1986.

Barnaby #6: J. J. O'Malley Goes Hollywood. New York: Ballantine, 1986.

Harold's Purple Crayon Treasury: Five Adventures with the Purple Crayon. Barnes and Noble Books, 1997.

Magic Beach. Appreciation by Maurice Sendak. Afterword by Philip Nel. Asheville, N.C.: Front Street, 2005.

CARTOONS
This list may well be incomplete.

Newtown High School Lantern
All cartoons are signed with a cursive *D* over a cursive *L*.
    "An Off Day," Mar. 1921, 25. Attributed to D. J. Leisk.
    "Kuku Karl and Hesa Nutt Visit the Museum," May 1921, 14.
    "Newtown H.S.," May 1921, 24.
    "Love Thy Neighbor," Dec. 1921, 12.
    "Vacation Number, 1922," May 1922, cover.
    "The L'antern Cl'ass Notes" (masthead), May 1922, 13.
    "Athletics" (masthead), May 1922, 17.
    "They Shall Not Pass," Dec. 1922, 17.
    "Athletics" (masthead), Dec. 1922, 25.
    Untitled, May 1923, cover.
    "Freshman Number, Oct. 1923," Oct. 1923, cover.
    "Athletics" (masthead), Oct. 1923, 14.

New Masses
"Harriet Here Is Practically an Authority on Communists. She Writes Pieces about Them
    in the New Yorker," 17 Apr. 1934, 4.
"It's the Real Thing, Mr. Millikan. Shall I Wire the New York Times?," 3 July 1934, 41.
Cartoon Depicting God and Angels, 3 July 1934, 41.
"They're Not Even Citizens," 10 July 1934, 29.
"Radiogram, Mr. Morgan. The White House Wants to Know Are You Better Off Than You
    Were Last Year?," 17 July 1934, 9.
Portrait of Bertrand Russell, 17 July 1934: 25.
Portrait of John Dewey, 17 July 1934, 26.
"Just Because Your Greedy Workmen Decide to Go on strike I Can't Have a New
    Mercedes. Somehow It Doesn't Seem Fair," 7 Aug. 1934, 22.
"Aw, Be a Sport. Tell the Newsreel Audience You Still Have Faith in the Lawd and Good
    Old Franklin D.," 28 Aug. 1934, 7. Reprinted in Robert Forsythe, *Redder Than the Rose*
    (New York: Covici, Friede, 1935), 232.
"My God, What Will Mr. Hearst Say? We left Out the Battleships This Week!," 11 Sept. 1934,
    24.
"Somehow I Don't Feel That the Eyes of the Nation Is on Us This Season." 2 Oct. 1934, 41.
    Reprinted in Robert Forsythe, *Redder Than the Rose* (New York: Covici, Friede, 1935),
    101.
"All Dat Dere Bad Grammar and Coise Woids in Me Letter to Dat Lousy Radical Paper Is
    on Account of Dat's d' only Kinda Language Dem Reds Can Understand," 20 Nov. 1934,
    11.
"First, We Tell His Majesty about the Flowers; Then Very Gently, Lead Up to the Marxism,"
    18 Dec. 1934, 26.
"But Regimentation Won't Hamper Your Individuality, Eustace; This Fascism Racket Will
    Give Real Freedom to Our Artistic Souls," 18 Dec. 1934, 29.
Full-Page, Eight-Part Cartoon without Caption, 25 Dec. 1934, 7.

"Was It Marx, Lenin, or Gen. Johnson Who Said: 'The General Strike Is Quite Another Matter'?," 1 Jan. 1935, 38.

"George Says You Can't Stop War. It's Man's Nature to Fight," 15 Jan 1935, 29.

"Mr. Hearst Says He'll Buy Your Farm Articles If You'll Just Change 'Arkansas,' 'Louisiana,' 'California,' and So On, to Soviet Russia," 28 May 1935, 26.

"You Gentlemen Take It Too Seriously. After All War Is Only a Game—Like Chess," 4 June 1935, 12.

"Nothing Doing! If He Ain't a Citizen He Can't Join!," 25 June 1935, 16.

"Next Year We'll Be Out There Throwing the Big Bad World for a Loss, Eh, Koscianiewicz?," 5 Nov. 1935, 22.

"Put in a Strong Word against the Union. The Big Boss Just Kicked in with a Century," 4 Feb. 1936, 18.

"The President's Secretary Says for You to File All Applications for Flood Relief in the Lower Right Hand Drawer," 7 Apr. 1936, 21.

"If You Haven't Read Escape from the Soviets You Don't Know How Lucky You and I Are Here in America," 7 Apr. 1936, 28.

"I'll Contribute If You Really Think That We Can Bring about Fascism in a Gentlemanly Way," 14 Apr. 1936, 15.

"Did You See What the Daily Worker Called Me Today, Brisbane? An Octopus!," 10 Nov. 1936, 15.

"No One Here Goes over My Head, Withers. Next Time You Pray to God for a Raise, You're Fired!," 20 Apr. 1937, 8.

"Jefferson Caffery, Master Meddler," 13 July 1937, 12.

"Copeland—Tammany's Choice?," 20 July 1937, 11.

"I Am a Real Red!," 27 July 1937, cover.

"We, the People," 7 Dec. 1937, 3.

"People's Front," 4 Jan. 1938, 12.

"Anti-Piracy Patrol," 15 Feb. 1938, 8.

"The Primary Candidate Who Tried to Make a Mountain Out of a Mole-Hill," 17 May 1938, 16.

"Wall Street & Company Accident Insurance Policy," 24 May 1938, 4–5.

"We Need Men Like You, Mr. Barton," 11 Oct. 1938, 15.

Nazi Soldier Marching, 29 Nov. 1938, 3.

"Pied Piper," 13 Dec. 1938, 15.

"Private Capital at Work," 7 Feb. 1939, 11.

"Wanna Help Your Great Big Senator Celebrate, Baby? Let's Go to a Show," 11 July 1939, 13.

"Warns Hitler News Item Chamberlain Warns Hitler News Item Chamberlain Warns Hitler News Item Chamberlain Warns Hitler News," 18 July 1939, 11.

"Tory Congressman Goes Home," 15 Aug. 1939, 8.

"That Dirty Russian Deserted Us!," 5 Sept. 1939, 20.

"A Social-Democrat Leader Does His Bit," 31 Oct. 1939, 11.

"This Is You, Williams, Defending Your Mother in Pennsylvania," 19 Dec. 1939, 7.

"This Home Is Unfair to Burglars," 26 Dec. 1939, 18.

"Wonderfullums Inc.," 2 Jan. 1940, 28.

"The Sun Never Sets on the British Flag," 23 Jan 1940, 18.

"ASPCA and the Lion," 5 Mar. 1940, 21.

"A Question Looks at Both Sides of a Liberal," 19 Mar. 1940, 10.
"Have You Written Any Good Books Lately?," 2 Apr. 1940, 16.
"Liberal at the Crossroads," 14 May 1940, 6.
Hitler and clock and globe, 24 Feb. 1942, 15.

Other Political Cartoons
"Despite Martin Dies's Warning, a Consumer Persists in Her Attempts to Undermine
    Confidence in American Advertising by Testing the Ripeness of an Avocado," *New
    Republic* 1 Jan. 1940.
"Honorable Ancestor," *PM*, 9 Feb. 1942, 6.

The Liitle Man with the Eyes in *Collier's*
"Table Tennis," 9 Mar. 1940, 28.
"Steam Shovel," 16 Mar. 1940, 26.
"Tiger," 23 Mar. 1940, 34.
"Murder Mystery," 30 Mar. 1940, 71.
"Speedboat," 6 Apr. 1940, 32.
"Miss," 13 Apr. 1940, 48.
"Taxis—With Fares," 20 Apr. 1940, 27.
"Foul! Strike Two," 27 Apr. 1940, 30.
"Three-Cushion Shot," 4 May 1940, 70.
"Straight Flush," 11 May 1940, 46.
"Minute Hand," 18 May 1940, 55.
"Leap Frog," 25 May 1940, 30.
"News Item," 1 June 1940, 27.
"Fifth Race," 8 June 1940, 31.
"Fly," 15 June 1940, 88.
"Belly Flopper," 22 June 1940, 64.
"Chess," 29 June 1940, 29.
"Empty Saddle," 6 July 1940, 48.
"High Building," 13 July 1940, 27.
"Target," 27 July 1940, 29.
"Dirt Road," 3 Aug. 1940, 35.
"High-Pressure Salesman," 10 Aug. 1940, 35.
"Telegraph Poles," 17 Aug. 1940.
"Hook," 24 Aug. 1940.
"Slice," 31 Aug. 1940.
"Sheep," 7 Sept. 1940, 27.
"Alarm Clock," 14 Sept. 1940, 29.
"Wood Splitter," 21 Sept. 1940, 32.
"Snub," 28 Sept. 1940.
"Aquarium," 5 Oct. 1940, 33.
"Collection Plate," 12 Oct. 1940, 57.
"No Riders," 19 Oct. 1940.
"French Pastry," 26 Oct. 1940, 50.
"Partner's Trump," 2 Nov. 1940, 30.

"Watched Kettle," 9 Nov. 1940, 64.

"Loop," 16 Nov. 1940, 29.

"Pinball," 23 Nov. 1940, 75.

"Knockdown," 30 Nov. 1940, 53.

"Brights," 7 Dec. 1940, 58.

"Program Rustler," 14 Dec. 1940, 47.

"Raconteur," 21 Dec. 1940.

"Gift," 28 Dec. 1940, 38. Note: Tie is green (in color ink).

"Entree—Price," 4 Jan. 1941, 35.

"Split," 11 Jan. 1941, 36.

"Bridge Argument," 18 Jan. 1941, 41.

"Traffic Cop," 25 Jan. 1941, 31.

"Begging Dog," 1 Feb. 1941, 57.

"Finesse," 8 Feb. 1941, 45.

"Celebrity," 15 Feb. 1941, 31.

"Smoke," 22 Feb. 1941, 67.

"Wet Paint," 1 Mar. 1941, 57. Note: Paint is dark green (in color ink).

"March Wind," 8 Mar. 1941, 53.

"Movies: Front Row," 15 Mar. 1941.

"Three Rings (and an Aerial Act)," 22 Mar. 1941, 61.

"April Fool," 5 Apr. 1941, 39.

"New Pursuit Plane," 12 Apr. 1941, 78.

"Street Salesman," 19 Apr. 1941, 60.

"Art Gallery," 26 Apr. 1941, 77.

"Dentist," 3 May 1941, 30.

"Tough Neighborhood," 10 May 1941, 65.

"Drawbridge," 17 May 1941, 65.

"Long Freight," 24 May 1941, 52.

"Singing Telegram," 31 May 1941, 46.

"Hat and Coat," 7 June 1941, 39.

"Banquet Cigars," 14 June 1941, 25.

"Yours Truly," 21 June 1941, 27.

"Black Cat," 28 June 1941, 73.

"Taximeter," 5 July 1941, 31.

"Waiter's Eye," 12 July 1941, 54.

"Dummy," 26 July 1941, 29.

"Insomnia," 2 Aug. 1941, 47.

"Fish Story," 9 Aug. 1941, 47.

"Double Play," 16 Aug. 1941, 46.

"Three Forks," 23 Aug. 1941, 42.

"Ten-Pounder," 30 Aug. 1941, 35. Note: *Ten* is crossed out and *Twenty* is written above.

"Roller Coaster," 13 Sept. 1941, 43.

"Hot Soup," 20 Sept. 1941, 73.

"Crooked Picture," 27 Sept. 1941.

"Exciting Movie," 4 Oct. 1941, 45.

"Shoeshine," 11 Oct. 1941, 89.

"After-Dinner Speaker," 18 Oct. 1941, 75.

"Smallest Piece," 25 Oct. 1941, 27.

"Burnt Tablecloth," 1 Nov. 1941, 43.

"Sidewalk Baby," 8 Nov. 1941, 69.

"Informal Flash Photo," 15 Nov. 1941, 89.

"Temperature?," 22 Nov. 1941, 73.

"Air Bump," 29 Nov. 1941, 44.

"Express Elevator—Up," 6 Dec. 1941, 72.

"Decrescendo—Fortissimo," 13 Dec. 1941, 53.

"Dripping Faucet," 20 Dec. 1941, 43.

"Handkerchiefs for Aunt Sarah," 27 Dec. 1941, 65.

"Boy with Snowballs," 3 Jan. 1942, 36.

"Scene of Last Night's Party," 10 Jan. 1942, 51.

"Double Combination Super-Frappé de Luxe," 17 Jan. 1942.

"Car in Pedestrian Lane," 24 Jan. 1942, 57.

"Our Planes," 31 Jan. 1942, 53.

"Three News Items and a Commercial," 7 Feb. 1942, 61.

"Buffet Supper," 21 Feb. 1942.

"Mirror," 28 Feb. 1942, 51.

"Soft Shoulders," 7 Mar. 1942, 53.

"Sour Note," 14 Mar. 1942, 43.

"Warning," 21 Mar. 1942, 63.

"Sugar Bowl," 28 Mar. 1942, 56.

"April Fool," 4 Apr. 1942, 37.

"Conga Line," 11 Apr. 1942, 53.

"Arm Band," 18 Apr. 1942, 57.

"New (and Pretty) Passenger," 25 Apr. 1942, 44.

"Too Easy Chair," 2 May 1942, 61.

"Empty Glass," 9 May 1942, 41.

"Flashing Light," 16 May 1942, 47.

"Motor Trip," 23 May 1942, 51.

"Victory Gardens," 30 May 1942, 50.

"Antique Chair," 6 June 1942, 55.

"Six-Year-Old-Charge on a Swing," 13 June 1942, 38.

"Only the Cat," 20 June 1942, 59.

"Letter Box," 27 June 1942, 41.

"Nothing," 4 July 1942.

"Tennis Duffer," 11 July 1942.

"Seat," 18 July 1942, 56.

"Ash Tray," 25 July 1942, 60.

"Sidewalk Menace," 1 Aug. 1942.

"'Please Pass It Along,'" 8 Aug. 1942.

"Fire Engines," 15 Aug. 1942.

"Crack of Light," 5 Sept. 1942.

"Office Switchboard—After Hours," 12 Sept. 1942.

"Zzz-zzzzzz-zz-zzzz," 19 Sept. 1942.

"Bad Dream," 26 Sept. 1942, 57.
"Mail Plane," 3 Oct. 1942, 47.
"Home Movies," 10 Oct. 1942, 69.
"Air-Raid Duty—12 to 4 A.M.," 17 Oct. 1942, 48.
"G-rrrrr!," 14 Nov. 1942, 56.
"Dinner Next Door," 19 Dec. 1942, 27.
"Air Raid Duty," 2 Jan. 1943, 65.
"January 2, 1942," 9 Jan. 1943. Note: The final 2 is crossed out.

Barnaby (syndicated comic strip)
Johnson was sole author from 20 Apr. 1942 to 31 Dec. 1945. From 1 Jan. 1946 to 13 Sept. 1947, Johnson served as story consultant, but Ted Ferro wrote and Jack Morley illustrated. From 15 Sept. 1947 to 2 Feb. 1952, Johnson wrote and Jack Morley illustrated, usually guided by Johnson's fairly detailed sketches. From 12 Sept. 1960 to 14 Apr. 1962, Johnson wrote and Warren Sattler redrew the art.

Barkis & Family (syndicated comic strip)
Ran from May to October 1955. Six strips were republished in *Nickelodeon Magazine*, November 2001, 48.

MAGAZINES
Barnaby Quarterly, July, Nov. 1945, February 1946.

PAMPHLETS (ILLUSTRATED BY JOHNSON)
Sister, You Need the Union! . . . And the Union Needs You! Detroit: International Union, United Automobile, Aircraft and Agricultural Implement Workers of America, ca. 1944.
The President's Speech Illustrated by Nineteen Artists. New York: Independent Voters Committee of the Arts and Sciences for Roosevelt, 1944. Includes one illustration by Johnson.
For the People's Health. New York: Physicians Forum, 1946.
The Saga of Quilby: A Ghost Story Especially Devised for Advertisers Who Stay Up Late (pamphlet designed to sell advertising space in *This Week* magazine). Ca. 1955.

ADVERTISEMENTS ILLUSTRATED BY JOHNSON
This list is incomplete.
"O'Malley Foiled by Crown Zippers." *Life*, 10 Apr. 1944, 82.
"Watch Ford in '48." *27 Annual of Advertising and Editorial Art.* New York: Pitman Publishing Corporation for Art Directors Club of New York, 1948.
"Ford's Out Front." Ca. 1947–48.
"Have You Considered Using Kimberly-Clark Coated Papers?" Ca. 1953.
". . . Before It Talks" (American Cancer Society). Ca. 1953.
Ladies Home Journal. 1950s. Box 15, Crockett Johnson Papers, Smithsonian Institution.

WORKS BY OTHER AUTHORS WITH ILLUSTRATIONS BY JOHNSON
Forsythe, Robert. *Redder Than the Rose.* New York: Covici, Friede, 1935.
Foster, Constance J. *This Rich World: The Story of Money.* New York: McBride, 1943.

"Small Cigaret Firms Tell 'Truth' about Shortage." *Advertising Age*, 18 Dec. 1944, 8 (*Barnaby* strip).

"Soap Opera." *Fortune*, Mar. 1946, 118–23, 146, 148, 151 (*Barnaby* strip).

Brown, Margaret Wise. *Willie's Adventures*. New York: Scott, 1954.

———. "Willie's Pocket." In *Through Golden Windows: Good Times Together*, ed. Nora Beust et al., 141–44. New York: Grolier, 1958.

Branley, Franklyn M., and Eleanor K. Vaughan. *Mickey's Magnet*. New York: Crowell, 1956.

Cook, Bernadine. *The Little Fish That Got Away*. New York: Scott, 1956.

Whyte, William H., Jr. "Budgetism: Opiate of the Middle Class." *Fortune*, May 1956, 133–37, 164, 166, 171–72.

ARTICLES

"Fantastic Companions." *Harper's Magazine*, June 1955, 32–34.

"A Geometrical Look at $\sqrt{\pi}$." *Mathematical Gazette*, Feb. 1970, 59–60.

"On the Mathematics of Geometry in My Abstract Paintings." *Leonardo* 5.5 (1972): 97–101, color plate facing p. 124. Rpt. *Visual Art, Mathematics, and Computing*, ed. Frank J. Malina, 143–47, 306. Oxford: Pergamon, 1979.

"A Construction for a Regular Heptagon." *Mathematical Gazette* 59 (Mar. 1975): 17–21.

REVIEWS BY JOHNSON

"Fables in Modern Dress." *New Masses*, 17 Nov. 1936, 22. Review of *Aesop Said So*, lithographs by Hugo Gellert.

"Dutch Uncle of the Arts." *New Masses*, 9 Nov. 1937, 24–25. Review of *The Arts*, by Willem Hendrik van Loon.

"From Gropper to Gothic." *New Masses*, 11 Jan. 1938, 24–25. Review of *Six Centuries of Fine Prints*, by Carl Zigrosser.

"Low's Cartoons." *New Masses*, 29 Aug. 1939, 20. Review of *A Cartoon History of Our Times*, by David Low.

"See My Lawyer." *New Masses*, 10 Oct. 1939, 31. Review of *See My Lawyer*, by Richard Maibaum and Harry Clork, starring Milton Berle, Eddie Nugent, and Teddy Hart.

"The Secrets of Ancient Geometry—And Its Use." *Leonardo* 5.4 (Autumn 1972): 362–63. Review of *The Secrets of Ancient Geometry—and Its Use*, by Tons Brunés.

PUBLISHED LETTERS

"Mathematics of Geometry in Crockett Johnson's Paintings." *Leonardo* 6.1 (Winter 1973): 92.

"Mathematics of Geometry in Abstract Painting (Cont.)" *Leonardo* 6.4 (Autumn 1973): 381.

PLAYS

Barnaby and Mr. O'Malley. Adapted by Jerome Chodorov. 1946. Two performances in Wilmington, Delaware, and two performances in Baltimore, September 1946.

Barnaby: A Play for Children in Two Acts, Adapted from the Original Barnaby Comic Strip by Crockett Johnson. Written by Robert and Lillian Masters. 1948. New York: French, 1950.

Harold and the Purple Crayon. Adapted by Jane Marlin Shepard, with music by Jon Ehrlich and lyrics by Ehrlich and Robin Pogrebin. Produced and performed by Theaterworks USA. 1990.

FILMS

Harold and the Purple Crayon. Directed by David Piel. Narration by Norman Rose. Music by Jimmy Carroll. Produced by David Piel in association with Robert Sagalyn and Stanley Flink. Brandon Films, 1959.

The Frowning Prince. Written and animated by Crockett Johnson. Rembrandt Films, 1960. Released by MacMillan Films, 1963. JEF Films International, 1995.

Barnaby. Won first prize at Venice Film Festival, 1967.

Harold's Circus. Graphic Curriculum, 1968. NBC, *Exploring.*

A Picture for Harold's Room. Directed by Gene Deitch. Animated by Bohumil Sejda. Music from the string quartet in B-minor by Leopold Kozeluh, played by Janacek Quartet. Produced by Morton Schindel. Weston Woods Studios, 1971.

Harold's Fairy Tale. Directed by Gene Deitch. Animation by Bohumil Sejda. Music by Karel Velebny. Produced by Morton Schindel. Weston Woods Studios, 1974.

TV

Barnaby and Mr. O'Malley. Screenplay by Louis Pelletier. Directed by Sherman Marks. Starring Bert Lahr as Mr. O'Malley and Ronny Howard as Barnaby. Mel Blanc provided McSnoyd's voice. CBS, 20 December 1959.

Harold and the Purple Crayon. Narrated by Sharon Stone. HBO Family Channel, 2001–2.

FILMSTRIPS

Harold and the Purple Crayon. Weston Woods Studios, 1963.

A Picture for Harold's Room. Weston Woods Studios, 1972.

The Frowning Prince. H. M. Stone Productions, 1972.

Harold's Fairy Tale. Weston Woods Studios, 1974.

PAINTINGS

Eighty Crockett Johnson paintings can be viewed on the Smithsonian Institution's *Mathematical Paintings of Crockett Johnson* website: http://americanhistory.si.edu/col lections/group_detail.cfm?key=1253&gkey=192&page=1. Those in the Smithsonian's collection are denoted by number on the Smithsonian Institution's website (SIW) and series number (SI). Another dozen or so are available at http://www.k-state.edu/eng lish/nelp/purple/art.html; these works are labeled CJHP. Others are in private collections. Sizes rounded off to the nearest quarter inch.

Aligned Triangles (Desargues). 25¼" x 48¾". 1970. SIW#1, SI#63.

Aligned Triangles and Projections. 32" x 32". 1968.

Alignment of Intersecting Traces (Desargues, 1593–1662). 1966.

Approximation of Pi to 0.0001. 24" x 32½" 1970–75. SIW#75, SI#101.

Archimedes Transversal. 32¾" x 32¾". ca. 1974. SIW#2, SI#104.

Area and Perimeter of a Squared Circle. 24" x 24". 1970–75. SIW#3, SI#95.

Area Measurement of a Parabola (Archimedes, 3rd c BC). 48" x 48". ca. 1967.

Biblical Squared Circles. 25¼" x 25¼". ca. 1972. SIW#4, SI#92.

Bouquet of Equal Areas. 48" x 48". n.d.

Bouquet of Triangle Theorems (Euclid, 4th c BC). 33" x 27". 1966. SIW#5, SI#26.

Calculus. 49" x 49". 1966.

Centers of Similitude (La Hire, 1640–1718). 33" x 22½". 1966. SIW#76, SI#14.

Collineation of Perpendiculars (Simson, 1687–1768). 48" x 42". ca. 1967.

Conic Curve (Appolonius, 3rd c BC). 33¼" x 29¼". 1966. SIW#6, SI#11.

A Construction for the Heptagon (Neusis II). 48" x 42". 1970–75. CJHP.

Construction of a Heptagon. 49¼" x 27¼". ca. 1975. SIW#7, SI#115.

Construction of Heptagon. 49" x 43". ca. 1975. SIW#8, SI#117.

Construction of Heptagon. 33" x 33". 1973. SIW#77, SI#116.

Construction of the Heptagon. 48½" x 42¼". 1975. SIW#9, SI#108.

Cross-Ratio (Poncelet, 1788–1867). 48" x 42". ca. 1967.

Cross-Ratio in a Conic (Poncelet). 33¼." x 48¾". SIW#11, SI#21.

Cross-Ratio in an Ellipse (Poncelet). 31" x 25½". SIW#10, SI#69.

Cube Doubled in Volume. 25" x 25". n.d.

Curve Tangents (Fermat, 1601–1665). 19" x 25". 1966. SIW#12, SI#12.

Division of a Square by Conic Rectangles. 33" x 33". 1970.

Division of the Square by Conic Rectangles. 25" x 25". 1970. SIW#13, SI#60.

Division of a One-by-Two Rectangle by Conic Rectangles. 41" x 24". 1970. CJHP.

Doubled Cube (Newton). 25¼" x 25¼". ca. 1970. SIW#14, SI#85.

Duality (Pascal-Brianchon). 25½" x 25½". 1966. SIW#15, SI#81.

Euclidian Values of a Squared Circle. 48¼" x 32¼". ca. 1970. SIW#18, SI#102.

Equal Areas, Their Triangular Square Root, and Pi. 48" x 47½". 1970–75. SIW#16, SI#90.

Equal Triangles. 28¼" x 25¼". 1972. SIW#17, SI#86.

Equation (Descartes, 1596–1650). 17" x 32". ca. 1967.

Equation Roots in Complex Numbers (Gauss, 1777–1855). 48" x 48". ca. 1967.

Every Positive Integer (Gauss, 1777–1855). 10" x 32½". 1966. SIW#19, SI#29.

Fluxions (Newton). 47¾" x 47¼". 1966. SIW#20, SI#20.

Fluxions, or the Differential Calculus (Newton, 1642–1727). 48" x 49". ca. 1967.

Fraction of Pi (to .0000003 . . .) in a Square of One (Construction of the 113:355 Ratio of Tsu Chung Chih, 500 AD). 23½" x 23½". CJHP.

Geometric Mean (Archytas). 15" x 24". 1968. SIW#21, SI#65.

Geometric Mean (Pythagoras). n.d.

Geometry of a Triple Bubble (Plateau, 1801–1883). 29" x 24¾". 1966. SIW#22, SI#23.

Golden Rectangle (Pythagoras). 25" x 25". 1968. SIW#23, SI#46.

Golden Rectangle (Pythagoras). 36" x 26½". 1970. SIW#24, SI#64.

Harmonic Series from a Quadrilateral (Pappus, 3rd c AD). 33" x 48¾". 1966. SIW#25, SI#24.

Heptagon 1:3:3 Triangle. 30¼" x 16¼". ca. 1973. SIW#26, SI#105.

Heptagon from Its Seven Sides. 23¼" x 16¼". 1973. SIW#27, SI#107.

Heptagon from Its Seven Sides. 23¾" x 16". 1973. CJHP.

Heptagon from Ten Equal Lines. 49¼" x 49¼". 1973. SIW#28, SI#109.

Heptagon 1:3:3 Triangle. 30¼" x 16¼". ca. 1973. SIW#26, SI#105.

Heptagon Stated by Seven Toothpicks. 26½" x 16¼". 1973. SIW#29, SI#106.

Hippias' Curve. 32¾" x 32¾". 1973. SIW#78, SI#114.

Homethic Triangles (Hippocrates of Chios, 5th c BC). 25½" x 17¼". 1966. SIW#30, SI#17.

Law of Drifting Velocities. 21" x 25". 1967. SIW#32, SI#99.

Law of Motion (Galileo). 24½" x 24½". 1970. SIW#31, SI#71.

Law of Orbiting Velocity (Kepler). 28¼" x 35¾". 1966. SIW#79, SI#76.

Law of Orbiting Velocity (Kepler, 1571–1630). 32" x 40". 1965. SIW#33, SI#22.

Locus of Point on Chord (Plato). 25" x 25". 1966. SIW#34, SI#41.

Locus of the Midpoint of a Chord (Plato 4th c BC). 24" x 24". ca. 1967.

Logarithms (Napier, 1550–1617). 22" x 26". 1966. SIW#35, SI#37.

Measurement of the Earth (Eratosthenes, 3rd c BC). 30" x 25½". 1966. SIW#36, SI#15.

Momentum of the Pendulum (Galileo, 1564–1642). ca. 1967.

Morley Triangle. 24" x 25¼". 1969. SIW#37, SI#74.

Multiplication through Imaginary Numbers (Gauss). 49½" x 49½". 1967. SIW#38, SI#40.

The "Mystic" Hexagon (Pascal, 1623–1662). 49" x 25". 1965. SIW#39, SI#10.

Nine-Point Circle (Euler). 24¾" x 41". 1970. SIW#40, SI#75.

Numbers in a Spiral. 32¼" x 33½". ca. 1965. SIW#41, SI#77.

One Surface and One Edge (Möbius). 25½" x 25½". 1965. SIW#42, SI#34.

One to One Hundred in a Spiral. ca. 1967.

Parabolic Triangles (Archimedes). 30" x 24". 1967. SIW#44, SI#78.

Parabolic Triangles (Archimedes). 49" x 25". 1969. SIW#43, SI#43

Paradox of One Surface and One Edge (Moebius, 1790–1868). 24" x 24". ca. 1967.

Pencil of Ratios (Monge, 1746–1818). 23¾" x 24". 1966. SIW#45, SI#18.

Pendulum Momentum (Galileo). 36½" x 49¼". 1966. SIW#46, SI#13.

Perspective (Alberti, 1404–1472). 25" x 30¼". 1966. SIW#47, SI#7.

Pi Squared and Its Square Root. 27½" x 33¼". 1970–75. SIW#48, SI#83.

Point Collineation in the Triangle (Euler, 1707–1783). 33¼" x 33". 1966. SIW#49, SI#28.

Polar Line of a Point and Circle (Apollonius, 3rd c BC). 24" x 32½". 1966. SIW#50, SI#38.

Polyhedron Edges + Faces = Vertices à 2 (Euler, 1701–1783). 28" x 22". ca. 1967.

Polyhedron Formula (Euler). 25" x 31". 1966. SIW#51, SI#39.

Problem of Delos (Meneachmus). 23¾" x 23¾". 1968. CJHP.

Problem of Delos II. 45" x 25". 1970.

Problem of Delos Constructed from a Solution by Isaac Newton (Arithmetica Universalis).
   39¼" x 33". 1970. SIW#52, SI#56.

Projections of Aligned Triangles (Desargues, 1593–1662). 33" x 33". ca. 1969. CJHP.

Proof of the Orbit as an Ellipse (Kepler, 1571–1630). ca. 1967.

Proof of the Pythagorean Theorem (Euclid, 4th c BC). 49¼" x 49¼". 1965. SIW#53, SI#2.

Reciprocation of Lines and Points (Pappus, 3rd c BC). 31¾" x 25¼". 1965. SIW#54, SI#6.

Rectangles of Equal Area (Pythagoras). 48¾" x 34¾". 1969. SIW#55, SI#48.

Relativity of Time and Space (Einstein, 1879–1955). 1966. 48" x 48". CJHP.

Right Triangle, Golden Rectangle, and Pythagorean Star. 37¾" x 47¾". 1972. CJHP.

Rotated Triangle and Reflexions. 24¼" x 30¼". 1970. SIW#56, SI#73.

Seventeen Sides—Gauss. 49" x 25". 1969. SIW#80, SI#70.

Similar Triangles (Thales, 7th c BC). 16" x 24½". 1966. CJHP.

Simple Equation (Descartes). 37¼" x 25½". 1966. SIW#57, SI#36.

Square Divided by Conic Rectangles. 33" x 33". CJHP.

Squared Circle. 47¾" x 48". 1969. CJHP.

Squared Circle. 52¼" x 52¼". 1968. SIW#64, SI#52.

Squared Circle. 48" x 48". 1969.

Squared Lunes (Hippocrates of Chios). 15" x 24½". 1968. SIW#65, SI#67.

Squared Lunes (Hippocrates of Chios). 26" x 25". ca. 1965. SIW#66, SI#68.

Squared Rectangle and Euler Line. 25½" x 23½". 1972. SIW#67, SI#94.

Square Root of Pi. 25" x 25". 1970–75. SIW#59, SI#89.

Square Root of Pi. 33" x 33". 1970–75. SIW#60, SI#100.

Square Root of Pi = 0.0001. 25" x 25". 1972. SIW#58, SI#52.

Square Root of Two (Descartes, 1596–1650). 21½" x 33½". 1965. SIW#61, SI#19.

Square Root of x. 48" x 48". n.d.

Square Roots of One, Two, and Three. 36" x 23½". 1969. SIW#62, SI#66.

Square Roots to 16 (Theodorus of Cyrene). 42½" x 33". 1967. SIW#63, SI#45.

Squares of a 3-4-5 Triangle in Scalene Perspective (Durer, 1471–1528). 32¼" x 25½". 1965.
    SIW#70, SI#8.

Squares of 1, 2, 3, 4, and Square Roots to 8. 25" x 25". 1970–75. SIW#68, SI#97.

Squares of 2, 4, 16 from Square Root of x. 48" x 48". 1972. SIW#69, SI#88.

Squares of the 3-4-5 Triangle (Pythagorus, 6th c BC). ca. 1967.

Star Construction. 20½" x 23¾". 1970–75. SIW#71, SI#103.

Symedians (Lemoine, 1840–1912). ca. 1967.

Transcendental Curve (Wallis). 12" x 23½". 1966. CJHP.

Transversals (Ceva, 1647–1734). 20" x 25". 1966. SIW#72, SI#31.

Transversals (Menelaus, 1st c BC). 24" x 21". ca. 1967.

Triangle and Lune of Equal Area (Hippocrates, 5th c BC). 24" x 24". ca. 1967.

Velocities and Right Triangles (Galileo). 49" x 24¾". 1972. SIW#73, SI#96.

Velocity on Inclined Planes (Galileo, 1564–1642). 49½" x 33". 1966. SIW#74, SI#42.

EXHIBITIONS

*Schematic Paintings Deriving from Axioms and Theorems of Geometry, from Pythagorus to
    Apollonius of Perga, and from Desargues and Kepler to the Twentieth Century*. Glezer
    Gallery. New York, 1967.

Squaring the Circle. Museum of Art, Science, and Industry. Park Avenue, Bridgeport,
    Conn., 1970.

IBM Gallery. Yorktown Heights, N.Y., 1975.

Theorems in Color. Museum of History and Technology, Smithsonian Institution.
    Washington, D.C., 1980.

COLLABORATIONS BETWEEN CROCKETT JOHNSON AND RUTH KRAUSS

Krauss, Ruth. *The Carrot Seed*. Illus. by Crockett Johnson. New York: Harper, 1945. Adapted
    for an audio version, ca. 1950.

Krauss, Ruth. *How to Make an Earthquake*. Illus. by Crockett Johnson. New York: Harper,
    1954.

Krauss, Ruth, and Crockett Johnson. *Is This You?* Illus. by Crockett Johnson. New York:
    Scott, 1955.

Krauss, Ruth. *The Happy Egg*. Illus. by Crockett Johnson. New York: Scholastic, 1967.

WORKS BY RUTH KRAUSS

BOOKS

A Good Man and His Good Wife. Illus. Ad Reinhardt. New York: Harper, 1944.

The Great Duffy. Illus. Mischa Richter. New York: Harper, 1946.

The Growing Story. Illus. Phyllis Rowand. New York: Harper, 1947.

Bears. Illus. Phyllis Rowand. New York: Harper, 1948.

The Happy Day. Illus. Marc Simont. New York: Harper, 1949.

The Big World and the Little House. Illus. Marc Simont. New York: Schuman, 1949.

The Backward Day. Illus. Marc Simont. New York: Harper, 1950.

I Can Fly. Illus. Mary Blair. New York: Simon and Schuster, 1950.

The Bundle Book. Illus. Helen Stone. New York: Harper, 1951.

A Hole Is to Dig: A First Book of First Definitions. Illus. Maurice Sendak. New York: Harper, 1952.

A Very Special House. Illus. Maurice Sendak. New York: Harper, 1953.

I'll Be You and You Be Me. Illus. Maurice Sendak. New York: Harper, 1954.

Charlotte and the White Horse. Illus. Maurice Sendak. New York: Harper, 1955.

I Want to Paint My Bathroom Blue. Illus. Maurice Sendak. New York: Harper, 1956.

Monkey Day. Illus. Phyllis Rowand. New York: Harper, 1957.

The Birthday Party. Illus. Maurice Sendak. New York: Harper, 1957.

Somebody Else's Nut Tree, and Other Tales from Children. Illus. Maurice Sendak. New York: Harper, 1958.

A Moon or a Button: A Collection of First Picture Ideas. Illus. Remy Charlip. New York: Harper, 1959.

Open House for Butterflies. Illus. Maurice Sendak. New York: Harper, 1960.

Mama, I Wish I Was Snow; Child You'd Be Very Cold. Illus. Ellen Raskin. New York: Atheneum, 1962.

A Bouquet of Littles. Illus. Jane Flora. New York: Harper and Row, 1963.

The Little King, the Little Queen, the Little Monster, and Other Stories You Can Make Up Yourself. New York: Scholastic, 1964.

Eyes, Nose, Fingers, Toes. Illus. Elizabeth Schneider. New York: Harper and Row, 1964.

The Cantilever Rainbow. Illus. Antonio Frasconi. New York: Pantheon, 1965.

What a Fine Day for . . . Illus. Remy Charlip. New York: Parents' Magazine Press, 1967.

This Thumbprint. Illus. Ruth Krauss. New York: Harper and Row, 1967.

There's a Little Ambiguity over There among the Bluebells and Other Theater Poems. New York: Something Else, 1968.

If Only. Eugene, Ore.: Toad, 1969.

I Write It. Illus. Mary Chalmers. New York: Harper and Row, 1970.

Under Twenty. Illus. Ruth Krauss. Eugene, Ore.: Toad, 1970.

Everything under a Mushroom. Illus. Margot Tomes. New York: Scholastic, 1973.

This Breast Gothic. Illus. Ruth Krauss. Lenox, Mass.: Bookstore, 1973.

Little Boat Lighter Than a Cork. Illus. Ester Gilman. Weston, Conn.: Magic Circle, 1976.

Under Thirteen. Lenox, Mass.: Bookstore, 1976.

When I Walk I Change the Earth. Providence, R.I.: Burning Deck, 1978.

Somebody Spilled the Sky. Illus. Eleanor Hazard. New York: Greenwillow, 1979.

Minestrone. New York: Greenwillow, 1981.

Re-Examination of Freedom. West Branch, Iowa: Toothpaste, 1981.

Big and Little. Illus. Mary Szilagyi. New York: Scholastic, 1987.

RE-ILLUSTRATED BOOKS

A Good Man and His Good Wife. Illus. Marc Simont. New York: Harper and Row, 1962.

I Can Fly. Illus. Jan Brett. New York: Simon and Schuster, 1981.

You're Just What I Need. Illus. Julia Noonan. New York: HarperCollins, 1999. Originally published as *The Bundle Book.*

Goodnight Goodnight Sleepyhead. Illus. Jane Dyer. New York: HarperCollins, 2004. Originally published as *Eyes Nose Fingers Toes.*

Bears. Illus. Maurice Sendak. New York: HarperCollins, 2005.

The Growing Story. Illus. Helen Oxenbury. New York: HarperCollins, 2007.

And I Love You. Illus. Steven Kellogg. New York: Orchard Books, 2010. Originally published as *Big and Little.*

PLAYS

This list is incomplete, and different groups of short plays were performed under the same title.

A Beautiful Day. Directed by Remy Charlip. Presented in four versions as part of the Pocket Follies. Pocket Theatre, New York City. Jun. 1963. Fifth version, directed by Remy Charlip, with music by Al Carmines. Judson Poets' Theater, Judson Memorial Church, New York. Dec. 1965. Performed again at the Judson Poets Theatre. Jun. 1966. Repr. with *Pineapple Play, There's a Little Ambiguity over There among the Bluebells,* and *The 50,000 Dogwood Trees at Valley Forge,* in Michael Benedikt, ed. *Theatre Experiment: An Anthology of American Plays.* Garden City, N.Y.: Anchor, 1968. 206–305. Repr. in Albert Poland and Bruce Mailman, *The Off Off Broadway Book: The Plays, People, Theatre.* New York: Bobbs-Merrill, 1972. 25–26.

There's a Little Ambiguity over There among the Bluebells, Pineapple Play, In a Bull's Eye, and one other one-act play (possibly *If Only*). Hardware Poets Playhouse, New York. Apr. 1964. Radio adaptation by the Word Players. Directed by Baird Searles. WBAI, New York. 23 May 1970. A larger collection of poem-plays bearing this title, conceived and directed by Joseph Gifford, ran at the Boston University Theatre. Music by Max Lifchitz. Part 1 included "The Poet and the Ashcan," "Seven Acts and Torch Song," "Weather: Cloudy with O.I.C.T.," "Practical Mother's Guide," "Sun Dance," "Whom Does the Little One Favor," "Everything Is Doubled Today," "The Date," "Winnie and Bill," "Hitch-Hike," "More!," "If Only," "French Omelette," "Dante and the Poet," "This Breast." Part 2 included "The Universe," "How to Write a Book," "Double Killing," "Young Man in Scanty Contemplation Clad and Miss Diana Palmer," "Suicide," "It'- s-s-s-s LOVE," "Quartet or Molly, Apollinaire and Friends," "Hands Are to Hold," "Le Poet and les Fleurs de France," "The Poet and His Id," "Yellow Umbrella," "Dream," "Re-Examination of Freedom." Mar. 1973

38 Haikus. Caffe Cino, New York. Aug. 1964.

The Cantilever Rainbow. Spencer Memorial Church, Brooklyn Heights, N.Y. Mar. 1965. Performed again at Caffe Cino at Café La Mama, New York. Apr. 1965. Also performed at Lee Strasburg's Actor's Studio. 1966.

Newsletters. Caffe Cino, New York. Mar. 1966.

If Only . . . : A Ruth Krauss Gala! Produced by the Westport Poetry Center, sponsored by the Westport Arts Council. WWAC Gallery, Town Hall, Westport, Conn. 12 Dec. 1969.

If I Were Freedom. Bard College, Annandale-on-Hudson, N.Y. 1976–77.

Re-Examination of Freedom. Boston University. 1976–77.

Small Black Lambs Wandering in the Red Poppies. New York City. Jun. 1982.

Ambiguity 2nd. Boston. 1985.

UNCOLLECTED POETRY

This list is incomplete. A partial list of journals that published Krauss's work includes *C*, *Floating Bear*, *Harper's Bazaar*, *Harper's Magazine*, *IN*, *Kulchur*, *Locus Solus*, *New World Writing*, *The Plumed Horn*, *Residu*, *Synanon Literary Journal*, *Wagner Literary Magazine*, *Wild Dog*, *XbyX*, *Yowl*.

"Four Prose Poems." *The Bards' Bugle* 1.1 (Dec. 1959).

"News" and "Uri Gagarin & William Shakespeare," *Locus Solus* 2 (Summer 1961): 153–55.

"Variations on a Lorca Form." *Harper's Magazine*, Oct. 1961, 88.

"Poem for the Depression." 1961. Folder 33, box 2, series I. Ruth Krauss Papers, Northeast Children's Literature Collection, Dodd Research Center, University of Connecticut, Storrs.

"Andy Auto Body" and "My Dream with Its Solar-Pulse gallop." *New School Poets* [ca. 1962–63]: 8–9.

"Duet." *XbyX*, July 1963.

"A Show a Play: . . ." *Wild Dog* 2.10 (Sept. 1964): 21–22.

"Seven Poem Plays." *Wild Dog* 2.11 (28 Oct. 1964): 27–33.

"Poem" and "Song." *Nadada* 1 (Aug. 1964): 6.

"Poem-Plays." *Kulchur* 18.5 (Summer 1965): 39–51.

"Practical Mother's Guide." *Kauri* 12 (Jan.–Feb. 1966): 5.

"Lost," "Poem," "Freedom Poem," and "This Breast." *Intransit: The Andy Warhol Gerard Malanga Monster Issue*. Eugene, Ore.: Toad, 1968. 162–63.

"Song" (from *Re-Examination of Freedom*). In *The World Anthology: Poems from the St. Mark's Poetry Project*. Ed. Ann Waldman. Indianapolis: Bobbs-Merrill, 1969. 59.

"News," "A Play," "Silence," and "Weather." *General Schmuck* 5 (Jan. 1975).

Two excerpts from *When I Walk I Change the Earth*, "Little Boat Lighter Than a Cork," "Song," "Duet," "Lullabye." In *On This Crust of Earth*. Ed. Ralph Nazareth and Lynda Sorensen. Stamford, Conn.: Yuganta, 1986. 1–8.

REVIEWS

JOHNSON, BARNABY (1943)

Kimbrough, Mary. "'Barnaby' Meets His Fairy Godfather in a New Book by Crockett Johnson." *St. Louis Star-Times*, 21 Oct. 1943, 17.

Mallet, Isabelle. "Godfather with Wings." *New York Times Book Review*, 31 Oct. 1943, 9.

Parker, Dorothy. "A Mash Note to Crockett Johnson." *PM*, 3 Oct. 1943, 16. Republished as the introduction to *Barnaby #4: Mr. O'Malley Goes for the Gold*. New York: Ballantine, 1986.

S[eaver], E[dwin]. "Books." *Direction* [n.d.]: 14. Barnaby Fan Mail II, folder 2, Crockett Johnson Papers, Mathematics Division, National Museum of American History, Smithsonian Institution.

KRAUSS, A GOOD MAN AND HIS GOOD WIFE (1944)

Korff, Alice Graeme. "Children's Books, 1944–1945." *Magazine of Art*, May 1945. Reel N/69-104, frame 590, Adolf and Virginia Dehn Papers, Archives of American Art, Smithsonian Institution.

JOHNSON, BARNABY AND MR. O'MALLEY *(1944)*
Binsse, Harry Lorin. "Children's Books—1944." *Commonweal*, 17 Nov. 1944, 127.
Conroy, Jack. "Leisk, David Johnson. Barnaby and Mr. O'Malley." *Booklist*, 1 Nov. 1944, 73.
Mallet, Isabelle. "Cartoonists in Review." *New York Times Book Review*, 24 Sept. 1944, 7.

KRAUSS, THE CARROT SEED *(1945)*
Buell, Ellen Lewis. *New York Times Book Review*, 18 July 1945, 18.
Virginia Kirkus' Bookshop Service, 15 Apr. 1945, 180.

KRAUSS, THE GREAT DUFFY *(1946)*
Fischer, Marjorie. *New York Times Book Review*, 10 Nov. 1946, 3.
Little, Florence. "For Small Children." *San Francisco Chronicle*, 10 Nov. 1946, 4.
Virginia Kirkus' Bookshop Service, 1 Oct. 1946, 490.

KRAUSS, THE GROWING STORY *(1947)*
Becker, May Lamberton. *New York Herald Tribune Weekly Book Review*, 14 Sept. 1947, 14
Darling, Frances C. *Christian Science Monitor*, 11 Nov. 1947, 16A.
Gerard, Lillian. *New York Times Book Review*, 16 Nov. 1947, 42.
Virginia Kirkus' Bookshop Service, 1 July 1947, 335.

KRAUSS, BEARS *(1948)*
Bechtel, Louise S. *New York Herald Tribune Weekly Book Review*, 14 Nov. 1948, 6.
Dedman, Emmett. "Celebrating Children's Book Week." *Chicago Sun Book Week*, 13 Nov.
    1948, 21.
Eaton, Anne Thaxter. *Christian Science Monitor*, 21 Dec. 1948, 11
Jordan, Alice M. "Mid-Winter Booklist." *Horn Book*, Jan.–Feb. 1949, 33–34.

KRAUSS, THE HAPPY DAY *(1949)*
Atlantic Monthly, Dec. 1949, 103.
Bechtel, Louise S. *New York Herald Tribune Book Review*, 13 Nov. 1949, 6.
Moore, Anne Carroll. *Horn Book*, Nov.–Dec. 1949, 520–23.

KRAUSS, THE BIG WORLD AND THE LITTLE HOUSE *(1949)*
Blasco, Doris M. *Library Journal*, 15 Dec. 1949, 1917.
Bulletin of the Children's Book Center, Jan. 1950, 16–17.
Palmer, Lois. *New York Times Book Review*, 15 Jan. 1950, 14.
San Francisco Chronicle, 13 Nov. 1949, 6.
Winn, Marcia. "How a Family Made a House Into a Home." *Chicago Sunday Tribune*, 13
    Nov. 1949, 12.

KRAUSS, THE BACKWARD DAY *(1950)*
Bechtel, Louise S. *New York Herald Tribune Book Review*, 12 Nov. 1950, 9.
Buell, Ellen Lewis. *New York Times Book Review*, 1 Sept. 1950, 36.

KRAUSS, THE BUNDLE BOOK *(1951)*
Lindquist, Jennie D., and Siri M. Andrews. *Horn Book*, Dec. 1951, 403.
Palmer, Lois. *New York Times Book Review*, 11 Nov. 1951, 42.
Virginia Kirkus' Bookshop Service, 1 Oct. 1951, 575.

JOHNSON, WHO'S UPSIDE DOWN? (1952)
Palmer, Lois. "Bewildered Kangaroo." *New York Times Book Review*, 9 Nov. 1952, 52.

KRAUSS, A HOLE IS TO DIG (1952)
Buell, Ellen Lewis. *New York Times Book Review*, 7 Sept. 1952, 31.
Lindquist, Jennie D. *Horn Book*, Oct. 1952, 315.

KRAUSS, A VERY SPECIAL HOUSE (1953)
Haviland, Virginia. *Horn Book*, Dec. 1953, 452–53.
Kieran, Margaret Ford. *Atlantic Monthly*, Dec. 1953, 97.

KRAUSS, I'LL BE YOU AND YOU BE ME (1954)
Bechtel, Louise S. *New York Herald Tribune*, 14 Nov. 1954, 32.
Buell, Ellen Lewis. *New York Times Book Review*, 31 Oct. 1954.

KRAUSS AND JOHNSON, IS THIS YOU? (1955)
Buell, Ellen Lewis. *New York Times Book Review*, 17 Apr. 1955, 28.
Bulletin of the Children's Book Center, Sept. 1955, 9.

KRAUSS, HOW TO MAKE AN EARTHQUAKE (1954)
Bulletin of the Children's Book Center, Sept. 1954, 4.
Donlon, Rae Emerson. *Christian Science Monitor*, 13 May 1954, 15.
Palmer, Lois. *New York Times Book Review*, 23 May 1954, 24.

JOHNSON, HAROLD AND THE PURPLE CRAYON (1955)
Buell, Ellen Lewis. "The Traveler." *New York Times Book Review*, 16 Oct. 1955, 34.
"Draws Anything." *Journal and Sentinel*, 13 Nov. 1955.
Haviland, Virginia. "Crockett Johnson, Author-Illustrator, *Harold and the Purple Crayon*."
    Horn Book, Oct. 1955, 362–63.

KRAUSS, CHARLOTTE AND THE WHITE HORSE (1955)
"Collector's Item." *Chicago Sunday Tribune*, 13 Nov. 1955, 7.
Horn Book, Oct. 1955, 363.
Kinkead, Katharine T. *New Yorker*, 26 November 1955, 205.
New York Herald Tribune, 13 Nov. 1955, 5.
Palmer, Lois. "Milky Way." *New York Times Book Review*, 13 Nov. 1955, 47.

KRAUSS, I WANT TO PAINT MY BATHROOM BLUE (1956)
Hormel, Olive Dean. *Christian Science Monitor*, 30 Aug. 1956, 7.
Libby, Margaret Sherwood. *New York Herald Tribune Book Review*, 9 Sept. 1956, 6.
Palmer, Lois. *New York Times Book Review*, 4 Nov. 1956, 38.

JOHNSON, HAROLD'S FAIRY TALE (1956)
Buell, Ellen Lewis. *New York Times Book Review*, 21 Oct. 1956, 48.
Goodwin, Polly. *Chicago Sunday Tribune*, 4 Nov. 1956.
Haviland, Virginia. *Horn Book Magazine*, Oct. 1956, 346.

Hormel, Olive Deane. *Christian Science Monitor*, 18 Oct. 1956.
Kinkead, K. T. *New Yorker*, 21 Oct. 1956, 227.
Libby, Margaret Sherwood. *New York Herald Tribune Book Review*, 23 Sept. 1956.

KRAUSS, MONKEY DAY (1957)
Berry, Mabel. *Library Journal*, 15 Dec. 1957, 3242–43.
Libby, Margaret Sherwood. *New York Herald Tribune Book Review*, 3 Nov. 1957, 11.
Virginia Kirkus' Service, 15 Jun. 1957, 410.
Woods, George A. *New York Times Book Review*, 17 Nov. 1957, 59.

JOHNSON, HAROLD'S TRIP TO THE SKY (1957)
Booklist, 1 Dec. 1957.
Buell, Ellen Lewis. *New York Times Book Review*, 13 Oct 1957, 51.
Goodwin, Polly. *Christian Science Monitor*, 7 Nov. 1957.

JOHNSON, HAROLD AT THE NORTH POLE (1958)
Kirkus, 1 Aug. 1958.
New York Times Book Review, 30 Nov. 1958.
Oakland Tribune, 2 Nov. 1958.

JOHNSON, HAROLD'S CIRCUS (1959)
Brown, Margaret Warren. *Horn Book Magazine*, June 1959, 204.
Buell, Ellen Lewis. *New York Times Book Review*, 26 Apr. 1959, 42.
Goodwin, Polly. *Chicago Tribune*, 26 Apr. 1959.

BARNABY *(TV, 1959)*
Gould, Jack. "Vet., Youngster Join Forces: Bert Lahr and Ronny Howard in Comedy." *New York Times*, 22 Dec. 1959.
"Tele Review." *Variety*, 22 Dec. 1959.

KRAUSS, OPEN HOUSE FOR BUTTERFLIES (1960)
Miles, Betty. *Saturday Review*, 15 July 1960, 37–38.
Virginia Kirkus' Service, 1 Apr. 1960, 288.
Woods, George A. *New York Times Book Review*, 8 May 1960, 30.

KRAUSS, MAMA, I WISH I WAS SNOW; CHILD, YOU'D BE VERY COLD (1962)
Christian Science Monitor, 10 May 1962, 2B.
Kirkus, 15 Jan. 1962, 53.
Woods, George A. *New York Times Book Review*, 13 May 1962, 5.

JOHNSON, HAROLD'S ABC (1963)
Bulletin of the Center for Children's Books, Nov. 1963.
Heins, Ethel L. *Horn Book*, Oct. 1963, 495.
Kirkus, 15 Jun. 1963.
New York Times Book Review, 10 Nov. 1963.

JOHNSON, THE LION'S OWN STORY (1963)

Buell, Ellen Lewis. *New York Times Book Review*, 12 Jan. 1964, 20.

R.M.B. "Dolls and Dogs, a Pig, and a Lion to Please the 6 to 10s." *Chicago Tribune*, 10 Nov. 1963, K22-A.

Taylor, Mark. "Reviewer Picks the Leaders in Children's Literature Sweepstakes." *Los Angeles Times*, 10 Nov. 1963, B16.

KRAUSS, A BOUQUET OF LITTLES (1963)

Sutherland, Zena. *Center for Children's Books Bulletin*, Feb. 1964, 96.

KRAUSS, PLAYS PERFORMED AT HARDWARE POETS (1964)

Walter, Sydney Schubert. "Theatre: Hardware Poets." *Village Voice*, 16 Apr. 1964, 10.

KRAUSS, THE LITTLE KING, THE LITTLE QUEEN, THE LITTLE MONSTER, AND OTHER STORIES YOU CAN MAKE UP YOURSELF (1964)

Gibson, Barbara H. *Library Journal*, 15 May 1969, 2090.

KRAUSS, THE CANTILEVER RAINBOW (1965)

Howard, Richard. "What Comes Naturally." *Book Week*, 27 Mar. 1966.

Kirkus, 15 Sept. 1965, 986.

Morrison, Lillian. *Library Journal*, 15 Dec. 1965, 5527.

"Poems That Please." *Christian Science Monitor*, 4 Nov. 1965, B11.

JOHNSON, CASTLES IN THE SAND (1965)

Izard, Anne. *Library Journal*, 15 May 1965, 2396.

Kirkus Reviews, 15 Feb. 1965, 171.

O'Doherty, Barbara Novak. "The World of Tangerine Cats and Cabbage Moons." *New York Times Book Review*, 9 May 1965; 4.

KRAUSS, A BEAUTIFUL DAY (THEATER, 1965)

Smith, Michael. "Theatre Journal." *Village Voice*, 16 Dec. 1965, 25.

JOHNSON, THE EMPEROR'S GIFTS (1965)

Hurwitz, Johanna. *Library Journal*, 15 Oct. 1965, 4606.

Finne, Rachel R. "The Emperor's Gifts." *New York Times Book Review*, 26 Dec. 1965, 18.

Kluger, Richard. "Hi-Jinks and Low." *Book Week*, 31 Oct. 1965, 16.

McCauley, Barbara S. "Heroes in All Sizes." *Christian Science Monitor*, 4 Nov. 1965, B3.

Sheehan, Ethna. "The Best Books of the Season for Children." *America*, 20 Nov. 1965, 637.

JOHNSON, GORDY AND THE PIRATE AND THE CIRCUS RINGMASTER AND THE KNIGHT AND THE MAJOR LEAGUE MANAGER AND THE WESTERN MARSHALL AND THE ASTRONAUT AND A REMARKABLE ACHIEVEMENT (1965)

Bulletin of the Center for Children's Books, Sept. 1966, 13.

Kirkus Reviews, 1 Nov. 1965, 1116.

KRAUSS, THE HAPPY EGG *(1967)*
Publishers Weekly, 28 Aug. 1972, 263.
School Library Journal, Dec. 1972, 71.

JOHNSON, ABSTRACTIONS OF ABSTRACTIONS *(EXHIBITION, 1967)*
B[enedikt], M[ichael]. "Reviews and Previews." *Art News*, Apr. 1967.
"Creator of 'Barnaby' in First Serious Show." *Bridgeport (Conn.) Sunday Post*, Apr. 1967.

KRAUSS, WHAT A FINE DAY FOR . . . *(1967)*
Gibson, Barbara. *Library Journal*, 15 Feb. 1968, 680.
Kirkus, 1 Nov. 1967, 1317.

KRAUSS, THERE'S A LITTLE AMBIGUITY OVER THERE AMONG THE BLUEBELLS *(1968)*
Baker, Robert. *Library Journal*, 1 Feb. 1969, 565.
Bermel, Albert. "Closet Openings." *The Nation*, 25 Aug. 1969, 156–57.

KRAUSS, I WRITE IT *(1970)*
N.M. "Things That Rhyme." *Christian Science Monitor*, 7 May 1970, B4.
Sutherland, Zena. *Saturday Review*, 22 Aug. 1970, 52.

KRAUSS, THERE'S A LITTLE AMBIGUITY OVER THERE AMONG THE BLUEBELLS *(THEATER, 1973)*
Clay, Carolyn. "Theatre: Masterful Bluebells at B.U." *Boston Phoenix*, 10 Apr. 1973, sec. 3, p. 14.
Henry, William A., 3rd. "Levels of Reality Explored in 'Bluebells' at BU Theater." *Boston Globe*, Apr. 1973. Ruth Krauss Papers, HarperCollins Publishers' Archives.

KRAUSS, EVERYTHING UNDER A MUSHROOM *(1973)*
Komaiko, Deborah. "3–6's: For Lookers and Listeners." *Christian Science Monitor*, 1 May 1974, F2.
Kuskin, Karla. *New York Times Book Review*, 5 May 1974, 46.
Publishers Weekly, 4 Feb. 1974, 72

KRAUSS, LITTLE BOAT LIGHTER THAN A CORK *(1976)*
Gregory, Helen. *School Library Journal*, Jan. 1977, 84.
Publishers Weekly, 13 Sept. 1976, 99.

KRAUSS, SOMEBODY SPILLED THE SKY *(1979)*
Hall, Donald. "The Third Hand." *New York Times Book Review*, 28 Apr. 1979, 25.
Kirkus, 15 Mar. 1979, 324.
Publishers Weekly, 22 Jan. 1979, 370.

KRAUSS, MINESTRONE *(1981)*
Kirkus, 1 Nov. 1981, 1346–47
Publishers Weekly, 21 Aug. 1981, 55.
Sanhuber, Holly. *School Library Journal*, Nov. 1981, 94
Stein, Ruth M. *Language Arts*, Sept. 1982, 606.

JOHNSON, BARNABY #1–6 (1985–86)

"The 'Barnaby' Books Bring Back the Magic." *Newsweek*, 29 July 1985.

"Barnaby Comic Strips to Be in Book Form." *New York Times*, 18 June 1985, C17.

Halliday, Bob. "Children's Books: Barnaby's Back." *Washington Post*, 8 June 1986, 10+.

WORKS ABOUT CROCKETT JOHNSON AND RUTH KRAUSS

Abel, Bob. "From 'Krazy Kat' to 'Barnaby': Revisiting Some of the Great Comics." *National Observer*, 28 Apr. 1968, 19.

"Animating Harold." Five-minute documentary included on the videocassette *Harold and the Purple Crayon and Other Harold Stories*. Wood Knapp Video, 1993.

"L'Auteur-Illustrateur." In *Harold et le Crayon Rose* by Crockett Johnson. Trans. Anne-Laure Fournier le Ray. Paris: Pocket Jeunesse, 2001. 2.

Bader, Barbara. "Crockett Johnson." In *American Picturebooks from Noah's Ark to the Beast Within*. New York: Macmillan, 1976. 434–42.

———. "Ruth Krauss; Ruth Krauss and Maurice Sendak." In *American Picturebooks from Noah's Ark to the Beast Within*. New York: Macmillan, 1976. 416–33.

B[aker], H[annah]. "Crockett Johnson." *Barnaby Quarterly* 1 (July 1945): 1.

Becker, Stephen. *Comic Art in America: A Social History of the Funnies, the Political Cartoons, Magazine Humor, Sporting Cartoons, and Animated Cartoons*. Intro. Rube Goldberg. New York: Simon and Schuster, 1959.

Beckwith, Ethel. "Barnaby, Brainy Set's Pet Comic, Grows in Darien." *Bridgeport (Conn.) Sunday Herald*, 1 Oct. 1944, 33.

———. "Monkey Business." *Bridgeport (Conn.) Sunday Herald Magazine*, 15 Dec. 1957: 4.

Blackbeard, Bill, and Martin Williams, eds. *The Smithsonian Collection of Newspaper Comics*. Washington, D.C.: Smithsonian Institution Press, 1977.

Bodmer, George. "Ruth Krauss and Maurice Sendak's Early Illustration." *Children's Literature Association Quarterly* 11.4 (Winter 1986–87): 180–83.

Broadman, Muriel. "Harold and the Purple Crayon." *Back Stage*, 30 Nov. 1990, 44.

Crago, Maureen, and Hugh Crago. *Prelude to Literacy: A Preschool Child's Encounter with Picture and Story*. Carbondale: Southern Illinois University Press, 1983.

Craven, Thomas, ed. *Cartoon Cavalcade*. New York: Simon and Schuster, 1943.

"Crockett Johnson." In *Major Authors and Illustrators for Children and Young Adults*. Ed. Laurie Collier and Joyce Nakamura. Detroit: Gale, 1993. 1436–38.

"Crockett Johnson." In *Third Book of Junior Authors*. Ed. Doris De Montreville and Donna Hill. New York: Wilson, 1972. 152–53.

"Crockett Johnson, Cartoonist, Creator of 'Barnaby,' Is Dead." *New York Times*, 13 July 1975, 38.

"Crockett Johnson's Art Is Tantalizing at MASI." *Bridgeport (Conn.) Sunday Post*, 18 Jan. 1970, 16.

"Cushlamochree!" *Newsweek*, 4 Oct. 1942, 102, 104.

Deitch, Gene. "The Picture Book Animated." *Horn Book*, Apr. 1978, 144–49.

Dove, Rita. "Maple Valley Branch Library, 1967." In *On the Bus with Rosa Parks*. New York: Norton, 1999. 32–33.

———. "Rita Dove." In *For the Love of Books: 115 Celebrated Writers on the Books They Love Most*, ed. Ronald B. Shwartz. New York: Grosset/Putnam, 1999. 70–75.

Dresang, Eliza T. *Radical Change: Books for Youth in a Digital Age*. New York: Wilson, 1999.

Ellington, Duke. "He Trusts Mr. O'Malley." *PM*, 1 Dec. 1942, 21.

"The End of a Fairy Tale." *Time*, 28 Jan. 1952, 77.

Erwin, Ray. "'Barnaby' Returns to Comic Strips." *Editor and Publisher*, 16 July 1960, 52.

"Escape Artist." *Time*, 2 Sept. 1946, 49–50.

Fadool, Cynthia, ed. *Contemporary Authors*. Vols. 57–60. Detroit: Gale, 1976.

"Fallen Star." *Newsweek*, 7 Feb. 1949, 54.

Fay, Francis X., Jr. "Ruth Ida Krauss Was Westport Resident: Noted Children's Book Writer Dies at 92." *Norwalk (Conn.) Hour*, 13 July 1993, 31.

"Features: William Joyce." *Salon.com*, 16 Dec. 1995. http://www.salonmagazine. com/16dec1995/features/kids.html.

Fisher, Charles. "Barnaby and Mr. O'Malley 'Developed.'" *Philadelphia Record*, 15 Nov. 1943, sec. 2.

"Geometric Abstraction." *Norwalk (Conn.) Hour*, 7 Jun. 1975, 22.

Glubok, Shirley. *The Art of the Comic Strip*. New York: Macmillan, 1979.

Goulart, Ron, ed. *The Encyclopedia of American Comics*. New York: Facts on File, 1990.

———. "A Little Bit of History . . ." In *Barnaby #1: Wanted, a Fairy Godfather*. By Crockett Johnson. New York: Ballantine, 1985. 209–13.

Harms, Valerie. "Interview with Ruth Krauss." *Parents' Choice*, Sept.–Oct. 1978, 8–9.

"Harold and the Purple Crayon." In *Everything I Need to Know I Learned from a Children's Book: Life Lessons from Notable People from All Walks of Life*. Ed. Anita Silvey. New York: Roaring Brook, 2009. 112–13.

"'A Hole Is to Dig?' Harold Should Know." *New Haven Register*, 12 July 1959, 2.

Hopkins, Lee Bennett. "Ruth Krauss [and] Crockett Johnson." In *Books Are by People: Interviews with 104 Authors and Illustrators of Books for Young Children*. New York: Citation, 1969. 121–24.

Horn, Maurice C. "The Crisis of the Forties." In *A History of the Comic Strip*. By Pierre Couperie, Maurice C. Horn, Proto Destefanis, et al. Trans. Eileen B. Hennessy. New York: Crown, 1968. 83–101.

"Johnson, Crockett." In *Current Biography 1943*. Ed. Maxine Block. New York: Wilson, 1944. 345–47.

"Johnson, Crockett, pseud." In *Illustrators of Children's Books, 1957–1966*. Comp. Lee Kingman, Joanna Foster, and Ruth Giles Lontoft. Boston: Horn Book, 1968. 126.

Jones, Stacy V. "Inventor of Barnaby Gets Patent for 4-Way Adjustable Mattress." *New York Times*, 29 Oct. 1955, 22.

Krauss, Ruth. "Ruth Krauss." In *More Junior Authors*. Ed. Muriel Fuller. New York: Wilson, 1963. 126.

Krauss, Ruth. "Ruth Krauss." In *Pauses: Autobiographical Reflections of 101 Creators of Children's Books*. Ed. Lee Bennett Hopkins. New York: HarperCollins, 1995. 39–41.

"Krauss, Ruth." In *Contemporary Authors: A Bio-Bibliographical Guide to Current Writers in Fiction, General Nonfiction, Poetry, Journalism, Drama, Motion Pictures, Television, and Other Fields*. Ed. James M. Ethridge and Barbara Kopala. Detroit: Gale, 1967. 553.

"Krauss, Ruth." In *Contemporary Dramatists*. Ed. James Vinson. New York: St. Martin's, 1973. 449–51.

"Krauss, Ruth." In *Foremost Women in Communications: A Biographical Reference Work on Accomplished Women in Broadcasting, Publishing, Advertising, Public Relations, and Allied Professions*. Ed. Barbara J. Love. New York: Foremost Americans, 1970. 356.

"Krauss, Ruth." In *Something about the Author*. Detroit: Gale, 1971. 1:135.

"Krauss, Ruth Ida." In *The Author's and Writer's Who's Who*. 6th ed. Ed. J. V. Yeats. London: Burke's Peerage, 1971. 468.

"Krauss, Ruth (Ida) 1911–." In *Major Authors and Illustrators for Children and Young Adults*. Ed. Laurie Collier and Joyce Nakamura. Detroit: Gale, 1993. 4:1364–66.

"Krauss, Ruth (Ida) 1911–." In *Something about the Author*. Detroit: Gale, 1983. 30:134–37.

"Krauss, Ruth (Ida) 1911–1993." In *Contemporary Authors: New Revision Series*. Ed. Pamela S. Dear. Detroit: Gale, 1995. 47:257–59.

"Krauss, Ruth (Mrs. Crockett Johnson)." In *American Authors and Books, 1640 to the Present Day*. Third rev. ed. Rev. by Irving Weiss and Anne Weiss. New York: Crown, 1972. 357.

"Leisk, David Johnson." In *Something about the Author*. Ed. Anne Commire. Detroit: Gale, 1971. 1:141.

"Leisk, David Johnson." In *Something about the Author*. Ed. Anne Commire. Detroit: Gale, 1983. 30:141–44.

"Leisk, David Johnson 1906–." In *Contemporary Authors*. Vols. 9–12. Ed. Clare D. Kinsman and Mary Ann Tennenouse. Detroit: Gale, 1974. 505

MacLeod, Anne Scott. "Johnson, Crockett." In *Twentieth-Century Children's Writers*. 3rd ed. Ed. Tracy Chevalier. Chicago: St. James, 1989. 499.

Marschall, Richard. "Barnaby" and "Leisk, David Johnson." In *The World Encyclopedia of Comics*. Ed. Maurice Horn. New York: Chelsea House, 1976. 97–98, 448–49.

———. "Barnaby" and "Leisk, David Johnson." In *The World Encyclopedia of Comics*. Rev. ed. Ed. Maurice Horn. Philadelphia: Chelsea House, 1999. 112–13, 474.

Martin, Anne. "Ruth Krauss: A Very Special Author." *Elementary English* 32.7 (Nov. 1955): 427, 428, 432, 434.

"MASI Shows Johnson 'Squared Circle.'" *Westport (Conn.) News*, 22 Jan 1970, Sec. 2, p. 20.

Nel, Philip. "Crockett Johnson and the Purple Crayon: A Life in Art." *Comic Art* 5 (Winter 2004): 2–18.

———. *The Crockett Johnson Homepage*. http://www.ksu.edu/english/nelp/purple/.

———. "'Never Overlook the Art of the Seemingly Simple': Crockett Johnson and the Politics of the Purple Crayon." *Children's Literature* 29 (2001): 142–74.

Nordstrom, Ursula. *Dear Genius: The Letters of Ursula Nordstrom*. Comp. Leonard S. Marcus. New York: HarperCollins, 1998.

Norris, Chan. "Meet the Man who Brought You Barnaby and Mr. O'Malley Together." *PM*, 20 Dec. 1942, 24.

North, Joseph, ed. *New Masses: An Anthology of the Rebel Thirties*. Intro. Maxwell Geismar. New York: International, 1969.

"O'Malley for Dewey." *Time*, 18 Sept. 1944, 50.

"Personal & Otherwise." *Harper's Magazine*, June 1955, 23.

Ron Howard: Hollywood's Favorite Son. Written, directed, and produced by Patty Ivins. Executive Produced by Kevin Burns. Twentieth Century Fox, 1999.

Rothschild, D. Aviva. "Barnaby and Mr. O'Malley." In *Graphic Novels: Bibliographic Guide to Book-Length Comics*. Englewood, Colo.: Libraries Unlimited, 1995. 35.

"Ruth Krauss, 91, Dies; A Writer for Children." *New York Times*, 15 July 1993, D22.

"Ruth Krauss: Let Me Tell You a Story." *See Saw Newsletter* 16 (Spring 1988): 3–4.

Sainer, Arthur. "Krauss, Ruth (Ida)." In *Contemporary Women Dramatists*. Ed. K. A. Berney. Detroit: St. James, 1994. 133–36.

Saunders, Sheryl Lee. "Johnson, Crockett." In *Children's Books and Their Creators*. Ed. Anita Silvey. New York: Houghton Mifflin, 1995. 335.

Sendak, Maurice. "Ruth Krauss and Me: A Very Special Partnership." *Horn Book* 70.3 (May–June 1994): 286–90.

Sharma, Prabha Gupta. "Ruth Krauss." In *Dictionary of Literary Biography*. Vol. 52, *American Writers for Children since 1960: Fiction*. Ed. Glenn E. Estes. Detroit: Gale, 1986. 228–32.

Soby, James Thrall, ed. *Arp*. New York: Museum of Modern Art, 1958.

Solomon, Deborah. "Beyond Finger Paint." *New York Times Book Review*, 17 May 1998: 24–25.

"Speaking of Pictures . . . : 'Barnaby' Has High I.Q. for Cartoon-Strip Humor." *Life*, 4 Oct. 1943, 10–11, 13.

Spiegelman, Art, and Françoise Mouly, eds. *Strange Stories for Strange Kids*. New York: HarperCollins, 2001.

Spitz, Ellen Handler. *Inside Picture Books*. New Haven: Yale University Press, 1999.

Spurgeon, Tom. "No. 68: Barnaby." *Comics Journal* 210 (Feb. 1999): 52.

Stroud, J. B. "Crockett Johnson's Geometric Paintings." *Journal of Mathematics and the Arts* 2.2 (June 2008): 77–99.

"Stroud Studies Crockett Johnson's Mathematical Artistry." *Davidson Update*, Oct. 1985, 7.

Tayler, Betty. "Barnaby's Creator Really Makes Bed He Plans to Lie In." *Bridgeport (Conn.) Sunday Post*, 22 Dec. 1955, B5.

Tyler, Betty. "As an Author Sees a Child's Thinking." *Bridgeport (Conn.) Sunday Post*, 22 May 1955, B4.

Van Allsburg, Chris. "Books I Remember." *HomeArts*. 20 Mar. 1999. http://homearts .com:80/depts/relat/allsbub1.htm.

Viguers, Ruth Hill, Marcia Dalphin, and Bertha Mahoney Miller, comps. *Illustrators of Children's Books, 1946–1956*. Boston: Horn Book, 1958. 135.

Waldman, Ann, ed. *The World Anthology: Poems from the St. Mark's Poetry Project*. Indianapolis: Bobbs-Merrill, 1969.

Waugh, Coulton. *The Comics*. New York: Macmillan, 1947. Rpt. Jackson: University Press of Mississippi, 1991.

Wepman, Dennis. "Barnaby." In *100 Years of Newspaper Comics: An Illustrated Encyclopedia*. Ed. Maurice Horn. New York: Gramercy, 1996. 46–47.

"Westporter's Painting Goes to Smithsonian." *Westport (Conn.) News*, 6 Jun. 1975, 7.

Williams, Gurney, ed. *Collier's Collects Its Wits*. New York: Harcourt, Brace, 1941.

OTHER SOURCES

"2 'Peace' Meetings Jeered by Pickets." *New York Times*, 27 Mar. 1949, 1, 47.

"27 Newtown High Students to Receive Letters for Track." *Queensborough Daily Star*, 25 June 1924, 12.

"50 Years Ago." *Norwalk (Conn.) Hour Online*, 20 Mar. 2008. http://www.thehour/story/ 308385409312189.php.

"200 Pay Tribute to Frank O'Hara." *New York Times*, 28 July 1966, 33.

"1000 Notables Protest Anti-Labor Probes." *Daily Worker*, 3 Jan. 1949, 2, 11.

"Aid to Family Life Aim of Conference." *New York Times*, 5 May 1948, 22.

"Albert A. Brager Married: Former Store Proprietor Wedded to Mrs. Blanche Krause [*sic*] by Rabbi Israel." *Baltimore [Morning] Sun*, 6 Mar. 1930, 3.

"Albert A. Brager to Wed Mrs. Bertha [*sic*] Krauss: Ceremony Uniting Two Former Store Proprietors Scheduled for Wednesday." *Baltimore [Morning] Sun*, 1 Mar 1930, 7.

"Albert A. Brager's Funeral Tomorrow: Services for Merchant and Charity Official to Be Held from Home." *Baltimore Evening Sun*, 28 Mar. 1936, 18.

Amateau, Albert. "Sidney Landau, 90, Textiles, Birds, and All That Jazz." *Villager*, 6–12 Feb. 2008. http://www.thevillager.com/villager_249/sidneylandau.html.

Ambrose, Stephen E. *Eisenhower*. Vol. 2, *The President*. New York: Simon and Schuster, 1984.

"American Cyanamid to Tell Paper Men of Process to Increase Wet Strength." *New York Times*, 17 Feb. 1958.

Anglund, Joan Walsh. *A Friend Is Someone Who Likes You*. New York: Harcourt, Brace, and World, 1958.

Antler, Joyce. *Lucy Sprague Mitchell: The Making of a Modern Woman*. New Haven: Yale University Press, 1987.

Barrier, Michael. *Hollywood Cartoons: American Animation in Its Golden Age*. New York: Oxford University Press, 1999.

Belkin, Pearl, and Gary Belkin. "Going through a Phrase Dept.: A Realistic Children's Book . . . for Realistic Children." Illus. Joe Orlando. *Mad*, Sept. 1961, 4–7.

Benedict, Ruth. "Primitive Freedom." *Atlantic Monthly*, June 1942, 756–63.

Benedict, Ruth, and Gene Weltfish. *The Races of Mankind*. 1943. New York: Public Affairs, 1946.

Bergman, Andrew. *We're in the Money: Depression America and Its Films*. 1971. Chicago: Elephant, 1992.

"Between Ourselves." *New Masses*, 28 Mar. 1939, 2.

"Between Ourselves." *New Masses*, 2 Apr. 1940, 2.

Blechman, R. O. *Dear James: Letters to a Young Illustrator*. New York: Simon and Schuster, 2009.

Bliss, G. H. *Climatological Data: Pennsylvania Section*. N.p.: U.S. Department of Agriculture, Weather Bureau, 1936.

Blum, Isidor. *The Jews of Baltimore: An Historical Summary of Their Progress and Status as Citizens of Baltimore from Early Days to the Year Nineteen Hundred and Ten*. Baltimore: Historical Review, 1910.

"Books and Authors." *New York Times Book Review*, 2 Dec. 1934, 18

Boone, Andrew R. "Type by Goudy." *Popular Science*, Apr. 1942, 114–19.

Bowditch, Eden Unger. *Images of America: Baltimore's Historic Parks and Gardens*. Charleston, S.C.: Arcadia, 2004.

Braun, Saul. "Sendak Raises the Shade on Childhood." *New York Times Magazine*, 7 June 1970, 34+.

Breton, André. *Selected Poems*. Trans. Kenneth White. London: Cape, 1969.

"A Brief History of the Ethical Culture Movement." *American Ethical Union* website. http://www.aeu.org/hist1.html.

Browder, Earl. "An Historic Report on the South." *New Masses*, 28 Aug. 1938, 3–4.

———. "The Isolationist Front." *New Masses*, 8 Mar. 1938, 3–4.

———. "What Is Communism? 8. Americanism—Who Are the Americans?" *New Masses*, 25 Jun. 1935, 13–14.

Brown, Jennifer M. "The Rumpus Goes On." *Publishers Weekly*, 18 Apr. 2005. http://www.publishersweekly.com/article/CA525095.html?pubdate=4%2F18%2F2005&display=archive.

Brown, Nona. "It's Been a Tough Winter, Even the Weathermen Say." *New York Times*, 1 Feb. 1948, E9.

Burke, Christopher. *Paul Renner: The Art of Typography*. New York: Princeton Architectural Press, 1998.

Burlingame, Roger. *Endless Frontiers: The Story of McGraw-Hill*. New York: McGraw-Hill, 1959.

Caffrey, Margaret M. *Ruth Benedict: Stranger in This Land*. Austin: University of Texas Press, 1989.

Canemaker, John. *The Art and Flair of Mary Blair: An Appreciation*. New York: Disney Editions, 2003.

———. "David Hilberman." 1980. http://www.michaelspornanimation.com/splog/?p=1090.

Carroll, Lewis. *Logical Nonsense: The Works of Lewis Carroll*. Ed. Philip C. Blackburn and Lionel White. New York: Putnam's, 1934.

"Cement: Noguchi's Polychrome Relief Achieves a Powerful Effect." *New Masses*, 15 Sept. 1936, 10.

Cerf, Bennett. *At Random: The Reminiscences of Bennett Cerf*. New York: Random House, 1977.

"The Challenge and the Answer." *New Masses*, 15 Sept. 1936, 20.

Chandler, Lester W. *America's Greatest Depression, 1929–1941*. New York: Harper and Row, 1970.

Chico, Beverly Berghaus. "The Cone Sisters: Claribel, 1864–1929; Etta, 1870–1949." In *Notable Maryland Women*. Ed. Winifred G. Helmes. Cambridge, Md.: Tidewater, 1977. 81–85.

"Chronologies of the Conflict." *Free Speech Movement Archives*. http://www.fsm-a.org/stacks/FSM_chron_index.html.

Chusid, Irwin. *The Mischievous Art of Jim Flora*. Seattle: Fantagraphics, 2004.

"City's Snow Costs Cut in 1948 Storm." *New York Times*, 30 Dec. 1948, 28.

Clarke, Gerald. *Capote: A Biography*. 1988. New York: Carroll and Graf, 2005.

Clowes, Daniel. *Ice Haven: A Comic-Strip Novel*. New York: Pantheon, 2005.

Cobb, William H. *Radical Education in the Rural South: Commonwealth College, 1922–1940*. Detroit: Wayne State University Press, 2000.

"Corona & Elmhurst." *Queensborough Daily Star*, 27 June 1924, 12.

Cronan, Carey. "Washington Close-Up." *Bridgeport (Conn.) Sunday Post*, 8 Apr. 1951, A12.

Culver, John C., and John Hyde. *American Dreamer: The Life and Times of Henry A. Wallace*. New York: Norton, 2000.

da Cruz, Frank. "The Parnassus Club." *Columbia University Computing History*. 24 Sept. 2004. http://www.columbia.edu/acis/history/parnassus.html.

Dart, Andrew K. "The History of Postage Rates in the United States since 1863." http://www.akdart.com/postrate.html.

"Deaths [Flaxer, Abram]." *New York Times*, 26 Feb. 1989, 36.

"Deaths [Leisk, Mary]." *New York Times*, 29 Dec. 1953, 23.

"Debate on Peace Formula Tonight." *Norwalk (Conn.) Hour*, 11 June 1947, 1, 12.

Denning, Michael. *The Cultural Front*. New York: Verso, 1996.

"Dinner Will Honor Gropper." *Daily Worker*, 2 Dec. 1944, 8.

Disney, Walter E. Testimony before House Un-American Activities Committee. 24 Oct. 1947. *CNN Cold War—Historical Document: Walt Disney Testifies*. http://www.cnn.com/SPECIALS/cold.war/episodes/06/documents/huac/disney.html.

Doggett, Marguerite V. *Newtown High School: Early History of Newtown High School, Graduates, Graduation Exercises, Early Education, Schools, Teachers, Educators, and Interesting Anecdotes of the Old Town of Newtown, Queens County, Long Island, New York*. Newtown, N.Y.: Newtown Historical Society, 1964.

Duchamp, Marcel. *The Writings of Marcel Duchamp*. Ed. Michel Sanouillet and Elmer Peterson. New York: Da Capo, 1973.

Dutt, R. Palme. "Britain and Spain." *New Masses*, 15 Sept. 1936, 3.

"Editorial: Styled for Today." *American Machinist*, 14 Sept. 1937, 769.

Edwards, Jim. "The Journalist and the G-Man." *Brill's Content*, Nov. 2000, 119, 152–54.

Eiseman, Alberta. "Authors to Fete Library." *New York Times*, 4 Sept. 1983, CN6.

"End of the Conversation." *Time*, 16 Mar. 1962. http://www.time.com/time/magazine/article/0,9171,940659,00.html.

"End Your Silence." *New York Times*, 18 Apr. 1965, E5.

"Events Today." *New York Times*, 4 Dec. 1944, 21.

Feiffer, Jules. *Backing into Forward: A Memoir*. New York: Doubleday, 2010.

Fein, Isaac M. *The Making of an American Jewish Community: The History of Baltimore Jewry from 1773 to 1920*. Philadelphia: Jewish Publication Society of America, 1971.

Fitzgerald, F. Scott. *The Great Gatsby*. 1925. New York: Scribner, 1995.

Folk, Thomas. *The Pennsylvania School of Landscape Painting*. Allentown, Penn.: Allentown Art Museum, 1984.

"Frank O'Hara, 40, Museum Curator." *New York Times*, 26 July 1966, 35.

"Fred Schwed Jr., Writer of Humor." *New York Times*, 11 May 1966.

Furman, Bess. "Johnston Stresses Family Life 'Crisis.'" *New York Times*, 6 May 1948, 32.

"Gene Wallace." *Bridgeport (Conn.) Telegram*, 6 Sept. 1954, 24.

"Georges Lepape: Illustrator." *Fashion Worlds*. http://fashionworlds.blogspot.com/2000_01_08_fashionworlds_archive.html.

Gesell, Arnold. *The First Five Years of Life: A Guide to the Study of the Preschool Child*. New York: Harper, 1940.

Gott, Tony, ed. *Shetland Family History Homepage*. http://bayanne.info/Shetland/.

Goudy, Frederic W. Introduction. In *Goudy: Master of Letters*, by Vrest Orton. Chicago: Black Cat, 1939. 19–23.

Goulart, Ron. *Cheap Thrills: An Informal History of the Pulp Magazines*. New Rochelle, N.Y.: Arlington House, 1972.

Graf, William. *Statistics of the Presidential and Congressional Election of November 2, 1948*. Washington, D.C.: U.S. Government Printing Office, 1949. Available at *Election Information: Election Statistics*. www.clerk.house.gov/member_info/electioninfo/1948electionpdf.

Gray, George. "Engineering Research Associates and the Atlas Computer." *Unisys History Newsletter* 3.3 (June 1999). https://wiki.cc.gatech.edu/folklore/index.php/Engineering_Research_Associates_and_the_Atlas_Computer_%28UNIVAC_1101%29.

"Group from Connecticut Meets Wallace and Urges Him to Run as Independent." *Hartford Courant*, 24 Dec. 1947, 1.

Gussow, Mel. *Edward Albee: A Singular Journey*. New York: Simon and Schuster, 1999.

Hall, Lee. *Abe Ajay*. Seattle: University of Washington Press, 1990.

Hambidge, Jay. *Practical Applications of Dynamic Symmetry*. Ed. and arranged by Mary C. Hambidge. New Haven: Yale University Press, 1932.

Harriman, Margaret Case. *And the Price Is Right*. Illus. Roy Doty. Cleveland: World, 1958.

Harvey, R. C. "Introducing Walt Kelly." *Pogo*. 1992. Seattle: Fantagraphics, 1999. 1:i–viii.

Hemingway, Andrew. *Artists on the Left: American Artists and the Communist Movement, 1926–1956*. New Haven: Yale University Press, 2002.

Hignite, M. Todd. "Daniel Clowes: In the Studio." *Comic Art* 1 (Fall 2002): 26–37.

Hirschman, Susan Carr. "1998 May Hill Arbuthnot Lecture." *Journal of Youth Services in Libraries* 11.4 (Summer 1998): 362–77.

Hoban, Russell. *Bedtime for Frances*. New York: Harper, 1960.

Hoover, J. Edgar. *Masters of Deceit: The Story of Communism in America and How to Fight It*. New York: Holt, Rinehart, and Winston, 1958.

Howard, Leslie. "What's in a Song?: The Dark Tale of Bonnie 'Loch Lomond.'" *Weekend Edition Sunday*, 24 July 2005. http://www.npr.org/templates/story/story .php?storyId=4766584.

Hungerford, Edward. *The Romance of a Great Store*. New York: McBride, 1922.

"Ickes for Free Speech—Even If His 'Pals' Are Not." *Philadelphia Record*, 25 Apr. 1946, 14.

"Increase Seats for Town Hall." *Norwalk (Conn.) Hour*, 9 June 1947, 1, 12.

Jack A. Goodman: A Few Words in Memory July 24th 1957 (memorial booklet). In possession of the author.

"Jack A. Goodman, Book Executive." *New York Times*, 23 July 1953, 27.

Jewell, Edward Alden. "Students Who Have Been Working Hard All Year Give an Account of Themselves." *New York Times*, 26 May 1929, 10.

Jones, Marjorie F. "A History of the Parsons School of Design, 1896–1966." Ph.D. diss., New York University, 1968.

"Judson Poets' Theater Productions." *Judson Memorial Church*. http://www.judson.org/ jpt_production_list.html.

Klapper, Melissa R. *Jewish Girls Coming of Age in America, 1860–1920*. New York: New York University Press, 2005.

Klehr, Harvey. *The Heyday of American Communism: The Depression Decade*. New York: Basic Books, 1984.

Klehr, Harvey, and John Earl Haynes. *The American Communist Movement: Storming Heaven Itself*. New York: Twayne, 1992.

Klutz, Jerry. "The Federal Diary." *Washington Post*, 19 May 1946, M5.

Koch, Kenneth. *The Collected Poems of Kenneth Koch*. New York: Knopf, 2005.

———. *Rose, Where Did You Get That Red?: Teaching Great Poetry to Children*. 1973. New York: Vintage, 1990.

Lanes, Selma G. *The Art of Maurice Sendak*. 1980. New York: Abradale/Abrams, 1993.

Lapsley, Hilary. *Margaret Mead and Ruth Benedict: The Kinship of Women*. Amherst: University of Massachusetts Press, 1999.

Leach, William. *Land of Desire: Merchants, Power, and the Rise of a New American Culture*. New York: Pantheon, 1993.

Lears, Jackson. *Fables of Abundance: A Cultural History of Advertising in America*. New York: Basic Books, 1994.

Leask, Anne Leask of. *The Leasks: Historical Notes on the Aberdeenshire, Orkney, and Shetland Families*. N.p.: Anne Leask of Leask, 1980.

Lehman, David. *The Last Avant-Garde: The Making of the New York School of Poets*. New York: Doubleday, 1998.

Lerner, James. "American League against War and Fascism." In *Encyclopedia of the American Left*. 2nd ed. Ed. Mari Jo Buhle, Paul Buhle, and Dan Georgakas. New York: Oxford University Press, 1998. 30–31.

Lieberman, Robbie. *The Strangest Dream: Communism, Anticommunism, and the U.S. Peace Movement, 1945–1963*. Syracuse, N.Y.: Syracuse University Press, 2000.

Linder, Douglas O. "Samuel Liebowitz." In *Famous American Trials: "The Scottsboro Boys" Trials, 1931–1937*. 1999. http://www.law.umkc.edu/faculty/projects/ftrials/scottsboro/SB_bLieb.html.

Linklater, Eric. *Orkney and Shetland: An Historical, Geographical, Social and Scenic Survey*. London: Hale, 1965.

"Lionel White 1905–." *Contemporary Authors Online*. Detroit: Gale, 2001.

Loewen, James W. *Lies across America: What Our Historic Sites Get Wrong*. New York: New Press, 1999.

"Looking Back at 1927." *Aviation*, 2 Jan. 1928, 22–25, 50–54.

Ludden, Jennifer. "A Conversation with Maurice Sendak." *All Things Considered* 4 June 2005. http://www.npr.org/templates/story/story.php?storyId=4680590.

Lyons, Leonard. "The Lyons Den." *New York Post*, 13 June 1944, 18.

"The MacDowell Colony: FAQ." http://www.macdowellcolony.org/about-FAQ.html.

Mankoff, Robert, ed. *The Complete Cartoons of the New Yorker*. New York: Black Dog and Leventhal, 2004.

Marantz, Kenneth. *A Bibliography of Children's Art Literature: An Annotated Bibliography of Children's Literature Designed to Stimulate and Enrich the Imagination of the Child*. Washington, D.C.: National Art Education Association, 1965.

"Marc Simont." *Contemporary Authors Online*. Detroit: Gale, 2002.

Marcus, Leonard S. *A Caldecott Celebration*. New York: Walker, 1998.

———. *Golden Legacy: How Golden Books Won Children's Hearts, Changed Publishing Forever, and Became an American Icon along the Way*. New York: Golden Books, 2007.

———. "Marc Simont's Sketchbooks: The Art Academy Years, 1935–1938." *Horn Book*, Mar.–Apr. 2004. http://www.hbook.com/magazine/articles/2004/mar04_simontmarcus.asp.

———. *Margaret Wise Brown: Awakened by the Moon*. 1992. New York: Quill/Morrow, 1999.

———. *Minders of Make-Believe: Idealists, Entrepreneurs, and the Shaping of American Children's Literature*. New York: Houghton Mifflin, 2008.

"Margaret Fishback, 85, Writer of Light Verse." *New York Times*, 28 Sept. 1985, sec. 1, p. 34.

Margolick, David. *Strange Fruit: Billie Holiday, Café Society, and an Early Cry for Civil Rights*. Philadelphia: Running Press, 2000.

"May Go to the Grand Jury: Corona People Want Flushing Bay Made Clean." *Brooklyn Daily Eagle*, 8 Sept. 1910.

McCloud, Scott. *Understanding Comics: The Invisible Art*. 1993. New York: HarperCollins, 1994.

McDonnell, Patrick, Karen O'Connell, and Georgia Riley de Havenon, eds. *Krazy Kat: The Comic Art of George Herriman*. New York: Abrams, 1986.

McGraw, James H. "Why McGraw-Hill Desires to Serve the Aviation Industry." *Aviation*, 2 Mar. 1929, 629.

Mellen, Joan. *Kay Boyle: Author of Herself*. New York: Farrar, Straus, and Giroux, 1994.

Meyers, Elissa Lin. "Cold War Illustrated." *New York Times*, 24 Jun. 2001, 24.

Mickenberg, Julia L. *Learning from the Left: Children's Literature, the Cold War, and Radical Politics in the United States*. New York: Oxford University Press, 2006.

———. "The Pedagogy of the Popular Front: 'Progressive Parenting' for a New Generation, 1918–1945." In *The American Child: A Cultural Studies Reader*. Ed. Caroline F. Levander and Carol J. Singley. New Brunswick, N.J.: Rutgers University Press, 2003. 226–45.

Mickenberg, Julia L., and Philip Nel. *Tales for Little Rebels: A Collection of Radical Children's Literature*. New York: New York University Press, 2008.

"Milk Strike Stops Flow into Chicago." *New York Times*, 7 Jan. 1934, F21.

Milkman, Paul. *PM: A New Deal in Journalism*. New Brunswick, N.J.: Rutgers University Press, 1997.

Murray, Lyn. *Musician: A Hollywood Journal of Wives, Women, Writers, Lawyers, Directors, Producers and, Music*. Secaucus, N.J.: Stewart, 1987.

"Musical Revivals Due Here in June." *New York Times*, 23 Apr. 1943, 10.

Naureckas, Jim. "New York Songlines: 10th Street." http://home.nyc.rr.com/jkn/nysonglines/10st.htm.

Neft, David S., Richard M. Cohen, and Rick Korch. *The Football Encyclopedia: The Complete History of Professional Football from 1892 to the Present*. New York: St. Martin's, 1994.

Nevins, Jess. "Pulp and Adventure Heroes: J." http://www.geocities.com/jjnevins/pulpsj.html.

———. "Pulp and Adventure Heroes: P." http://www.geocities.com/jjnevins/pulpsp.html.

"Newtown High Decides to Play and Wins Easily." *Queensborough Daily Star*, 29 Mar. 1924, 10.

"Newtown High School, Elmhurst, January Regents' Honor Roll." *Queensborough Daily Star*, 14 Feb. 1924, 5.

The Newtown High School Handbook. New York: Arista, [1921].

"Newtown H.S. Graduates Its Largest Class." *Queensborough Daily Star*, 27 June 1924, 12.

"Newtown Loses Baseball Stars; Other Teams Intact." *Queensborough Daily Star*, 27 June 1924, 14.

"Newtown Swamps Schools in Meet; One Record Broken." *Queensborough Daily Star*, 9 June 1924, 8.

"New Yorkers Are Moving to Win the Peace." *Daily Worker*, 24 Jun. 1946, 5

"Next Sunday." *New York Times*, 6 Mar. 1960, X7.

Nicholson, James R. *Shetland*. 4th ed. London: David and Charles, 1984.

Noguchi, Isamu. *A Sculptor's World*. New York: Harper and Row, 1968.

"Noted Professionals Back May Day; Parley Spurs Parade Preparations." *Daily Worker*, 22 Apr. 1946, 4.

"Nugent's Comedy to Open on June 5." *New York Times*, 13 May 1944, 16.

O'Connor, Tom. "News Tailored to Fit." *The Nation*, 16 Apr. 1949, 438–40.

"Offers $500 for Blood to Save Mother." *PM*, 26 Feb. 1948, 17.

"On Vietnam." *New York Times*, 5 June 1966, E5–E7.

Orton, Vrest. *Goudy: Master of Letters*. Chicago: Black Cat, 1939.

Orwell, George. "Why I Write." In *A Collection of Essays*. 1946. New York: Harcourt Brace, 1981. 309–16.

Parke, Richard H. "Culture Sessions Center on Conflict of East and West." *New York Times*, 27 Mar. 1949, 1, 44, 45, 46, 47.

———. "Global Unity Call, Cheered by 18,000, Ends Peace Rally." *New York Times*, 28 Mar. 1949, 1–4.

Parsons, Art. *A Library Is to Know*. Illus. Leo Martin. Jacksonville, Ill.: New Method, 1961.

Perry, Ralph Barton. *The Thought and Character of William James*. Boston: Little, Brown, 1936.

Philbrick, Herbert A. *I Led 3 Lives: Citizen—Communist—Counterspy*. New York: McGraw-Hill, 1952.

"Phyllis Rowand." *New York Times*, 17 Jun. 1963, 25.

"Pickets Denounce Soviet, Communism." *New York Times*, 26 Mar. 1949, 1, 3.

"The Pioneer Manufacturer." *Aviation*, 31 Oct. 1927, 1049.

Pittman, Betsy. "Finding Aid for Marc Simont Papers." Dodd Research Center, University of Connecticut. http://www.lib.uconn.edu/online/research/speclib/ASC/findaids/Simont/MSS19970002.html.

"Plans Reception for Henry Wallace." *Norwalk (Conn.) Hour*, 6 Jun. 1947, 12.

"Post Time." *Time*, 19 May 1961. http://www.time.com/magazine/article/0,9171,872407,00.html.

Price, David H. *Threatening Anthropology: McCarthyism and the FBI's Surveillance of Activist Anthropologists*. Durham, N.C.: Duke University Press, 2004.

"Prognosis: Available." *Time*, 15 Dec. 1961. http://www.time.com/time/magazine/article/0,9171,827081,00.html.

Pruce, Earl. *Synagogues, Temples, and Congregations of Maryland, 1930–1990*. Baltimore: Jewish Historical Society of Maryland, 1993.

"Public Speaking Zooms." *The Commoner*, May 1939, 4.

Randolph, Vance. "Utopia in Arkansas." *Esquire*, Jan. 1938, 60, 147, 148, 150, 152.

Ray, Deborah Wing, and Gloria P. Stewart. *Norwalk: Being an Historical Account of That Connecticut Town*. Canaan, N.H.: Phoenix for Norwalk Historical Society, 1979.

Raymond, Frank. *Rowayton on the Half Shell: The History of a Coastal Village*. West Kennebunk, Me.: Phoenix for Rowayton Historical Society, 1990.

Read, Herbert. *Art and Industry: The Principles of Industrial Design*. New York: Harcourt, Brace, 1938.

"Recovering from Submersion." *New York Times*, 26 Nov. 1934, 17.

Redfield, A. [Syd Hoff]. "'When the Locomotive of History Makes a Sharp Turn'—V. I. Lenin." *New Masses*, 28 Nov. 1939, 16–17.

Reinhardt, Ad. "Twelve Rules for a New Academy." In *Ad Reinhardt, 1960: Twenty-Five Years of Abstract Painting*. New York: Parsons Gallery, 1960. N.p.

Richter, Dan. *Moonwatcher's Memoir: A Diary of 2001: A Space Odyssey*. New York: Carroll and Graf, 2002.

"RKO Will Produce 'Barnaby' as Film." *New York Times*, 1 Jun. 1946, 9.

"Rockwell Kent Biography." *Rockwell Kent Home Page*. Plattsburgh State Art Museum, State University of New York at Plattsburgh. 2006. http://clubs.plattsburgh.edu/museum/rk_bio.htm.

Roosevelt, Franklin D. "Address at Oglethorpe University." 22 May 1932. In *The Public Papers and Addresses of Franklin D. Roosevelt*. Vol. 1, 1928–32. New York City: Random House, 1938. 639.

Roosevelt, Theodore. *America and the World War: Fear God and Take Your Own Part*. New York: Scribner's, 1926.

Rovere, Richard. "What Every Appeaser Should Know." *New Masses*, 5 Sept. 1939, 5–6.

"Rowayton Arts Center." *Rowayton Arts Center*. http://www.rowaytonartscenter.org/ homepage.htm.

Sandler, Gilbert. *Jewish Baltimore: A Family Album*. Baltimore: Johns Hopkins University Press in Association with the Jewish Museum of Maryland, 2000.

Schallert, Edwin. "Dorothy McGuire Set for 'White Collar Girl.'" *Los Angeles Times*, 3 May 1944, A10.

Schama, Simon. *A History of Britain: The British Wars, 1603–1776*. London: BBC, 2001.

Schneider, Daniel E. *The Psychoanalyst and the Artist*. 1950. New York: Mentor, 1962.

Schwed, Fred, Jr. *The Pleasure Was Mine: The Journal of an Undisappointed Man*. New York: Simon and Schuster, 1951.

———. *Where Are the Customers' Yachts?; or, A Good Hard Look at Wall Street*. Illus. Peter Arno. 1940. New York: Simon and Schuster, 1955.

Sendak, Maurice. *Caldecott and Co.* 1988. New York: Noonday, 1990.

Scotland Online. *Scotland's People*. http://www.scotlandspeople.gov.uk/.

Seeley, Evelyn. "Barnaby's Coming to Town, and So Is His Talking Dog." *PM*, 1 Sept. 1946, 14.

Seldes, George. *Freedom of the Press*. Indianapolis: Bobbs-Merrill, 1935.

Seyfried, Vincent F. *Corona: From Farmland to City Suburb, 1650–1935*. N.p.: Edgian, 1986.

Shelley, Percy Bysshe. "A Defence of Poetry." 1821. In *Shelley's Poetry and Prose*. Ed. Donald H. Reiman and Sharon B. Powers. New York: Norton, 1977. 478–508.

Shiefls, Art. "600 at Win-Peace Parley Chart Drive." *Daily Worker*, 30 Jun. 1946, 7.

Sklenicka, Carol. *Raymond Carver: A Writer's Life*. New York: Scribner, 2009.

Small, Melvin. *Antiwarriors: The Vietnam War and the Battle for America's Hearts and Minds*. Wilmington, Del.: Scholarly Resources, 2002.

Smith, Michael Steven. "Smith Act Trials, 1949." In *Encyclopedia of the American Left*. Ed. Mari Jo Buhle, Paul Buhle, and Dan Georgakas. New York: Oxford University Press, 1998. 755–57.

Snodgrass, W. D. "Tact and the Poet's Force." 1958. In *Claims for Poetry*. Ed. Donald Hall. Ann Arbor: University of Michigan Press, 1982. 417–33.

Stoddard, Sandol. *I Like You*. Illus. Jacqueline Chwast. Boston: Houghton Mifflin, 1965.

Sullivan's Travels. Written and directed by Preston Sturges. Perf. Joel McCrea, Veronica Lake. Paramount Pictures, 1941.

Swyrich Corporation. "The Ancient History of the Distinguished Surname Krauss." www .houseofnames.com, 2009.

Teachout, Terry. *The Skeptic: A Life of H. L. Mencken*. New York: HarperCollins, 2002.

"Text of the Platform as Approved for Adoption Today by the Progressive Party." *New York Times*, 25 July 1948, 32.

"Text of Wallace Letter to Stalin Calling for Peace Program." *New York Times*, 12 May 1948, 14.

"This Is the Kind of Book I Like." *New York Times Book Review*, 26 Oct. 1947, 23.

"This Little Gag Went . . ." *Time*, 12 Aug. 1946. http://www.time.com/time/magazine/article/0,9171,793176-1,00.html.

Thompson, Stith. *The Folktale*. New York: Dryden, 1946.

———. *Motif-Index of Folk Literature*. Bloomington: Indiana University Press, 1955–58.

———, ed. and annot. *Tales of the North American Indians*. Bloomington: Indiana University Press, 1929.

Thomson, William P. L. "Population and Depopulation." In *Shetland and the Outside World, 1469–1969*. Ed. Donald J. Withrington. Oxford: University of Aberdeen and Oxford University Press, 1983. 151.

"To Our Readers: Announcing the New 'Fight.'" *Fight against War and Fascism*, Mar. 1936, n.p.

"To the President of the United States: Teachers Appeal for Peace in Vietnam." *New York Times*, 4 Jan. 1966, 12.

Toledano, Henry. "Earliest Pictorial Jackets." http://modernlib.com/Identifiers/earlyPictorialJackets/earlyPictorialJackets.html.

———. "The Modern Library: A Talk Given at the Book Club of California, 312 Sutter St., Suite 150, San Francisco, CA." 23 Sept. 2002. http://www.dogeared.com/General/ToleHistorySpeech.html.

Torres, Ana Maria. *Isamu Noguchi: A Study of Space*. New York: Monacelli, 2000.

Tracy, W. H. "Climatological Data." Dec. 1947. *Climatological Data: New England Section*. U.S. Department of Agriculture, Weather Bureau, 1947. 94.

———. "Climatological Data." Jan. 1948. *Climatological Data: New England Section*. U.S. Department of Agriculture, Weather Bureau, 1948. 23.

———. "Climatological Data." Feb. 1948. *Climatological Data: New England Section*. U.S. Department of Agriculture, Weather Bureau, 1948. 23.

"The Treasury's Position." *New York Times*, 1 Jan. 1934, 22.

Truman, Harry S. "President's Speech to Family Conference." *New York Times*, 7 May 1948, 10.

———. "Statement by the President upon Approving the Housing Act." 10 Aug. 1948. In *The American Presidency Project*. Ed. John T. Woolley and Gerhard Peters. http://www.presidency.ucsb.edu/ws/?pid=12975.

Twain, Mark. *Pudd'nhead Wilson and Those Extraordinary Twins*. 1894. New York: Harper, 1922.

"Two Plays Tonight Involve the Bard." *New York Times*, 3 June 1946, 34.

U.S. Code 2385 (Advocating Overthrow of Government). U.S. Code Collection, Cornell University Law School. http://www.law.cornell.edu/uscode/18/2385.html.

U.S. Department of Commerce and U.S. Bureau of Foreign and Domestic Commerce. *Statistical Abstract of the United States, 1932*. Washington, D.C.: U.S. Government Printing Office, 1932.

U.S. House of Representatives, Committee on Un-American Activities. *Report on the Communist "Peace" Offensive: A Campaign to Disarm and Defeat the United States*. Washington, D.C.: Committee on Un-American Activities, 1951.

———. *Review of the Scientific and Cultural Conference for World Peace*. Washington, D.C.: U.S. Government Printing Office, 1950.

———. *Testimony of Bishop G. Bromley Oxnam: Hearing before the Committee on Un-American Activities*. Washington, D.C.: U.S. Government Printing Office, 1954.

Village Creek Home Owners Association: 50th Anniversary Celebration. South Norwalk, Conn.: Ink, 2000.

"Visions of Warhol by Jonas Mekas, Willard Maas, Marie Menken, Ronald Nameth." *Electronic Arts Intermix.* http://www.eai.org/eai/tape.jsp?itemID=8361.

"Walden Past: History of Camp Walden." 22 Sept. 1999. http://www.campwalden.com/waldenpast.html.

"Wallace Raps Truman Doctrine, Foreign Policy." *Norwalk (Conn.) Hour,* 12 June 1947, 1, 6.

"Wallace Returns from Europe Trip." *Bridgeport (Conn.) Post,* 4 Nov. 1947, 2.

Ware, Chris. "Skeezix for Sale: A Semi-Comprehensive Catalogue of 'Gasoline Alley.'" In *Walt & Skeezix 1925 & 1926.* By Frank O. King. Montreal: Drawn and Quarterly Books, 2007. n.p.

"We Are for Wallace." *New York Times,* 20 Oct. 1948, 32.

Wertz, Richard W., and Dorothy C. Wertz. *Lying-In: A History of Childbirth in America.* New Haven: Yale University Press, 1989.

"Westport Arts Center: About Us." http://www.westportartscenter.org/i_page?page=about_us.

"Why the Pact Was Signed." *New Masses,* 5 Sept. 1939, 10–12.

"Wife and Children Get Brager Estate: Will Provides for Division of Property after Widow's Death." *Baltimore Evening Sun,* 1 Apr. 1936, 36.

Williams, Sidney Herbert, Falconer Madan, and Roger Lancelyn Green. *The Lewis Carroll Handbook.* Hamden, Conn.: Shoe String, 1979.

Williams, William Carlos. "A Sort of Song." 1944. In *Selected Poems.* Ed. Charles Tomlinson. New York: New Directions, 1985. 145.

Wilson, Amy. "Marlton House: Building History." Fall 1998. http://marltonhouse.org/history.php.

Wilson, Robin. *Lewis Carroll in Numberland: His Fantastical Mathematical Logical Life.* New York: Norton, 2008.

Wilson, Woodrow. Speech at League of Nations. 25 Sept. 1919. http://www.presidentialrhetoric.com/historicspeeches/wilson/leagueofnations.html.

"Win the Peace for Whom?" *Time,* 16 Sept. 1946. http://www.time.com/time/magazine/article/0,9171,888295,00.html.

"With the Readers." *Fight against War And Fascism,* Apr. 1936, 5.

"Writer Is Rescued as Seas Swamp Dory: Richard Barry in Mishap at Asbury Park, Trying to Get Aid for Drifting Cruiser." *New York Times,* 25 Nov. 1934, 32.

Yohannan, Kohle, and Nancy Nolf. *Claire McCardell: Redefining Modernism.* New York: Abrams, 1989.

Young, Art. *On My Way: Being the Book of Art Young in Text and Picture.* New York: Liveright, 1928.

Zolotow, Sam. "Canada Lee to Act White Role in Play." *New York Times,* 16 Sept. 1946, 10.

———. "New Variety Show Arriving Tonight." *New York Times,* 15 Jun. 1944, 17.

ACKNOWLEDGMENTS

You should tell the audience when to clap, if they don't know. One way is to start clapping yourself.
—RUTH KRAUSS, "A Few Rules for Giving a Show," *How to Make an Earthquake* (1954)

I began this project in 1999. There are a lot of people to thank.

I am particularly grateful to those who shared their time and memories of Ruth and Dave, especially Maurice Sendak, a frequent collaborator and weekend guest in the 1950s who knew them well; Nina Stagakis, the daughter of their good friends who became like a daughter to them; the late Mary Elting Folsom, who knew Dave and his first wife in the 1930s; Betty Hahn, the wife of Ruth's late cousin, Richard, who remained very close to her throughout her life; and the late Else Frank, Dave's sister and my sole witness to his childhood. Maurice and Nina not only answered many questions but even read an early draft of part of the manuscript.

For sharing memories of, correspondence from, or other information about Crockett Johnson or Ruth Krauss, I thank Leone Adelson, Isabella Blake, Miriam Bourdette, Pat Brooks, Gail Cathey, Ina Chadwick, Remy Charlip, Sas Colby, Bernadine Cook, Norman Corwin, Jackie Curtis, Karen Curtis, Bianca Czaderna, Gene Deitch, Barbara Dicks, Sally Dimon, Jon Ehrlich, Dallas Ernst, Anne Eyes, David Eyes, Frank Fay, Jules Feiffer, Sally Fisher, Harley Flanders, Antonio Frasconi, Miguel Frasconi, Pablo Frasconi, Valerie Harms, Peggy Heinrich, Bet Hennefrund, David Hilberman, Susan Carr Hirschman, Syd Hoff, Ann Holmes, Lee Hopkins, Tom Hopps, Roussie Jacksina, Amy Kaiman, Leonard Kessler, Binnie Klein, Henry F. Klein, Mark Kramer, Sidney Kramer, Janet Krauss, Sidney Landau, Amos Landman, Emily Levine, Grace Lichtenstein, Sid and Doris Lund, A. B. Magil, Harry Marinsky, Ann McGovern, Bob and Helen McNell, Harriet McKissock, Alice McMahon, Elisabeth Merrett, Ben Gray Moore, Ben Gray Moore Jr., Ralph Nazareth, Wendy Newton, Maureen O'Hara, Doris Orgel, Fran Pollak, Lilian Moore Reavin, Anna Reinhardt, Dan Richter,

Mischa Richter, Andy Rooney, Marge Rooney, Gilbert Rose, Warren Sattler, Morton Schindel, Marion Schnabel, Elizabeth Schneider, Gene Searchinger, Dale Shaw, Norma Simon, Marc Simont, Vicki Smith, Howard Sparber, Shelley Trubowitz, Peter Wang, Joanna Czaderna Wood, and Charlotte Zolotow.

For reading and commenting on portions of this work, I thank Todd Hignite (of *Comic Art*), Stephen Roxburgh and Katya Rice (of Front Street), Jennifer A. Hughes, Karin Westman, and the anonymous readers for *Children's Literature* 29 (2001). For some creative-writing wisdom, I thank Katy Karlin. For excellent suggestions (many of which I've used) on how to revise the first five paragraphs, I thank Dan Steffan.

I could not have gained glimpses into the early lives of Crockett Johnson and Ruth Krauss without the generous assistance of Linda Graetz, Harold Frank, David Frank, and Lani Frank.

Many people have been extraordinarily generous with their time and knowledge. J. B. Stroud, who is *the* expert on Crockett Johnson's mathematical paintings shared his vast knowledge. Leonard Marcus, an experienced navigator of the thickets of biographical research, has provided invaluable guidance on many occasions. My agent, George Nicholson, offered this project his enthusiastic support, read and offered suggestions to improve the first complete draft, and helped find it a home.

Particular thanks go to Kate Jackson, who granted me access to HarperCollins's archives, and to Stewart I. Edelstein and Monte E. Frank, who granted me access to materials held by the Estate of Ruth Krauss and who have granted me permission to reproduce Johnson's and Krauss's works.

I'm grateful to many others who granted me access to archival material, especially Peggy Kidwell (Smithsonian Institution), Wendy Wick Reaves and Amy Baskette (Smithsonian National Portrait Gallery), Terri Goldich and Wendy Hennequin (Dodd Research Center, University of Connecticut, Storrs), Tzofit Goldfarb (HarperCollins Publishers), and John Hyslop (Long Island Division, Queens Borough Public Library).

Other people and institutions also very kindly permitted me to examine archival material: Bob E. Rutan (Macy's Annual Events); Donna L. Davey and Andrew H. Lee (Tamiment Library, New York University); Daniel Sokolow, Rimma Skorupsky, and Susan Gormley (McGraw-Hill); Emilyn L. Brown (New York University Archives); Iris Snyder (Special Collections, University of Delaware Library); Kathleen Manwaring (Special Collections, Syracuse University Library); Bill Santin (Columbia University); Jocelyn K. Wilk (Columbiana Library, Columbia University Archives); Bill Kimmel and

X. Theodore Barber (Parsons School of Design); Bob Giles (Nieman Foundation for Journalism, Harvard University); Brian A. Sullivan (Harvard University Archives); Bob McAuley (*Aviation Weekly*); Mark Rosenzweig (Reference Center for Marxist Studies); Ric Grefé (American Institute of Graphic Arts); Layne Bosserman (Enoch Pratt Free Library, Baltimore); Elizabeth Schaaf (Peabody Archives, Friedheim Music Library); Kathy Cowan (Maryland Institute College of Art); Sara W. Duke and Martha Kennedy (Prints and Photographs Division, Library of Congress); Georgia Higley (Serial and Government Publications Division, Library of Congress); Sandy Schechter (Museum of Comic and Cartoon Art, New York); Dee Jones (de Grummond Collection, University of Southern Mississippi); Kathy Jacob and Ellen M. Shea (Schlesinger Library, Radcliffe Institute, Harvard); Helen Herz Cohen, Wendy Cohen, Elesa Nelson, Jill Zeikel, Renee Keels, Marnie Benatovich, and Trish Siembora (Camp Walden); and Lynda Claassen (Mandeville Special Collections Library, Geisel Library, University of California at San Diego).

For scanning images, I thank Nancy Crampton, Harrison Judd, Nicola Shayer (Dodd Research Center, University of Connecticut), Robert E. Thomas (Tamiment), Henry Yan (Smithsonian), and Jonathan Barli and Rick Marschall (Rosebud Archives). For helping me track down the holders of rights, assisting with related queries, or granting permission to use images, I thank Roger Adams (Rare Books, Kansas State University); Candice Bradley, Cassidy Flanagan, and Jean McGinley (HarperCollins); Jeff Dymowski (Creative Photographers); Frank J. Gerratana; Gary Johnson (Newspaper and Current Periodical Room, Library of Congress); Jack Kramer (*New Haven Register*); Eleanor Lanahan; Jennifer Lavonier; Joseph McQuaid (*New Hampshire Union Leader*); Danielle Musgrove and TaSonja Hibbler (American Cancer Society); Linda Briscoe Myers (Harry Ransom Center, University of Texas at Austin); Elisabeth Pankl (Hale Library, Kansas State University); Patrick Rodgers (Rosenbach Museum); Amy J. Staples and Kareen K. Morrison (Eliot Elisofson Photographic Archives, National Museum of African Art, Smithsonian); and Jane Thiel (Kimberly-Clark Worldwide).

For answering queries, sharing information, and helping me learn more about Johnson and Krauss's lives and times, I thank Rona Ackerman, Brian Alverson, Marcia Ascher, Ann M. Ashmore, Dmitri Belser, Penny Bergamini, David Bonner, Franklyn Branley, Paul Buhle, John Caldwell, Danielle Cavanna and Alyssa Crouse (Westport Arts Center), Katie Chase (Westport Historical Society), Irwin Chusid, Dan Clowes, William Cobb,

Harold Coogan, Joe D'Amico (Henry Holt and Company), Pete Dillon, Kai Erikson, Nancy Fadis (Eames Collection), Betty Fraser, Martin Gardner, Leonard Garment, Martin Garment, Si Gerson, Linda Greengrass and Kristin Freda (Bank Street College of Education), Grace A. Halsey, Charles Hatfield, Michael Patrick Hearn, Jason E. Hill, Mary Ann Hoberman, Thacher Hurd, Charles Keller, Melissa R. Klapper, Peter Leavitt, Ellen Lupton, Scott McCloud, Marjorie Melikian (Historical Committee, First Presbyterian Church, Newtown), Mike Michaels, Steffie Michaels, Julia Mickenberg, Paul Mishler, Mark Newgarden, Kirsten Nicolaysen, Susan B. Obel (Theatreworks USA), Nathan Oser, Karen Petersen, Hal Prince, Robin Lynn Rausch (Library of Congress), Meg Rich (William Sloane Papers), Stanley Rubin, Tim Samuelson, Brie Shannon, Claire Sherman, Bob Singleton, Christopher Skelly, Lane Smith, Steve Smith, Paul Solomon, Lois Redding Stranahan, Lee Talley, Hilda Terry, Mark Tonra, Terry Trilling, Chris Ware, Hedy White, Helaine White, January White, Roger Willcox, John Wolbrecht, and Matt Wood. Very special thanks go to two Barnabys for sharing details about the productions in which they starred: Jared Brown (radio, 1949) and Thomas Hamilton (stage, 1946).

For invaluable research assistance, I thank Bill Alger, Jennifer D. Askey, James M. Babcock, George Bodmer, Brad Bunnin, Amy Burr, Molly Butler, Richard Cohen, Nancy Crampton, Tony Crawford, June Cummins, Tim Dayton, Carson Demmans, Elizabeth Dodd, Dennis Duarte, Paul Fernbach, Richard Flynn, Rachel Folsom, Melissa Glaser, Liz and Tony Gott (Genealogy, Bayanne House, Yell, Shetland, Scotland), Michael Helgesen and Arthur J. Leask (of the Clan Leask Society), Irwin T. Holtzman, Martin Janal and Eve Hochwald, Micah Janzen, Michael Joseph, Arjun Kharel, Chris Lamb, Monica Langley (Charleston Public Library), Bob Leftwich, Bob Levin, Scott Lewis, Anne Longmuir, Mike Lynch, Aaron Marcus, David Margolick, Bill McCann, Jill Morgan, Peter Muldavin, Patrick Murtha, Colin Myers, Eric Nadworny, Linda Nel, Rick Norwood, Hugh O'Connell, Rachel Olsen, Shannon Ozirny, Adam Paul, Anne Phillips, Leena Reiman, D. A. Sachs, Carla Schuster, Kate Skattebol, Bill Slankard, Stephen Smith, Cliff Starkey, Jan Susina, Lisa Tatonetti, Joseph Thomas Jr., Maria Torio, Brian Tucker, David Turner, Ivan Ulz, Detlef Urbschat, Christopher Wheeler, Jerry Wigglesworth, Cari Williams, Marsha Williams, and Naomi Wood.

For institutional support at Kansas State University, I thank English department heads Linda Brigham, Larry Rodgers, and Karin Westman and administrative assistants Lisa Herpich and Mary Siegel. I thank Kansas State University for Small Research Grants in the fall 2000, spring 2001, fall 2001, and fall 2003; the University of Connecticut for a Sigmund Strochlitz Travel Grant in 2004; and the Smithsonian for a postdoctoral fellowship at the National Portrait Gallery in 2005. I also thank those who wrote letters on my behalf: Jay Cayton, Richard Flynn, Jerry Griswold, Anne Phillips, and Jan Susina. I am grateful to those who read through versions of what would become the book proposal, among them Scott Peeples, Jen Henderson, Linda Brigham, and Karin Westman.

For putting me up (and up with me), I thank Edward and Lucy Appert; Matt Dunne; Gloria Hardman (Hi, Mom!); Chris Kenngott and Melissa Songer; Darin McKeever and Perry Pearson McKeever; Terry, Bill, and Christopher Sherwin; William Speed Weed; Jake, Dave, Amanda, and Chelsea Whalen; and Ted Whitten and Sonya Hals.

Parts of this book have previously appeared, in somewhat different form, in *Children's Literature* 29 (2001); in *Comic Art* 5 (Winter 2004); and as the afterword to Crockett Johnson's *Magic Beach* (2005). I have presented other portions of this book at various conferences over the past dozen years, and I thank the audience members who listened and provided feedback to me on those occasions. In addition, my many teachers in the art of biography have included the Washington Biography Group (http://www.patmcnees.com/work16.htm).

At the University Press of Mississippi, I thank Seetha Srinivasan for her long-standing interest in this project. Walter Biggins read the first draft diligently and offered thoughtful, valuable critical advice: If the level of detail still overwhelms, that's my fault, not his. I also thank Ellen D. Goldlust-Gingrich for her rigorous copyediting and editing.

I've tried to keep track of all assistance received; apologies to anyone I've forgotten!

INDEX